Education
in Vietnam

The **Institute of Southeast Asian Studies (ISEAS)** was established as an autonomous organization in 1968. It is a regional centre dedicated to the study of socio-political, security and economic trends and developments in Southeast Asia and its wider geostrategic and economic environment. The Institute's research programmes are the Regional Economic Studies (RES, including ASEAN and APEC), Regional Strategic and Political Studies (RSPS), and Regional Social and Cultural Studies (RSCS).

ISEAS Publishing, an established academic press, has issued more than 2,000 books and journals. It is the largest scholarly publisher of research about Southeast Asia from within the region. ISEAS Publishing works with many other academic and trade publishers and distributors to disseminate important research and analyses from and about Southeast Asia to the rest of the world.

The **Vietnam Update** is a series of annual conferences that focus on recent economic, political and social conditions in Vietnam and provide in-depth analysis on a theme of particular relevance to Vietnam's socio-economic development. The first Vietnam Update was held at the Australian National University in 1990. In recent years, the series has been organized in conjunction with ISEAS.

The **Research School of Pacific and Asian Studies (RSPAS)** is Australia's pre-eminent centre for research and postgraduate training on the Asia-Pacific region. Priority areas of the School are Southeast Asia, Northeast Asia and the Southwest Pacific. There are nine major disciplines represented in the School: Anthropology, Archaeology, Economics, History, Human Geography, International Relations, Linguistics, Political Science and Strategic & Defence Studies. One of the four original research schools that formed The Australian National University when it was established in 1946, RSPAS has maintained a strong record of research excellence.

VIETNAM UPDATE SERIES

Education
in Vietnam

EDITED BY
JONATHAN D. LONDON

INSTITUTE OF SOUTHEAST ASIAN STUDIES
Singapore

First published in Singapore in 2011 by ISEAS Publishing
Institute of Southeast Asian Studies
30 Heng Mui Keng Terrace
Pasir Panjang
Singapore 119614

E-mail: publish@iseas.edu.sg
Website: http://bookshop.iseas.edu.sg

The responsibility for facts and opinions in this publication rests exclusively with the editor and contributors and their interpretations do not necessarily reflect the views or the policy of the Insititute or its supporters.

ISEAS Library Cataloguing-in-Publication Data

Education in Vietnam / edited by Jonathan D. London.
    Based on Vietnam Update Conference held at the Australian National University in 2007.
    1.   Education—Vietnam—Congresses.
    I.   London, Jonathan.
    II. Australian National University.
    III. Institute of Southeast Asian Studies.
    IV. Vietnam Update Conference (2007 : Canberra, Australia)
DS559.912 V66 2007   2011

ISBN 978-981-4279-05-5 (soft cover)
ISBN 978-981-4279-06-2 (PDF)

Typeset by International Typesetters Pte Ltd
Printed in Singapore by Utopia Press Pte Ltd

CONTENTS

FOREWORD

Few concerns are of greater importance in Vietnam than education. It could be characterized as the unifying preoccupation of that country. Today, more personal and public resources are devoted to education than to almost any other comparable form of social activity; nearly every citizen has experienced schooling at some level. Education has been integral to Vietnam's history and remains central to its people's identity and aspirations for the future. For years, fierce debates have raged over the quality, accessibility, direction and management of education. The debates reveal dissatisfactions that are expressed more openly than perhaps in any other sector of society. However, all protagonists in Vietnam's perennial education debates are united by the passionate belief that education is critical to individual advancement and to the wellbeing of the nation.

The pressure on education to serve as a vehicle of individual and collective advancement is more acute than ever as the society becomes more complex and globally integrated. Major changes have occurred in the funding of education, and a host of reforms undertaken in curriculum design, examination procedures, teacher training, and educational administration. Private and foreign schools have entered the educational marketplace and the number of Vietnamese seeking education overseas continues to soar. Today Vietnamese people face unprecedented educational choices, but also substantial risks and costs. Do parents and students feel this is money well spent? Are their opinions being heard at policy levels? Is education meeting the needs of its diverse population and satisfying the expectations of its employers, civil service and social organizations?

Can it be said that educational achievement is fostering social mobility in Vietnam?

The 2007 Vietnam Update was organized to respond to these questions. Held at the Australian National University, it was titled: "Education in Vietnam: Changes and Challenges". The majority of the proposals submitted in response to the call for papers were from Vietnamese academics, reflecting the keen debate on education that is presently underway in Vietnam. Six of the invited speakers were from Vietnam. The remainder were specialists on education in Vietnam from other countries. The Update consisted of sessions on educational financing, the political economy of education reform, skills training, school case studies, and higher education. The audience members included development specialists, public servants, diplomats, journalists, academics, university students and NGO workers.

This book is the product of that workshop and it is fitting to acknowledge the many organizations and individuals who provided the financial and logistical support that made it possible. Funding for speakers from Vietnam and for the bulk of the workshop expenses was provided by the Australian overseas aid agency, AusAID. The Institute of Southeast Asian Studies, Singapore, covered the travel costs of the remaining speakers. Additional support for organization of the workshop was provided by the four units of the College of Asia and the Pacific, ANU, that co-operated to host the 2007 Update.

Particular thanks must go to Thai Duy Bao who acted as the convener of the Update. David Marr drafted the call for papers, provided detailed comments on individual papers, and chaired the wrap-up discussion. Ben Kerkvliet secured and oversaw the Update funding. The academic organizing committee also included Li Tana, Ashley Carruthers, and Philip Taylor of the Australian National University, and David Koh and Russell Heng of the Institute of Southeast Asian Studies, Singapore. The real work of organizing, however, was done by the capable team of Oanh Collins, Lyn Ning, Pham Thu Thuy, and Lynne Payne, who handled the many logistical arrangements with great professionalism.

Jonathan London's offer to edit the Update volume was enthusiastically welcomed by the organizing committee. This book is the end result of years of his dedicated and patient efforts. Jonathan wishes to thank Ngo Tuyet Lan and Jennifer Eagleton, at City University of Hong Kong, for their assistance on research and copy-editing respectively, and Bui Thai Quyen for her assistance with research and data collection in Hanoi. The academics whom he asked to read and comment on some of the chapters include Vu Quang Viet, Hue-Tam Ho Tai, Jonathan Pincus, David Marr, Ben Kerkvliet, and Philip Taylor. Jonathan wishes also to thank the contributors for their receptiveness to undertaking multiple revisions.

Philip Taylor
Australian National University

ABOUT THE CONTRIBUTORS

Bùi Thái Quyên is currently a PhD candidate at the Vietnam Academy of Social Science and a Lecturer at the Faculty of Management and Tourism, Hanoi University. She received a Masters Degree in Development Economics in 1998. She has more than ten years of experience in socioeconomic studies in Vietnam, including education, healthcare, poverty elimination and social safety net.

Jim Cobbe is Professor of Economics at Florida State University. He has conducted research on education and other issues in Africa, the Caribbean, Asia, and the Persian Gulf. From 2000 to 2004, Cobbe served as education economist for the European Union's Support to the Ministry of Education and Training Project in Hanoi. In 2007 and 2008, Cobbe was a Fulbright scholar and spent the academic year at the College of Business and Public Administration of the University of Dā Nẵng. His PhD is from Yale.

Alexandre Dormeier Freire earned a PhD in development studies at the University of Geneva. He is a senior lecturer, Asian academic coordinator of the IMAS (International Executive Master in Development Studies) and fellow researcher at the Graduate Institute of International and Development Studies, Geneva. Since 2000, he has been working on education issues in Indonesia and Vietnam with a special focus on skills development, labour market, social transformations, and social inequalities and has conveyed various researches in these fields.

Marea Fatseas is Managing Director of Ideas Connect. She has lived and worked in Vietnam at different times over the past twenty-five years as a student, an Australian Embassy official responsible for developing bilateral education and training cooperation, and as a consultant on development assistance projects in the education sector.

Hồ Vũ Khuê Ngọc is Senior Lecturer at University of Dã Nẵng, Vietnam and PhD candidate at Ritsumeikan University, Japan. Her major interests include higher education and cross-cultural issues in education.

Jonathan D. London (editor) directs the Vietnam Project at the Centre for Southeast Asian Studies, City University of Hong Kong, where he is assistant professor in the Department of Asian and International Studies. London has authored scholarly articles on contemporary Vietnam's education and health systems and a forthcoming book on Vietnam's welfare regime. He has conducted education-related research for international organizations, such as UNICEF. He holds a PhD in Sociology from the University of Wisconsin-Madison.

Nguyễn Minh Hồng (PhD) is Dean of the Faculty of Electrical and Electronic Engineering, Hung Yen University of Technical Teacher Education, Vietnam. He has been active in numerous higher education projects across the country.

Elizabeth St. George (PhD) is Visiting Fellow with the Department of Political and Social Change, The Australian National University. St. George has conducted research on higher education in Vietnam for over a decade and currently works for the Australian Agency for International Development in Jakarta.

Trần Thị Bích Liễu (PhD) is Lecturer in Education Management at the University of Education, Vietnam National University in Hanoi and Vice Director of the Centre for Education Research and Practice. She has served as Director of the Centre for Educational Assessment and Accreditation, National Institute for Educational Management.

Trương Huyền Chi is an anthropologist based in Hanoi. Her research interests include societies in transition, transnational narratives and memories, and education of ethnic minorities. She holds a PhD from the University of Toronto and was a postdoctoral fellow at Harvard University.

1

EDUCATION IN VIETNAM
Historical Roots, Recent Trends

Jonathan D. London

Over the last two decades Vietnam has experienced profound changes in all manner of its social institutions. This volume of essays examines developments in the sphere of education. Broadly understood, education refers to social activities that impart knowledge, skills, or morality. Education can thus take place in innumerable guises and settings. The essays in this volume are focused on Vietnam's education system, understood as the entire set of processes and institutions that govern formal schooling, training, and research activities in Vietnam, and their social and educational outcomes.

The historical lineages of education in Vietnam stretch back over a thousand years. The country has had an organized education system for more than 500 years. Regional differences in education systems that emerged in (what is today) Vietnam in the nineteenth and twentieth centuries and the associated politics of education during this period are equally if not more important for understanding education in contemporary Vietnam. In macrohistorical terms, major influences on education in Vietnam include the development and incomplete decay of Confucian institutions, colonialism and anti-colonial struggle, post-colonial state formation, twentieth century wars, the development and subsequent erosion of state-socialist institutions and, most recently, the development of a state-dominated market economy within a Leninist political framework. Against such a varied and complex historical backdrop, the last two decades is a small bit of time indeed. And yet, changes in Vietnam's education since the late 1980s have been momentous, both reflecting and effecting broader social change.

The publication of this volume comes at a time when Vietnam's education system is at a crossroads. Rapid economic growth over two decades has permitted unprecedented increases in the scale and scope of formal schooling. And yet there is a prevailing sense that Vietnam's current education system is inadequate to the country's needs. These are not abstract concerns. Education is not a stand alone sector but a major institution that functions and develops interdependently with other major institutions. What happens in Vietnam's education system has broad implications for social life in the country.

Contemporary Vietnam's education system is fascinating. Seeing why requires moving beyond platitudes to analysis of substantive educational issues. The platitudes are familiar but deserve consideration. One is that respect for education is somehow essential to the Vietnamese character (*bản sắc người Việt*). Another — especially popular among Vietnam's political leaders — is that education is the "national priority", the "national strategy", or the "national policy" (*quốc sách hàng đầu*). International development agencies chime in with saccharine praise of Vietnam's educational "achievements" before their inevitable laundry lists of "shortcomings".

Taken at face value, these sayings are valid enough. Education *has* figured prominently in Vietnam's social history; education *is* a major focus of the state; and, residual problems notwithstanding, over the last two decades, Vietnam *has* registered significant "improvements" across many indicators of educational development. But as the essays in this volume demonstrate, Vietnam's education system is more interesting and complex than the well-worn clichés suggest. In Vietnam today, there are a wide variety of views engaged in a sprawling and urgent debate about what is happening, why, and what might be done about it.

Current debates on Vietnam's education system seem to be fuelled by three broad and related sets of anxieties. The first concerns the relation between education and livelihoods. As the country has grown wealthier, opportunities for schooling have increased greatly. But demand for education and training has increased even faster, while the costs, qualities, distribution, and accessibility of education remain uneven across regions and different segments of the population. Education in Vietnam — as in other countries — has long been viewed as a pathway to a better life; an avenue to social mobility. But, as elsewhere, education can also function as an obstacle to such social mobility, as a giant sorting mechanism that generates, reproduces, or transforms existing social inequalities. In an age of rapid economic growth, consumerism, and geographic mobility, Vietnam's education system may be thought of as a vast social field in which aspirations and constraints collide.

A second source of debate are the anxieties concerning education policies. Beyond thin consensuses regarding the importance of education and the need for further educational reforms, there are conflicting diagnoses of what ails Vietnam's education system and substantively divergent prescriptions for change. Quite often, entrenched interests, bureaucratic rigidities, and ideological factionalism seem only to promote continued organizational inertia. In other respects, the intensity and sophistication of education policy debates have increased. There are, it is clear, both new and old dilemmas and new and old problems, many of which are addressed in the current volume.

A final concern relates to the quality of education in the context of rapid increases in the scale of, and demand for, education. Maintaining or improving quality in the context of rapid growth is a challenge familiar to educators around the world. It is recognized, for example, that uneven access to and the quality of preschool education is undermining the achievement capabilities of children from poor and marginalized groups. Significant steps to improve preschool education are only now taking hold. Completion of primary and lower-secondary education is becoming the norm, but there are large disparities in the quality of primary and secondary education, and in educational achievement across and within regions. Tertiary education in Vietnam is rapidly becoming mass education, even as the country lacks a single university of international standard. Thousands of vocational training centres have sprouted up across Vietnam, but the country is only now developing systems of accreditation. In the meantime, credentialism and commercialism fuel over-rapid growth. There is, as can be observed, no shortage of important and controversial issues concerning education in Vietnam.

The analysis of education in Vietnam can be approached from innumerable perspectives and this volume does not pretend to offer a comprehensive treatment or all the answers. But it is hoped that the chapters in this volume will contribute to existing knowledge of the country's education system and, in so doing, to broader understandings of social conditions in contemporary Vietnam. The remainder of this chapter introduces Vietnam's education system through an overview of its historical development and current organization, a summary of recent trends, and a survey of relevant literature. The individual contributions to this volume are then introduced in turn.

THE HISTORICAL LINEAGES OF VIETNAM'S EDUCATION SYSTEM

To study contemporary Vietnam's education system is to scratch the surface of something much larger and older.[1] But the history of education in Vietnam cannot be treated as a mere "backdrop" to the present. On the contrary, the history of Vietnam's education system is essential to the analysis and understanding of its present. The following discussion attempts to provide the reader with some of the salient elements of this history. It helps link evidence and understandings of Vietnam's educational past with evidence and understandings of its present.

Confucian Institutions and Their Historical Legacies

To say that Vietnam's Confucian heritage has shaped its education system is to risk essentializing, as is common in many contemporary debates. Indeed, the difficulty of stating concisely the significance of Confucianism to the development of education in Vietnam owes to the complex nature of Confucianism itself, the intellectual content, practical manifestations and effects of which varied considerably over time and place. Confucianism has meant different things to different people. In certain periods and places and among certain groups Confucianism was of marginal or even no significance.[2] And yet, on balance, Confucianism, Confucian institutions, and their historical legacies — real and imagined — have played a vital role in debates about the development of education system in Vietnam and of Vietnamese social institutions more broadly.[3] That said, and before entering a more detailed discussion, it must be acknowledged that the account below is not expert. It does not offer a substantive analysis of different streams of thought in Vietnamese Confucianism or a serious engagement with scholarship on these themes.[4] Finally, it should be stated that our discussion starts with a consideration of Confucianism, not because it is the most important for understanding the present, but because of its early influence on trajectories of educational development in Vietnam.

To generalize, Confucianism blended education and normative governance. Confucian institutions imposed constraints by linking organized education and the study of classics to governance and authority relations. Confucian ideals and institutions shaped attitudes and behaviours concerning education, but in non-determinant ways, contingent on actors' interests, capacities, and circumstances. Perhaps most important, the development of education systems in Vietnam, as in China and Korea, occurred in interdependent relation with the development of authority relations — proto-national, local, and familial. Grasping this helps us to appreciate the historical significance of education in Vietnam.

Vietnam's introduction to Confucianism occurred through Chinese influence. Chinese domination of what is today northern Vietnam between the first and tenth centuries gave the country what Alexander Woodside has called "a comprehensive initiation into the scholarship, political theories, familial organization patterns, bureaucratic practices, and even the religious orientations of Chinese culture" (Woodside 1971, p. 7). Chinese-inspired civil service exams, based on Chinese Buddhist and Confucian classics, began no later than the eleventh century. The use of written Chinese, the development of an intellectual (or Confucian) scholar "class" (*tầng lớp nho sĩ*), and the incorporation of villages into the pre-modern (or "feudal") state were critical steps in the development of Vietnam's village culture, customs, and codes (Bùi Xuân Đính 1985).

In Vietnam, as in China and Korea, the organized study of Confucian classics and the regular conduct of competitive examinations became integral to the development and functions of dynastic states. As Woodside (2005) has shown, the use of exams and other merit-based criteria allowed imperial courts in these three mandarnites to develop rules-based bureaucracies, contributing to a "precocious de-feudalization" of authority relations that enhanced dynastic states' power. In other respects, impacts of Confucianism on the development of education in Vietnam reflected the peculiarities of

Vietnamese social life. The expulsion of the Chinese in the tenth century was followed by roughly 900 years of largely autonomous development, punctuated by defeats of several Chinese and Mongol attempts to invade. During this period, rulers of the Lý (1010–1225), Trần (1225–1400), Lê (1428–1788), Mạc (1527–92),[5] and Nguyễn (1802–1945) dynasties continued to use formal examinations and other Chinese-inspired mechanisms to recruit and regulate their bureaucracies. John Whitmore (1997) has provided a particularly interesting analysis of literati culture and its significance with respect to political integration in "Đại Việt" between the fifteenth and nineteenth centuries.

The practical significance of Confucianism and Confucian institutions with respect to education needs to be clarified. Up until the nineteenth century, education in Vietnam occurred largely in privately run village schools led by Confucian scholars, who trained local candidates (*cử tử* or *sĩ tử*) — always boys or men — for exams and eventual careers as clerks, bureaucrats, or mandarins. Beyond the village schools were state-sponsored prefectural schools (*tràng/trường học*), provincial schools, and the imperial college (*Quốc tử giám*). But education in Vietnam more often took place in village schools (usually situated in the residence of village scholars) rather than in state academies.

How was the "Vietnamese experience" different from that in China? Village teachers in Vietnam tended to be more independent of the bureaucracy. Vietnam's examination system was not as extensive as China's, less hierarchal, and eligibility for participation in exams was less contingent on lineage. In both China and Vietnam, education tended to be elitist. But the celebration of literacy in Vietnam was associated with the economic and cultural standing of the village more than a particular lineage. While educational opportunities were fewer among the poor, it was not uncommon for village associations in the country to maintain separate "study fields" (*học điền*) to finance the education of ambitious, but materially poor students (Woodside 1991). Vietnamese education was, by comparison, less specialized and divisions between academic elite and village instructors were less distinct.

Dynastic states sought to use education and teaching to penetrate village life, with mixed success. Early nineteenth century Nguyễn rulers sought to inculcate ten moral maxims regarding the conduct of village life by demanding their regular recitation in village communal houses (*đình*) (Woodside 1971, p. 189). But local literati were often able to promote their own interests; local customs and local discretions determined which maxims to embrace and which to flout, which students were worthy of material support or exemptions from labour and military requirements, and who would sit for exams (Woodside 1971).

The resilience of local institutions to outside authority (explained, *inter alia*, by the insularity of village life, the physical isolation of frontier settlements, and principled opposition) helps to explain the varying relevance of Confucianism to the development of education in Vietnam across time and place. Moreover, however important to village life Confucian institutions may have been, they always existed alongside other important institutions, including village codes under different names (e.g., *khoán ước, khoán từ, khoán lệ, điều lệ, hương lệ, tục lệ*, etc.), councils of elders, and local indigenous customs. Village codes, which provided rules for an impressive range of social activities, frequently regulated educational matters, including the level of support for local scholars and finding substitutes to fulfil military obligations (Bùi Xuân Dính 1985). Hence, different localities' peculiarities might manifest in distinctive engagements with and critiques of Confucian thought and institutions. Among non-Viet (and non-Chinese) ethnic groups, the force of Confucian thought and institutions was much more limited, and education was more likely to take place within familial or religious settings, as opposed to formal training.

During the Lê dynasty, the number of examinees at the doctoral exam (*thi hội*) reached 5,700 in the year 1514 and 6,000 in the year 1640 (Ngô Dúc Thọ 2003, pp. 75–77). By the nineteenth century, an estimated 4,000 scholars in Vietnam competed in regional exams held every three years (Woodside 1971, p. 179). While the examination system continued to function,[6] dynastic states encountered difficulty recruiting enough scholars of sufficient quality to staff imperial courts, and their efforts to use village literati and village teachers to meet their own imperatives were frequently frustrated. Imperial educational officials appointed to administer education at the provincial and district levels were sometimes less well trained (and therefore not respected) by those they sought to administer.

Confucianism is associated with the veneration of education and its development occurred in an age where access to education was limited. Despite the greater openness of education in Vietnam as noted above, only a small minority of Vietnamese children studied. Although Vietnamese custom did allow education for non-elites, Confucian ideas and institutions nonetheless often promoted and reproduced hierarchies of power, wealth, and status. With rare exceptions such as the famous case of Nguyễn Thị Duệ,[7] girls and women were largely excluded and those who did receive instruction in the classics were mostly expected to learn and recite certain "virtues of feminine behaviour", such as how to stand and sit, speak, cook and sew, and submit to male authority. Boys, by contrast, had a standard and fairly extensive syllabus of Confucian classics they were expected to master.

Critiques of Confucian institutions have played an important role in Vietnam's social history and educational history in particular. Elite malfeasance was a common inspiration of many of Vietnam's greatest literary figures, such as the eighteenth century writers Nguyễn Du, Hồ Xuân Hương, and Cao Bá Quát, each of whom were both products and critics of the country's classical educational traditions. The brilliance of these writers lay not in their mastery of classical texts *per se* but in the artistry of their social commentary.

Overall, the impact of Confucianism on education in Vietnam defies generalization. Despite the limited accessibility of education, the use of classical education as an instrument of local and extra-local power imbued much of the country's population with respect for intellectual tradition and certain methods of learning. The proportionately small number of people involved in formal studies meant that education took place through other means, especially through oral traditions, such as songs, storytelling, and epic poems, many of which offered biting commentary on social and political affairs. Exclusionary aspects of classical education and the difficulty of mastering Chinese characters or Vietnamese *chữ nôm* ("southern script") meant that vast majorities of Vietnamese remained functionally illiterate (Woodside 1971). And yet, Confucian thought and Confucian-inspired social institutions had wide impacts on the development of education systems in Vietnam and legacies of these impacts remain.

Colonialism, Anti-colonialism, and Education

French colonialism destabilized, destroyed, and transformed Vietnamese institutions, including those governing education. As will be noted, French influence on education preceded the institutionalization of colonial rule. The institutionalization of colonial rule amounted to an attack on Vietnamese authority relations and was, by extension, an attack on the traditional educational system. By militarily defeating and subsequently coopting the imperial bureaucracy and scholar gentry, French colonial authorities precipitated the demise of Vietnam's Confucian institutions. By the 1920s, French authorities had undertaken a restructuring of the country's school system designed to serve colonial imperatives more efficiently. But the exclusionary, restrictive, and exploitive character of these arrangements drew criticism. Indeed, Vietnamese struggles against French education policies were critical to the development of anti-colonial sentiment. Ironically, French colonialism contributed not only to the demise of Confucian institutions, but also to the rise of a new and increasingly radicalized anti-colonial intelligentsia, members of which would ultimately overturn French rule.

French influence on education in Vietnam was spatially and temporally uneven. European missionary schools existed in various parts of the country by the eighteenth century. But it was the establishment of explicitly Franco-"Annamite" schools in the French protectorate of Cochin China (what is today southern Vietnam), beginning in 1861, that marked the beginning of a significant French influence on organized education. As Trần Thị Phương Hoa (2009) has pointed out, explicitly assimilationist Franco-Annamite schools were in operation prior to the establishment of the official colonial administration. By 1869, there were some 126 Franco-Vietnamese primary schools in Cochin China, with more than 4,000 students (Thompson 1937, cited in Trần 2009, p.7). Importantly, the introduction of these schools occurred in the south several decades prior to the establishment of any similar schools in (what is today) central and northern Vietnam, and there were many more such schools in the south. By 1887, according to Trần (ibid) there were only forty-two Franco-Vietnamese schools in Tonkin. Instruction was in Romanized Vietnamese script, Quốc Ngữ. Of these forty-two schools, only thirteen were primary schools, four of which were designated for girls. The remaining twenty-nine schools were geared to adults, for the training of colonial functionaries, such as clerks and interpreters. Undoubtedly, the greater exposure of the south to French education affected and accentuated regional differences in social structure and trajectories of change.

French colonialism advanced in stages, with the creation of the Cochin China colony in 1860 (in what is today southern Vietnam), and the establishment in 1884 of the protectorates of Annam and Tonkin in (what is today) central and northern Vietnam, respectively. French colonialism and local responses to it precipitated the demise of Confucian social institutions, as the French attack on Vietnamese authority amounted to an attack on hierarchical authority relations and hence education at both the national and local levels. The subsequent cooptation and marginalization of the Vietnamese Confucian literati and the active participation of many members of this elite stratum in the maintenance of oppressive colonial hierarchies generated popular contempt. Historians of Vietnamese anti-colonialism provide richly detailed accounts of how literati who appeared to collaborate with French authorities became living symbols of moral bankruptcy and subservience and lightening rods of social criticism.[8] The famous Vietnamese doctor, historian, literary critic, and dissident Nguyễn Khắc Viện decried Vietnamese Confucians' proclivities towards conservatism and fixation on individual self-improvement while ignoring institutional constraints, a view characteristic of prevailing leftist critics (Nguyễn Khắc Viện 1993).

Collaboration or toleration were not the only options, as many members of the scholarly elite questioned or openly rejected French colonialism, if in very different ways. The ultimately unsuccessful *Cần Vương* (Aid the King) Movement of 1885–89, for example, was coordinated by scholars such as Phan Đình Phùng, Phan Chu Trinh, Phan Bội Châu, Trần Qui Cấp and Huỳnh Thúc Kháng, who sought to restore sovereign authority to the Nguyễn throne. French-educated conservative scholars of the early twentieth century sought, by contrast, to advance education reforms without fundamentally challenging established power structures. Vietnam's two most famous anti-colonial scholars of this era, Phan Chu Trinh and Phan Bội Châu (neither of whom was French educated)[9] drew direct attention to the relation between French education policies and colonial domination.[10] Anti-colonial dissent politicized education. The tax revolts in 1908 led to an almost ten-year closure of colleges established in the same year.

Indeed, French education reforms undertaken between 1917 and 1919 exacerbated rather than eased tensions. While the nineteenth century saw regional differentiation in education (including the aforementioned development of Franco-Vietnamese schools), these early twentieth century reforms effectively ended the old education system (comprised of village schools and hierarchical regional academies); replacing it with a new arrangement that included, in Cochin China, a separate French and Franco-Vietnamese school system and, in Tonkin and Annam, "traditional academies" (Hue-Tam Ho Tai 1992, p. 11). All three types of schools were placed under the authority of the French "Office of Public Instruction" which, in addition to overseeing public schools and approving or rejecting the operation of village and prefectural "traditional" schools, controlled curricula and the management of human resources. According to one estimate, education accounted for seven to eight per cent of the French Indo-China budget.[11]

The Franco-Vietnamese school system, established in 1917, was designed principally to keep Vietnamese out of French schools and to train Vietnamese for administrative occupations in a way that would not threaten French superiority (Kelly 1975).[12] Advancing from elementary to primary education within this system was impossible without elementary education in French, but this was offered in only a small number of schools. By the 1920s, it is estimated that no more than 3 per cent of the population had completed primary school, equivalent to a third- or fourth-grade education. The trial and punishment in the 1920s of both Phan Chu Trinh and Phan Bội Châu and the funeral of Phan Chu Trinh (in 1925) were major political events that fuelled critiques of the colonial education system. Yet between 1920 and 1938, little more than 10 per cent of all students would make it beyond the third grade, while less than 10 per cent of children were attending school (Marr 1981, see especially pp. 32–44). As Truong Huyen Chi notes later in this volume, Kelly demonstrated that instead of promoting national integration, schooling promoted regional inequalities and class tensions (Kelly 1982, p. 52).

While schooling in colonial Vietnam was limited, some question the conventional depiction of early twentieth-century Vietnam as overwhelmingly illiterate. Scholars agree that by the early twentieth century literacy rates in Vietnam had begun to increase, thanks to popularization and increasing availability of printed material in the Romanized Vietnamese language system (*quốc ngữ*). As Woodside (1983) has pointed out, statements that 95 per cent of Vietnam's population was illiterate in 1945 appear to some as a decidedly Confucian equation of literacy and academic learning.

On the other hand, it was clear that anti-colonial politics fuelled an interest in education. Hồ Chí Minh was not the first to claim that the longer Vietnamese remained an ignorant people (*ngu dân*), the longer they would remain in servitude. Indeed, demands for more inclusive educational institutions and calls for Vietnamese to educate themselves fuelled the development of anti-colonial movements of the early twentieth century and figured prominently in the political struggle for national independence (Marr 1981). A small number of semi-privileged young Vietnamese who managed to make it through secondary education went on to seize the political initiative, rejecting colonial careers for revolutionary politics, which they frequently pursued through educational activities. Though there were only three upper-secondary schools nationally (in Hue, Hanoi, and Saigon) their significance to Vietnam's political history was immense. Well known students of the Trường Quốc Học in Huế included Hồ Chí Minh, Phạm Văn Đồng, Trần Phú, Võ Nguyên Giáp, and Đào Duy Anh.

Colonial structures of domination proved fertile ground for the development of a small, young, and radical intelligentsia, who rejected traditional Confucian ideas and institutions in favour of liberal and socialist ideas. This new intelligentsia, largely from petit-bourgeois families, took form through exposure to new ideas and to the indignities of the colonial experience. They were unwilling to settle for careers as clerks, interpreters, or tax collectors and increasingly sought to overturn French rule. By the twentieth century, a trickle of such Vietnamese ventured overseas for education, most importantly to France, Japan, and China, where they gained exposure to liberal, nationalist, and revolutionary ideas, as well as political and military training. Members of this young intelligentsia formed political parties, such as the Vietnam Quốc Dân Đảng (Nationalist Party), inspired by the ideology of Sun Yat-sen and founded by Phan Bội Châu in 1924, and the Marxist-Leninist Indochina Communist Party (ICP), which was formed during the late 1920s and was officially (and secretly) established under the authority of Comintern in Kowloon, Hong Kong, in 1930.

Outside the established education system, education played a key role in the independence struggle. In 1940, the communist-led *Việt Minh Đồng Minh Hội* (Việt Minh) announced their commitment to a fully literate population and to compulsory schooling at the primary level. As early as 1938, communist party committees in Tonkin launched efforts to promote literacy and party ideology through clandestine schools. As the 1940s unfolded, literacy training emerged as an integrated feature of the Việt Minh's political platform and a powerful tool for inculcating revolutionary values. Notably, the Việt Minh's literacy campaigns especially sought to reach out to non-Kinh ethnic minorities which, among other things, signalled the importance of achieving "unity" (*đoàn kết*) among the "great Vietnamese family of peoples" (Woodside 1983, p. 407).

After declaring Vietnam's independence in 1945, these efforts continued through compulsory literacy training in Việt Minh-controlled areas. Between 1946 and 1950, amid French efforts to reclaim northern Vietnam by force, the Việt Minh and sympathetic forces provided literacy training to some ten million previously uneducated Vietnamese (Woodside 1983, p. 401). In the 1950s and early 1960s, the Việt Minh and National Front similarly organized literacy classes and educational activities across the south, from the central mountains to the Mekong delta.[13]

State Formation, War, and Education Systems in a Divided Vietnam

The worldwide expansion of education during the twentieth century was a phenomenon closely linked to the development of modern states. The close relation between education systems and processes of state formation owes in large measure to the fact that education systems can be multifunctional instruments of state power. States can use education to promote diverse imperatives, including social order and consent, economic growth, and welfare. In post-World War II Vietnam, processes of educational development and state formation went hand in hand. Education in Vietnam during this period is only given a cursory glance here. In the account that follows, broad developments are offered instead of details on influential persons and events.

In the 1940s and 1950s Vietnam experienced the formation of two new states — the Democratic Republic of Vietnam (DRV) in the north and the Republic of Vietnam (RVN) in the south — and with them, two separate education systems. General poverty combined with the onset of war limited the scope of education, while the administration and daily operations of the system took place in the context of social upheaval. As Thaveeporn Vasavakul has shown in her comprehensive study of education and state building in North and South Vietnam between 1945 and 1965, the fledgling states that developed on either side of the seventeenth parallel developed educational systems that reflected the nationalist, class-based, and organizational biases of their respective political elite (Vasavakul 1994). These biases were shaped not only by ideological convictions, but the exigencies of an intensifying civil and international war.

In northern Vietnam, the development of the education system was part and parcel of the DRV's Soviet-inspired development strategy. By 1949 and 1950, the Việt Minh set about designing a new school system. In principle, universal education was to be guaranteed as a right of citizenship and wholly financed by public means. Curricula were, after 1950, simplified to focus on perceived organizational and productive requirements of the wartime situation.

The development of mass education in the Democratic Republic of Vietnam is frequently represented as a success story. Indeed, school enrolments increased rapidly during the 1950s and even during the wartime 1960s. Though constrained by lack of resources and war, Vietnam's communist leaders maintained a thoroughly instrumentalist and ultramodernist view of education. Education was (and in most respects remains) seen as an instrument of state power for the achievement of progress and socialist revolution. Education would contribute to the development of the "new socialist man" (and, presumably, woman).

But in other respects, the successes were illusory and the relevance of schooling to the "worker" and peasant questionable. The transition from the "guerrilla-style" (*du kích*) or *blitzkrieg* mass literacy courses of the 1950s to a stable bureaucratically organized education system proved difficult (Woodside 1983). The urban bias of the DRV's development model, the overwhelming paucity of resources, and war placed severe limits on the quality of education across regions. Successes of the 1950s in promoting literacy and school enrolments among ethnic minority groups in the northern mountainous regions declined. The development of education in the north during this period is revisited in Chapter Two of this volume.

The first education reforms in southern Vietnam predated Hồ Chí Minh's declaration of independence. By March 1945, the Japanese had permitted the establishment of the so-called State of Vietnam, or "Imperial Vietnam" (Đế quốc Việt Nam), whose first prime minister, Trần Trọng Kim, was a conservative academician and former colonial education administrator under the French. However short, Trần's six-month reign saw the transition of the southern curriculum to the Vietnamese language and Vietnamese oversight, albeit in a faithful translation of the French educational programme. By 1949, the Ministry of Education of the southern government had under its jurisdiction three primary superior schools (*collèges*) and 573 primary schools. The number of post-primary and primary school students numbered 2,686 and 119,600 respectively, but did not include some 5,000 students enrolled in private schools and over 23,000 enrolled in Chinese schools, mostly in Chợ Lớn (Vasavakul 1994, p. 51). Thaveeporn Vasavakul's previously cited comparative study of education in the north and south contains an exhaustive description of the southern education system, including organization, curricula, and finance.

With the establishment of the Republic of Vietnam in 1954 came great excitement over a new independent education system in the south, but also controversy, confusion, and disorder with respect to education policy. A recent collection of articles by Nguyễn Thanh Liêm, a former vice-minister of Education and Youth in the Republic of Vietnam, provides a fascinating glimpse of the situation in the south during this period. The volume includes contributions from more than twenty-five former educators and education officials and provides details for the period between 1955 and 1975. Upon its formation, the Republic of Vietnam (RVN) undertook successive rounds of education sector reforms. These achieved certain quantitative indicators of progress. Modelled after the French, the RVN's education system saw rapid growth. Between 1960 and 1970, the proportion of children that completed primary education in the Republic doubled, from 30 to 60 per cent, while by 1973 there were more than 100,000 students enrolled in over fifteen community colleges and universities (Nguyễn Thanh Liêm 2006, p. 6). War and increasing chaos in the south gradually eroded the southern education system before its collapse in 1975.

Education after 1975

After 1975, the state authorities waited until 1981 to adopt a unified national education system. Dire social conditions and acute shortages across the entire country meant that quality of education was lacking and there was uneven access across regions. The gradual imposition of a Soviet-style education system to the south of the country was one among many major changes in southern society in the post-war period. The exclusion of former teachers and of children from families and localities associated with the RVN, along with "re-education" camps, were indicative of the politicization of education in the immediate post-war south.

In many areas of post-war south, the same guerrilla education tactics used in the 1940s and 1950s were redeployed and so the development of education frequently depended on local initiative. As a primary school principal in Quảng Nam province recalled in a 1999 interview, "after the war, getting the school operating was a priority; getting children to come to school was difficult though and we had no money; but we were young and no one really cared about money at that time" (London 2004). The end of the war and social mobilization in the south contributed to rapid increases in school enrolments. Between 1976 and 1981, enrolments grew by some 260,000 pupils per year and by 1981, statistics indicated that almost a quarter of the entire population was enrolled in either primary or lower-secondary schools (Woodside 1991).

Over time, however, the development of the national education system was limited by acute financial constraints. By the 1980s, Vietnam had developed a sprawling education system and boasted enrolment figures comparable with countries ten times as wealthy. But the poor performance and gradual erosion of Vietnam's state socialist economic institutions undermined the fiscal foundations upon which the provision and payment for education depended. The quality of education remained hamstrung by threadbare conditions, particularly in rural areas and especially in remote regions. School attendance figures masked the fact that a "school day" for most children in rural areas consisted of no more than two or three hours.

While no detailed analysis of curricula can be offered here, some comments on the content of education during this period seem appropriate. In hindsight, many Vietnamese have questioned the practical relevance of the school curricula during the 1970s and 1980s, and many believe this deficiency remains. In the post American-war context, Vietnam's leaders demonstrated rhetorical flair in their emphasis on practically oriented "socialist" education. But the development of vocational education consistently fell short of such rhetoric. Heavy emphasis was placed on literature (including readings of "classics" not written for children), the celebration of nationalist symbols, heroes and legends, and other subjects far removed from the students' daily lives.

Some attribute these curricular peculiarities to Vietnam's leaders' intellectual failure to grasp the real significance of a skilled labour force. This, it is argued, is a consequence of the deeply engrained tradition of scholarly elitism which, whether in the study of analects or dialectics, tended to treat intellectual pursuits as a pathway from the world of manual labour to state power — what one scholar has aptly described as "the incomplete disappearance of Mandarin instincts" (Woodside 1991). In 1989, an academic writing in the leading party journal on the theme of education reforms for the next twenty years emphasized the need to reorient education policies towards vocational education, but still evidenced an underlying elitism, stating the need to steer those with "intellectual capability" towards careers as "scientific, technical, and economic cadres", while equipping the majority of students, those with a "fixed level of cultural development", with "essential and appropriate knowledge to step into a life of labour" (Nguyễn Quang Vinh 1989).

In the late 1980s, as Vietnam's economy descended into turmoil, the education system struggled to function. In the face of dire economic conditions, declining quality, the advent of school fees, and new economic opportunities, scores of young Vietnamese abandoned their studies, with many professional educators following suit. By the early 1990s, Vietnam's education system was in disarray. Further discussion of the education system in Vietnam during this period is provided in Chapter Two. A discussion of developments since the early 1990s immediately follows an overview of the organizational and operational attributes of contemporary Vietnam's education system.

THE ORGANIZATION AND OPERATION OF VIETNAM'S EDUCATION SYSTEM

Many of the organizational and operational attributes of Vietnam's education system are similar to those of other countries, while others are unique to Vietnam. The formal administrative organization of Vietnam's education system is fairly centralized, though there has been a recent movement towards greater decentralization. By contrast, the actual workings of the education system (including policy implementation processes and educational activities) are highly decentralized, owing to the nature of education and the broader features of social organization in Vietnam. The curriculum is fully standardized and broadly resembles that found in other countries. Other aspects of the curriculum — such as its content — can only be understood in relation to the peculiarities of Vietnamese history.

The Administrative Organization of the Education System

The state — understood here as the interpenetrated complex of party, government, bureaucracy, and all affiliated state organs — plays a dominant leadership role in the ordering and coordination of the education system, as it is by far the leading provider of education through various state-owned or state-managed schools.

The education system's administration is subordinated to formally centralized and hierarchical bureaucratic structures. One remarkable feature of the education system was the longevity of its leadership. Nguyễn Văn Huyên, for example, served as minister of Education from 1946 until 1975 (his successor, Nguyễn Thị Bình, served from 1976 until 1987). Until

1990, the Ministry of Education and the Ministry of Higher Education and Vocational Education were separate. In 1990, the Ministry of Education and Training (MOET) became the main national agency responsible for education matters, except those involving specialized institutes, universities, and schools falling under other functional parts of the state (such as medical schools, military, and maritime institutes).

MOET's responsibilities include the drafting of education planning strategies, the management of the education budget and human resources, and the formulation of laws and policies. These are approved by the National Assembly in accordance with the directives of the Communist Party of Vietnam (CPV). MOET works with other line ministries to determine investments in education and plays the leading role in determining the content of curricula.

At the local level, education matters are left to province-level departments of education and district-level offices of education. These are doubly accountable to MOET's organizational hierarchy, on the one hand, and to the People's Committees at their respective levels of government, on the other. At the province level and in the major cities (Hanoi, Ho Chí Minh City, Haiphong, and Danang), educational affairs are administered by departments of education (*Sở Giáo Dục*), whose responsibility is to implement national policies and manage resources. At the district or urban ward level, offices of education (*phòng giáo dục*) are accountable both to their local people's committee and to the provincial department of education. Provincial department of education are responsible for the direct oversight of upper-secondary education, whereas districts oversee lower levels. District-level offices of education manage school districts; populous districts may contain multiple school districts. At the commune (administrative village) level, People's Committees are responsible for mobilizing children for primary education and managing kindergarten and nursery schools. Virtually all communes have a "social affairs" cadre who may be involved in various education-related issues, and village heads (*trưởng thôn*) may also be involved in educational matters.

While all communes in Vietnam have a primary school and arrangements for preschool education, school districts may incorporate all or parts of several different communes. This is common in rural and sparsely populated areas, particularly at the level of secondary and upper-secondary education, where students from several communes will be pooled together in a school. The increasing number of non-state schools — including so-called "people founded" (*dân lập*) schools (for which the state may provide land or subsidies) and self-sufficient private (*tự thực*) schools — are more common in urban areas and draw students from different jurisdictions. As in any other country where place of residence affects location of schooling, families in Vietnam manoeuvre their children into schools of choice through diverse tactics.

Beyond secondary education, many districts and all provinces and major cities have an assortment of tertiary institutions, such as post-secondary colleges (*cao đẳng*), vocational schools, and colleges and universities. Vietnam's colleges (*trường cao đẳng*) are administered by provincial authorities. They typically enrol between one and two thousand students and offer single-focus training programmes for teachers and other professions. These colleges account for roughly 20 per cent of students enrolled in post-secondary education. Universities, by contrast, are established under the authority of the prime minister and administered by MOET and other functional ministries, such as health, finance, and defence.

Like virtually all other spheres of life in Vietnam, education and the education system are highly politicized. The CPV and its organs permeate all aspects of the education system. Party organizations for students and teachers exist at all levels of education, save preschool. Examples include the Ho Chi Minh Pioneers (*Đội thiếu niên tiền phong Hồ Chí Minh*) at the primary and lower-secondary school level and the Ho Chi Minh Communist Youth League (*Đoàn Thanh niên Cộng sản HCM*), active in secondary schools and above.

Educational Structure

The structure of Vietnam's education system is broadly consistent with that found in other countries and is given in Figure 1.1.

Figure 1.1 describes the structure and age-appropriate sequence of the education system as established by MOET. This structure has gone relatively unchanged since the early 1980s, though lower-secondary education has gradually been separated from primary education.

Bureaucratic Organization and Operation

The formal bureaucratic organization of the education system tells us only so much about its actual operational features. Vietnam's education system is a sprawling complex of thousands of linked organizations operating in diverse local circumstances. By 2008, the education system (that is, all public and non-public schools, institutes, and universities) accounted

FIGURE 1.1
Vietnam's Education System Structure

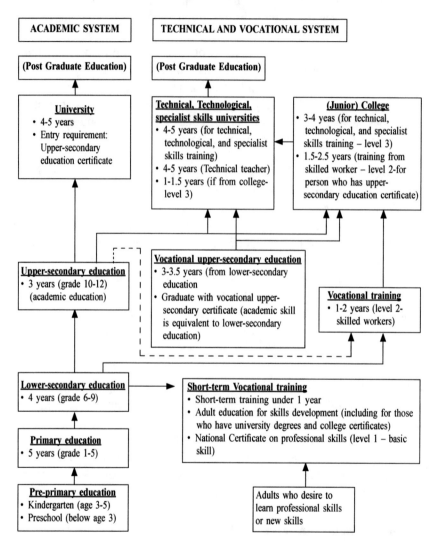

Note: If a student wishes to move from the technical and vocational system to the academic system or vice versa, he/she must pass a special transfer training programme, which is designed to be appropriate to each level of education.

Source: Adapted and translated from *Chien Luoc Phat Trien Giao Duc Viet Nam.*

for well over 20 million students and 1.5 million personnel. In 2006, the country had some 11,582 kindergartens, 14,834 primary schools, 9,635 lower-secondary schools, 2,044 upper-secondary schools, 307 combined lower- and upper-secondary schools, as well as over 300 universities and colleges and some 269 professional secondary schools (*trung cấp chuyên nghiệp*). The National Academy of Sciences and Technology and the National Academy for Social Sciences, which fall outside the administration of MOET, encompass twenty-eight and twenty-nine separate research institutes, respectively.

Taken alone, the general education system (consisting of primary, lower-secondary, and upper-secondary education) included some 16.2 million students and 789,000 teachers (GSO 2007). Each of Vietnam's sixty-four provinces and 593 districts has local education administration units, employing thousands of "education cadres" (*cán bộ*). There is, in addition to the formal education system, a vast system of informal education in the form of after-hours private tuition.

Despite recent reforms, the formal administrative organization of the education system is quite centralized. Critics of this centralization decry "controlism" (*chủ quản*), understood as a range of behaviours by central authorities that stifle local innovation. No doubt, the centralizing pretensions of MOET have not disappeared. In a 2006 interview, one MOET official asserted that from his office it was possible to know what was being taught at any hour of any day in any corner of Vietnam. On the other hand, decentralization in a poorly regulated setting, such as Vietnam's poses its own risks. Given ongoing concerns about cost, quality, and equity, the move towards decentralization raised important questions about the appropriate future roles of MOET. Central-local tensions exist over a wide range of concerns, including curriculum and quality controls, personnel, and finance.

And yet decentralization has and continues to be a salient operational feature of the education system, in some respects owing to the nature of education, in other respects owing to the nature of the Vietnamese state. Two different types of decentralization need to be specified. There is a long tradition of informal *de facto* decentralization in which local units of the state respond to local circumstances and exigencies. The war and poverty that Vietnam experienced during the middle parts of the twentieth century required local education administrators and teachers to develop innovative and, at times, illicit improvisational strategies simply to survive periods of acute shortages.

Since 1996, Vietnam has been undergoing a process of administrative decentralization, which has had important effects on the education system. The Budget Laws of 1996 and 2002 marked a significant change in granting local authorities (especially provinces) increased discretion over education spending, provided (in principle) that centrally determined norms are met. Decree 43, which took effect in 2006, encourages schools and other local public service delivery units to expand their own non-budgetary sources of income through various revenue enhancing activities (such as the establishment of service companies and special services) and to adopt a "business-model" of management. As we will observe throughout this volume, the issues of decentralization and (especially) school autonomy are the subject of considerable debate in Vietnam today.

A comprehensive analysis of MOET would be fascinating if not impossibly complicated. The organization is unquestionably in transition. But its direction is sometimes difficult to discern. Many aspects of its organization show that there is significant organizational learning going on. Then again, in late 2008, MOET released its "Draft of National Education Strategic Planning 2009–2020", which was immediately subject to heavy public criticism. The document, which had been revised more than ten times within MOET before its public release, managed largely to ignore several earlier (and better regarded) education policies. MOET ultimately had to withdraw this strategy document. Controversies have also erupted concerning control over education budgets. Ironically, while the MOET strategy document called for administrative centralization (going against its own quite recent rhetorical statements about the need for decentralization), MOET is rapidly losing control over education expenditure, which is increasingly being ceded to provinces.

TRENDS IN THE EDUCATION SYSTEM SINCE 1989

Since the late 1980s, Vietnam's education system has changed considerably. The most important of these changes have been (1) large and sustained increases in education spending; (2) shifts in the principles and institutions governing the provision and payment for education; and (3) continuous if uneven expansions in the scale of the education system, as indicated by enrolments and other measures. These trends have manifested themselves differently across different regions and different segments of the population. We next examine the nature and significance of these trends in turn.

Increasing Education Expenditure

The rapid economic growth that Vietnam has experienced since the late 1980s has permitted significant and sustained increases in total education spending, where "total spending" includes public, private/household, and spending from other sources, such as official development assistance (ODA).[14]

Public spending on education has grown significantly in both absolute terms and as a proportion of GDP. Between 1990 and 2006, recurrent budgetary spending on education increased from 1 to 3.5 per cent of GDP (MPI 2006). Between 2001 and 2006 the government's annual budget for education trebled. By 2008, education accounted for roughly 23 per cent of the state budget and the government has indicated its intention to maintain this level for the foreseeable future. The government has also signalled its intent to bring total public spending on education up to 6.9 per cent of GDP by 2010, compared with roughly 1.8 per cent in 1994.[15] In the 2007 education budget, primary education accounted for some 28 per cent, lower- and upper-secondary for a combined 36 per cent (24 and 11 per cent respectively), followed by tertiary education (16 per cent), vocational and professional secondary education (four per cent each), continuing education (two per cent), with the remainder going to "other" categories.

Like most developing countries, Vietnam sees a large proportion (over 80 per cent) of its recurrent public spending on education going to teachers' wages.[16] Recent years have seen several rounds of wage increases, reflected in a more than fourfold increase in recurrent expenditures. Salaries and wages vary considerably across regions and different parts of the education system, however. Finally, the very slow growth in teachers' pay over the 1990s created hardships for teachers and contributed to the institutionalization of such practices as illegal fees, the private provision of after-hours "extra-study" classes by nominally "public" teachers, and various forms of academic corruption. Future policies on teachers' pay have wide-ranging implications for the costs and quality of education in Vietnam and it will be interesting to see whether future pay increases will mitigate the current trends towards the commodification and commercialization of "public" education.

Increased public spending on education has also gone to finance construction and various programmes targeting poor and vulnerable segments of the population. Between 2001 and 2007, capital expenditure on education (mainly for new construction and facility upgrades) increased more than fourfold, while education spending on so-called target programmes increased more than fivefold. The construction boom, along with the reorganization of schools and school districts, has resulted in increasing numbers of schools of all levels. Importantly, public education spending has been broadly redistributive in that education budgets effectively rely on interprovincial fiscal transfers through the central budget. On the other hand, the educational and infrastructural needs of poorer regions are more acute than those of wealthier areas, and budgetary transfers, though they have increased, are often inadequate for local needs.

Increased household expenditure has grown alongside increases in average per capita incomes and earnings, which has grown from roughly US$200 in the early 1990s, to a projected US$1,000–US$1,050 today. Though estimates vary, evidence suggests household spending on education approaches or exceeds public spending, and that, proportionally, household spending on education in Vietnam is higher than in other countries in East Asia, save Cambodia.[17]

As we would expect, there are sharp differences in household spending across regions and different income/expenditure quintiles of the population. Whether and how these discrepancies affect enrolment and academic performance is addressed later in this introduction and in the different chapters comprising this volume. Table 1.1 shows estimated annual per

TABLE 1.1
Average Estimated Real Expenditure per Student in Past 12 Months
('000 Vietnam Dong, per capita expenditure/income quintiles)

	2004	2006	2008
Poorest	413	467	671
Near Poor	647	934	1,129
Middle	689	1,086	2,302
Near Rich	1,523	1,778	1,932
Rich	2,545	3,000	4,319

Source: GSO 2010.

capita expenditure on education per student in Vietnam for the period 2004 to 2008, across five different expenditure quintiles of the population.

Table 1.1 illustrates how household educational expenditures of Vietnam's wealthiest quintile are roughly six times those of the lowest. These differences reflect not only regional variance in school fees and other charges, but also the varying sums households across and within regions pay for private "extra-study" classes. For example, by 2008 it was not uncommon for households in Ho Chi Minh City or Hanoi to pay more than US$100 per month on "extra study" classes — an unimaginable sum for poor households in any region.

International development organizations have invested substantially in Vietnam's education system, through both grants and technical assistance. The World Bank and Asian Development Bank (ADB) have been the most important donors, with the World Bank focusing on primary and (since 1998) tertiary education and the ADB on secondary education.[18] Up until 2007, the World Bank had provided some US$535 million in educational assistance (including grants, loans on concessional terms, and technical assistance).[19] Other international organizations such as UNICEF and bilateral development agencies have contributed significant funds and expertise. Important bilateral donors to Vietnam's education system have included Canada, the United Kingdom, Holland, Japan, Norway, Singapore, and the United States. Examples of large foreign-sponsored education projects include a US$139 million in credit for the primary education of disadvantaged children in 2003, organized by the World Bank and sponsored by bilateral donors; and bilateral support for the Mekong 1000 project, which aims to train 1,000 Vietnamese government staff. Up until 2007, the World Bank's credits to higher education projects has exceeded US$140 million. In 2009, the government announced plans to build four "international standard" universities, with a loan of US400 million from the World Bank and ADB. These will be Vietnam's first public, non-profit, foreign-managed universities.[20]

Grants and technical assistance are aligned with grant makers' normative commitments. Hence, for example, in addition to various projects aimed at curricular reform and teacher training, and primary education for poor and vulnerable children, the World Bank's emphases have broadly been on measures to enhance cost efficiency and increase the role of markets. Through the International Finance Corporation (IFC), the Bank has invested and will continue to invest in private education.[21]

Another somewhat strange, but noteworthy, arrangement is the US–Vietnam Education Fund, which allows Vietnam to pay the RVN debt to the United States back into a special education fund, which can then be used to fund overseas scholarships for (as it turns out) hand-picked state-affiliated Vietnamese.

Non-governmental organizations (NGOs) have also played an important role. While NGOs have not been a major source of education finance, they have played important roles in steering funds, piloting innovative programmes, and raising awareness of education sector needs.[22] Overall, increases in education spending have contributed to increases in the scale of the education system. But the significance of spending increases is better understood in relation to the shifting principles governing education finance.

Changes in the Principles Governing the Provision and Payment for Education

Since 1989, Vietnam has experienced a shift from an education system based on principles of universalism and public finance to a hybrid system combining state and non-state provision of education, and public and private (that is, household) responsibility for education finance. While the state remains by far the largest provider of education, state policies have sought to shift financial responsibility for education payment onto households. The transition from public financing to the current hybrid system was hastened by the demise of state socialism in the late 1980s. In addition to public and household expenditure, the state has sought to promote what it calls the "socialization" (*xã hội hóa*) of education, understood here as broad-based social mobilization of resources for education, not public finance of education. For the above reasons, the analysis of education finance in Vietnam defies conventional categories, such as public and private.

Vietnam's market transition in the late 1980s entailed the rapid erosion of collectivist institutions that had formerly been responsible for education finance. Over the course of the 1990s, growth in public spending on education was significant, but moderate. State policies in the early 1990s sought to stabilize the education system by allowing for the introduction of fees (in 1989) and the limited "non-state" provision of education through so-called "people-founded" schools. In subsequent years, local authorities and schools resorted to chronic scarcities by introducing and increasing fees of various types (tuition fees, construction "contributions", medical insurance, water and sanitation, and other fees — legal and illegal). The 1990s also saw the emergence (or rather re-emergence) of so-called "semi-public" schools and classrooms — a category of schools that (ironically enough) existed in the Republic of Vietnam, and which is financed through a combination of state subsidies and fees. Perhaps most importantly, across the country, teachers resorted to teaching of so-called "extra-study" classes after school hours, and income from such activities increasingly became their most important source of income.

In essence, the collapse of state socialism produced an institutional vacuum in the area of education finance; certain national and local *ad hoc* responses grew into institutionalized features of the education system. While public expenditure on education has increased, these increases have not been sufficient to address needs, while household expenditure tends to benefit children from wealthier households disproportionately. To address the residual funding gap, the state has sought to promote the "socialization" of education. Enthusiasts of socialization understand it to be a peculiarly Vietnamese form of social mobilization, embodying the values of community and mutual assistance under the leadership of the Party (see, for example, BGDĐT 1999; Chu Văn Thành 2004, 2007). They have a point. Social mobilization in the name of education is not new to Vietnam, as some forms of compulsory community contributions to schools existed even during the state-socialist period and earlier. On the other hand, critics of "socialization" see it as the state shirking its responsibilities. Either way, the need for socialization appears to arise mainly from the absence of a mature tax system and the limited allocative capacities of the central state.

Given the shifting of responsibilities for education payment, the expanding role of non-state provision of education, and the mobilization of funds from other sources, it is no surprise that education finance in Vietnam is a messy practice. Fees and private payments for public education are pervasive. Various forms of "non state" schools (such as "people-founded schools" and private "self-sufficient schools") are almost always organized and operated by people within or closely associated with networks of state power and can draw substantially on state resources. "Socialization" resembles charitable donations in some instances and regressive taxes in others. In short, the analysis of education finance in Vietnam defies conventional public-private categorizations.

Increasing Scale and Scope, Shifting Inequalities

Rapid increases in enrolment indicate that Vietnam's education system is growing in scale. Once-huge disparities between regions and rural and urban zones have declined. Enrolment for girls has surpassed that for boys. Increases in the proportion of children attending school at their age-appropriate grade — the so-called net enrolment rate — indicates that formal schooling is becoming a more institutionalized feature of social life. Yet enrolment data have important limitations, both general and owing to specific conditions in Vietnam. Enrolment data supplemented with other data provide us with a general understanding of trends and differentials across Vietnam's education system and within different educational levels.

The Value and Limitations of Enrolment Data

Enrolment data are useful for gauging general trends and differentials in school attendance, but are not particularly informative about other basic concerns. An understanding of trends and differentials in Vietnam's education system requires an appreciation of the value and limits of enrolment data.

In Vietnam as in many countries, increases in school enrolment are taken as indicators of progress. Internationally institutionalized development rubrics, such as the Millennium Development Goals, tend to reinforce this view. The emphasis on enrolment rates in Vietnam may be especially strong, owing to decades of state-socialist developmentalism in which physical production targets were the standard barometers of performance. The emphasis on enrolment rates as progress creates strong incentives for Vietnamese state agencies, officials, and teachers to report exaggerated enrolment and graduation figures and shuttle students through the system, regardless of learning outcomes. In Vietnam, this tendency to exaggerate successes has been appropriately dubbed "achievement syndrome" (*bệnh thành tích*), which detracts from the credibility of enrolment figures, even those quoted in high-level planning documents.[23]

The volume and quality of enrolment data in Vietnam have no doubt improved. The most widely cited enrolment data come from the large-scale foreign-sponsored household surveys, such as the Vietnam Living Standards Survey (VNLSS) and the Vietnam Household Living Standards Survey (VHLSS). While these surveys may provide the most credible enrolment data, they are not without important problems. Perhaps most notably, these surveys may miss large numbers of migrant households as well as non-official residents. Many of these "missing households" are poor and their children's educational status go unreported (Pincus and Sender 2008). Finally, enrolment data alone are unable to account for wide variances in the costs, qualities, and distributions of education. Pairing enrolment data with other sorts of data provides a better understanding of developments in Vietnam's education system.

System-wide Trends

In spite of deficiencies in the data, it is reasonable to assert that over the last two decades, Vietnam has seen rapid increases in school enrolments at virtually all education levels. Table 1.2 lists net (that is, age appropriate) school enrolment data for primary, lower-secondary, and upper-secondary education for the period 1993–2006. 2008 data, which became available only in 2010, show less significant changes.

As Table 1.2 indicates, Vietnam has registered steady increases in net enrolment at the primary, lower-secondary, and upper-secondary levels. Increases in lower- and upper-secondary education have been striking, rising by 2.5 and seven times respectively. The increasing scale of higher education is equally impressive. As of 2008, there were over 1.3 million Vietnamese enrolled in tertiary institutions, compared with 162,000 in 1993. When the data are disaggregated to account for urban/rural and regional differences, a more interesting, but no less impressive, picture emerges, as illustrated in Tables 1.3 and 1.4.

TABLE 1.2
Estimated Net Enrolment Rate (NER), 1993–2008

	1993	1998	2002	2006	2008
Primary	86.7	91.4	90.1	89.3	88.3
Lower-secondary	30.1	61.7	72.1	78.8	78.4
Upper-secondary	7.2	28.6	41.8	53.9	54.2

Sources: VLSS 1997–98 (GSO 2000, p.52); VLSS 1992–93 (GSO 1994, p. 50); 2004 and 2006, the author calculated percentages on the basis of VLSS (2004; 2006); * indicates MICs Data 2006, VHLSS 2008 (GSO), VHLSS 2010, GSO.

TABLE 1.3

Estimated NER by Level of Education in Urban and Rural Areas, 1993–2008

	1993	1998	2002	2006	2008
Primary					
Urban	85.58	95.92	94.1	89.7	89.2
Rural	76.56	91.96	89.2	89.1	88.1
Lower-secondary					
Urban	55.8	81.9	80.8	82.8	82.6
Rural	31.8	57.2	69.9	77.7	77.1
Upper-secondary					
Urban	30.2	54.9	59.2	66.3	66.4
Rural	6.9	21.9	37.7	50.3	50.6

Sources: VLSS 1997-98 (GSO 2000, p. 52); VLSS 1992–3 (GSO 1994, p. 50); 2004 and 2006, the author calculated percentages on the basis of VLSS (2004; 2006); * indicates MICs Data 2006, VHLSS 2008 (GSO), VHLSS 2010, GSO.

TABLE 1.4

Estimated NER by Level of Schooling Region, 2008

	Primary	Lower-Secondary	Upper-secondary
Country-wide	88.3	78.4	54.2
Regions			
Red River Delta	91.3	85.2	69.5
Northeast	89.7	79.9	52.5
Northwest	81.4	63.9	33.4
North Central	89.3	81.6	57.4
South Central	87.9	82.0	58.4
Central Highlands	85.6	69.9	44.4
Southeast	88.5	79.0	54.7
Mekong Delta	86.7	71.5	40.4

Source: VHLSS 2010.

Table 1.3 lists net enrolment rates for primary, lower-secondary, and upper-secondary enrolment by urban and rural areas. As we observe, disparities between urban and rural areas have declined at all levels of the general education system.

Table 1.4 indicates enrolment levels across different regions of Vietnam. While the data are not given here, interregional variation in enrolment levels have declined across all levels of the general education system. On the other hand, gaps between regions have become larger in upper-secondary education. In higher education, large differentials between regions remain. As recently as 2005, the gross enrolment rate in higher education in Vietnam's north-west region was 6 per cent, three times less than in the Red River Delta.

One striking feature of enrolment in Vietnam is the relative parity that exists in boys' and girls' enrolment from kindergarten through upper-secondary education into tertiary education. As recently as the mid-1990s, nationwide enrolments in lower- and upper-secondary education were a full five percentage points lower for girls. Today, the primary school and secondary completion rate for girls and boys is virtually equal. In Vietnam's south-eastern wealthiest region, female enrolment in (lower and upper) secondary education is, at 83.9 per cent, significantly higher than male's, at 73.7 per cent (UNICEF-GSO 2008, p. 96). Nationally, female net enrolment in upper secondary education is 56.4 per cent, whereas male enrolment is 51.5 per cent (VHLSS 2008). Female enrolment in higher education is higher than male enrolment, in both colleges and (undergraduate) university education. On the other hand, enrolment parity does not mean that gendered inequalities have ceased to exist. Research by Belanger and Liu (2004), for example, suggests that in poorer families, boys' education tends to be privileged over girls. An interesting question is whether and to what extent household expenditure on "extra study" differs among boys and girls across and within households.

As will be observed across different levels of education, ethnic minorities continue to lag behind those in the ethnic *Kinh* and *Hoa* groups. The reasons for this include the physical remoteness of many ethnic populations, lags in developing public infrastructure (including schools) in remote areas, as well as various forms of cultural and linguistic barriers, and discrimination. Past efforts to "universalize" primary education among ethnic minorities did not always contribute to better educational outcomes. The rush to boost primary education (and enrolment figures) among ethnic minorities in the 1990s, for example, involved new arrangements that allowed students to "pass" two grades in a single year, and five grades in as few as 120 weeks for ethnic minority students.

In the past, Vietnam's education system was characterized by sharp differences in the quality of education. Quality is, of course, a slippery term that can be assessed in many ways, including differences in amount of schooling, the adequacy of school, infrastructure, teachers' qualifications, and the relevance of the curriculum, to name a few. Vietnam has seen advances across most of these dimensions.

Until quite recently, many schools in rural and remote areas were makeshift facilities. New school construction, infrastructural upgrades, and gradual declines in population growth have reduced the incidence of double- and triple-shift schools and allowed for longer school hours. As recently as the late 1990s, it was common for children in remote areas to have no more than two hours of schooling a day in a thirty-three week school year — one of the shortest school years in the world (Oxfam 1998). By contrast, in April of 2009, MOET announced that some 35 per cent of primary students in thirty-five poor mountainous provinces would study a full school day, like students in wealthier provinces. While investments in school construction have reduced this phenomenon, it remains common in preschool education in many rural areas. Today, large proportions of schools in rural areas lack adequate water and sanitation facilities. With respect to the quality of instruction, gaps remain. In remote and rural areas, schools are often understaffed while the skills of those employed fall short of national standards and local needs.

Another dimension of quality concerns the relevance of the curricula. If Vietnam is to chart a path of sustainable, rapid, and equitable development, it must — at the very least — develop a skilled workforce capable of creating value and competing internationally. But there is wide questioning in Vietnam about the adequacy and appropriateness of the educational curriculum at virtually all levels. Talk of the need for curricular reform is nothing new, but the sense that there is a need for change is perhaps stronger today than in the past. Today, Vietnam's leaders frequently speak of their intent to develop a "knowledge economy". This stands in stark contrast with the current thrust of prevailing pedagogy and practice, where the emphasis is still on rote memorization and attempts to innovate are actively or structurally discouraged.

As the foregoing discussion suggests, the scale of the education system has grown while the magnitudes of certain educational inequalities in Vietnam have declined. An examination of developments within different educational levels provides a more nuanced picture.

Trends and Differentials Across Educational Levels

Preschool Education

Across the various educational levels, it is arguably preschool — including nursery school (*mầm non*) and kindergarten (*mẫu giáo*) — that has seen the most disorganized growth. However recent years have seen something of a reversal. Until the late 1980s, nursery school and kindergarten education was — in principle — provided and paid for by collectivist institutions, such as agricultural cooperatives, enterprises, and other state organizations. When these institutions unravelled, so too did institutional arrangements governing early childhood education. Central government efforts to develop lagged over the course of the 1990s and preschool education has generally been underfunded. Nonetheless, preschool and kindergarten education has gradually been reintegrated into the administrative and financial operations of the educational system.

Making sense of the data on preschool education in Vietnam is complicated, to say the least. The term administrative category "kindergarten" (*mẫu giáo*) is a misnomer, for it really refers to preschools, which include both kindergarten and nursery schools. Today, roughly three million children regularly attend preschool and kindergarten. There are in Vietnam nearly 12,000 preschools, roughly half of which are public and half so-called "people-founded" (sometimes also called "private"). Within these 12,000 are roughly 9,000 nursery schools (35 per cent of which are people-founded) and some 3,000 kindergartens (which are 70 per cent "public").[24]

Public and private expenditure on preschool and kindergarten education has increased alongside economic growth, but public spending on early childhood education remains marginal compared with that for other education levels. In 2002, the government mandated that early childhood education must account for at least 10 per cent of total education spending, but as of 2006, only seventeen of sixty-four provinces were able to reach this target (UNICEF 2008, p. 9). Not surprisingly, many aspects of early childhood education have been subject to market principles. State-managed preschools charge fees for service in most areas and are staffed by underpaid young women on short-term contracts.[25]

In general, attendance for early childhood education is lower than might be expected as a recent UNICEF-sponsored survey is revealed. By 2006, an estimated 57 per cent of children aged thirty-six to fifty-nine months were regularly attending some form of school with wide gaps across different segments of the population (MICS 2006). Roughly 75 per cent of urban children in this age group attended some form of schooling, compared with just over half in rural areas (UNICEF 2008). There was significant variation across regions, with the highest rates in the Red River Delta (80 per cent) and north central regions (67 per cent). Interestingly, the lowest rates are found in the Mekong Delta (roughly 40 per cent) and the south central coastal region (44 per cent). While the low rate for the Mekong region may be attributed to geographical barriers, the low figure for the south central coast is not readily explicable. Vietnam's poorest regions — the north-west and central highlands also fared poorly, with just 50 and 44 per cent of the children attending some form of early childhood education.

In rural and remote regions, the material circumstances of early childhood education can be extremely rudimentary. In poor regions, many preschools and kindergartens lack water or electricity and use open pits as toilets. Some preschools make use of other facilities, such as commune "cultural houses". Many localities are unable to meet local preschool needs. In fieldwork carried out in Lao Cai province in 2008, local authorities related their need to turn tens of three and four-year-old students away for lack of adequate facilities.

Addressing inequalities in early childhood education will mean diminishing the currently strong association between income and schooling on the one hand, and parents' level of education and schooling on the other. More than 80 per cent of wealthier households send their children to preschool, as do over 83 per cent of mothers with an upper-secondary education. By contrast, less than half of mothers with no upper-secondary education send their preschool-aged children to school. Sex discrimination in early childhood education does not appear to be a problem, at least not within the Kinh ethnic group. Nationally, preschool and kindergarten attendance is higher for girls than boys, at 61 and 53 per cent respectively. An estimated 39 per cent of small children from non-Kinh ethnic groups were attending school, compared with 60 per cent for Kinh, although these figures may overestimate actual enrolment.[26] Still, these and other poor regions have seen increases in state efforts to boost early childhood education in poor regions and among poor groups through conditional cash payments and other schemes.[27]

Current efforts to promote preschool education are motivated by the observed consequences of inadequate preschool education, particularly among the poor. Children with some preschool education tend to perform significantly better than those without it. In Vietnam, only 60 per cent of children under five live in houses with a minimum of three non-children's books, and only 24.7 per cent of children under five live in houses with children's books (UNICEF-GSO 2008, p. 93). Currently, Vietnam's state and international donors such as the World Bank are assigning greater priority to preschool education, driven by the recognition that early childhood education is essential for increasing the academic performance of vulnerable groups and promoting further poverty reduction.

Primary Education

For decades, primary education was the central focus of Vietnam's education policy. The constitution and education law stipulate that primary education is compulsory and provided free to all citizens. In 2008, Vietnam's government declared that primary education had been "universalized" (*phổ cập giáo dục tiểu học*), by which it meant that practically all Vietnamese children had access to primary education.[28]

The actual picture is more complicated. It suggests that while all Vietnamese have access to primary education and the vast majority complete primary education, significant numbers of children do not complete primary education at the age-appropriate grade and a non-trivial number do not complete it at all. Survey data indicate that by 2006, 93.5 per cent of children aged six were attending primary school, while the net primary enrolment rate was estimated at 88 to 89 per cent, meaning that the majority of children attending primary school were studying in their age-appropriate grades (VHLSS 2006). A UNICEF survey found that 81.7 per cent of children of primary completion age (age 11) were indeed completing the last year of primary education and that, of all children starting the first grade, 97.5 per cent would eventually reach grade five (UNICEF-GSO 2008, p. 97). By 2008, there were nearly seven million primary school students, though a decline in birth rates over the next ten years will mean a gradual shrinkage in the scale of primary education.

Compulsory primary education has gradually eroded regional and income disparities. Urban/rural discrepancies in primary enrolment are gone, even as disparities in the costs and quality of primary schools remain. A 2006 survey actually found higher net-enrolment rates among six-year olds in rural areas (UNICEF–GSO 2008, p. 96). Primary enrolment in Vietnam exceeds 90 per cent across all major regions and social groups,

TABLE 1.5
Net Primary Enrolment, 1993–2006

	1993	1998	2002	2004	2006
Poorest	66.9	84.8	84.5	83.0	85.4
Near Poor	77.57	94.47	90.3	91.3	88.3
Middle	81.49	94.82	91.9	90.2	90.1
Near Rich	84.96	96.27	93.7	92.9	90.1
Rich	84.77	96.81	95.3	89.7	90.1

Sources: VLSS 1997-98 (GSO 2000, p. 52); VLSS 1992–3 (GSO 1994, p. 50); 2004 and 2006, the author calculated percentages on the basis of VLSS (2004; 2006).

excluding ethnic minorities and the very poor. In important respects, state financed primary education is the most progressive component of Vietnam's education system. The relation between income and primary enrolment has also declined over time. By 2006, the difference between the poorest and wealthiest quintiles of the population was around five per cent, as illustrated in Table 1.5.

However, comparisons across regions, income/expenditure groups, and ethnicities reveal that many disparities remain. Gross completion ratios for primary education are significantly higher (at 89 per cent) in urban areas than in rural areas (80 per cent) (UNICEF-GSO 2008, p. 98). Vietnam's poorest regions — the north-west and central highlands — and one of its richest (in income terms) — the Mekong delta — exhibit some of the lowest primary enrolments, reflecting geographical and ethnic obstacles unique to those regions. Estimated net primary enrolment rates for these regions in 2008 were 81, 86, and 87 per cent respectively. Once again, these enrolment figures do not capture disparities in the quality or material circumstances of primary education across regions. It is also the case that laws and policies notwithstanding, primary schools still collect fees of various kinds and that these fees weigh more heavily on those who can least afford to pay them. This issue has received considerable attention in Vietnamese-language literature, which is reviewed immediately following this section.

Secondary Education

Increases in lower- and upper-secondary enrolment since the early 1990s have been striking. Between 1993 and 2008, net lower-secondary enrolment more than doubled (from 30 to 79 per cent), while upper-secondary enrolment increased sevenfold.[29] As of 2006, 91 per cent of children who completed the last grade of primary school continued onto (though not necessarily complete) lower-secondary school (UNICEF–GSO 2008, p. 99). Only roughly five per cent of secondary-school-aged children were attending primary school, though this figure is higher across poor regions and poor segments of the population. Non-state schools, that is, people-founded and private schools, play an increasingly important role in the provision of secondary and especially upper-secondary education. By 2007 in Hanoi, for example, non-state schools accounted for over forty per cent of upper-secondary enrolment — a surprising figure, indeed.[30]

By 2010, the government aims to "universalize" lower-secondary education, though in 2008 only forty of sixty-five provinces were on track to do so. Though it is clear that Vietnam is a long way from ensuring that all children have access to upper-secondary education, the government's target for doing so is 2015. By 2008, there were nearly six million lower-secondary students and over three million upper-secondary students instructed by some 312,000 lower-secondary and 135,000 upper-secondary teachers respectively. As of 2008, there were some 275 vocational secondary schools, administered by various line ministries and under the supervision of MOET. Vocational education is addressed in the next subsection.

Disparities in secondary school enrolments have declined across regions and groups. At both the lower- and upper-secondary levels, the gaps in enrolment between urban and rural areas have narrowed considerably, to around 10 per cent. At the lower-secondary level, there have been impressive declines in regional enrolment inequalities. Between 1992 and 2008, net lower-secondary school enrolment increased in the north-west mountainous region from 30 to 64 per cent, in the central highlands from 21 to 70 per cent, and in the Mekong from 22 to 72 per cent. In the same regions, net upper-secondary enrolment increased from 10 to 33 per cent, 2 to 44 per cent, and 6 to 40 per cent respectively.[31]

Still, significant regional, socio-economic, and ethnic disparities remain. Given various fees and extra-study expenses, the costs of education have increased significantly, reaching their apex in upper-secondary education. In effect, lower- and upper-secondary education functions as a sorting mechanism, excluding many poor children, thereby increasing the likelihood that their poverty will endure. For many children in Vietnam's poor households, completing upper-secondary education remains enormously difficult. Children from poor households and ethnic minority groups remain much less likely to attend secondary schools. Transitions from primary to lower-secondary or from lower-secondary to upper-secondary education are when students are most likely to drop out or discontinue their studies. The gap in net enrolment rates for the poorest and richest households is over 25 per cent for lower-secondary education and over 55 per cent for upper-secondary enrolment. 2008 and 2009 have seen a surge in dropouts, as inflation, declining earnings, and rising prices associated with economic turbulence have impinged on expenditures on education.

Although enrolments have increased among children from ethnic minority groups, children from such backgrounds — especially girls — continue to face obstacles to continuing their studies. A recent UNICEF–UNESCO report found that girls from ethnic minority backgrounds had systematically lower educational attainment, despite the increasing availability of schools in their areas. Research revealed that major obstacles included financial barriers, the perceived need to work, poor quality of education, inadequate infrastructure, and the parents' low regard for education in comparison to other imperatives. However, the research also noted significant variability across ethnic groups, suggesting caution in making sweeping generalizations.[32]

Tertiary and Vocational Education

Vietnam has seen rapid increases in tertiary and vocational enrolment and a proliferation of colleges, universities, and vocational schools. Between 1999 and 2008 the number of universities in Vietnam more than doubled, from sixty-nine to 160, while the number of vocational schools (colleges) nearly trebled, from eighty-four to 209.[33] Today, over 1.6 million Vietnamese are attending colleges and universities in Vietnam, nearly double that of ten years ago. The role of non-state education has increased as well. Of the 330 colleges and universities in 2007, about fifty were non-state, accounting for roughly 12 per cent of tertiary students. By 2020, government targets stipulate that non-state providers of higher education will account for 40 per cent of enrolments. There is also intense debate on financing higher education and whether or not some public universities ought to be privatized.[34]

While tertiary and vocational education are the fastest growing segments of the education system, they are arguably also the segments most in dire need of reform. The higher education system is failing to meet the increasing demand for skilled labour. Within universities, staff tend to be undertrained, underpaid, and have few opportunities to pursue research. Vietnam is generally weak on research in both physical and social sciences and lacks a single university of international standard. Recently, the Ministry of Education and Training has focused on the goal of rapidly developing higher education, through such measures as training 20,000 PhD holders by 2020.

But there are doubts about what can be achieved, given outstanding problems in the education bureaucracy and within universities themselves. Academic freedom is tightly bound. The education bureaucracy is widely accused of undermining local initiatives, though higher education leaders are themselves inexperienced in decision making. In rural areas, especially remote regions, there are few outlets for higher education and most schools that do exist tend to offer training that is incommensurate with ongoing processes of economic diversification. Until recently, Vietnamese who were trained overseas were more likely to return to bureaucratic posts than industry or applied work.[35] Sustained improvements in living standards require a shift towards the production of higher value-added commodities, but undertaking such a shift requires a skilled workforce and a higher education system that the country presently lacks. There are also major questions about the role of foreign-operated tertiary institutions. Numerous foreign universities (including many from the United States) are anxious to establish operations in Vietnam (Overland 2009).

CURRENT LITERATURE, CURRENT ISSUES, AND THE CONTRIBUTIONS OF THIS VOLUME

The literature concerning Vietnam's education system has grown rapidly and a comprehensive overview is not possible. Rather, the survey presented here distinguishes several major genres of literature, indentifies key debates and, in the course of doing so, introduces and situates the contributions to this volume.

Genres of Literature on Vietnam's Education System

Current literature on Vietnam's education system falls into several distinctive genres, including policy documents and analysis, press reports, academic literature, and materials published online.

Until the late 1990s, most Vietnamese educational literature remained largely descriptive policy literature. General overviews provide useful summaries of the education system's development (for example, MOET 1991), though much of the literature tends to be in the traditional reporting format of listing statistics, stating successes and shortcomings, and concluding with the unquestionable correctness of the party line (for example, UBQGCNMC 1994). Former Education Minister Phạm Minh Hạc's *Vietnam's Education on the Threshold of the 21st Century* (1999), available in both Vietnamese and English, is exemplary of this genre. Lê Văn Giạng's more recent book (2003) provides a 1,000-year historical overview. More detailed policy literature can be found in leading Vietnamese state education journals, such as *Nghiên Cứu Giáo Dục* (Education Research), *Thông tin Khoa học Giáo dục* (Educational Science Information), and *Thông tin Quản lý Giáo dục* (Educational Management Information). Ideological pronouncements on education appear regularly in party journals and newspapers, such as *Tập Chí Cộng Sản* (Communist Review) and *Nhân Dân*.

Recent years have seen the emergence of more varied and critical policy literature. The analysis is more empirically grounded, rigorous, and critical. Such literature emanates from both within and outside the state education apparatus. Various books and articles on education exhibit new ways of thinking and an eagerness to view problems in Vietnam from a comparative international perspective (for example, Trần 1996). A number of books approach education from the perspective of public administration reform (for example, Vũ 1998; Lê 2003), while others focus on the special problems of education in a market economy (for example, Nguyễn 2006). Rather than fading away, retired state officials and former educators and academicians weigh in forcefully in current debates, frequently through newspaper articles and online postings (for example, Bùi Trọng Lễu 2006).

Recent years have seen the publication of collections of analyses on education in books and online. A recent collection of essays titled *Những vấn đề giáo dục hiện nay* (Current Problems in Education) includes over thirty spirited essays, many of which are quite critical of current education policies (NXBTT 2007). This collection includes a sharply critical 2004 piece by Vietnam's most famous nonagenarian, Võ Nguyên Giáp, who decries the inadequacies of education in the country today. Other contributions argue for the need to raise or lower fees, increase or decrease public financing, and pose suggestions for improving the quality and relevance of education at all levels. Literature on higher education is growing especially rapidly (for example, Vũ Quang Việt 2007; Hồ Tú Bảo et al. 2008).

At the outset of 1990s, English publications on education in Vietnam largely consisted of translated MOET documents on such themes as "Education for All". The arrival of international development organizations in the early 1990s was accompanied by new survey research and more sophisticated economic analyses, frequently based on assumptions reflecting the interests of those organizations. The World Bank's 1996 analysis (World Bank 1996) of education finance was the first such study. Since then scores of econometric analyses have been published by academic economists, especially those affiliated with and reflecting the market expanding mission of the World Bank (for example, Glewwe 1999; Moock et al. 2003). The ADB has been a major provider of financial and technical assistance and has carried out large-scale education studies, for example, on lower-secondary education teacher training (ADB 1998). Several UNDP (United Nations Development Programme) analyses of public services have touched on problems in education finance from the perspective of users (for example, UNDP 1999). In 2008, the World Bank completed a major study on higher education and skills (World Bank 2008).

The transition to a market economy implied both economic restructuring and changing skills requirements. In the late 1990s, several important studies of skilling and vocational education pointed out issues that policymakers are still struggling to address today. Martin and Oudin's 1996 analysis of skills development and labour markets in rural Vietnam (ORSTOM-MOLISA 1996) emphasized the need for training to be responsive to the diverse needs of different regions and communities, encouraged collaboration among firms and public and private providers of skills training, and suggested the need for apprenticeship schemes, which might link them. Pandey's 1998 analysis emphasized the need for skills development among women to promote economic diversification and increased agricultural productivity in rural areas and the development of small and medium-sized enterprises in all areas (Pandey 1998).

Today, each round of survey data is quickly followed by a corresponding round of quantitative analyses of education (for example, Nga 1999).

Among other international organizations, UNICEF has also carried out several important surveys and analyses of problems in education. Non-governmental organizations involved in education-related projects have produced quite informative reports on their activities.

English-language academic scholarship on education in Vietnam is growing rapidly, displaying increasing diversity. A complete discussion is not possible. The late 1990s saw the emergence of scholarly articles on education, including Nguyễn Văn Chính's analysis of education and opportunity costs (Nguyen Van Chinh 1991) and Judith and Ralph Biddington's 1997 analysis of education for all (Biddington and Biddington 1997). Demographers and econometricians have used survey data to measure general trends and differentials in education (for example, Anh et. al. 1995), as well as specific relationships, such as effects of family size on educational achievement (Anh et al. 1998), economic growth and the demand for education (Glewwe and Jacoby 2004), education and earnings (Moock et al. 1998), and social class and school conditions on boys' and girls' enrolment (Phuong 2006), to name a few. Philip Taylor's work on state policies and peasants (2007) discusses regional variations in education. Taylor questions the validity of the official perception of "low" education levels among ethnic minorities and provides concrete evidence of alternative, non-official education systems in existence among some ethnic minority groups — among the Khmer in particular. Taylor's introduction to the 2004 volume on social inequality in Vietnam and other chapters in that volume also touch on education.

Other recent scholarly articles have pursued such diverse concerns as education and identity formation (Salomon and Vu 2007) and pedagogy in multigrade schools in remote areas, and the globalization of universities and community (vocational) colleges (Oliver and Pham et al. 2009). In the past decade, several doctoral dissertations have addressed educational concerns, including studies of education and stratification (Nguyen Phuong Lan 2004), work (Brisner 2004), social capital (Duong 2004), and political decision making (Lucius 2009). Lucius's analysis is particularly interesting, as it examines how socialization (in the classic sociological sense) through state education, mass organizations, and compulsory military training schemes shapes state decision making modalities. The present author has sought to grasp continuity and change in the principles and institutions governing the provision and payment for education (London 2003; 2007; Chapter Two of this volume). Scholarship on education in Vietnam in languages other than English and Vietnamese is not covered in this review.

While education has always received attention in Vietnam's print media, the coverage today is surprisingly, and perhaps increasingly, critical. Newspapers are filled with populist critiques of everything from escalating education costs to corruption among teachers and administrators, to cheating students. Established in 1953, *Giáo Dục & Thời Đại* (Education & Era) is the longest running education newspaper and now appears in an online version.[36] Long (2006) presents a compilation of news articles from various sources on the theme "Renewing consciousness and developing Vietnamese education in a market economy". Another recent book consists of letters to editors on educational matters, under the title *Giáo dục, Những Lời Tâm huyết* (Education: Heartfelt Words).[37]

Today, perhaps the most interesting literature on education in Vietnam is found on the Internet. One of the most interesting websites is *edunet*,[38] a site managed by MOET. On this site, Vietnamese from across the country participate daily in vibrant debates and sometimes exchange direct and sharply critical discussions with policy leaders. Remarkably, policy leaders often respond to these remarks at length. This is the kind of policy dialogue that is hard to find even in much wealthier and ostensibly more democratic societies.

Issues, Debates, and the Contributions to this Volume

The chapters in this volume pursue diverse concerns within three broad thematic areas. These include the governance of education and education finance, issues in the general education system, and issues in higher education and vocational training. The discussion below identifies major issues and debates across three thematic areas covered in this book as a way of introducing and situating the individual contributions to this volume.

The Governance of Education and the Political Economy of Education Finance

The next two chapters broadly examine the governance of education and the political economy of education finance. The governance of education refers to the coordination and ordering of activities within Vietnam's education system. Governance is dependent on a variety of social, political, economic, and cultural institutions, which may exhibit continuity and change over time. Education finance refers to institutional arrangements and activities governing payment for education in Vietnam.

One of the most striking changes in the recent history of education in Vietnam has been in the institutional arrangements governing the provision and payment for education. These changes should not be seen in isolation from other major developments in the political and economic spheres. In Chapter Two, the present author examines continuity and change in the principles and institutions governing the provision and payment for education in Vietnam under the CPV.

Current debates concerning education and the economy in the country ask what kind of education Vietnam requires in order to promote sustained economic growth along with an equitable distribution of its benefits. What kind of workforce or "human resources" does Vietnam require? But there are other — much less abstract — economic concerns, such as the impact of education expenditure on household economics, tradeoffs between education and work, and education and food, to name a few. In Chapter Three, Jim Cobbe offers a refreshingly sceptical and accessible economic analysis of these issues.

Issues in Primary and Secondary Education

Chapters Four, Five and Six examine selected issues in general education (that is, primary and secondary) education, with individual chapters on "people-founded" schools, dropouts, and schooling in an ethnic minority context. One of the most important developments in general education is the increasing role of non-state schools, including people-founded and private schools. In Chapter Four, Trần Thị Bích Liễu examines the strategies these schools deploy in their efforts to improve and expand their operations.

The next chapter on general education concerns school dropout. School dropout rates were highest in the late 1980s and early 1990s, a period of crisis in the education system during which the dropout rate from secondary schools approached 40 per cent in some areas. Although Vietnam saw subsequent declines in dropout rates, actual dropout figures can be misleading as children who discontinue their studies at the end of any school year are not included in dropout figures. Across time, dropout rates have been consistently higher in rural areas, among the poor, and in ethnic minority groups. Widely-cited reasons for dropping out of school include perceptions of the low value of education, distance to school, costs of schooling, gender norms among some groups, and the poor quality of education, real or perceived. Dropout numbers are highest in upper- and lower-secondary education, where the costs of school attendance also increase. Dropout rates saw significant declines between 1999 and 2006 but have since surged upwards, as Bùi Thái Quyen shows in Chapter Five. Recent research suggests that increases in the cost of housing, food, health care, and other services are cutting into spending on education, though no sharp escalation in dropout numbers is apparent (UNICEF 2008).

The educational status of ethnic minorities in Vietnam has consistently lagged behind ethnic Kinh and overseas Chinese (*Hoa Kiều*). Research on education and ethnic minority groups suggests a diverse range of economic, cultural, and linguistic barriers. Long-standing barriers such as physical remoteness of minority populations to schools, have declined over time, alongside the state's efforts to make schools more available. The higher incidence of dropouts among non-Kinh minorities is frequently attributed to their comparatively lower economic status, but also various ethno-linguistic barriers (including a wide lack of bilingual education as well as direct and indirect forms of discrimination). Nor have these problems eased with economic growth. A 2003 news report noted that the plight of Khmers in the education system was so dire that temples were playing a more important educative role than schools (Tran Bính 2002). As Trương Huyền Chi demonstrates in Chapter Six, linguistic and cultural barriers, as well as the structural exclusion of ethnic minorities in the schools and in the local political economy, combine to promote and reproduce educational and social stratification.

Issues in Higher Education and Vocational Training

The final chapters in this volume examine selected issues in higher education, including higher education reform, university autonomy, collaboration between educational institutions and industry, and vocational education in the context of Vietnam's membership of the World Trade Organization (WTO).

As the urgency of higher education reform grows more acute, the Vietnam's government has renewed efforts to reform higher education. In 2005, MOET released a fifteen-year master plan for the development of higher education, and in the same year issued Resolution 14 on higher education reform. These were by no means the first attempt at reforming the higher education system in the era of Đổi Mới, as an earlier attempt was launched in 1991 intended to address many of the same problems. It is fair to say, however, that the current round of higher education reforms is more sweeping and dynamic, even as its prospective outcomes remain unclear. There are many issues in higher education that are currently being debated.

One of the major themes of higher education reform efforts has been the uncertain division of authority between universities and the Ministry of Education. In Chapter Seven, Elizabeth St. George puts these processes in perspective with an analysis of higher education governance. One of the key challenges of higher education institutions is to produce graduates equipped with skills needed in Vietnam's changing labour market. In one of the more interesting foreign-sponsored projects, the Dutch Government has been assisting Vietnam in the development of professional education. A key aspect of this work is to develop programmes that more effectively link higher education curricula with the "world of work". In Chapter Eight, Nguyễn Minh Hồng addresses efforts to improve the relevance of higher education curricula to the practical needs of students and employers. Nguyen has discovered that many of the obstacles are due to the rigidity of the bureaucracy, particularly that within universities.

In Chapter Nine, Hồ Vũ Khuê Ngọc, who has found that the University of Đà Nẵng is busy reinventing itself in the face of new market opportunities, explains the top-down and bottom-up nature of Vietnamese educational institutions' responses to globalization and how they are viewed by university staff.

Another interesting dimension of collaboration between academia and industry concerns environmental governance. Vietnam is said to be among the most vulnerable countries to threats posed by climate change and rising ocean levels. In Chapter Ten, Marea Fatseas investigates the link between environmental research institutes and industry. Her analysis includes discussion of general sustainability concerns and examinations of specific collaborative projects.

While the demand for skilled labour continues to increase, state education policies are struggling to keep pace. In the meantime, the globalization of Vietnam's economy and Vietnam's WTO commitments are raising new questions about trade in educational services. In Chapter Eleven, Alexandre Dormeier Freire addresses many of these concerns through an analysis of skills formation and globalization.

The analysis of education in Vietnam can be approached from innumerable perspectives. This introductory chapter aimed to provide an introduction to education in Vietnam, if perhaps in quite general and lengthy terms. What this collection of essays aims to provide is an analysis of several key issues in contemporary Vietnam's education system, pertaining to the political economy of education, the provision and payment for primary and secondary education, and the development of vocational and tertiary education in a context of rapid social and economic change. It is hoped that this volume will contribute to existing knowledge of Vietnam's education system and to a broader understanding of social conditions in contemporary Vietnam.

Notes

1. An education system of some form is likely to have existed in Vietnam no later than 250 BCE, though available evidence is too thin to permit thorough analysis. As one observer (who did not wish to be named) put it, education in Vietnam is a mix of the present and the past (*kim cổ*).
2. Perhaps especially minority ethnic groups.
3. As Alexander Woodside (1983, p. 401) has argued, "Confucian societies were based on the principle of chính giáo ("government" merged with "teaching"), the belief that political leadership and the power of moral and intellectual indoctrination must always be fused together."
4. Examples of expert English language scholarship on Vietnamese Confucianism includes Whitmore (1984), Taylor (1997), Taylor and Whitmore (1995), and Cooke (1994).
5. The Lê and the Mạc existed in parallel during a period called "Nam-Bắc triều" (Southern-Northern courts), from 1527–92. Between 1529 and 1592, the Mạc held twenty-two exams, while the Lê could organize only seven exams in the same period.
6. Woodside (1971, pp. 169–223) gives a particularly rich description of the imperial education and examination systems as they existed in the middle 19th century. With respect to the development of Vietnam's education systems, by the 1840s, it is estimated that Vietnam had twenty-one provincial educational commissioners, sixty-three prefectural educational officers, and ninety-four educational officers, two-thirds of whom were stationed in provinces from Nghệ An north (KĐĐNHĐSL 1842–51, cited in Woodside, ibid).
7. In the late 16th century Nguyễn Thị Duệ, from Hải Duong, passed the last exam held under Mạc dynasty, though she did so under a man's name.
8. For an especially vivid account, see Ho Tai (1982), pp. 10–11.

9. Phan Chu Trinh studied the classics and attained Candidate degree level (Phó bảng) in the 1901 exam, while Phan Bội Châu passed exams at the prefecture level.

10. Phan Chu Trinh was born to a wealthy scholar from Quang Nam, but lost his father at age nine. Phan Chu Trinh's political views developed from a more to a less patient attitude towards French colonialism, culminating with outright challenges to the legitimacy of French occupation. Phan Boi Chau (1867–1940) was founder of the Duy Tân Hội (Reformation Society) and Đông Du ("Go East") movement that encouraged nationalist Vietnamese youth to study in Japan. Later, he founded the Vietnam Quang Phuc Hoi (Vietnam Restoration League). Phan Bội Châu was himself a descendent of a family of outstanding (though economically poor) scholars in Nghệ An Province.

11. According to Nguyễn Thế Anh. *Việt Nam Thời Pháp Đô Hộ*. Saigon 1971. Cited in Trần Kin Đinh et al., *Cơ Cấu Xã Hội Trong Quá Trình Phát Triển Của Lịch Sử Việt Nam.* (Social Structure and Development in Vietnam's History) (Hanoi: Nhà Xuất Bản Chính Trị Quốc Gia. Hanoi, 1998).

12. In one famous study of education in colonial Southeast Asia, the scholar J.S. Furnivall estimated that the French colonial regime provided rudimentary schooling to only slightly more than two per cent of the population, making it worse than any other colonial government in the region (Furnivall 1956, p. 211: cited in Woodside 1983, p. 404).

13. David Elliot's *The Vietnamese War* includes a fascinating account of these educational activities in the Mekong (Elliott 2003, pp. 87–88, 600–01).

14. Official poverty rates have declined, from 58 per cent in 1993 to less than 11 per cent (under a higher poverty ceiling) in 2006. Poverty declines in Vietnam were even steeper than in China (according to the Ministry of Planning and Investment's report of March 2006), making what was just recently among Asia's poorest countries into Asia's most recent entrant into "middle income country" status.

15. The 1994 figure is cited in Nguyen Thi Canh (1997), p. 28.

16. According to the Ministry of Education and Training, <http://www.moet.gov.vn/?page=11.6&view=9268>.

17. Trần Hữu Quang (2007), for example, cites the figure of 41 per cent, based on government sources. Given that primary education is (in principle) entirely state-funded, the share of household spending might be higher for other educational levels. Whatever the case, this is one of the highest shares on household spending in Asia. See also Kattan and Burnett (2004).

18. For example, the first large-scale World Bank project, a US$70-million primary education project, focused on textbook development and teacher training. The project was widely regarded as a failure, according to ADB (1998).

19. World Bank (2010). Figures obtained from the online Projects Database and calculated by the author. <http://web.worldbank.org/external/projects/main>. Accessed October 2009.

20. <http://www.diendan.org/thay-tren-mang/400-trieu-usd-xay-dung-bon-truong-111h-201ctrinh-111o-quoc-te201d/view> (Accessed May 2009).

21. For example, the Bank-affiliated International Finance Corporation has, along with the ADB, invested in the Royal Melbourne Institute of Technology's private university in Ho Chi Minh City. The World Bank, Report No: 24621-VN, Memorandum of the president of the International Development Association and the International Finance Corporation to the executive directors on a Country Assistance Strategy of the World Bank Group for the Socialist Republic of Vietnam, 16 September 2002, Vietnam Country Management Unit, East Asia and the Pacific Region.

22. Only a few examples of NGO activities can be mentioned here. One, a 1997 OXFAM UK/Ireland study of education in a Mekong Delta district of Tra Vinh province, assisted with providing housing for teachers, the great majority of whom were Kinh from outside areas and working (at the time) with quite low salaries, but required to fend for themselves on housing arrangements (OXFAM 1998). The international charity Catholic Relief Services has actively promoted the cause of inclusive education for children with physical disabilities.

23. Take Vietnam's 2006–10 five-year socioeconomic development plan, which stated that 97.5 per cent of children were attending primary school at the right age. As we will see, this is an exaggeration (MPI 2006, p. 35).

24. Day care has been shifted mostly to non-state provision. As of 2008, only thirty-six public crèches (nhà trẻ) remained. (There are nearly 42,000 preschool groups (so-called nhóm trẻ), 75 per cent of which are "people-founded" and therefore entirely people-paid.)

25. As of 2007, 170,000 of 172,000 instructors were women.

26. The multicluster index survey includes the wealthier and well educated Hoa Kiều within the broad category non-Kinh.

27. Decision 112 (2006) provides for cash payments to children of eligible poor and minority households.

28. Lao Động. Chưa khắc phục được triệt để tình trạng học sinh bỏ học. <http://www.laodong.com.vn/Home/Chua-khac-phuc-duoc-triet-de-tinh-trang-hoc-sinh-bo-hoc/200810/110397.laodong>. (Last accessed 15 October 2008).

29. VHLSS (1993, 1996, 2002, 2006).
30. But nonetheless true. Interview with Văn Như Cương, Hanoi, 2008.
31. Sources: VLSS 1997–98 (GSO 2000, 52); VLSS 1992–3 (GSO 1994, 50); and for the years of 2004 and 2006, the author calculated on the basis of VLSS (2004; 2006).
32. UNICEF Transition Study.
33. <http://www.moet.gov.vn/?page=11.5&view=930> (Accessed October 2008).
34. For example, see Bùi Trọng Liễu. *Vì sao không nên cổ phần hóa đại học công?* <http://www.diendan.org/viet-nam/co-phan-hoa-truong-111ai-hoc-cong/> (Accessed May 2008).
35. It is estimated that by 2007 more than 45,000 Vietnamese had university degrees from "Western" universities. Until now, education authorities have not taken advantage of this resource. For a recent study of higher education and internationalization, see Pham The Nghi (2006).
36. <http://www.gdtd.com.vn/>. Last accessed April 2009.
37. Giáo dục: Những lời tâm huyết. No author. Nhà xuất bản thong tấn, 2006.
38. <http://edu.net.vn>

References

ADB. Report on Lower-Secondary Curriculum and Teacher-Training System. Lower-Secondary Education Development Project, 1998.

Aikman, Sheila, Pat Pridmore. "Multigrade Schooling in 'Remote' Areas of Vietnam". *International Journal of Educational Development* 21 (2001): 521–36.

Bélanger, Danièle and Jianye Liu. "Social policy rèoms and daughers' schooling in Vietnam". *International Journal of Educational Development* 24 (2004): 23–38.

Biddington, Judith and Ralph Biddington. "Education for All: Literacy in Vietnam 1975–1995". *Compare: A Journal of Comparative and International Education* 27, no. 1 (1997): 43–61.

Bộ Giáo dục và Đào Tạo. *Số Liệu Thống Kê Giáo Dục Và Đào Tạo, 1945–1995* (Statistical Data of Education and Training, 1945–95). Unpublished statistical brief. Hanoi: Center for Education Information and Management, Ministry of Education and Training, 1995.

Bộ Giáo Dục và Đào Tạo. *Xã Hội Hóa Công Tác Giáo Dục: Nhận Thức và Hành Động.* Hanoi: Viện Khoa Học Giáo Dục.

Bùi, Trọng Liễu. "Giáo dục đào tạo: Mấy chục năm điều trần". <http://www.chungta.com/Desktop.aspx/GiaoDuc/DeXuat-GiaiPhap-GD/Giao_duc_dao_tao-May_chuc_nam_dieu_tran/>. (Last accessed November 2007).

————. "Vì sao không nên cổ phần hóa đại học công". <http://www.diendan. org/viet-nam/co-phan-hoa-truong-111ai-hoc-cong/>. (Last accessed May 2008).

Bùi Xuân Đính. *Lệ Làng Phép Nước.* Hanoi: Nhà Xuất Bản Pháp lý, 1985.

Chu Văn Thành ed. *Dịch Vụ Công: Đổi Mới Quản Lý và Tổ Chức Cung Ứng Ở Việt Nam Hiện Nay.* Hanoi: Nhà Xuất Bản Chính Trị Quốc Gia, 2007.

———— *Dịch Vụ Công và Xã Hội Hóa Dịch Vụ Công.* Hanoi: Nhà Xuất Bản Chính Trị Quốc Gia, 2004.

Cooke, Nola. "Nineteenth Century Vietnamese Confucianism in Historical Perspective: Evidence from the Palace Examinations (1463–1993). *Journal of Southeast Asian Studies* 25 (1994): 2.

Đoàn Huệ Dung. "Centralism — The Dilemma of Educational Reforms." In *Rethinking Viet Nam*, edited by Duncan McCargo. London: Routledge 2004.

Elliott, David W.P. *The Vietnamese War: Revolution and Social Change in the Mekong Delta, 1930–1975.* Armonk, NY: M.E. Sharpe, 2003.

Furnivall, J.S. *Colonial Policy and Practice: A Comparative Study of Burma and Netherlands India.* New York: New York University Press, 1956.

General Statistics Office. *Vietnam Households Living Standards Survey, 1992.* Hanoi: Statistical Publishing House, 1994.

————. *Viet Nam Households Living Standards Survey, 1998.* Hanoi: Statistical Publishing House, 2000.

————. *Viet Nam Households Living Standards Survey, 2001–2002.* Hanoi: Statistical Publishing House, 2003.

————. *Viet Nam Households Living Standards Survey, 2004.* Hanoi: Statistical Publishing House, 2005.

————. *Vietnam Households Living Standards Survey, 2004.* Hanoi: Statistical Publishing House, 2008.

Glewwe, Paul and Jacoby Hanan G. "Economic Growth and the Demand for Education: Is There a Wealth Effect?" *Journal of Development Economics* 74 (2004): 33–51.

Glewwe, Paul and Harry Anthony Patrinos. "The Role of the Private Sector in Education in Vietnam: Evidence From the Vietnam Living Standards Survey". *World Development* 27 (1999): 887–902.

GSO. *Viet Nam Household Living Standards Survey (VHLSS) 2008.* Hanoi: General Statistics Office, 2010.

Hồ Tú Bảo and associates. *Đề án cải cách giáo dục Việt Nam: Phân tích và đề nghị của nhóm nghiên cứu giáo dục Vietnam.* <http://tapchithoidai.org/ thoidai13/200813_nhomghieencuu.html> (Last accessed November 2008).

Hue-Tam Ho Taī. *Radicalism and the Origins of the Vietnamese Revolution.* Cambridge: Harvard University Press, 1992.

Kattan, Raja Bentaouet and Nicholas Burnett. "User Fees in Primary Education". *Education Sector, Human Development Network.* World Bank, July 2004.

Lao Động. "Chưa khắc phục được triệt để tình trạng học sinh bỏ học". <http://www.laodong.com.vn/Home/Chua-khac-phuc-duoc-triet-de-tinh-trang-hoc-sinh-bo-hoc/200810/110397.laodong>. Accessed 15 October 2008.

Lê Chi Mai. *Cải Cách Dịch Vụ Công ở Việt Nam.* (Public Services Reform in Vietnam). Hanoi: Nhà Xuất Bản Chính Trị Quốc Gia, 2003.

Lê Quốc Hùng. *Xã Hội Hóa Giáo Dục: Nhìn Từ Góc Độ Pháp Luật.* (Socialization of Education: Viewed from a Legal Perspective). Hanoi: Nhà Xuất Bản Tư Pháp, 2004.

Lê Văn Giạng. *Lịch Sử Giảm Lược: Hơn 1000 năm nền giáo dục Việt Nam.* Hanoi: Nhà Xuất Bản Chính Trị Quốc Gia, 2003.

Li, Tana. *Nguyen Cochichina: Southern Vietnam in the Seventeenth and Eighteenth Centuries.* Ithica, Southeast Asia Program, Cornell University, 1998.

London, Jonathan D. "Vietnam's Mass Education and Health Systems: A Regime's Perspective." *American Asian Review* 21, no. 2 (2003): 125–70.

Lucius, Casey. *Vietnam's Political Process: How Education Shapes Political Decision Making.* London. Routledge Contemporary Southeast Asia Series, 2009.

Marr, D. *Vietnamese Tradition on Trial, 1920–1945.* Berkeley: University of California Press, 1981.

Matthieu Salomon, Vu Doan Ket. "Đổi mới, education and identity formation in contemporary Vietnam." *Compare* 37 (2007): 345–363.

Ministry of Education and Training of Vietnam (MOET). *Education in Vietnam, 1945–1991.* Ha Noi, 1991.

———. *Statistical Data of Education and Training, 1981–1990.* Hanoi: Ministry of Education and Training, 1992.

Ministry of Planning and Investment. *The Five Year Socio-Economic Development Plan, 2006–2010.* March 2006.

Moock, Peter R., Harry Anthony Patrinos, and Meera Venkataraman. "Education and earnings in a transition economy: the case of Vietnam." *Economics of Education review* 22 (2003): 503–10.

Ngô Đức Thọ. *Văn Miếu Quốc tử Giám và 82 bĩa tiến sỹ* (2003).

Nguyễn Khắc Viện. *Bàn về đạo Nho.* First published in French in 1993, and republished in Vietnam. Hanoi: Nhà xuất bản Thế giới. 2000.

Nguyen, Phuong L. "Effects of social class and schoool conditions on educational enrolment and achievement of boys and girls in rural Viet Nam". *International Journal of Educational Research* 45 (2006): 153–75.

Nguyễn, Thanh Liêm. *Giáo Dục Ở Miền Nam Trước 1975.* Santa Ana: Lăng Ông Duqxa Tả Quân Le Văn Duyệt Foundation (2006).

Nguyễn, Thế Anh. "Việt Nam Thời Pháp Đô Hộ." in *Cơ cấu xã hội trong quá trình phát triển của lịch sử Việt Nam* (Social structure and Development in Vietnam's History), edited by Trần Kim Đinh et al. Hà Nội: Nhà xuất bản Chính Trị Quốc Gia, 1998.

Nguyễn, Thế Lông. *Đổi Mới Tư Duy, Phát Triển Giáo Dục Việt Nam trong Kinh Tế Thị Trường.* (Renew Consciousness, Develop the Education of Vietnam in a Market Economy). Hanoi: Nhà Xuất Bản Lao Động, 2006.

Nguyễn, Thị Canh. "Vấn đề giáo dục và đào tạo trong nền kinh tế chuyển đổi Việt Nam" (The problem of education and training in Vietnam's transitional economy). *Phát Triển Kinh tế.* No. 86 (1997): 28.

Nguyễn, Quang Vinh. "Tiếp tục cải cách giáo dục phổ thông." *Tạp chí cộng sản,* 6, 1989.

Nguyen, V.C. "Looking for the Future: Work versus Education". Unpublished Paper. Amsterdam: Amsterdam School for Social Science Research, Centre for Asian Studies, 1997.

Oliver, Diane E., Pham Xuan Thanh, Paul A. Elsner, Nguyen Thi Thanh Phuong, and Do Quoc Trung. "Globalization of Higher Education and Community Colleges in Vietnam". In *Community College Models.* The Netherlands: Springlink, 2009. Available online at <http://www.springerlink.com/content/q20t1721114u407x/>.

ORSTOM-MOLISA. *A Qualitative Survey of Skills Development in Rural Vietnam.* French Institute of Research for Development in Cooperation. John Yeves-Martin and Xavier Ouain — MOLISA, 1996.

Overland, Martha Ann. "American Colleges raise the flag in Vietnam". *Chronicle of Higher Education,* 55, no. 36 (13 May 2009).

Oxfam Great Britain. "Education for Poor Children: Research Findings from Lao Cai Province, Vietnam". Oxfam Great Britain, Vietnam Country Programme, 1998.

Phạm Minh Hạc. *Giáo Dục Việt Nam: Trước Ngưỡng Cửa Thế Kỷ XXI.* Hanoi: Nhà Xuất Bản Chính Trị Quốc Gia, 1999.

Phạm Thế Nghị. Các giải pháp thúc đẩy hội nhập quốc tế của giáo dục đại học Việt Nam 2006. <http://www.gdtd.com.vn> (Last accessed April 2009).

Santosh Mehrotra, Enrique Delamonica. "Household Costs and Public Expenditure on Primary Education in Five Low Income Countries: A Comparative Analysis". *International Journal of Educational Development* 18 (1998): 41–61.

Tai, Hue Tam-Ho. *Radicalism and the Origins of the Vietnamese Revolution.* Cambridge: Harvard University Press, 1992.

Tam Hieu. ed. *Những Vấn Đề Giáo Dục Hiện Nay: Quản Điểm & Giải Pháp.* (Current Problems of Education: Perspectives & Solutions). Hanoi: Nhà Xuất Bản Tri Thức, 2007.

Taylor, Keith W. "The Literati Revival in Seventeenth Century Vietnam". *Journal of Southeast Asian Studies* 18 (1987): 1.

Taylor, Keith W. and John K. Whitmore, eds. *Essays into Vietnamese Pasts*. Ithaca: Cornell University Press, 1995.

Taylor, Philip, ed. *Social Inequality in Vietnam and the Challenges to Reform.* Singapore: Institute of Southeast Asia Studies, 2004.

————. "Poor Policies, Wealthy Peasants: Alternative Trajectories of Rural Development in Vietnam". *Journal of Vietnamese Studies* 2, no. 2 (2007): 3–56.

Thompson V. *French Indochina*. New York: Macmillan, 1937.

Thông Tấn. *Giáo Dục: Những Lời Tâm Huyết* (Education: Passionate Words). Hanoi: Nhà Xuất Bản Thông Tấ, 2006.

Trần, Bình. "Đầu tư tổng thể cho giáo dục đồng bào Khơme." *Thời Đại*, 14, no. 9, 3 March 2002.

Trần Thị Phương Hoa. "Franco-Vietnamese Schools and the Transition from Confucian to a New Kind of Intellectuals in the Colonial Context of Tonkin". Harvard Yen-Ching Institute Working Paper, 2009. <http://www. harvard-yenching.org/publications-and-projects/working-papers-series/>. Accessed May 2009.

Trần Đình Nghiêm and Bộ Giáo Dục và Đào Tạo. *Chiến Lược Phát Triển Giáo Dục Trong Thế Kỷ XXI: Kinh Nghiệm Quốc Tế* (Strategies to Develop Education in the 21st Century: International Experience). Hanoi: Nhà Xuất Bản Chính Trị Quốc Gia, 2002.

Trần Kim Đinh, Đỗ Đức Hùng, Nguyễn Văn Khánh, Nguyễn Đình Lê, Phùng Hữu Phú, Vũ Văn Quân, and Trương Thị Tiến. *Cơ cấu xã hội trong quá trình phát triển của lịch sử Việt Nam* (Social structure and Development in Vietnam's History). Hanoi: Nhà xuất bản Chính trị Quốc gia, 1998.

Trần Văn Tùng and Lê Ai Lam. *Phát Triển Nguôn Nhân Lực: Kinh Nghiệm Thế Giới và Thực Tiễn ở Nước ta* (The Development of Human Resources: World Experience and Practice in our Country). Hanoi: Viện Kinh Tế Thế Giới. Nhà Xuất Bản Chính Trị Quốc Gia, 1996.

Truong Thi Kim Chuyen, Thai Thi Ngoc Dung, and Bach Hong Viet. "Educational Enrolments in Lower Secondary School". In *Living Standards During an Economic Boom, The Case of Vietnam*, edited by Dominique Haughton and Jonathan Haughton. Hanoi: United Nations Development Programme, 2001.

Truong Si Anh, John Knodel, David Lam, and Jed Friedman. "Family Size and Children's Education in Vietnam". *Demography* 35 (1998): 57–70.

Truong Si Anh, John Knodel, Le Huong, and Tran Thi Thanh Thuy. "Education in Vietnam: Trends and Differentials". Population Studies Center, University of Michigan, 1995.

UBQGCNMC. *Về Giáo dục cho mọi người ở Việt Nam* (About Education for Every Person in Vietnam). National Committee Against Illiteracy. Hanoi: National Politics Publishing House, 1994.

UNICEF et al. "The transition of ethnic minority girls from primary to secondary education". Hanoi, UNICEF Vietnam, MOET of Vietnam, UNESCO Vietnam, 2008.

United Nations — MOLISA. *Basic Social Services in Viet Nam (Dịch vụ xã hội cơ bản ở Việt nam)*. Hanoi: United Nations, 1999.

Vasavakul, Thaveenporn. "Schools and Politics in South and North Vietnam: A Comparative Study of State Apparatus, State Policy and State Power (1945–1965)". PhD Dissertation, Cornell University, 1994.

Vo Than Son, Truong Thi Kim Nguyen, Doan Thuan Hoa, Nguyen Thi Thuy, *et al.*, Dominuque Jonathan Haughton, and Phuong Nguyen. "School Enrollments and Drop Outs". In *Living Standards During and Economic Boom*, edited by Anonymous. Hanoi: UNDP GSO, 2001.

Vũ Cao Đàm. *Suy Nghĩ về Khoa Học và Giáo Dục trong Xã Hội Đương Đại Việt Nam* (Thoughts on Science and Education in Contemporary Vietnam). Hanoi: Nhà Xuất Bản Khoa học và Kỹ Thuật, 2007.

Vu Huy Tu, Lê Chi Mai, and Voi Kim Sơn, eds. *Quản ly Khu Vực Công* (Public Sector Management). Hanoi: Nhà Xuất Bản Khoa học và Kỹ Thuật, 1998.

Whitmore, John K. "Social Organization and Confucian Thought in Viet Nam". *Journal of Southeast Asian Studies* 15, no. 2 (1984): 296–306.

———. "Literati Culture and Integration in Dai Viet, c. 1430-c. 1840". *Modern Asian Studies* 31, no. 3, Cambridge University Press, 1997.

Woodside, Alexander. "The Triumphs and Failures of Mass Education in Vietnam." *Pacific Affairs* 56: (1983): 401–27.

———. *Vietnam and the Chinese Model: A Comparative Study of Vietnamese and Chinese Government in the First Half of the Nineteenth Century*, edited by anonymous. Cambridge, Mass.: Council on East Asian Studies, Harvard University, 1971.

———. "The Contributions to Rural Change of Modern Vietnamese Village Schools". Pp. 223 In *Reshaping Local Worlds: Formal Education and Cultural Change in Rural Southeast Asia*, edited by C.F. Keyes. Yale University Southeast Asia Studies, 1991.

———. *Lost Modernities: China, Vietnam, Korea, and the Hazards of World History*, edited by anonymous. Cambridge, Mass.: Harvard University Press, 2006.

World Bank. *Vietnam Education Finance Sector Study*. Washington, D.C.: World Bank, East Asia Pacific Region, Human Resources Operations Division, 1996.

———. *Vietnam: Higher Education and Skills for Growth*. Report No. 44428-VN. No place, Human Development Department, East Asia and Pacific Region, 2008.

2

HISTORICAL WELFARE REGIMES AND EDUCATION IN VIETNAM

Jonathan D. London

Welfare refers to human well-being and to the satisfaction of basic human needs. Welfare regimes are specific institutional arrangements governing the creation and allocation of welfare. Welfare regimes analysis is a body of political economy scholarship that seeks to explain the determinants and stratification effects of welfare regimes across different historical settings. A core assumption of welfare regimes analysis is that social class — and in particular political settlements among social classes — figure centrally in the determination and stratification effects of welfare regimes. This chapter extends the concepts and theoretical methods of welfare regimes analysis to an investigation of education and educational inequalities in Vietnam under Communist Party of Vietnam (CPV), which has ruled in the north of the country since the 1940s and on a countrywide basis since 1975.

Welfare regimes depend on more or less stable institutional arrangements and can rise and fall. But all welfare regimes are "causally specific" to the political and economic regimes that contain them

(Esping-Andersen 1987, p. 7). Over the roughly sixty years of its rule, the CPV has presided over the development of two distinctive forms of political economy and, within them, two distinctive welfare regimes. Between the 1940s and the 1980s, Vietnam experienced the development and erosion of a *state-socialist* political economy — first in the north and then in the south — distinguished by its democratic-centralist modes of political integration and its redistributive modes of economic integration. Since the late 1980s, Vietnam has experienced the development of a *market-Leninist* political economy in which democratic-centralist modes of political integration exist in combination with market economic institutions (London 2009).[1] As I demonstrate in this chapter, under these distinctive forms of political economy, Vietnam has experienced important changes in the principles and institutions governing welfare, education, and social and educational inequalities.

The chapter is organized in three sections and advances three related arguments. The first section summarizes core concerns, concepts, and theoretical suppositions of welfare regimes analysis. Engaging theoretical literature on welfare regimes (Esping-Andersen 1990; Gough 2004), state-socialism (Kornai 1992; Szelenyi and Manchin 1987), market transitions (Szelenyi and King 2005), and institutional economics (Polanyi 1957), I contend that welfare regimes analysis has value for an analysis of education and educational stratification in contemporary Vietnam so long as it includes a theorization of the rise and demise of socialist political, economic, and welfare institutions and how exit paths from state-socialism and legacies of state-socialism affect the development of subsequent welfare regimes. Correspondingly, the second section relates core features of state-socialist political economies and their welfare regimes, identifies ideographic features of Vietnamese state-socialism and its welfare regime, and examines principles and institutions governing the provision and payment for education and educational inequalities in Vietnam under state-socialism. The third section clarifies the core institutional attributes of market-Leninism, identifies idiographic features of Vietnam's market-Leninist political economy and its associated welfare regime, and clarifies the principles and institutions governing the provision and payment for education and educational inequalities in contemporary Vietnam.

I
EDUCATION IN VIETNAM: TOWARDS AN ANALYSIS OF HISTORICAL WELFARE REGIMES

Education is a component of well-being and welfare regimes analysis is a useful way of conceptualizing and explaining institutional arrangements governing education in different historical settings. While welfare regimes analysis developed first through comparative analysis of welfare states and social security systems in advanced capitalist countries (Esping-Andersen 1990), recent scholarship has extended welfare regimes analysis to the study of other kinds of welfare and to the analysis of welfare regimes in diverse historical settings, including "developing" (that is, poor or late-industrializing countries) and "transitional societies" (that is, formerly state-socialist settings) (Gough and Wood 2004). Arguably, welfare regimes (that is, stable institutional arrangements governing the creation and allocation of welfare and its stratification effects) exist in *any* historical formation, whether it be "feudal" or pre-capitalist or state-socialist. Drawing on contemporary welfare regimes scholarship and the economic writings of Karl Polanyi (1949; 1957), I propose the concept of "historical welfare regimes", which refers to the claim or reality that welfare regimes of some sort exist in any stable social formation (London 2008).

Welfare regimes analysis is theoretical in the sense that it is concerned with developing empirically grounded explanations. More specifically, welfare regimes analysis is concerned with:

1. Explaining the historical determinants of the ways in which "institutional responsibility" for different types of welfare and welfare-producing goods (for example, food, shelter, income, social insurance, education, and health) is distributed across different institutional spheres (that is, state, economy, family, and secondary associations);

2. Explaining the effects of this "welfare mix" with respect to social stratification (that is, institutionalized inequalities) and hence life-chances; and

3. Accounting for similarities and differences in the attributes of welfare regimes across different social and historical settings.

As indicated, the concepts and theories of welfare regimes analysis developed initially through studies of variation in welfare states. It is important to consider this work, even if briefly, as doing so helps clarify the core theoretical claims of welfare regimes. In his seminal contribution, *The Three Worlds of Welfare Capitalism* (1990), Gøsta Esping-Andersen identified three welfare regime types across Western Europe and North America (liberal, conservative, and social democratic), whose social policies granted citizens different forms and degrees of protection from markets.[2] The developments of these distinctive regime types were not accidental, Esping-Andersen argues. Rather, they were rooted in processes of class formation and were the products of political coalitions among classes and the formation of "political settlements" that defined the relation between state and economy and the rights of the state to tax and redistribute (Esping-Andersen 1999).[3]

The relation between state and economy (*viz.* political and economic institution) is critical, as a country's welfare institutions — including its social policies — exist and develop in an interdependent relation with preponderant political and economic institutions. Undoubtedly, cultural institutions (understood as shared values and beliefs that affect behaviour) are also critical determinants of welfare. But cultural arguments are famously difficult to substantiate and, without some disciplining, can be decidedly vacuous. For example, cultural explanations fail to account for the divergence in the welfare regimes of culturally-similar settings or in the same setting across time. While the United States and United Kingdom may share certain cultural attributes and also similar welfare regimes, other culturally similar settings differ (for example, North and South Korea, Taiwan and China, or Quang Nam province in 1908 and today). Just as social analysis that is devoid of cultural considerations should raise our suspicions, so should social analysis that relies exclusively or even primarily on cultural arguments.

It is reasonable to question the relevance of welfare regimes analysis for countries such as Vietnam and to specify the conditions under which extending welfare regimes analysis beyond advanced welfare states can be a fruitful enterprise. As indicated, in recent years scholars have extended welfare regimes concepts to the analysis of welfare in so-called "developing" and "transitional" country settings (Gough 2000; Gough and Wood 2004).[4] Anticipating charges such as "wrong headed" or "naive", these scholars plainly stated that their intent was "never to apply the welfare regime idea *tout court*" but rather to extend the conceptual apparatus of welfare regimes to see what institutional categories it generated in non-rich countries (Gough and Wood 2004, p. 5). Conceptually, "second generation welfare regimes analysis" has indeed helped to clarify the often considerable institutional differences between and among the political economies and welfare regimes of advanced capitalist countries, late-industrializing countries, and very poor countries.[5] Such differences include, but are not limited to, the roles, capacities, and significance of the state in the determination of welfare regimes,[6] late industrializing and poor countries' greater vulnerability to global economic shocks, the more limited scope of state-social policies in countries with limited extractive and allocative capacities, the greater role of international institutions in the political economies and welfare institutions of poor countries, and the greater importance of informal welfare institutions outside the world's richest countries.

The arguments I develop concerning education in Vietnam are based on two criticisms of welfare regime which are meant to be constructive. The first is that second-generation welfare regimes analysis takes an unnecessary step back from welfare regimes analysis as a research programme. To date, second-generation welfare regimes analysis has tended towards description rather explanation. They lack historical and class analysis. To be fair, Gough and Wood have noted that their analyses were intended to be largely conceptual and heuristic. And they and others might well object to extending the *theoretical claims* of welfare regimes analysis — which involve class-based arguments about political settlements — to the analysis of welfare regimes outside the "worlds of welfare capitalism". But as Esping-Andersen has shown, welfare regimes tend to rise and fall with fundamental realignments of a country's political and economic institutions (Esping-Andersen 1987). I am not alone in assuming that class and social competition among classes and other social grouping always figure fundamentally in the determination and realignment of a country's political and economic institutions. Hence, I believe class analysis (or more modestly, the analysis of social competition) is a necessary ingredient of any welfare regimes analysis.

A second criticism of second-generation welfare regimes analysis concerns so-called "transitional settings" or what I call "formerly state-socialist settings". (After all, what social setting is not in transition?). Gough and Wood (2004) did a service in recognizing the distinctive features of such settings. But greater elaboration is needed. Literature on "market transitions" has shown that state-socialist institutions erode unevenly and incompletely and that the way this occurs can shape and constrain (if not determine) subsequent patterns of institutional change (see, for just one example, Stark 1998). This suggests that an analysis of welfare regimes in formerly state-socialist settings necessarily entails an analysis of the principles and institutions governing welfare under state-socialism and how the erosion of state-socialism shapes the formation of new political economies and their corresponding welfare regimes.

In a volume focused on Vietnam, I do not want to wade too far into theoretical literature (though perhaps I already have!). Nonetheless, I want to close my discussion of welfare regimes by explaining their relation to social inequality. An insight emerges in the comparative analysis of social policies under state-socialist (redistributive) and market economies: namely, that in any setting, preponderant modes of political and economic integration are also the primary mechanisms generating social inequalities (Szelenyi and Manchin 1987).

As Szelenyi and Machin (1987, p.111) have shown, when it comes to social inequalities, state-socialist (redistributive) economies and market economies are each other's mirror image. Under state-socialist regimes, institutional responsibility for welfare lies overwhelmingly within the sphere of planned economy, with self-exploiting households and (black) markets assuming secondary roles. In state-socialist regimes, bureaucratic institutions of central planning are the primary means of allocation and the principal mechanisms generating social inequalities; household strategies of accumulation and accumulation through involvement in (black) markets may provide an alternative means of economic security and may counteract the stratifying effects of bureaucratic allocation.

In market economies, by contrast, institutional responsibility for welfare lies overwhelming within the sphere of the market, which is to say that people must secure their well-being through markets. As markets are the principal means of allocation, market institutions are the principal mechanisms driving social inequalities. In market economies, household self-exploitation and redistributive state policies (including social policies) may provide alternative forms of economic security and may mitigate market-based inequalities. Racism, sexism, and other forms of discrimination transcend state-socialist and market-based political economies. It is now left to us to appreciate the specific features of state-socialist and market-based political economies in Vietnam and how the evolution and involution of state-socialism and subsequent developments affected the creation and allocation of education and attendant patterns of social and educational inequalities.

II
EDUCATION IN VIETNAM'S STATE-SOCIALIST WELFARE REGIME, 1945–89

Between 1917 and 1989, more than thirty countries experienced the development of distinctively state-socialist political economies. The settings in which this occurred varied considerably along a range of dimensions, including degree of industrialization, geographical attributes, population size, and cultural characteristics, among others. In some instances, the development of state-socialism owed chiefly to processes emanating from within a given country; in other places it owed more to external forces (Kornai 1992, p. 27). What these regimes shared, however, was a specific combination of institutional attributes, which have been identified and analysed in ideal-typical terms by Janos Kornai (1992). There are surprisingly few attempts to theorize welfare or social policies in state-socialist societies systematically, even though there are many case studies.

Kornai's analysis is useful to the extent that it recognizes the promises of economic security characteristic of all state-socialist regimes and the reasons such promises are rarely met. But outside country-specific studies (for example, Philion 1998), there have been no efforts to theorize state-socialist welfare regimes explicitly, at least in the sense used in this essay. Social inequalities are, as discussed, tightly related to welfare regimes. For this reason, Ivan Szelenyi's works on state-socialist social policies and their attendant social inequalities (Szelenyi 1978; 1987) provide an especially useful starting point for theorizing welfare regimes under state-socialism. Drawing on Polanyi's (1957) analysis of historical variation in economic institutions, Szelenyi (1987) affirmed that in any social context, market, redistributive, and reciprocal institutions exist side by side, but one of these will play a preponderant integrative role. In any social context, preponderant modes of political and economic integration will also be the chief mechanism driving social inequalities. Taken together, the contributions of these scholars (all Hungarians!) and others help to delineate the basic institutional contours of state-socialist welfare regimes as a distinctive kind of historical welfare regime.

Conceivably, state-socialist welfare regimes constitute a family of welfare regimes, within which there are various types (for example, industrial state-socialist, agrarian state-socialist, Maoist versus Stalinist, etc.). While a full taxonomy is beyond the scope of this chapter, an appreciation of the ideal typical features of state-socialist welfare regimes provides a useful foundation for understanding the principles and institutions governing education and education inequalities in Vietnam under the CPV up until the late 1980s. Naturally, the specific features and outcomes of Vietnam's state-socialist welfare regime reflect the country's unique social history.

State-Socialist Welfare Regimes

State-socialist regimes and their attendant welfare regimes are distinguished by a specific set of institutional attributes and stratification outcomes. With respect to political institutions, all state-socialist regimes have been established (from within or without) under the authority of communist parties inspired by Lenin. All have displayed formal political institutions fashioned in accordance with the formal principles of democratic-centralism, whose actual institutionalized features are more repressive than democratic. In principle, "democratic centralism" entails the local selection of political leaders and the use of hierarchical party governance structures as a "bottom-up" conveyer belt by which democratic aspirations of the people are transmitted to the political centre for further democratic deliberation by putatively representative organs. In practice, democratic centralism tends to function in a top-down manner. Elected local leaders are selected and approved by local and higher levels. Top-down decision making is the rule rather than the exception. Nationally and at local levels of governance, political power is concentrated. Real public deliberation is non-existent.

In economic terms, state-socialist regimes are integrated through the bureaucratic allocative institutions of central planning. Under state-socialism, the circulation of value is to be administered by central authorities. The premise is that central planning is more efficient than markets. The announced aim of state-socialist central planning is to allocate resources in a way that promotes economic efficiency (through economies of scale) while reducing social inequalities (through the elimination of capitalist relations of production). The establishment of central planning entails the elimination of private property, the collectivization of all production factors under state ownership, and the collectivization of all productive activities under state managed production units, including various types of state-owned enterprises and state-managed agricultural collectives. The actual institutionalized outcomes of these institutional arrangements depart from those intended. Most notably, central planning turns out to generate powerful incentives for rent-seeking and hoarding, which leads to systemic scarcity, while poor incentives within production units depress output and productivity growth.

State-socialist regimes displayed distinctive welfare regimes in which state agencies (including functional agencies and production units) assumed a dominant (and, in principle, exclusive) role in the creation and allocation of welfare. State-socialist citizenship rights typically exhibit extraordinarily progressive welfare principles, such as the right to work and the right to social and economic security, including food, shelter, health care, and education. These rights are enshrined in the revolutionary constitution of the socialist state. But a large gap exists between formal political rights concerning welfare, and actual conditions. As Kornai notes, although some of these promises are met, the complete fulfilment of the promises "never occurs and can never occur" — resulting in tensions between promises and performance and creating "an oppressive burden" for the party (Kornai 1992, p. 54).

The look and feel of the state-socialist welfare regime in real life differed from its formally specified designs. In many instances, state-socialism delivered on its formally specified goals, if within limits. In principle, institutional responsibility for welfare under state-socialism was firmly within the sphere of the state; in reality, the systemic failures of state-socialism meant that personal networks, black markets, and households also played prominent roles in the creation and allocation of welfare. This is because in most countries the economic institutions of state-socialism failed to generate sufficient resources, compromising both material wealth and the quality of social services. In rural areas, economic security and survival frequently relied on subsistence production, involvement in the black market, and other survival strategies outside the planned economy, while the provision and payment for essential services depended on the collective efforts of local populations. In urban and especially rural areas, promises of social services coexisted with an egalitarianism of poverty and inefficiencies in the delivery of services (Deacon 2000).

State-socialist welfare regimes generated distinctive patterns of social inequality that reflected political inequalities, reliance on bureaucratic allocative mechanisms, and the dualism promoted by state-socialist development strategies. Administrative allocative institutions — state bureaucracies of one sort or another under party membership — were the principal mechanisms governing social inequality (Szelenyi 1978; 1987). At the broadest level, this was reflected in the dualist principles underlying state-socialist economic policies, which subordinated exploited agrarian populations for the advancement of industrialization and to the benefit of urban and administrative classes.[7] Membership in the communist party or a position in the bureaucracy frequently resulted in improved access to political, economic, and informational resources, as well as status and other intangible resources (Walder 1992). Created to destroy class exploitation and social inequalities, state-socialist regimes levelled many inequalities, but also gave birth to a new class system in which redistributors emerged as a dominant class across an uneven urban-rural divide. While state-socialist regimes oversaw land reforms, the extension of state-financed services, and other progressive policies, the formal and real functioning of these regimes demonstrated that there was nothing inherently egalitarian about state redistribution.

The Political Economy of Vietnam's State-Socialist Welfare Regime

The principles and institutions that governed the provision and payment for education in Vietnam from the 1940s and 1950s in the north and on a countrywide basis after 1975 resembled those of an ideal typical state-socialist welfare regime. But the precise features of this regime reflected Vietnam's unique circumstances, including its overwhelmingly agrarian economy, and the conditions of national partition and protracted guerrilla war under which the welfare regime developed. The country's partition and wars, its low levels of industrialization, and its sheer social and physical diversity meant that the precise attributes and practical force of state-socialist principles and institutions varied within the country across time and place. State-socialist institutions in Vietnam were fragile in some areas, stronger in others, and eroded over the course of the 1980s. Nonetheless, across the north of Vietnam from the 1950s and across the country after

1975, it was most fundamentally the core principles and institutions of state-socialism (as defined above) that governed the creation and allocation of education and the character of social and educational inequalities. The specific attributes of Vietnam's political, economic, and welfare institutions under state-socialism are next examined in turn.

The political foundations of Vietnam's state-socialist welfare regime emerged with the ascendance of the CPV. Founded in 1930, the CPV was from its beginning a political coalition of petit-bourgeois revolutionaries, peasants, workers, and other class elements mobilized under the banners of national self-determination and socialist revolution.[8] As the party expanded its membership, it became more, though not entirely, representative of the country's population.[9] Fundamentally, the CPV's rise to power was due largely to native forces, even as or because colonialism had transformed Vietnam's political economy. In its own view, the CPV was the sole legitimate champion of national self-determination and a more just social order. During the 1950s and 1960s, the party gained immense popular backing, particularly (though by no means exclusively) in the north. In southern Vietnam, political support for the party was more fragile, owing to the mixed political allegiances of southerners and some ill-will generated both during and after the war.[10] Over the course of its history, the CPV has ensured its supremacy by repressive means, even if the intensity of repression has waxed and waned over time.[11]

The substance of the CPV's economic policies were recognizably state-socialist even as outcomes diverged from plans. The formation of the Democratic Republic of Vietnam (DRV) in the north of Vietnam after 1945 and especially after 1954, and the extension of this state to the rest of the country after 1975 (as the renamed Socialist Republic of Vietnam) involved the implementation of policies that achieved massive institutional realignments.[12] The state-socialist development model the CPV pursued until the late 1980s was designed to achieve rapid industrialization and avoid the perceived traps of dependent capitalist development. This was to be achieved by promoting a dual economy in which agriculture would feed industry, as detailed above. War, the poor performance of state-socialist economic institutions, external economic embargoes, and a prevailing paucity of resources combined to undermine state-socialist plans.[13]

Severe shortages and supply bottlenecks, along with poor infrastructure and other factors, led to the development of a highly fragmented and decentralized economy that was meant to be centralized. The collectivization of agriculture improved economic security for scores of peasants and boosted agricultural production in northern Vietnam during the late 1960s. But over the long haul, both agricultural and industrial policies failed to produce the promised outcomes. Given its wars and paucity of resources, the scale and scope of state industrial enterprises were more limited than in other state-socialist regimes, while the force of state-socialist policies in Vietnam varied across time and place. After 1975, accumulated war damage, the costs of a new war in Cambodia, and the political and economic blockade imposed by China and the United States helped drive the country further into poverty. By the 1980s, local units of government and production units increasingly resorted to spontaneous or improvisational survival strategies (Fforde and deVylder 1996) and in so doing gained increasing autonomy from the central authority.

The development of state-socialism in Vietnam transformed the country's welfare regime, albeit in a context of war and post-war devastation. State-socialist economic institutions subjected human well-being to new formal and informal rules. In the north of Vietnam during the 1950s and 1960s, land reform and the advent of some state- and collectively-financed social services (for example, preventive health services and education) produced tangible if spatially and temporally uneven welfare gains, even in the context of war and its aftermath. The extension of state-socialist economic and social policies to the post-war south produced some confusion and ill-will (owing to the confiscation of property, among other reasons). Nationally, destruction wrought by war and anaemic economic performance limited the scope and quality of such services. A fuller illustration of Vietnam's state-socialist welfare regime is developed below in the analysis of principles and institutions governing education. Overall, Vietnam's state-socialist welfare regime was something of an "insecurity regime" (Wood 2004), in that the basic needs of most of the population were under constant direct and indirect threats. Rural populations had inferior services. Both before and after 1975, large segments of the population were periodically subject to threats of disease and famine.

In the north and then in the south, Vietnam's state-socialist welfare regime reduced some forms of inequality and promoted others. The dualist structure of the economy ensured low returns to agriculture. Across the political economy, state managers with control over the means of bureaucratic allocation exercised class power. Ethnic minority groups, though incorporated in some state schemes (for example, literacy training), experienced social exclusion in other respects. Before 1975 in the north and after 1975 in the south, Vietnamese with "suspect" class backgrounds or affiliations were subject to economic and social exclusion. All of these characteristics of Vietnam's state-socialist welfare regime were evidenced in the principles and institutions governing the provision and payment for education up until the collapse of the welfare regime in the late 1980s.

Education and Educational Inequalities under State-socialism

The rise of a state-socialist welfare regime beginning in northern Vietnam in the 1940s and 1950s and in southern Vietnam after 1975 involved fundamental changes in the principles and institutions governing the provision and payment for education, including changes in mechanisms governing educational inequalities. In the north and later the south, this was a transition from arrangements under which formal schooling was a privilege of a relative few to a mass education system, in which a state-financed education was to be compulsory for all children and enshrined in law. In this respect, the institutionalization of state-socialism in northern and southern Vietnam truly revolutionized arrangements governing the provision and payment for education. But while the development of state-socialist education regime occasioned steady increases in educational enrolments, the outcomes of state education policies were at variance with those envisioned. Social turbulence owing to war, acute economic scarcity, and the intended and unintended consequences of certain education policies contributed to these outcomes. Additionally state-socialist institutional arrangements governing education generated distinctive inequalities. The withering of state-socialist economic institutions over the course of the 1980s eviscerated the fiscal foundations of essential public services, plunging Vietnam's education system into crisis.

The Institutionalization and Outcomes of the State-socialist Education

In the 1940s and 1950s and in the south after 1975, the CPV initially pursued mass education through literacy campaigns, which were undertaken using "guerrilla" and other revolutionary tactics, such as compulsory literacy classes on a village basis. Building an education system, by contrast, would involve the development of a large-scale educational bureaucracy, the recruitment and training of hundreds and thousands of teachers, and the troublesome problem of education finance (Woodside 1987).

Preliminary efforts in this direction took place as early as 1945 and 1946, as the Party in this period began developing its education bureaucracy, planning a Vietnamese curriculum, and establishing ideological contents of such a curriculum with great attention paid to patriotic and socialist themes. These elements of a nascent national education policy would be implemented in so-called "free zones" — that is, those under CPV control. The first education "reform", between 1950 and 1952, established the basic curriculum and organization of the education system. During this period, the CPV began building on the pre-existing patchwork of informal village schools and the smaller number of colonial schools that gradually fell under their control. A second education reform was ratified after the DRV's independence was secured and explicitly set out the twin aims of the education system: "building socialism in the north" and supporting the defeat of the United States and their puppets to unite the country.

A third set of reforms, introduced in 1958, reflected the political character of the emerging state-socialist regime. Focused on building "socialist schools", this set of reforms emerged largely as a reaction to the political fallout from the land reform debacles of 1956 and the suppression of the Nhân Văn Giải Phẩm dissident movement, one of whose demands was that education be left to educators, not party apparatchiks. Specific contents of the 1958 reforms included compulsory political education for educators and students, the harmonization of school curricula with the contents of five-year plans, the affirmation of the exclusive leadership role of the CPV, and various measures to reinforce ideological compliance (then the Worker's Party) (Lê V.G. 2003, p. 169). Steps were taken to integrate schooling with productive activities, including harvesting, irrigation, and so on. Graduates of tertiary schools would be assigned jobs according to state plans.

But from the perspective of welfare regimes, the significance of the 1958 reforms lay in the establishment of formal principles and institutions governing education finance. The state would assume all costs for the provision of education (with voluntary contributions from the people). No fees would be charged at any level. No private schools would exist. Schools in rural areas were to be funded on the basis of resources from local economic units (principally agricultural collectives) and supplemented by transfers from the central budget (mostly for infrastructure and, to a lesser extent, to supplement teachers' wages). In urban areas, schools were financed by transfers from the local and central budgets. As such, schools in rural areas had a greater dependence on the performance of local economic institutions.

The growth of enrolments in Vietnam under the state-socialist regime followed a trajectory of rapid expansion during the 1950s and 1960s, slow growth and post-war expansion in the 1970s, and stagnation and crisis in the mid-to-late 1980s. By 1957, the number of primary school students in northern Vietnam was three times the number of primary students in the entire country in 1939. In 1939, only 2 per cent of primary school students advanced to higher educational levels. By 1957, this figure had risen to 13 per cent (Pham 1999, p. 51). Vietnamese histories sympathetic to the party speak of legions of youth (*rất nhiều thanh niên*) coming across the 17 parallel to study as an act of resistance, though no figures are offered as to what *rất nhiều* might mean (Lê G.V. 2003, p. 119).

Massive dislocations that accompanied the onset of U.S. bombing in northern Vietnam in 1965 did not throw the education system into turmoil. On the contrary, the urgency associated with the war effort created conditions for more effective mass mobilization and the scale of formal schooling actually expanded.[14] Urban schools destroyed by U.S. bombs were rebuilt in the countryside, where they were less vulnerable to attack.[15] Rural schools functioned with little resources. Between 1965 and 1975, gross enrolments and staffing in northern Vietnam saw increases at all levels (MOET 1995*a*, pp. 7–8). That Vietnam's education system developed as quickly as it did in the context of a war of national independence and amid severe poverty and scarcity is a testament to the determination and mobilizational capacities of national and, especially, local leaders, and to popular enthusiasm for education.

After 1975, under the banner of the new and unified Socialist Republic of Vietnam, the CPV implemented education policies that aimed to ensure access to education for all Vietnamese and to expand the country's higher education in the service of socialist industrialization. In the south, the 1975–76 school year started on schedule, albeit in a surreal political context. According to official statistics, Vietnam continued to achieve important gains in terms of accessibility to formal schooling.[16] By the mid-1980s, education indicators were comparable to countries with income levels ten times that of Vietnam's. Conditions were threadbare and, in the south, the political climate in localities could be tense. Indeed, official statistics are inadequate for grasping the realities of schooling in the post-war period. State statistics and official documents did not call attention to prevailing inequalities in the spatial distribution of education provision across regions, the limited scope and quality of schooling, or access to education among different population segments.

With respect to institutional responsibilities for the provision and payment for education, the situation in northern Vietnam between the 1945 and the mid 1970s could be summarized as follows: Formal policies dictated a gradual movement towards state provision of a compulsory standard education for all children through state-run schools and funded through the central budget, and in rural areas, through combinations of budget allocations and resources from local agricultural collectives. Of the different levels of education, kindergarten education was the most dependent on resources from the collectives, while primary and lower- and upper-secondary education depended on budget transfers from district and provincial education departments, whose budgets were determined by the Ministry of Education.

In practice, institutional arrangements were more complex and varied across time and place, in response to local conditions and wartime contingencies. Despite early efforts to extend literacy training to ethnic minorities, access to education in remote rural areas remained patchy and many areas remained without functioning schools into the 1970s. In less remote and more populous rural areas, the functioning of schools (including teachers' wages and rations) depended on resources from local collectives. Conditions were often threadbare, meaning earthen floors, thatched roofs, three-hour school days, and among the shortest academic years in the world. Across locations, primary and lower secondary schools received additional financial support from communes, varying from 5 to 15 per cent, or even more. In urban areas, precincts funded kindergartens, while primary and secondary schools depended on arrangements described above. In wartime, schools in urban areas were disrupted. Though better funded, schools in urban areas also functioned with limited resources and under threadbare conditions.

From a contemporary vantage point, it is easy to forget the texture of social life in urban and rural Vietnam of this period and what it meant for education. Three points warrant particular emphasis. First, the combined effects of wars, prolonged economic isolation, and the poor performance of state-socialist economic institutions severely constrained the scope and quality of formal schooling. In most rural areas, going to school consisted of three hours of studies in dirt-floored thatched huts. Second, while education policies were progressive in principle — and were indeed more egalitarian than policies pursued in many other societies — they also promoted and reinforced inequality by conferring greater access to better services for urban dwellers over rural ones and, even more pronouncedly, for those with party ties.[17] Finally, after 1975, significant segments of southern Vietnam faced exclusionary practices on the basis of their families' past political allegiances. There is an abundance of anecdotal evidence that families and entire villages with past ties to the Republic of Vietnam regime were denied access to schooling.

The education system that developed under the state-socialist regime reflected and promoted social inequalities, both with respect to the accessibility and quality of formal education. The education system reproduced inequalities between town and country. Urban residents had comparatively good access to schooling, financed through the state budget; rural populations had inferior schools, often dependent on the meagre resources generated by agricultural collectives. Ethnic minority groups, comprising some fifteen per cent of the population, experienced varying degrees of exclusion due to their settlement in remote areas, as well as linguistic differences and the paltry amount of state resources committed to their education, compared with their needs. In the post-bellum south, children from families with ties to the old regime were frequently denied educational opportunities beyond a basic level.

Education and State-socialist Involution

Market transitions involve fundamental realignments of a country's political and economic institutions and result in the emergence of a new welfare regime. While a given welfare regime may accommodate minor changes, fundamental changes in the principles and institutions governing the provision and payment for welfare signal the emergence of a new regime (Gough 2004). How did the erosion of state-socialism in Vietnam affect education?

Vietnam's transition to a market economy was a ten-year process of institutional decay that undermined the basic coherence of the economy and ultimately threatened the survival of the state.[18] After 1975, war damage, international isolation, and economic scarcity undermined the viability of state-socialist developmentalism. By the 1980s, economic producers (including state owned enterprises and agricultural collectives) adopted increasingly brazen deviations from central planning norms. The central government sought to contain these "spontaneous" reforms by introducing successive rounds of top-down reforms designed to control, limit, and steer change processes that were already occurring. Politically, the gradual disintegration of the planned economy and its fiscal institutions weakened the powers of the central state *vis-à-vis* the localities and compromised the central state's fiscal integrity, resulting in a prolonged fiscal crisis that ended only with the abandonment of core state-socialist institutions.

Economic reforms towards the late 1980s, such as output contracts in agriculture and new trade laws for state owned enterprises, boosted economic outputs and improved incentive by allowing economic producers to engage in market exchange. But once this limited liberalization gained momentum, it also had the effect of draining economic resources from the central budget, further undercutting central planning in the financial bases of state functions, including education. Vietnam's 1980 constitution stipulated the state's commitment to developing compulsory education at no direct charge. But such plans, along with indicators of progress regarding the extension of formal schooling during the mid-1980s, masked the fragility of the state-socialist economic institutions on which formal schooling depended. Between 1980 and 1990, Vietnam registered only a minor increase in its gross enrolment, even though the country gained millions more school-age children. By the end of the decade, dropout rates soared, particularly at the secondary level of education.

The shift to household production in agriculture and the expansion of markets across sectors stimulated economic growth, but did not address fundamental problems regarding the financing of essential social services. With hyperinflation and evaporating state budgets during the 1980s, real public investments in education stagnated and then fell sharply in real terms. Education sector workers faced declining wages from an already low base and in many localities, local authorities resorted to financing arrangements under the heading "the state and people work together" (*nhà nước và dân cùng làm*). It did not take long for households to grow both suspicious and weary of such arrangements, though this was only a hint of things to come. Teachers went increasingly long stretches without compensation (in cash and kind) and expanded their economic activities outside of the school. As the flow of resources into the education system dwindled, so did the quality of education and morale among teachers. Many left teaching altogether in search of a living wage.

As the 1980s wore on, the institutional arrangements responsible for financing education gradually disintegrated as the planned economy unravelled.[19] The plight of schools in rural areas was especially acute. As the dissolution of agricultural collectives gathered pace, so did declines in school resources. Formal policies indicated the state's increasing reliance on economic resources outside of the planned economy. Decision No. 15-CP, dated 14 January 1981, titled "amendment to the social welfare mechanism for teachers in primary and secondary education sector", stipulated the establishment of "school protection funds" (quỹ bao trợ nhà trường) called on "the state and society" to contribute to education, from household savings to production units' welfare funds. By 1984 Circular No. 19-TT/LB dated 23 July 1984 was issued, requiring "contributions" (in both money and kind) from children's parents and from centrally and locally managed production units within a given area.[20] According to the recollection of one teacher,[21] "monthly wages" included 13.5 kg of rice per teacher to be purchased at the price of 3.8 hào/kg (hào = 1 đồng), 0.5 kg of meat (called meat, but in fact, mostly fat, usually fried and used for oil), and 0.5 kg of sugar. These constraints on teachers were harsh, but perhaps no harsher than those faced by most Vietnamese. Special funds collected in communities were helpful to help pay these salaries, as schools often did not receive budgetary funds in time.

How are we to make sense of education and educational inequalities under Vietnamese state-socialism? Under state-socialism, the CPV-led state realized many important gains in education and did so in the face of overwhelming challenges. But by 1989, Vietnam's thirty-five-year experiment with state-socialism came to a rapid and unexpected conclusion. The withering of state-socialist economic institutions necessitated a reworking of the financial and fiscal basis of formal schooling. In 1989, the CPV took its first step away from the universalist principles that had guided education policies since the 1950s, when the National Assembly met in a special session to pass a constitutional amendment permitting the state to charge school fees. Whether sharp declines in enrolment at the time predated or were exacerbated by the introduction of fees is the subject of some debate. What is clear is that enrolment rates fell sharply while dropout rates soared. Between 1989 and 1991, dropouts increased dramatically by up to 80 per cent in secondary schools in some areas, while nationally, new enrolments declined sharply and would not reach 1985 levels until the mid-1990s.

III
EDUCATION IN VIETNAM'S MARKET-LENINIST WELFARE REGIME

Vietnam's transition from state-socialism to a state-dominated market economy has occasioned the rise of a market-Leninist welfare regime distinguished by a specific and, in some respects, contradictory mix of state-socialist, neoliberal, and corporatist principles and institutions. Understanding the development of this regime, its precise institutional attributes, and its stratification effects provides a foundation for an analysis of continuity and change in the principles governing the provision and payment for education and education inequalities in Vietnam since 1989.

Welfare Regimes in the Path from State-socialism

Transitions from state-socialism involve a redefinition of the relationship between the state and the economy and the rise of a new welfare regime. But the precise institutional attributes of the new regime depends on the particular circumstances of a country's exit path from state-socialism, the intensities and kinds of institutional legacies of state-socialism that remain, and the dynamics of the political economy that emerges in state-socialism's aftermath. Indeed, the character of a country's exit path from state-socialism affects the subsequent development of a country's political economy and its attendant welfare-regimes.

Theoretical literature on transitions from state-socialism has clarified basic differences in transitions from state-socialism and their consequence with respect to subsequent patterns of institutional change. Analysis of the political economies and welfare regimes of Eastern Europe and Russia is beyond the scope of this work. But an awareness of the basic dimensions of variation in transitions from state-socialism is necessary. Szelenyi and King (2005) have observed at least three distinctive pathways from state-socialism, including a European path, a Russian path, and an East Asian (read "Chinese") path. In much of Central and Eastern Europe, they argue, the erosion of state-socialist institutions culminated in political revolutions and the formation of new states, based on a political alliance of liberal intellectuals and neoliberal economic technocrats, supported by foreign investors, but largely insulated from former nomenklatura elements. Szelenyi and King have dubbed this type of transition a "revolution from without". In Russia, by contrast, remnants of the state-socialist nomenklatura joined forces with emerging oligarchic business interests to seize political and economic power in a "revolution from above". Among other things, this entailed the primitive accumulation of formerly public assets and the establishment of an authoritarian and now quasi-fascistic regime. In the so-called East Asian path (and here the authors focus on China, only mentioning Vietnam), communist parties survived the bottom-up dissolution of state-socialist economic institutions. This was a so-called "transformation from below", in that changes in grassroots economic institutions, associated productivity improvements, and spillovers into savings and investment propelled the transition. Notably absent is any element of political revolution. Indeed, many of the institutional features of state-socialism survived the market transition, particularly, though not exclusively, in the political sphere.

In both Vietnam and China, the communist parties survived the dissolution of state-socialism with their political monopolies intact and proceeded to use markets, and instrumentally to promote state imperatives. The way they have done so has varied and can only be understood in relation to the dynamics of each political economy (London 2009).[22] Political leaders in both countries insist on their commitment to "socialism", which they identify with broad notions of public ownership and shared wealth, rather than with the existence of a planned or market economy *per se*.[23] Such an understanding of "socialism" is interesting but, in important respects, too detached from reality to be useful. For it is politically mediated and dramatically inegalitarian private accumulation within the shell of formally "public" institutions that is the hallmark of market-Leninist political economies. Political principles of Leninism remain the preponderant mode of political integration and are an important determinant of market power, while markets — alongside redistribution — have emerged as a dominant mode of economic integration. Leninism and politically-mediated markets are principal arbiters of social inequalities.

Comparative analyses of China and Vietnam are suggestive of the generic and distinctive attributes of these market-Leninist regimes (see, for example, London 2008). In both Vietnam and China, contemporary welfare regimes are characterized by a contradictory, but stable combinations of redistributive, neoliberal, and communist-corporatist principles that are unique from welfare regimes in other settings.[24] Redistributive elements of Market-Leninist welfare regimes include the maintenance of large-scale state planning institutions, fiscal republicanism that share state revenues across localities, and centrally funded social policies.[25] Neoliberal elements of market-Leninism involve the selective embrace of market-led governance in certain fields, including (at times) essential services, such as electricity, water, and health care. Finally, communist-corporatist elements of market-Leninist regimes refer to economic and welfare policies that target strategically important political constituencies (for example, retired state managers, industrial workers, war veterans, and soldiers' mothers) and which reinforce dogmatic Leninist ideologies. Whether and to what extent this combination of elements can be called "socialist" is open to debate. Certainly, individual elements of market-Leninist regimes can be found elsewhere. The distinctive combination of redistributive, neoliberal, and communist-corporatist principles is unique to Vietnam and China (London 2009). The development, attributes, and stratification of Vietnam's market-Leninist welfare regime is now examined in greater detail.

The Political Economy of Vietnam's Market-Leninist Welfare Regime

Vietnam's transition from state-socialism has involved a redefinition of the relation between the state and the economy and, with it, the development of a new welfare regime. Broadly, economic growth associated with Vietnam's market transition has improved welfare and living standards. But the country has seen fundamental changes in institutional arrangements governing welfare and in the mechanisms governing social inequalities.

Understanding Vietnam's contemporary welfare regime requires an appreciation of the country's political economy. The country's transition to a state-dominated market economy — and the country's intensifying intercourse with processes and institutions of global capitalism — have occasioned rapid economic growth and significant, if uneven, welfare improvements across different regions and segments of the population. But Vietnam's transition from state-socialism has not entailed a decline in the political and economic power of the state. Rather, the CPV has managed to use combinations of politics and markets to promote its political imperatives.

The fiscal crisis of the middle and late 1980s all but paralysed the state and reduced the leverage of the central state in planning. But the CPV and its state have since harnessed market economic institutions to bolster economic accumulation. While coalitions of provincial leaders (especially from the south) and enterprise managers detain political clout, the central state has gained unprecedented fiscal powers by virtue of its control of trade and budgeting, although it has transferred political authority over budgeting back to localities in some fields. Politically, important legacies of state-socialism remain: state planning institutions remain strong, state agencies (from business enterprises to schools) remain thoroughly interpenetrated by party cells and, "grassroots democracy" and freedom of the press lay a harmonious façade of accountability over what remains an illiberal and secretive polity.

Continuity and change in Vietnam's political institutions can be better seen with respect to state attempts to regulate the economy and welfare. Vietnam's market reforms are complex and have been detailed elsewhere, but their main impact has been to promote the development of a state-dominated market economy. Failures in the country's centrally planned economy in the 1980s spurred a coalition of southern reformers and provincial leaders to champion greater market reforms. The sequencing of enterprise reforms prior to agricultural reforms, the subsequent modest scope of gains in agriculture after the reforms, and the absence of anything comparable to China's famed township and village enterprises gave surviving SOEs (state owned enterprises) a dominant market position. Structurally, the largest proportion of the population is in household-based agriculture. State agencies and state owned enterprises remain the most powerful economic players, and many have benefited through collaborations with foreign investors. The state permits and promotes oligopolies in industry and trade. Vietnam has an increasingly lively but (in comparison to China) small-scale private sector. Indeed, state economic policies appear to aim at securing state control over the commanding heights of the economy and simultaneously preventing the development of an independent bourgeoisie by promoting a corporate national bourgeoisie within and on the borders of the party and state.[26] Even at local levels of governance, those within or with superior access to state decision-making bodies are favoured in the new market economy.

The essential spatial duality of the economy has remained, though the economic relation between rural and urban areas no longer centres on gains from agriculture being invested in industry. Towns and cities have transformed from largely domestically-oriented centres of administration and industry to globally-linked centres of business and administration with peri-urban agglomerations of labour intensive manufacturing. Rural areas feature decollectivized small-holder agriculture geared towards subsistence and production for the markets and larger-scale plantation agriculture dominated by state-owned and foreign-invested enterprises. The most rapid economic growth and industrialization has been concentrated in and around Ho Chi Minh City and Hanoi and their environs, boosting local revenues of provinces and municipalities in those areas while transforming agricultural lands into surreal industrial landscapes.

Redistributive measures such as the redistribution of revenues from wealthy to poor provinces have mitigated regional inequalities to an extent. While significant, the scope of these transfers has not been sufficient to offset market-driven uneven development. Indeed, provinces with high revenues streams enjoy residual claimancy rights, under which they retain control over revenues in excess of centrally mandated revenue contributions (World Bank 1996a; Socialist Republic of Vietnam and World Bank 2005). Nor are interprovincial transfers always necessarily welfare-enhancing, as such transfers can be linked to state-financed construction projects of questionable economic benefit to local populations.

With respect to welfare, a fundamental difference with the past lies with economic growth. Over the last two decades, Vietnam has experienced rapid, if uneven, economic growth and significant, if uneven, improvements across virtually all indicators of living standards. Economic growth does not tell us about the welfare regime, however, which is defined by institutional responsibility for the creation and allocation of welfare and its stratification effects.

Contemporary Vietnam's welfare regime combines redistributive, neoliberal, and communist corporatist elements. The welfare regime is liberal in that households' economic security depends principally on income from wage labour and commodities production, with public transfers of income and assets and subsistence agriculture playing secondary roles. With respect to essential welfare services — such as education and health — the welfare regime is more complex. On the one hand, the state provides and pays for a floor of essential welfare services (for example, preventive health, basic education) and is currently expanding insurance schemes to protect against covariate and idiosyncratic shocks. Beyond basic services, state policies have shifted institutional responsibility for financing essential social services onto households. The state has deployed safety nets mechanisms to address the needs of certain segments of the population, including officially certified poor persons and members of valued political constituencies.

In essence, the CPV has sought to promote a hybrid regime in which state, market, household, and third-party (insurance) elements share institutional responsibility for the provision of and payment for welfare. The state has promoted a transition to this new regime in a decidedly *ad hoc* manner, describing the shifting of institutional responsibility for the provision of and payment for essential services as a process of "socialization" (*xã hộ hóa*). "Socialization" is a term whose definition Vietnamese officials have customized or reinvented to describe certain normative ideas concerning appropriate institutional arrangements for the governance of essential social services. When Vietnamese policymakers refer to "socialization" they are referring to three inseparable processes — none of which involves the public finance of social services, as socialization is understood throughout the rest of the world. "Socialization" refers (1) to the selective withdrawal of the state from certain activities which non-state entities are deemed capable of performing more effectively while ensuring a desired outcome; (2) to a process of social mobilization (*huy động xã hội*) that will "liberate" the state from excessive burdens by "bringing into play" (*phát huy*) maximum resources and energy from all sectors of society, and (3) to the assumption that the Party, state, and "people" will collectively manage the process in a way that is accountable and produces optimal results.[27]

In practice, "socialization" is more complex still. There are several reasons. Three will be stated here. First, "socialization" is an umbrella term that state officials use to refer not only to the withdrawal of the state from the provision of certain services but also to a wide variety of mechanisms whereby state providers of services seek to mobilize resources outside of the state budget. Everything from introducing fees for public services, to promoting joint ventures between public and private service providers, to promoting foreign investment is dubbed "socialization". Second, in general policy statements, the "social mobilization" component of "socialization" is almost always vague. There is no agency. "Socialization" enthusiasts see it as a process that is neither "top-down" nor "bottom-up" and whereby all segments of society participate in the provision of services. This may work well in diagrams, but it bears little resemblance to reality. Which brings us to the third decisive element of "socialization" — its use as a term to describe, justify, and promote *ad hoc* institutional arrangements involving fuzzy combinations of public resources and private interest under party leadership.[28] "Socialization" may be a temporary phenomenon, as its existence owes in large part to the absence of a well functioning tax system and to the limited resources and weak allocative capacities of the state. As we will see in the analysis of education, the greatest practical effect of "socialization" has been to shift institutional responsibilities for essential welfare services away from the state. In many instances, the burden is shifted onto households.

Mechanisms governing social inequalities in contemporary Vietnam reflect historical and contemporary patterns of uneven development, as well as the stratifying effects of market-Leninist institutions. On top of pre-existing regional inequalities, Vietnam's market transition has contributed to the generation, reproduction, and intensification of regional inequalities in per capita income terms. But the country has also experienced a reconfiguration of social class that is in important respects an outgrowth of specific accumulation strategies pursued by the state. Party membership and membership in other state organization remain important determinants of life chances, affecting employment, access to capital, and access to welfare-enhancing goods, services, and information. The country has also seen the emergence of a commercial petit-bourgeois. But uneven development and institutional arrangements governing politics, economy, and welfare have contributed to inequality within and across urban and rural areas. The country has seen the development of a tiered system of essential social services in which access to services beyond a basic level is contingent on out-of-pocket cash payments. In economically depressed parts of the country, where growth in household earnings have lagged, the quantity and quality of services are typically inferior to that available in urban areas. In the sphere of essential services, the state ensures a basic floor of services, while services beyond this basic level are subject to market principles. State safety net programmes target certain segments of the population (within limits) and strategically important political constituents. These principles and institutions are evidenced in the sphere of education.

Education and Educational Inequalities under Market-Leninism

Vietnam's economic growth over the last two decades has permitted continuous expansion in the scale and scope of schooling, as detailed in the introduction. Rapid economic growth has enabled continuous growth in total spending (that is, state and non-state) on education, including substantial investments in infrastructure and establishment of schools in previously underserved areas. Gross and net enrolments are up across all levels of education and most segments of the population. Table 2.1 is suggestive of the many kinds of educational inequalities that exist in Vietnam. As has been made clear, many of the inequalities that exist in Vietnam today are not new (for example, rural-urban inequalities). But the development of a new welfare regime in Vietnam has meant important changes in formal and informal principles and institutions governing the educational inequalities. As was shown in Chapter One of this volume, many forms of educational inequalities in Vietnam have declined. The relative parity between girls and boys is particularly noteworthy. On the other hand, enrolment inequalities are only part of the story and there are many forms of inequality that the state's ameliorative "safety-nets" policies and target programmes have only partially mitigated.

Policy Principles and Their Intended and Unintended Consequences

Under Vietnam's market-Leninist regime, state policies have shifted an increasing share of institutional responsibilities for the provision and payment for education away from the state. More specifically, education policies have shifted an increasing responsibility for the provision of education onto "markets" by permitting and promoting the development of so-called "non-public" or "extra-public" (*ngoài công lập*) schools, including "people's founded" (*dân lập*) and private (*tư tực*) schools at the pre-primary, secondary, and tertiary levels. State policies have, at the same time, shifted an increasing share of the responsibilities for education finance from the state onto households by permitting and promoting the collection of various school fees.

The two most fundamental changes in principles governing the provision and payment for education concern the introduction of the fees-for-service principle and the gradual expansion of non-public schooling. First, since 1989, fees for schooling have expanded continuously so that

TABLE 2.1
Primary and Secondary Education Indicators, 2006

	Percentage of children aged 36–59 months currently attending early childhood education	Percentage of primary school entry age currently attending grade 1	Primary net attendance ratio			Lower-Secondary and Upper-Secondary Net attendance ratio		
			Male	Female	Total	Male	Female	Total
Gender								
Male	53.3	95.5						
Female	61	91.5						
Regions								
Red River Delta	80	98.5	97	96.8	96.9	88.1	87.4	87.7
North East	46	86.8	97.7	96.4	97.1	75.9	70.1	73.1
North West	50	88.7	94.2	94.5	94.4	69.6	69	69.3
North Central	66.9	94.1	98.4	96.3	97.3	85.5	86.7	86.1
South Central	43.8	92	94.7	92	93.4	81.7	79.2	80.5
Central Highlands	44.4	94.1	90.8	95.4	93	72.3	77.7	74.9
South East	63	91	89.9	93	91.4	74	83.9	79
Mekong Delta	39.8	95.7	95.9	96.2	96	67.1	68	67.5

Area								
Urban	74.7	91.6	94.6	94.6	94.6	86.2	91.4	88.8
Rural	51.4	94	95.6	95.6	95.6	76	76.2	76.1
Mothers' education								
None	46.5	92.9	93.8	94.3	94.1	65.7	66.7	66.2
Completed primary	51.7	94.2	95.9	95.6	95.8	79.3	80	79.6
completed lower secondary	71.7	96.3	97	96.4	96.7	87.9	89.5	88.7
Completed upper secondary	83.1	-83.9	94.9	95.7	95.3	94.7	95	94.9
Mother not in household						70.3	65.2	67.9
Income Quintiles								
Q1 (poorest)	35.7	93.1	95	93.1	94.1	62.3	57.3	59.9
Q2	48.9	94.7	96	95.2	95.6	71.8	74.7	73.2
Q3	56.7	94.3	93.9	97.6	95.7	79.7	80.8	80.3
Q4	61.7	93.5	98.3	95.2	96.8	84.4	85.7	85
Q1 (richest)	80.7	91.9	94	96.1	94.9	89.4	93.6	91.5
Ethnicity								
Other	39.6	90.5	93.8	93.8	93.8	67.8	61.6	64.9
Kinh/Hoa	60.9	94.1	95.7	95.7	95.7	80	82.6	81.3
Total	57.1	93.5	95.4	95.4	95.4	78.1	79.6	78.8

Source: UNICEF 2008, tables ED1–ED4, pp 209–15.

an average household can expect to pay five or six different types of school fees, in addition to other expenses discussed below.[29] As a result, education has become a significant and at times overwhelmingly large expenditure item for households.[30] By 1996, household expenditure was estimated to account for 43 per cent of total (that is, state and household) expenditures on education (World Bank 1996) and today's estimates are that roughly 50 per cent of the total spending on education is out of pocket spending. A 2003 study from the Vietnam Academy of Social Sciences reported that the average expenditure for a middle school student includes: VND72.2 thousand in school fees; 66.7 thousand for other contributions; 53.1 thousand for uniforms; 65 thousand for books; 56.8 thousand for other study materials; 107.5 thousand for extra study; and 30.3 thousand for other expenses; adding up to an average grand total of VND454.8 thousand a month, an amount equivalent to the lion's share of a low-wage worker's salary (VKHXHNV 2003). Table 2.1, lists other data on household education expenditure.

A second important policy change concerns the permission for and promotion of non-public provision of education, including "non-state" (that is, private) provision of non-primary education and various forms of "semi-public" arrangements, according to which a public school has two or more schedules of fees for different students. These components of socialization reduce financial burdens on the state while increasing burdens on certain households (MOET 2002, cited in UNDP Hanoi 2006). Resolution 90 of the National Assembly, which was adopted in 1993, introduced a full set of rules permitting the foundation of non-state school forms, including semi-public (*bán công*) schools, semi-public classes within public schools, and people-founded (*dân lập*) private schools.[31] Semi-public schools and classes are partially subsidized through the state budget, but students have to pay three to four times more than public school students.[32] In practice, this is a blueprint for a two-tiered dualist education system.

Some critics of "socialization" worry that its basic effect is to shift an increasing share of the costs of schooling onto households. As one commentator notes:

> Beyond the spirit of supporting children in their studies and promoting a close relation between the school, family, and society ... the real meaning of [socialization] that everyone knows is to contribute' [đóng] money to the school: contribute the fee, contribute to the supplemental funds like

the construction fund, sanitation, water, parking, electricity (through the parents' school committee), ... for text books and materials, various kinds of extra study ... All these contributions have the signature of the parents next to the word "voluntary"! (*Người Hà Nội* newspaper, quoted in Nguyễn Thế Long 2006).

In practice, "socialization" is interpreted and acted upon by different individuals and organizations in different ways. Sometimes the term is used to refer to people investing funds to open a school (usually under the heading "people founded" school) for students unable to qualify for public schools. At other times, socialization is used to describe efforts to promote foreign investment in education (*Người Hà Nội* newspaper, quoted in Nguyễn Thế Long 2006). Confusion over the meaning of the term can frustrate even those with long experience in the education sector. As a former education minister lamented, concepts such as "socialization" make policymakers look like "chickens lost in the rice paddy" (Vũ Ngọc Hải 2004).

Mechanisms Governing Educational Inequalities

Educational inequalities in Vietnam include unevenness in the accessibility and quality of education across regions and population segments, inequalities within the education system owing to state policies and their intended and unintended effects, and the general movement towards an education system in which opportunities are increasingly contingent on household's ability to afford out-of-pocket expenditures. While some of these inequalities are reflected in survey data, the mechanisms governing educational inequalities are not.

Data on education finance were presented in Chapter One and will not be repeated here. What bears emphasis is that Vietnam's rapid economic growth has expanded the overall amount of resources available for investment in education and the country has seen increases in education spending by the state, households, and international donors.[33] Once again, however, increases in the scale of investments have been accompanied by a shifting of the burden of education finance from the state onto households. Some analysts have argued that the state's emphasis on achieving universal provision of primary education has improved the "progressiveness" of education provision for the simple reason that poorer households in Vietnam tend, on average, to have more children (World

Bank 2004). This may be true. But it is also the case that the shifting responsibility for education finance that state policies have effected has produced new problems.

Already, Vietnam's households invest a sizeable portion of their incomes in their children's schooling. The increased average household earnings that Vietnam experienced during the 1990s were reflected in expenditure data on education. Although inflation in the country between 1993 and 1998 was a cumulative 44.6 per cent, household expenditure on primary, lower secondary, and upper secondary education during the same period increased by 70, 65, 70 per cent, respectively.[34] Annual household expenditure on education rose 14 per cent between 1998 and 2002 (General Statistics Office 2003). According to estimates, household expenditure now accounts for over 50 per cent of all spending on education. However, household expenditure on education varied sharply between urban and rural areas and across seven different geographical regions.[35] Household expenditure on education was, on average, three times greater in urban areas than rural ones, while the wealthiest quintile of the population spent more than six times that of the poorest (General Statistics Office 2003). Hence, economic growth and improved household earnings have led to increased education expenditure, but these expenditure levels reflect the uneven spatial distribution of economic growth and growing inequalities in household income (see Figure 2.1).

Fees are one major cause of rising household expenditures on education. Although the state charges lower fees for education in rural areas (and especially in poor regions), fees in both urban and rural areas have increased over time. Moreover, fees increase as students advance through the grades of mass education, meaning that poorer households in urban and rural areas are confronted with increased costs over time, making the incentive to stay in school questionable for many households as their children proceed up the school ladder. As indicated, fees are several times greater for students attending semi-public or people-founded schools. Although these categories represented less than one per cent of all primary education and just five per cent for lower-secondary education, 32 per cent of upper-secondary students were enrolled in semi-public schools by 2003, and the numbers are growing (MOET 2005).[36]

In addition to tuition, local (that is, district and commune) authorities also collect annual construction "contributions", compulsory payments that are earmarked for school upkeep and renovation. Non-tuition costs can be

FIGURE 2.1
Household Income in Vietnam, 1996–2008

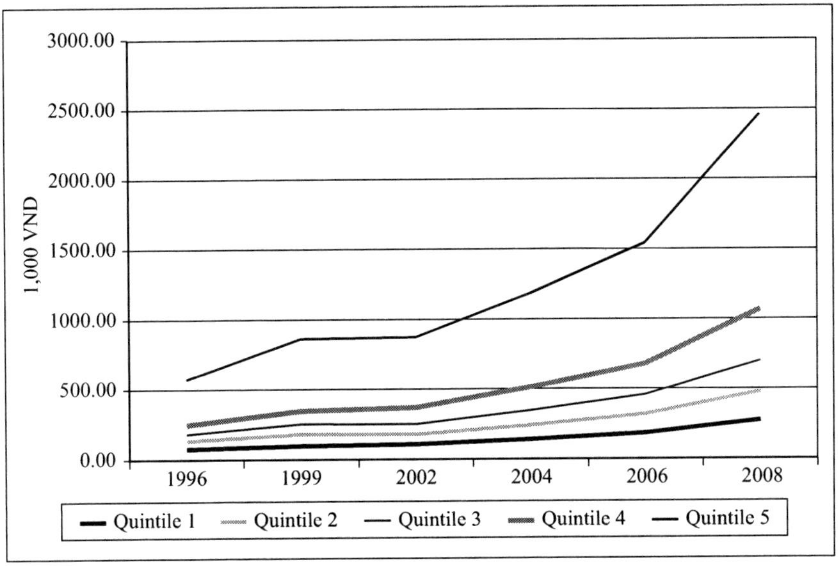

Source: General Statistics Office, various years. Data in current prices.

more onerous for poorer households and thus the cost of education can remain burdensome even when fees are exempted or reduced. In essence, then, formal fees and other government cost recovery schemes represent an important, but only a limited portion of total household expenditures on education.

The trend towards the commodification of education has also been exacerbated by some unintended consequences of state policies, perhaps the most striking example of which is the pervasive informal economy called "extra study" (*học thêm*), in which public-school teachers provide class-based instruction for fees outside of school hours. While international agencies have begun to collect data on some aspects of "extra study" (such as household expenditures), they do not in my view grasp its significance. In practical terms, extra study classes can be as important as the formal school system itself. Any Vietnamese parent will agree. Rules prohibiting students studying with their public school teachers in extra study classes are loosely applied. As recently as this year, parents in Hanoi reported sending children to study after hours with their normal "public" school teacher. On the demand side, competitive examinations and the real and perceived improvements in the economic returns of education have prompted households to invest progressively more in extra study.

While there is a great demand for extra study and many teachers benefit from its existence, its practice is in many important respects contrary to the state's socialist rhetoric. Basically, wealthier households are more able to afford extra study and thus, students from wealthier households enjoy an advantage over their poorer classmates in competitive examinations. Extra study privileges students in urban areas, in particular, where households have more disposable income. In relatively wealthy urban households (especially in Ho Chi Minh City and Hanoi), it is not uncommon to pay hundreds in U.S. dollars per year on extra study.[37] Likewise, teachers in urban areas benefit from extra study more than their rural counterparts. In 2000, one high school teacher in Da Nang indicated he earned US$1,000 a month from his extra teaching, compared with US$40 a month from his salary at the time.[38] In poor rural areas, we might expect that low household incomes would limit the growth of extra study. Still, by the late 1990s, most rural area school systems also featured a parallel informal economy. In some rural areas, expenditures on extra study can be a household's largest expenditure item, after food and fuel. Seventy per cent of in-school youth in Vietnam between the ages of fourteen and twenty-one report going to a private tutor (Ministry of Health et al. 2005).

In some respects, extra study in Vietnam is comparable to experiences in other Asian countries. But three features of extra study in Vietnam distinguish it from other countries. First, it is occurring in the context of a much poorer society — the majority of households in Vietnam must weigh the advantages of expenditure on extra study versus expenditure on basic subsistence needs. Second, there is an element of conflict of interest — if not institutionalized corruption — as Vietnam's students face pressure to take extra study courses from their own public school teachers.[39] Those who do not enrol in (and pay for) extra classes stand a much poorer chance of doing well in public schools and competitive entrance examinations.

Finally, the importance of these "supplemental" lessons sometimes surpasses that of the formal curriculum.[40] The result is not only inequality between rich and poor households, but a pervasive sense of inequity, even as overall school participation rates are improving in objective terms. It is notable that in the recently released *Survey Assessment of Vietnam's Youth*, 44.1 per cent of youth not attending school cited financial reasons, while 25 per cent of those who dropped out of school reportedly did so for financial reasons (SAVY 2005).

Efforts to Reduce Educational Inequalities and their Limits

From its beginnings, the CPV has always professed a commitment to providing equitable access to education. In the context of the country's new market economy, the Party has overseen the development of policies designed to extend educational benefits to poorer segments of the population, especially ethnic minority groups and others in poor, remote, and "difficult" regions, and children from households with recognized contributions to the "revolution".[41] These policies have taken two principal forms: the National Target Programmes (NTP) and Program 135 aimed at ethnic minority groups. The NTP programmes — formerly known as Hunger Eradication and Poverty Reduction (HEPR) — are targeted in two senses. On the one hand, they attempt to focus benefits on specific population groups (as mentioned above). On the other hand, they aim to contribute to Vietnam's achievement of its Millennium Development Goals and progress in the eyes of the CPV and international donor agencies.

NTP-PR and P135 have sought to promote education with assistance for the construction of schools and various forms of financial assistance, including the exemption of school fees and other contributions for officially income-poor and ethnic minority children. Additional forms of assistance include conditional cash payments to income-poor households that send their children to preschool or boarding schools.[42] Ethnographic research underscores the limitations of these policies. In practice, the NTP-PR and P135 policies are having a significant impact, but they are frequently overwhelmed by other factors that conspire to deprive children of educational opportunities. By 2004, an estimated 12–20 per cent of poor households in Vietnam receive some education benefits through HEPR, and roughly 12 per cent of these recipients indicated that they would not have sent their children for schooling had they not received tuition exemptions.[43]

But the cost of schooling, geographic barriers, and (intended and unintended) discrimination continue to undermine the educational prospects of Vietnam's children, particularly those in ethnic minority and other socio-economically vulnerable groups. Despite fees reductions and exemptions schemes, the cost of education remains a major obstacle to schooling. According to one calculation, roughly one-fourth of the poorest quintile and a fifth of the second poorest quintile of the population received full exemptions (SRV & World Bank 2005, p. 14). At the grassroots level inclusion in fees exemption schemes requires being officially recognized as a poor household. Moreover, while fees exemptions eliminate an important component of the costs of education, poor households almost invariably lack the means to pay for other costs (for example, food, transport, informal payments, etc.), let alone that required to participate in extra study. Despite consistent state claims that these programmes effectively protect the poor, they have important limitations. These programmes may mitigate educational inequalities, but they do not address fundamental sources of inequality.

CONCLUSION

The development of a quasi-universalist formal education system in Vietnam under centrally planned state-socialism was a project built on stable class alliances, produced historic gains in literacy and primary education, and enabled the CPV to achieve major political imperatives, including the promotion of welfare, social order, and political legitimacy. But over time, state-socialism generated new class hierarchies, and education policies and their conduct promoted major educational inequalities, many of which were due to state-socialist mechanisms of distribution. Vietnam's transition from centrally planned state-socialism to an internationally linked market economy enabled rapid increases in the scale of formal education and — in important respects — improved the quality and accessibility of education. But the emergence of a new economy transformed the character of class relations — both within and outside the state. This phenomenon, in combination with new education policies and other factors, contributed to the emergence of new inequality-generating mechanisms, which in some cases replaced and in others, added to the inequality legacies of state-socialism.

In this chapter, I have introduced welfare regimes analysis as a way of conceptualizing changes in the principles and institutions governing education in Vietnam. In the empirical analysis I sought to explain the principles and institutions governing schooling in Vietnam in relation to continuity and change in the country's political and economic institutions. I illustrated how the CPV's quasi-universalistic education policies under state-socialism gradually degenerated and were ultimately replaced by policies that shifted an increasing share of the costs of education from the state onto households.

I believe that the institutionalized inequalities within Vietnam's education system and its system of formal schooling reflect and are being exacerbated by a newly emerging class configuration. This class configuration is a product of accumulation strategies undertaken by a Market-Leninist regime under which a state business elite and a growing urban-based petty bourgeoisie have thrived on market opportunities. In contemporary Vietnam, education at a basic level is accessible to all. But educational opportunities beyond that level are much more difficult to grasp for those towards the bottom of the country's developing class hierarchy. As inequalities in Vietnam's education system become further institutionalized, we might expect that they will perpetuate and exacerbate rather than ameliorate present class cleavages. Whether and how the CPV responds to these trends will tell us a lot about the nature of the CPV and its unique brand of market-Leninism.

In both China and Vietnam, the relation between the state and the economy are mediated by Leninist institutions. In both countries, responsibility for the creation and allocation of different types of welfare is distributed across the state, market, and household spheres in combinations that defy conventional categorizations. In both countries, markets play a fundamental role in the determination of welfare, even as the Leninist state's retention of key redistributive functions and secretive party institutions actively structures market-based accumulation and welfare institutions and, hence, social inequalities. In market-Leninist regimes, the state retains a role in the creation and allocation of welfare through its social policies, but private (that is, market-based) provision of essential welfare goods (including education) also occurs, though often within the shell of state (nominally "public") institutions. Institutional responsibility for the payment for many essential welfare goods (such as education, health, and housing) is shifted onto households. Once again, it is important to appreciate Vietnam's distinctiveness as well as its social diversity. Welfare institutions look and feel different in the northern province of Lào Cai compared with the southern province of Sóc Trăng.

With such internal diversity and with such differences from China, why is Vietnam usefully construed as having a market-Leninist welfare regime? My provisional response is that, in market-Leninist regimes, political inequalities associated with communist party membership remain an important mechanism of social stratification and mediate market-based inequalities, which nonetheless emerge as a major and, in many respects, dominant mechanism of stratification. Like social policies under various forms of welfare capitalism, social policies under market-Leninist regimes are designed to counteract market-based inequalities and at the same time promote the subjective legitimacy of, and consent to, state power. But within market-Leninist regimes, the politics of redistribution have a specific ideological content of social policies (including education) and cannot be dissociated from the accumulated social history of the political regime. As the case of education in Vietnam shows us, the character of social policies under market-Leninism varies and exhibits socialist, neoliberal, and corporatist element. Their ideological rationale is decidedly mixed, as is their ability to generate recognizably "socialist" outcomes in the context of a market-based economy.

An analysis of the role of class politics in the determination of Vietnam's welfare regimes have been presented here only in broad strokes. My main claims have been programmatic and conceptual; that is, that by identifying the generic features of state-socialist and market economies and by appreciating their particular instantiations in Vietnam, we can better understand the principles and institutions governing education and educational inequalities in Vietnam over time.

Notes

1. The journalists Nicolas Kristof and Sheryl WuDunn (1994) were, to my knowledge, the first to use the term *market-Leninism* in a published work. I arrived at the term independently in the mid-1990s, though I am sure others did too. I really don't care whether I was original. In the meantime, I have sought to specify the meaning of market-Leninism with the understanding that, as a sociological concept, it would only be useful if it has real analytical purpose: that is, that it identifies some real institutional properties. See London (2009) for a fuller elaboration.

2. In *liberal regimes* (such as the United States and Canada), welfare needs are secured primarily through the market (economy), while the institutional spheres of state and family play important but more marginal roles. In *conservative-*

    corporatist regimes (such as Germany and Italy), the family plays a central role in the creation and allocation of welfare while the state assumes an important subsidiary role and the market is comparatively marginal. Finally, in *social democratic* welfare regimes (such as Sweden), the state plays a central role in welfare provision, while the welfare roles of the family and market are comparatively marginal.

3. The example of the United States is illustrative of both how welfare regimes develop and how they change. The New Deal emerged in the 1930s as the product of a "red" — "green" coalition of labour and farmers; it resulted in the development of a large-welfare state, even as other class forces effectively prevented the state from adopting truly universalistic social security programmes and blocked future welfare state development. In the post-World War II period, the New Deal withered in the face of new middle-class political alliances (Esping-Andersen 1990, p. 31).

4. Though not without losing sight of important differences between developing and transitional country settings and countries with advanced welfare states. Such differences include, forms of economy, political institutions, state capacities, the role of informal institutions, and so on (Gough 2004).

5. Wood (2004), for example, introduces the interesting notion of "insecurity regimes" to refer to welfare regimes in which human security (that is, economic security and basic needs) is under constant threat.

6. In this context it bears emphasizing that in any social formation, and probably particularly in developing countries, states heavily influence, but do not alone determine welfare regimes. States shape institutions, but institutions shape and limit states too.

7. Specifically, agricultural producers had to sell their produce at artificially low prices to the detriment of household welfare, local revenue, and the quantity and quality of services in rural areas (Vo 1990).

8. The Communist Party of Vietnam was established in exile (in Kowloon, Hong Kong) in 1930, but shortly thereafter renamed and reestablished itself as the Indochina Communist Party (ICP, Đảng Cộng sản Đông Dương) under the authority of the Comintern. In 1951 the party was renamed the Việt Nam Workers' Party (*Đảng Lao Động Việt Nam*), before reverting to the name CPV in 1976. For practical reasons, I refer to the party throughout as the CPV.

9. If the party had a class character in its early stages, it was not mainly proletarian or even peasant-based. The density of party membership in Vietnam remained comparatively low (as a proportion of the population) and was and remains regionally uneven. Northerners and indeed certain regions of the north have and remain overrepresented in party ranks, as Carl Thayer has pointed out in a personal communication.

10. In the post-war south, the party's efforts to implement land reforms met with myriad forms of resistance (Ngo 1991; White 1986). As Benedict Kerkvliet (2005) has recently shown, even in northern Vietnam of the 1960s, the state's efforts at coercive collectivization met with various forms of resistance.

11. For more on Vietnam's politico-administrative hierarchies, see Porter (1993), Phong and Beresford (1998), and Kerkvliet (2005).

12. The Democratic Republic of Vietnam (DRV) was founded in 1945 and recognized internationally by the Geneva Accords in 1954.

13. See Beresford (1989a; 1989b; 1997); Fforde (1999), Fforde and deVylder (1996).

14. According to anecdotal evidence, boys drafted into the army were often awarded upper secondary school diplomas after one year of education.

15. See Ministry of National Defense (1990).

16. For example, between 1975 and 1980, gross enrolments in primary, lower secondary, and upper secondary education increased by 19 per cent, 25 per cent, and 28 per cent, respectively (General Statistics Office 2001), while between 1981 and 1990, the number of primary school teachers in Vietnam increased by some 20 per cent, including an increase of 35 per cent in the southern part of the country (MOET 1992, p. 40).

17. Ethnic minority groups account for roughly 15 per cent of the population and, with the exception of the wealthier Chinese, were far less likely to have access to education due to their settlement in remote and neglected regions, cultural barriers, and other reasons.

18. This account draws largely on the work of Adam Fforde (1999) and Melanie Beresford (1997).

19. The continuing poor performance of Vietnam's economy was compounded by the country's political and economic isolation under the U.S.-Sino embargo.

20. Circular No. 19-TT/LB dated 23 July 1984. With respect to the funds, 65 per cent would be used to supplement the government budget for physical repairs and funds for teaching materials; 20 per cent was to be used for welfare and rewards, while five per cent was to be used for fund management. Ten per cent was directed to the district education office.

21. Personal notes. 2009 interview with teacher from northern Vietnam. Name and place withheld.

22. To suggest these regimes are *market-socialist* is to understate the importance of the communist party in organizing the economy and to overstate the importance of socialist principles in the design of public policies. To call them "capitalist" is to suggest the supremacy of liberal economic institutions (e.g. private property) and the presence of a dominant capitalist class. To call it "capitalism" with Vietnamese or Chinese characteristics is too vague to be

meaningful. While market reforms in both Vietnam and China grew out from the cracks in state-socialist economic institutions, their market-economies have been and continue to be heavily shaped by the political logic of the communist party, hence market-Leninism.

23. This is characteristic of Deng Xiaoping's thinking, which has greatly influenced Vietnamese thinking on the matter. See the translation of Cung Kim Quốc et. al. *Chủ Nghĩa Xã Hội Cũng co thể Áp Dụng Kinh Tế Thi Trường (Socialism can also apply market economics). Nhà Xuất Bản Chính Trị Quốc Gia.*

24. Redistributive principles refer to the mobilization and reallocation of resources by a central authority. Neoliberal principles refer to the expansion of market institutions. Communist-corporatism refers to patron-client politics within a communist political regime. Jonathan Stromseth coined this term in his dissertation on state business in Vietnam.

25. In China, the fiscal federalism that prevailed for much of the 1990s (the so-called "eat in separate kitchens" policy) was blamed for the rapid degradation of essential social services, but the central government has more recently announced massive redistributive initiatives affecting infrastructure, health, and education.

26. One is reminded of Becker and Sklar's (1999) volume on "postimperial politics" and even shades of Becker's earlier (1982) analysis of the "corporate national bourgeoisie" in Peru's "bonanza development".

27. There are innumerable publications concerning socialization. The account here draws mostly on Lê Quốc Hùng. *Xã hội hóa Giáo Dục: Nhìn từ Góc Độ Pháp Luật.* (Hanoi: Nhà Xuất Bản Tu Pháp, 2004). See also, Chu Văn Thành, ed., *Dịch vụ công và xã hội hóa dịch vụ công: Một số vấn đề lý luận và thực tiễn.* (Hanoi: Nhà Xuất Bản Chính Trị Quốc Gia)(no date).

28. This means, that in the "post-subsidy period" (*hậu thời kỳ bao cấp*), as the Vietnam state does not have sufficient resources to finance many essential social services, "socializing" or "privatizing" certain state functions will reduce burdens on the state budget and allow the state to perform its core functions more efficiently and effectively.

29. When first introduced in 1989, school fees were set at the cash equivalent of 4 kg and 7 kg of rice per month for lower and upper secondary students, respectively. By 1993, the state eliminated school fees at the primary level, but increased fees for lower- and upper-secondary education.

30. Survey data on household education expenditure reveal that by 1996–97, school fees accounted for 46.1 per cent and 61.7 per cent of yearly education expenditures per lower- and upper-secondary student, respectively (General Statistics Office 1999). Other education expenditure includes spending on books, transport, as well as after school "extra study" (discussed in the next section).

31. The semi-public status is for students who perform below a certain level in lower, and upper-secondary school entrance examinations. People-founded schools are, by contrast, financially autonomous from the state education budget, but are subject to state curriculum requirements and typically more expensive. Both semi-public and people-founded forms are permitted at all levels of education except the primary level.

32. During fieldwork in Quang Nam Province in 2000, I found that semi-public students in public schools paid five times the tuition fees of public students.

33. International organizations include bilateral donors and multilateral development agencies, as well as non-governmental organizations. Together, they represent a significant source of education finance, with the development agencies intimately involved in shaping education policy. The role of international organizations in Vietnam's education is to be discussed elsewhere due to space consideration.

34. According to the Ministry of Finance, inflation for the years 1994, 1995, 1996, 1997, and 1998 ran at 14.7 per cent, 12.4 per cent, 4.5 per cent, 3.8 per cent, and 9.2 per cent, respectively.

35. Vietnam's seven geographical regions include the two richest regions — the south-east (including Ho Chi Minh City) and Red River Delta (including Hanoi and Hai Phong) — and five other geographical regions.

36. By 2003, some 58 per cent of kindergarten students were enrolled in non-state schools (MOET 2005).

37. According to the 1998 Vietnam Living Standards Survey, extra study expenses, on average, comprised roughly 18 per cent of household education expenditures for lower-secondary students and 28 per cent for upper-secondary students. These figures are misleading. First, there is considerable evidence that extra study has increased since 1998. Second, average expenditures on tutoring do not take into consideration the wide disparities in expenditure on extra study between rich and poor. During my own research in 2000 in central Vietnam's Quang Nam province, it was observed that many rural households expended VND100,000 per month on extra study for secondary school students compared with VND17,000 for school fees.

38. Notes from personal communication with an upper-secondary teacher in Danang in May 2000.

39. There is much anecdotal evidence supporting this claim, though no systematic survey has been conducted. In recent years, some provinces have instituted rules that teachers may not have their own students in the extra study classes.

40. This is more eloquently captured in Vietnamese as *"hoc them la chinh va hoc chinh la phu"* [Extra is the main part, main part is the minor] as one

Vietnamese put it <http://diendan.edu.net.vn/PrintPost.aspx?PostID=17353>, (accessed December 2006).

41. The seventh Party Congress in 1991 explicitly recognized the problem of education and health access for the poor (UN Development Program-Deutsche Gesellschaft für Technische Zusammenarbeit 1999).

42. Decision 112 establishes monthly payments of VND70,000 to certified income-poor households for the preschool attendance of their children, of VND140,000 for households with children attending semi-boarding schools.

43. Although the HEPR scheme was designed to incorporate democratic participation at the grassroots level, the implementation of the programmes has been frequently top-down (Vietnam Consultative Group 2004, pp. 27–30).

References

Becker, David G. "'Bonanza Development' and the 'New Bourgeoisie': Peru under Military Rule". *Comparative Political Studies* 15 (1982): 243–88.

Becker, David and Richard L. Sklar, eds. *Postimperialism and World Politics*, Praeger, 1999.

Beresford, M. "Vietnam: Socialist Agriculture in Transition". *Journal of Contemporary Asia* 20, no. 4 (1989*a*): 466–86.

———. *National Development and Reunification in Vietnam*. London: Macmillan, 1989*b*.

———. "Vietnam: The Transition from Central Planning". In *The Political Economy of Southeast Asia*, edited by G. Rodan, K. Hewison and R. Robison, pp. 179–204. Oxford: Oxford University Press, 1997.

Davis, P.R. "Rethinking the Welfare Regime Approach". *Global Social Policy* 1, No. 1 (2001): 79–107.

Drori, Gili S., John W. Meyer, and Hokyu Hwang. *Globalization and Organization: World Society and Organizational Change*. Oxford: Oxford University Press, 2006.

Esping-Andersen, Gosta. "The Comparison of Policy Regimes". In *Stagnation and Renewal: The Rise and Fall of Social Policy Regimes,* edited by Gosta Esping-Andersen, Lee Rainwater and Martin Rein. Armonk, New York: M.E. Sharpe, 1987.

———. *Three Worlds of Welfare Capitalism*. Cambridge, UK: Polity Press, 1990.

———. *Social Foundations of Post-Industrial Economies*. Oxford: Oxford University Press, 1999.

Fägerlind, Ingemar and Lawrence J. Saha. *Education and National Development.* Oxford: Pergamon Press, 1983.

Fforde, A. "The Institutions of the Transition from Central Planning". In *Institutions and Economic Change in Southeast Asia: The Context of*

Development from the 1960s to the 1990s, edited by C. Barlow, pp. 118–31. Cheltenham: Edward Elgar, 1999.

Fforde, A., and S. deVylder. *From Plan to Market: The Economic Transition in Vietnam*. Boulder, CO: Westview Press, 1966.

General Statistics Office. *Vietnam Households Living Standards Survey, 1997–1998*. Hanoi: Statistical Publishing House, 1999.

———. *So lieu dan so va Kinh te xa hoi, 1975–2000* [Population and socio-economic data, 1975–2000]. Hanoi: Statistical Publishing House, 2001.

———. *Vietnam Households Living Standards Survey, 2001–2002*. Hanoi: Statistical Publishing House, 2003.

———. *Vietnam Households Living Standards Survey, 2004*. Hanoi: Statistical Publishing House, 2005.

Gough, I. "Welfare Regimes: On Adapting the Framework to Developing Countries". Unpublished manuscript, University of Bath, the United Kingdom, 1999.

Gough, I. and G. Wood, with A. Barrientos, P. Bevan, P. Davis, and G. Room. *Insecurity and welfare regimes in Asia, Africa and Latin America: Social policy in development contexts*. Cambridge: Cambridge University Press, 2004.

Harvey, David. *The Limits to Capital*. Oxford: Blackwell, 1982.

Kerkvliet, B.J.T. *The Power of Everyday Politics: How Vietnamese Peasants Transformed National Policy*. Ithaca, NY: Cornell University Press, 2005.

Kristof, N.D. and Sheryl, WuDunn. *China Wakes: The Struggle for the Soul of a Rising Power*. New York: Times Books/Random House, 1994.

London, Jonathan D. "Vietnam's Mass Education and Health Systems: A Regimes Perspective". *American Asian Review 21*, No. 2 (2003): 125–70.

———. "Social Provision and the Transformation of the Socialist State: Mass Education and Health Provision in Vietnam's Market Transition". Ph.D. dissertation, Department of Sociology. University of Wisconsin-Madison, 2004.

———. "Reforming Higher Education in Vietnam". Unpublished Brief, 20 Years of Doi Moi Roundtable. United Nations Development Program, 2006.

———. "Historical Welfare Regimes and Welfare Regimes in the Wake of State-socialism". Unpublished paper, presented at the Annual Meetings of the American Sociological Association. Boston MA, 31 July–4 August 2008.

———. "Vietnam and the Making of Market-Leninism". *The Pacific Review 22*, no. 3 (July 2009): 375–99.

Marr, D. *Vietnamese Tradition on Trial, 1920–1945*. Berkeley: University of California Press, 1981.

Ministry of Education and Training of Vietnam. *Statistical Data of Education and Training, 1981–1990*. Hanoi, 1992.

———. "So lieu thong ke giao duc va dao tao, 1945–1995" [Statistical data of education and training, 1945–95], Unpublished statistical brief, 1995*b*.

————. "Statistical Data of General Education: School Year 1995–1996". Unpublished statistical brief, 1995.

————. *"Bao cao: Chuyen de giao duc"* [*Report on Education*]. Unpublished brief, 2000.

————. *Sectoral Report*, 1993–2002, 2002.

————. *"So lieu thong ke giao duc"* [*Statistical education data*]. <http://edu.net. vn/data/thongke/>. Accessed 20 May 2005.

Ministry of Health, General Statistics Office, United Nations Children's Fund, & World Health Organization. *Survey Assessment of Vietnamese Youth*. Hanoi: Ministry of Health, 2005.

Ministry of Labour, War Invalids & Social Affairs. *"Tinh hinh thuc hien chuong trinh xoa doi giam ngheo cac tinh khu vuv mien trung va tay nguyen 6 thang dau nam* 1999" [The situation of implementing the hunger eradication and poverty reduction programmes in the Central Region and Central Highlands in the first six months of 1999]. Unpublished report, 1999.

Ministry of National Defence. *Khang chien chong my cuu nuoc* [The uprising to defeat America and save the country]. Hanoi: Nha Xuat Ban Su That Vietnam, 1990.

Ngo, V.H. "Post-war Vietnam: Political Economy". In *Coming to Terms: Indochina, the United States, and the War*, edited by D. Allen and N.V. Long, pp. 65–88. Boulder, CO: Westview Press, 1991.

Nguyen, N.N. "Trends in the Education Sector from 1993 to 1998". World Bank Policy Research Working Paper No. 2891. Washington, D.C.: World Bank. September, 2002.

Nguyen, T.C. *Van de giao duc va dao tao trong nen Kinh te chuyen doi Vietnam* [The problem of education and training in Vietnam's transitional economy]. *Phat Trien Kinh Te*, 861, 1997: 28–31.

Nguyen, V.C. "Looking for the Future: Work versus Education". Unpublished paper, Amsterdam School for Social Science Research, Centre for Asian Studies, the Netherlands, 1997.

Philion, Stephen. "Chinese Welfare State Regimes". *Journal of Contemporary Asia* 28, *Iss. 4* Manila: (1998): 518–19.

Phong, D. and M. Beresford. *Authority Relations and Economic Decision-Making in Vietnam: An Historical Perspective*. Copenhagen, Denmark: Nordic Institute of Asian Studies, 1998.

Polanyi, Karl. *The Great Transformation: The Political and Economic Origins of Our Times*. Boston: Beacon Press, 1994.

————. *Trade and Market in the Early Empires: Economies in History and Theory*, edited by K. Polanyi, Conrad M. Arensberg and Harry W. Pearson. Glencoe, Illinois: Free Press, 1957.

Porter, G. *Vietnam: The Politics of Bureaucratic Socialism*. Ithaca, NY: Cornell University Press, 1993.

Poverty Working Group. *Attacking Poverty: Vietnam Development Report, 2000.* Washington, D.C.: World Bank, 1999.

Socialist Republic of Vietnam & World Bank. *Managing Public Expenditure for Poverty Reduction and Growth: Public Expenditure Review and Integrated Fiduciary Assessment.* Hanoi: Financial Publishing House, 2005.

Stark, David. *Postsocialist Pathways: Transforming Politics and Property in East Central Europe* (with László Bruszt). New York and Cambridge: Cambridge University Press, 1998.

Szelenyi, Ivan. "Social inequalities in state socialist redistributive economies: Dilemma for social policy in contemporary socialist societies of Eastern Europe". *International Journal of Comparative Sociology*, No. 1–2 (1978): 63–87.

Szlenyi, Ivan and R. Manchin. "Social policy under state socialism". In *Stagnation and Renewal: The Rise and Fall of Social Policy Regimes,* edited by Gosta Esping-Andersen, Lee Rainwater and Martin Rein, pp. 102–39. Armonk, New York: M.E. Sharpe, 1987.

Tilly, C. *Durable Inequality.* Berkeley and Los Angeles: University of California Press, 1998.

UNDP Hanoi. "Impacts of Basic Public Services Liberalization on the Poor and Marginalized People: The Case of Health, Education and Electricity in Vietnam". August 2006.

UNICEF Viet Nam. Multiple Indicator Cluster Survey of Children in Viet Nam. Hanoi, 2008.

United Nations. *Looking Ahead: A Common Country Assessment.* Hanoi: United Nations, 1999.

United Nations Development Program — Deutsche Gesellschaft für Technische Zusammenarbeit. "First Forum on the National Target Programme on Hunger Eradication and Poverty Reduction". Unpublished paper, 1999.

United Nations & Ministry of Labour, War Invalids and Social Affairs. *Dich vu xa hoi co ban o Vietnam* [Basic social services in Vietnam]. Hanoi: United Nations, 1999.

Vietnam Consultative Group. "Governance: Vietnam development report 2005". Joint Donor Report to the Consultative Group Meeting. Hanoi: Vietnam Consultative Group, December 2004.

Vo, N.T. *Vietnam's Economic Policy since 1975.* Singapore: Institute of Southeast Asian Studies, 1990.

Vo, T.S., T.K.N. Truong, T.H. Doan, and TT. Nguyen. "School Enrolments and Dropouts". In *Living Standards during an Economic Boom,* edited by D. Haughton, J. Haughton and P. Nguyen. Hanoi: United Nations Development Program and Statistical Publishing House, 2001.

White, C.P. "Everyday Resistance, Socialist Revolution and Rural Development: The Vietnamese Case". *Journal of Peasant Studies* 13, No. 2 (1986): 49–63.

Woodside, A. *Lost Modernities: China, Vietnam, Korea, and the Hazards of World History*. Cambridge: Harvard University Press, 2006.

Wright, E.O. *Class Counts: Comparative Studies in Class Analysis*. Cambridge: Cambridge University Press, 1997.

————. "Class, Exploitation, and Economic Rents: Reflections on Sørensen's 'Sounder Basis'". In *American Journal of Sociology* 105, No. 6 (2000): 1559–71.

World Bank. "Vietnam: Fiscal Decentralization and the Delivery of Rural Services". Report No. 15745-VN. Washington, D.C.: World Bank, East Asia and Pacific Division, Country Department I, Country Operations Division, October 1996a.

————. *Vietnam Education Finance Sector Study*. Washington, D.C.: World Bank, East Asia Pacific Region, Human Resources Operations Division, 1996b.

————. "Global Poverty Down by Half Since 1981 But Progress Uneven as Economic Growth Eludes Many Countries". 2004, <http://www.worldbank.org.vn/news/press46_01.htm>. Accessed 20 May 2005.

3

EDUCATION, EDUCATION FINANCING, AND THE ECONOMY

Jim Cobbe

INTRODUCTION

The government of Vietnam emphasizes expanded investment in human capital to accelerate economic growth. This is appropriate in a country where sustaining rapid economic growth is the stated priority of the government. Human capital is widely seen as a key ingredient for growth, although in recent years the quality of schooling has emerged as at least as important as the quantity (for example, Hanushek 2008). In recent years, education policies have changed a great deal in Vietnam, as have the administrative and financial structures to support it. Upper secondary and higher education have expanded rapidly, while disparities in the provision and financing of primary and lower secondary education have probably increased across different segments of the population, despite official commitments to universalize access to basic education and make it more equal. The policy for many years has been to increase the fraction of government expenditure devoted to public education, and the target of 20 per cent was exceeded in 2008. However, and at the same time, education policies have increased the share of the cost of education borne by students, their families, and communities, a process somewhat ironically described as "socialization".

This chapter examines economic aspects of education, but it is impossible to ignore other factors. It will start with a discussion of enrolment trends and three background issues that have implications for what happens in education: rapid demographic change and urbanization; rapid but geographically uneven economic growth; and the specifically Vietnamese constitutional, administrative, and political structures within which education exists. That is followed by sketches of trends arising from general government policies that impact on how education operates and the effects it has on peoples' lives. These involve changes in education financing, decentralization, deregulation, and governance. The chapter then turns to issues of education proper: access and imbalances; quality; actual and potential schisms and conflicts within the education sector and between different stakeholder groups; equity; and finally, whether or not the education sector is giving society and most groups within it good value for the huge resources it consumes.

Before launching into all this, let us make a brief aside about data quality. In all countries, data on the education sector are somewhat suspect. There are many reasons obtaining accurate enrolment and attainment data is difficult, and when it comes to financial and economic data on the sector, things are often even more difficult. Public financing of educational institutions is often far from transparent, with arcane budgetary and accounting rules and arbitrary distribution and accounting of costs over many levels and institutions.[1] Making sense of education data is particularly difficult when substantial portions of total costs are borne privately by students and their families, both in out-of-pocket expenses and in opportunity costs, such as foregone earnings and foregone household production. In Vietnam, these problems are especially acute because of the general level of poverty, the relative autonomy and independence of lower levels of government, the prevalence of significant elements of educational expense that are unofficial or downright illegal, and the difficulty of estimating opportunity costs appropriately when the foregone opportunities are mostly in self-employment or household production.[2]

What follows will be my reading of the broad evolution of recent educational trends, without pretending to provide detailed references or data, although the appendix tables do give some official and other data — but those data should be interpreted with caution.

ENROLMENT TRENDS AND BACKGROUND ISSUES

Numerically precise data on enrolments are published annually by both the General Statistics Office and MOET, and in recent years they have been close to consistent, with the minor differences probably due to slightly different dates for reporting. Data for recent years from both sources are in Tables 3.1 and 3.2 (see Appendix).[3] Enrolment patterns reflect two major trends: the *Đổi Mới* process and subsequent economic growth, and the freeing up of many restrictions and enrolment caps, including very substantial changes in how educational institutions are financed and how they determine how many students, and who, to enrol; and the demographic trends of the past thirty years or so, during which time the country has undergone a rapid transition toward the low birth rates characteristic of most East Asian countries.

Available data suggest demographic changes in Vietnam have, in addition to economic growth, strongly altered enrolment trends. The United Nations estimates that Vietnam's total fertility rate[4] peaked at about 7.25 in 1970, but had declined to 2.5 by 2000 and perhaps 2.30 by 2005. Because older women were more fertile in their youth, this implies that many younger women are already having fewer than two children each. Correspondingly, the population under age fifteen, estimated at 33 per cent of the total in 2001, is projected by the United Nations to fall to only 25 per cent by 2015. Urbanization has also accelerated under *Đổi Mới*; the United Nations estimates that the proportion of the population in urban areas increased by only two percentage points, from 18.3 per cent to 20.3 per cent between 1970 and 1990; but reached 26.7 per cent in 2005, reflecting a threefold increase in urban growth. GSO estimates that the urban population grew from 11.8 million in 1986 to 23.4 million in 2007, so the absolute increment of the urban population was almost as large (11.6 million) as the increment of rural population (12.5 million — from 49.3 to 61.8 million). The lower birth rates have produced falling total primary school enrolment since the mid-1990s as shown in the tables; note that lower-secondary enrolment is now falling as well. The combination of lower birth rates and outmigration to cities and towns has resulted in many rural primary schools losing pupils at a quite rapid rate, even as schools in towns are often overcrowded. In poorer provinces, such as Thanh Hóa, this can result in difficult staffing problems as schools lose financing for posts that teachers are occupying. It is important to note that Vietnam still has one of the most rural populations in the world, and it is in the rural areas that most poverty is found in the country.[5]

Beyond primary school, the story is somewhat different. Prior to *Đổi Mới*, enrolment at higher levels of the education system was strictly planned, with institutions receiving instructions as to how many students to enrol and then receiving funding on the basis of that number of students. However, in the early 1980s, the country's economic crisis resulted in declines in enrolment and levels of activity: schools had insufficient operating funds, and finances for teacher salaries were also insufficient.[6] This situation continued into the early 1990s, but then the trend dramatically reversed as government budgets, and more importantly, the economy and personal incomes, recovered and then grew. Primary education is now officially almost fully "universalized", although there remain pockets of disadvantaged and ethnic minorities who are still not in school.[7] Dropout and repetition rates in primary schools have fallen dramatically, although these are not good indicators of either school quality or demand for education since they are easily influenced by policy adjustments, such as those designed to ensure the country meets universalization standards. Those standards include dropout and completion rates, encouraging districts and provinces (and perhaps MOET) to massage the numbers in one way or another.[8] Official policy now is that lower-secondary education should also be universalized, with the target of meeting a 99 per cent enrolment rate for eleven to fifteen-year-olds by 2010.[9]

Upper-secondary and higher education enrolment has been increasing dramatically since the early 1990s. This was achieved by a variety of methods: expansion of public institutions, although not always with commensurate expansion of staffing, physical facilities, or budgetary resources; permitting semi-public classes (in public schools, but with students paying higher tuition fees) and semi-public schools and people-founded schools; and permitting the establishment of higher educational institutions by a variety of groups, including foreign institutions and joint degree programmes in a few cases. This shifting of enrolment to non-public institutions is most marked at the pre-primary level,[10] and upper-secondary level, where about a third of all schools are now non-public.

One of the more impressive aspects of the expansion is that after an initial lag, staffing at upper-secondary and university levels seems to have almost caught up with the expansion of student numbers, with the number of teachers at upper-secondary level almost doubling from 1999–2000 to 2006–07, and the number of university teachers increasing by over two-thirds in the same period. One consequence of this rapid expansion of the teaching force is that high proportions of teachers at these levels are young and inexperienced. On the other hand, the new staff has been recently trained and do not have the cynicism of older teachers who went through the bad periods of the 1980s and early 1990s.

This expansion of the teaching force has, in fact, occurred at all levels, including primary schools until 2003–04, despite the fall in enrolments. It has also resulted in falling pupil/teacher ratios at all levels. By 2006–07 the overall national rates were 20.4 at primary level, 20.0 at the lower-secondary level and 24.8 at the upper-secondary level. If we take the ratio of full-time students at universities to university instructors, that ratio has risen somewhat recently after falling in the first part of this decade, but is far lower than many assert and assume (see data in Table 3.2 of the appendix).[11] Of course, crude pupil-teacher ratios tell one nothing meaningful about actual instructional time that pupils receive,[12] or about the size of class in which they receive instruction, which is widely believed to have an impact on quality, and certainly has an impact on parent and student satisfaction. Nevertheless, Vietnamese pupil-teacher ratios are now comparable to other countries in the region, and considerably better than in most other countries of similar income level.

However, one of the main ways in which the expansion of enrolment was achieved was by the introduction of double and triple shifting, especially in secondary schools. Historically, half-day schooling was common in primary schools, in part a response to inadequate salary levels for teachers (it gave them time to farm or hold another job). Official policy is to move to full-day schooling at all levels and everywhere, but apart from the physical infrastructure obstacles (one needs more classrooms to eliminate double or triple shifting if enrolment is not falling fast, and this can be very difficult to achieve in urban areas because of the non-availability and cost of suitable land), there are other difficulties standing in the way.

Currently, most teachers in Vietnam actually teach in their regular job for fewer hours per week and per year than in most other countries; for example, one estimate for lower-secondary schools is an average of fourteen hours a week of actual classroom time. Part of the reason for this is double shifting, which tends to shorten the school day for each shift, and teaching one shift is considered a regular job. But this also means pupils are getting less direct instruction than is desirable — and is likely to mean lower quality results. Eliminating triple and double shifting and increasing the amount of instruction per year will mean teachers have to teach more; but they are not likely to be happy about that unless they are also paid more, which, of course, is a problem. It is particularly a problem because the current existence of double shifting implies that teachers can use their off-shift to either offer private "extra tuition" classes, or take a second job at a private or other non-public school when they are not teaching in their regular job.

Perhaps the most glaring example of this is connected with the attempts to move primary schooling to a full day. Many primary schools that were not double-shifted have in fact offered full-day schooling for some time, but parents who wanted it had to pay and those payments supplemented teacher salaries. To think that one could now just simply say primary school will henceforth be full-day and you teachers will teach the full day, but not get paid more, and lose the supplements from payments for full-day schooling, is to engage in a pipe dream. In these and other instances, the resources are obviously not available to increase teacher remuneration commensurately with the increase in workload that is probably necessary to lift the duration of officially provided public education to close to international norms.

In higher education, and vocational-technical (and "professional secondary") institutions, the system of the 1980s was that not only did institutions get a quota of students to enrol, students were also earmarked for employment positions in terms of numbers, and sometimes individually, at an early stage, although adjustments could be made for individuals on details of who went where.[13] This system began to unravel in the 1990s, as institutions were permitted to enrol "beyond quota" and "semi-private" students to help meet the demand for places. Such students did not receive government scholarships (under the old system, all students of higher and vocational/technical education were, at least in theory, on government scholarships) and were charged varying amounts of tuition fees. By 2007, the system had almost totally reversed, with institutions instructed to enrol a given number of regular students, on which public funding is based. The vast majority of students pay tuition fees, although some still receive scholarships and increasing numbers qualify for loans. Institutions are free to do close to what they like with respect to part-time courses, non-degree courses, or cooperative programmes with other institutions, for all of which they keep all or most of the fees, and which are important sources of income for academic staff.

The very rapid economic growth Vietnam has experienced since the mid-1990s has had many results, not least, the vastly increased demand for private schooling, and the much greater ability of the state to finance public education. However, growth has been very uneven, and internal income inequality, both on a regional basis and between individuals, has increased perhaps even more dramatically than national average income. While the country has made impressive strides in reducing poverty, it has also seen the emergence of a substantial high-income urban group, at the same time as large proportions of especially the rural population remain below or near the official poverty line. Education is a potential force to mitigate the effects of income inequality, particularly across generations, and definitely played that role in the 1975–90 period, when the children of workers and peasants officially received preference, but now that role appears to be increasingly attenuated.

At the school level, and increasingly with respect to higher education as well, a complicating factor in educational policy in Vietnam are the tensions in the administrative, political, and constitutional structure. Under the constitution, People's Councils at all levels — national, provincial, district, and commune — are sovereign within their sphere of responsibility though in principle all are accountable to the national level. The implication in education is that the central Ministry of Education and Training (MOET) is responsible for "professional" issues at all levels, but has no direct operational or budgetary control over most institutions, which "belong" to lower levels. When it comes to finance, the allocations of central funds to the provinces for school education are made centrally and ultimately by the Ministry of Finance, not MOET. The centre does not make allocation decisions for lower levels, although it attempts to provide guidance and influence them. At provincial, district, and commune levels, the People's Councils have constitutional and real authority over expenditure and personnel, with the actual decisions being strongly influenced by the permanent administrative bureaucracy.[14] The most recent Public Expenditure Review (World Bank 2005) estimates that in 2002, 98 per cent of public expenditure for general education was channelled through local government.

The centre does issue "norms" on spending and staffing and other matters, but they are not necessarily adhered to at the local level. Many norms are outdated, and attempts to overhaul the norms for education have repeatedly floundered. The basic problem is that there are both financial norms and physical norms (meaning pupil-teacher ratios, class sizes, teaching hours per week, as well as building and equipment norms), and the two are often inconsistent and unrealistic in practice at current salary, price, and enrolment levels. To adhere to the physical norms would not be affordable at current financing levels; and to adhere to all the financial norms implies that education could not deliver what it is supposed to. So it is almost inevitable that norms will not be fully observed,[15] while attempts at adjusting them tend to get bogged down over what level of physical norms is both acceptable and affordable. So-called "Fundamental School Quality Levels" (FSQLs), strongly promoted by some foreign donors including the World Bank, are in effect an attempt at an end-run around the problem of outdated and ineffective "norms" and MOET's unrealistic standards for "excellent schools".[16] Better off provinces can always supplement the centre's allocations, but the majority of provinces cannot afford to.[17] Provinces do not always or consistently do what the centre wants them to, nor do districts always or consistently do what the province wants them to.

Although the administrative system is relatively standard, even that is not completely uniform across provinces. Typically, primary schools and lower-secondary schools come under districts, and senior-secondary schools and colleges (and now, some universities) under provinces, while most public universities are under MOET.[18] There is intended to be one primary school in each commune, and at least one lower-secondary school in each district. Communes often have influence over schools physically in their areas, to the extent that they may even provide them with supplementary resources. In addition, there are educational institutions, especially but not only, in vocational-technical education that come under the Ministry of Labour, Invalids, and Social Affairs (MoLISA) or other line ministries. However, in some provinces upper-secondary schools have been delegated to district control. In theory, the Party is an overall watchdog for maintaining some consistency, but intra-Party differences that lead to divergences in actual practice and behaviour in other matters are just as likely to be displayed in education.

GENERAL POLICY TRENDS

Changes in Education Finance

Both the absolute amount allocated to education in the state budget, and education's share of the total, has increased substantially over the past fifteen years, with the total estimated to reach VNĐ72.5 trillion (about $4.5 billion) or 22 per cent of the state budget in 2008. This was from a very low level, so the result has not been that institutions or their staff consider themselves adequately funded. And nor do most outside observers. The key difficulty is one common in education internationally, namely that by far the greatest part of expenditure is personnel costs. The opening of the economy and labour market has meant that successful workers and entrepreneurs outside the state sector can now command incomes many times greater than state salaries. It is open to debate what portion of the education labour force would actually succeed in the non-education private sector, but in a society where education is regarded as an appropriately major determinant of individual outcomes, these income disparities cause dissatisfaction amongst education staff and huge problems for the finance of education. Government policy can be interpreted as seeking to shift a growing proportion of the total cost to students and their families, although sometimes in ways that have had counter-productive effects.

Tuition as such is not charged at primary level, but is retained at all other levels. There are numerous other charges that exist in primary schools as well as other levels, some official and others unofficial. These include construction fees, parent-teacher association fees, and charges for such amenities as drinking water and electricity. Also widespread, although officially discouraged, is "extra tuition" with either the students' normal teacher or in after-school classes run by others. Tuition rates escalate as pupils move up through the system, and at university level they account for a substantial portion of school budgets. Available data suggest that at all levels families do bear a substantial and growing portion of the total cost of schooling, although at primary level, the share has actually fallen recently because of increases in teacher salaries.[19]

The reasoning of public rhetoric is that while primary and lower-secondary levels of education are intended to be universal and, therefore, at least primary schooling should be free to maximize access,[20] the benefits of upper-secondary, vocational/technical, and higher education accrue in increasing amounts to the users, so the users should make larger contributions to the cost. On this basis, the share of the state budget for education and training (E&T)[21] going to higher education has actually fallen in recent years to around 10 per cent or less of the total, although recent pronouncements about the need to expand higher education even more, and to improve quality and build four "international standard" universities, suggest that this trend may likely reverse. However, the universities and their students need reform of their financing and regulation systems, as well as quality improvement, and that process is not yet very advanced.[22]

With the encouragement of donors, efforts have been made to shift educational funding to a Medium Term Expenditure Framework (MTEF), a fashionable approach to attempting to plan for government expenditure. Unfortunately, like many other donor-promoted initiatives, it seems very unlikely that the MTEF exercises are either fully accepted by the key ministries involved, or reflects the reality of how budget decisions are made in Vietnam. In brief, the system is that guidance is issued downward, based in part on formulas that take some account of population and local conditions, and then budget requests filter upward, at each stage involving some form of consultation or negotiation between education and finance authorities. Ultimately, the key decisions are made by the central government, and then the provincial allocations are made by the Ministry of Finance (MOF) and communicated through MOET. But it is widely accepted that the final stage, the determination of provincial allocations, is subject to intense lobbying and negotiation between provincial authorities and the centre, with the result that the actual distribution of state budget funding cannot be explained fully by any formula or MTEF, but is the outcome of a political process. This is of course normal, but somewhat throws off the usefulness of central financial planning, although in any case, with the exception of National Target Programmes, no state budget funds can actually be earmarked for a specific purpose after they reach the lower levels.

This does not prevent the central ministries from trying to dictate how funds should be used once they reach lower levels, and in deficit provinces — that is, most of the country — the centre can have a lot of influence over what happens, if it knows or cares. However, information flows are such that it is often incorrect to assume the centre does — with the exception of matters that are very prominent in the public eye. Local behaviour can vary substantially from official central guidance on the basis of local norms without attracting much, if any, attention from the centre.[23]

Decentralization

Another important policy trend that has relevance for education is the process of greater decentralization of authority and decision making powers. One can argue this is more rhetoric than real as the centre has never held much sway over actual behaviour except in very limited spheres. But there is undoubtedly a trend to say publicly that more discretion is being given to provinces, districts, and institutions, while at the same time, there is clearly a desire in the centre to exercise more control over budgetary and expenditure decisions at the local level.

This, together with changes in the budget law and regulations with respect to fiscal autonomy of institutions, has resulted in substantial variation in what actually happens with respect to both state budget funds reaching schools, and the monitoring of what they do with them. Because the funds flow down through the finance hierarchy, subject to consultation at each level with education and training agencies and decisions by the People's Council, what actually gets to a school is not necessarily what was intended at the higher level. Similarly, education and training agencies do not necessarily know very quickly what each school has at its disposal, nor how the schools are spending it.[24] To put it more simply, nobody can be quite sure how actual expenditures at school level are distributed across levels and types of purchase within provinces, although provinces may believe they know.

ACCESS AND IMBALANCES

Access to primary school is now mostly a problem only in disadvantaged rural areas, basically mountainous and remote regions, islands, and some parts of delta regions where transport is highly problematic. The policy is that each commune should have a primary school, and each district a lower-secondary school, and this has been achieved. Where population densities are very low, this may involve a school with several locations, that is, a main school and several satellites covering only some grades, which of course tends to result in multigrade classrooms and difficult quality, staffing, and administrative issues. However, differences in enrolment ratios at the lower levels of schooling are now largely believed to be outcomes of economic and language[25] differences, and are being addressed by both government and donor programmes.[26] Of course, in such areas, access to secondary school and higher education becomes increasingly problematic, but this is a worldwide issue. There is a long history of some public policy in Vietnam to address the more extreme aspects of this, notably boarding schools and special programmes for ethnic minority students. Unsurprisingly, disparities persist. For ethnic minorities, perceptions of and real discrimination and prejudices in education, society, and the job market contribute to the disparities.

There is also a question of access imbalances between rural and urban areas, and to some extent, within urban areas. Urban areas in an absolute sense obviously provide better access than rural areas to senior-secondary and higher education because transport to the institution will almost always be easier in towns and cities. However, within cities, and particularly the rapidly growing ones, there are also access issues that align with income differences. Where low-income, high-density residential areas have grown rapidly, schools may be overcrowded or multishift and this can produce access problems for low-income residents. As press reports frequently tell us, schools also vary within urban areas in perceived quality and in the level of costs of attendance (because of fees that are in practice, if not officially, "required"), with the two usually correlated. The "good" ones often have to turn away many pupils who desire admission, and anecdotally are usually located in areas where higher-income families tend to reside.

QUALITY

One consequence of the demographic trends mentioned earlier is often overlooked but will be important in the next decade or so. This is simply that age cohorts are now shrinking, as the enrolment in primary schools shows clearly. As these shrinking cohorts move up through the education system, they will automatically make it easier either to improve the proportion of the cohort continuing in education, or to increase resources per student and thereby work on improvements in quality. This, together with the rapid economic growth in the country, which shows no signs of stopping, suggests that in the medium term one should have great confidence in the potential to improve the education system substantially. However, in the short run there is widespread consensus that the quality of education is a real problem that requires attention.

At the school level, there have been extensive attempts to measure pupil attainment, and some of the results of the most extensive are summarized in Table 3.3 in the appendix, although they are not fully reliable and should be treated with considerable caution. Much donor and MOET effort has been expended on curriculum renovation and quality improvement, but it is unclear how effective these efforts have been. A paradox exists: the traditional veneration of education and educators is still widespread, but there is simultaneously much and arguably growing concern about the performance of teachers and the quality of the education.

This may be less of a paradox than it seems. What employers in the most dynamic parts of the economy now want is rather different: they want workers who know the subjects they are supposed to, and can take direction and discipline — the attributes the old system was very good at nurturing — but who can also take initiative, are willing to accept responsibility and make decisions on their own, and who display some of the "soft skills" required to work in teams and deal with customers, subordinates, and superiors in the flexible, rapidly changing sectors of the economy. In sectors that are being emphasized because of their growth prospects, notably manufacturing and tourism, foreign language skills are also much desired.

Many educators are aware of this clash between old and new, but it is neither universally accepted as a desirable change, nor do many teachers, at any level, really know how to change their behaviour to encourage their pupils to make the necessary shift in their attitudes and therefore fit the new mould rather than the old one, which implied simple mastery of the stated subject. To be fair, it is not clear that anyone is sure how to do it, but one can suggest with some confidence that in a system where progression to the next stage is determined by examination performance and the examinations test mastery of the subject, the incentives do not support the change. To the extent students want to be able to do well in examinations, and schools are judged by their success in getting good results for their students on those examinations, students, teachers, and administrators will all resist experiments and changes that they doubt will improve examination performance.

The only exception to this conclusion, but unfortunately one that can only operate slowly, is in higher education. At this level, employers and prospective employers can and do get very explicit about what they want in the graduates they wish to recruit, and complaints about the quality and skills of many graduates are widespread, and appear to have acted as a wake-up call for government. Perhaps the best known example concerns the well publicized initial recruitment attempts of Intel for its huge one-billion-dollar investment in manufacturing capacity. Intel planned from the start to send recruits overseas for a year of training, but stated publicly that only about forty engineering graduate applicants met their requirements, although they were prepared to hire up to 500 and received over 1,000 applications.

As the higher education sector becomes more competitive, and institutions compete for tuition income and, therefore, the best students and enrolment generally, the success or otherwise of the institutions' graduates in the labour market will become increasingly important to them, and eventually universities themselves will wish to change their instructional techniques to equip their graduates better for employment. Currently, in practice, there is no great pressure on the universities to do this and their internal structures and incentive systems do not encourage staff to make the necessary reforms. Many younger academic staff, especially those trained abroad, may want to change the way their programmes prepare students to equip them better with appropriate skills, but neither know for sure how to do it, nor are in a position to initiate such changes if their more senior colleagues see no need for them. Sustained quality improvement in universities probably requires the reforms that are promised, and sustained quality improvement in the school system will probably require reforms on how selection for entry into especially the "better" universities is done.

CONFLICTING INTERESTS

It is wrong to assume that everybody has the same interests when it comes to education. Families want easy access, low costs, and good quality. Students do not want to have to study "too hard" to succeed. Teachers would like higher income, more prestige, and not to have to work more hours than they do currently. Employers want recruits to the labour force who have the desired skills, and would much rather the state and families, rather than they themselves, pay for the necessary training costs.[27] The state wants education to be low cost, high quality, and to support both general state goals and the efficiency and growth of the economy. High-income families are more concerned about quality and prestige while low-income families care about the costs they have to bear. Low-income families are more likely to care most about primary and lower-secondary schools providing children who go no further in the system with useful skills; high income families, with how well they prepare pupils for examinations, and the quality of senior secondary schools and higher education. Clearly, these interests are often in conflict.

However, one of the consequences of a one-party state with relatively undeveloped civil society institutions is that these conflicts are little discussed and often unrepresented in what passes for public debate. Almost the only exception to this in practice are the large, and especially foreign, employers, who are increasingly willing to express their views about education. At the local level, all schools are supposed to have parent-teacher associations, and although these are often dominated by teachers and administrators, they do provide a channel for feedback and accountability. However it would seem obvious that the interests of the teachers do not necessarily coincide with those of the state or the institutions that employ them, and there is no independent teachers' union or academic staff organization at higher education levels.[28] It is possible that the absence of channels for the varied interest groups to express their interests makes the formulation and implementation of policy more difficult.

EQUITY

There is ample evidence that enrolment and achievement vary along these lines: the more remotely and rural, a family is situated, or the lower its income, the less likely it is that its child will be enrolled at any level of schooling or graduate from it. The same goes for those belonging to an ethnic minority. However, in this crude sense, the evidence suggests quite strongly that not only is government at all levels aware of the inequalities, but that they are genuinely committed to doing something about them and have had considerable success, particularly in comparison to other countries of similar income level. Relatively, it is probably better to belong to a poor family of an ethnic minority in a remote part of Vietnam than it is to have the equivalent status in Thailand or Indonesia. This is an issue on which good reliable data are particularly hard to come by, but the numbers from the World Bank showing progress in closing the gaps in upper-secondary enrolment between 1993 and 2002 are probably indicative of the progress that has been made.

However, one can question the appropriate interpretation of "equity" in the debates about education and its financing. One extreme interpretation is to look solely at the equity implications between individuals of state contributions to the cost of education, when considering say those who complete primary education versus those who complete higher education. A desire for equity on that dimension argues for more complete state funding of primary and perhaps lower-secondary education, and a reduction in state funding for the educational missions of higher education institutions — the trend of recent years.

An alternative view of equity is equity between identifiable groups based on say, ethnic, rural/urban, income level, class origin, and gender. This view of equity implies assessing equity outcomes more in terms of the composition of graduates from each programme, and the reduction of barriers to completion by under-represented groups. It is this vision of equity that most obvious policy initiatives of government address. Yet a third way of looking at equity is to worry about intergenerational equity, where it is clear that most of the current students in the higher levels of education have a very high probability of higher lifetime incomes than current average taxpayers — so why should they be subsidized? Official policy is somewhat murky on what the equity objectives of the government are, but it is also probable that perceptions of what they should be differ among different groups, and yet are evolving — but it is unclear how that evolution will manifest itself.

IS IT WORTH IT?

This discussion of equity raises the more general question of whether the very large amounts of resources devoted to formal schooling and education are generally worth it, in the sense that they produce returns to the economy and society which are at least as good as what could have been achieved using them in other ways. It is probably axiomatic that the vast majority of both officialdom and the populace strongly believe that if anything, more resources should be devoted to education, and the willingness of families to devote large amounts to education from their own pockets supports this conclusion. However, this belief should not be axiomatic, and is not necessarily true. The underlying problem is that when the educational qualifications of those entering the labour force are escalating more rapidly than the educational requirements of new employment opportunities, what is best from the point of view of individuals and their families may not be optimal from the point of view of the society as a whole, unless one takes a very long time horizon as one's reference, and believes that the external benefits of education are extremely large.

One way to see the problem is to ask whether it is possible to waste resources on education and formal schooling, and the answer is obviously yes — few would argue for switching all the money spent on, say, health, to education. A more useful way to get at it is to consider two different extreme approaches to interpreting the role of formal education in the economy, its growth, and individual income determination. At the one extreme is what one can think of as the "tournament" view or the "rent-seeking" explanation of behaviour: the economy grows at a given rate, and generates a given number of "good" jobs; the role of education is to determine who gets the "good" jobs. In this view, if the education system produces more graduates than the number of jobs for which they are qualified, the resources used to produce those who get jobs below their qualifications have been wasted.

At the other extreme, which we could call the "growth factor" view, one of the determinants of economic growth is the availability of human capital, that is, educated people. So the more of these education produces, the faster the economic growth. Of course, as education expands, often there will be recent graduates who fail to obtain employment that meets their expectations of what they are qualified for, but this is normal. Over time in most societies, formal educational qualifications required for a given job title tend to escalate, and the more educated persons will move into jobs for which they would earlier have been regarded as overqualified. Again over time they will be more productive than the workers with lower qualifications they replace. In addition, at least some of the workers who feel themselves overqualified will innovate and, in effect, accelerate economic growth and create new job opportunities.

Neither of these extreme views is likely to be wholly true, but it is also likely that both contain some insight into the interaction between formal education and economic growth. If the most obvious way to improve one's children's life chances is for them to get as much education as possible and land one of the "good" jobs in the economy, then it makes sense for parents to invest in their children's education even if the probability of getting one of those jobs is much less than one. The larger the public subsidy to education, and the larger the ratio of the net benefits of the "good" jobs to those of the less desirable occupations, the stronger the incentive for parents to invest their own resources in education, as well as encourage the government to improve the education their children get.

Our ignorance of the exact relationship between the qualifications of the labour force and the performance of the economy, and the impossibility of ever being able to predict the future, mean that judging whether the education system is in any sense optimal in terms of its size, resources, and structure is an impossible task in terms of producing a firm conclusion in which one can have confidence. However, there are bits of evidence that one can turn to which give some suggestions as to possibilities.

Labour market information in Vietnam is not easily or frequently available by education level and age. However, a survey conducted in 2004 found that in the age group 22 to 25, only 9.6 per cent of those with gainful activity were in professional or technical jobs, and only 5.5 per cent were "office staff". Almost half were in unskilled positions, and close to 30 per cent in various kinds of "trained craft or similar" positions. For all those with gainful activity aged 14 to 25, more than 35 per cent were self-employed, with another 20 per cent working for family enterprises. State firms employed 6.7 per cent and private firms 8.7 per cent. Although some university graduates are self-employed, the majority are likely to be working for private or state firms, and given that those firms employ many youthful workers who do not have higher education qualifications, the anecdotal information on the difficulty upper-secondary and higher education graduates encounter now in finding appropriate employment seems very likely to be true. This suggests that in current circumstances, where it is often widely alleged that as many as half of the recent university graduates fail to find employment, it is plausible that already in Vietnam, much schooling at the higher education level takes place to give graduates a better chance of acquiring a good job in competition with others in the labour market, rather than providing skills and capabilities that will raise productivity sufficiently to justify the investment in human capital involved for the cohort of students overall. In turn, this suggests that the reform of higher education, and attempts to improve quality throughout the system, should perhaps receive more emphasis than further expansion.

CONCLUSION

Economists are notorious for practising what has long been called the dismal science. In truth, we know far less about the things that are important about education and how education interacts with the economy than is often presumed. What we do know with some confidence is mostly little better than obvious platitudes: a more educated labour force is likely to facilitate faster economic growth; more education that is of higher quality, on average, results in higher income for individuals; the pattern of educational access and attainment tends to be similar to the pattern of income levels and opportunity; reducing educational disparities tends to reduce economic disparities; investing in quality in education may be rewarded; families will tend to send children to school for longer, the lower the cost and the greater the perceived rewards; teachers will tend to do more of the things they are rewarded for.

The only issue this chapter raises that is perhaps not so obvious is that from a strictly economic perspective, it is possible to spend too much of society's resources on the quantity of schooling provided, and it is possible, and currently in Vietnam perhaps even plausible, that spending more on quality improvement, and less on enrolment expansion, would be better for economic growth. Whether the population would agree is uncertain, especially if at the higher levels, the "tournament" view of the function of education is widely held. In any case, continued attention to quality improvement and to the reform of incentive and governance structures, both projects of the government, is highly desirable.

APPENDIX

TABLE 3.1
Student Enrolment as of December of the School Year

Year/level	1990/91	1995/96	2000/01	2004/05	2006/07
Primary	11,882,900	10,228,800	9,741,100	7,744,800	7,029,400
Lower Secondary		4,312,700	5,863,600	6,616,700	6,152,000
Upper Secondary		1,019,500	2,171,400	2,761,100	3,075,200
Professional Secondary		165,600	255,400	465,300	468,800
College and University	129,600	297,900	795,600*	1,182,000*	1,456,700*

Note: * (The 2006/07 data for colleges and universities are preliminary.) This is the number in *public* institutions; in 2000/01 there were a further 103,900, in 2004/05 137,800, and in 2006/07, 209,500 in non-public institutions; these numbers include both full-time students and those undergoing in-service training or other short-term or part-time courses, who have also grown rapidly in numbers. Full-time students numbered 173,100 in 95/96, 552,500 in 2000/01, 729,400 in 2004/05, and 917,200 in 2006/07. The number of full-time students in non-public institutions grew from 100,100 in 2000/01 to 162,300 in 2006/07.

Source: Socialist Republic of Vietnam, General Statistics Office (*Statistical Yearbook*, various years, and webpage <http://www.gso.gov.vn/default_en. aspx?tabid=474&idmid=3>.

TABLE 3.2
Published MOET data for 1999–2000 to 2007

Item	99–2000	00–01	01–02	02–03	03–04	04–05	05–06	06–07	07–08
Pre-primary enrolment	2,497	2,480	2,488	2,547	2,589	2,754	3,025	3,147	3,284
Primary enrolment	10,063	9,751	9,337	8,841	8,350	7,773	7,322	7,041	6,995
Lower secondary enrolment	5,767	5,918	6,254	6,498	6,612	6,671	6,459	6,218	6,100
Upper secondary enrolment, academic	1,976	2,200	2,334	2,458	2,616	2,802	2,977	3,111	3,184
Full-time upper secondary technical and vocational enrolment	129	149	148	240	298	366	407	433	
College enrolment, full-time	133	149	167	166	184	188	241	264	
University enrolment, full-time	376	403	412	438	470	501	547	677	
Pre-Primary teachers	142,954	146,871	144,257	145,934	150,335	155,699	160,172	163,809	
Pre-Primary P/T	17.5	16.9	17.2	17.5	17.2	17.7	18.9	19.2	
Primary teachers	340,871	347,833	354,624	358,606	362,627	360,624	353,608	344,521	
Primary P/T	29.5	28.0	26.3	24.0	23.0	21.6	20.7	20.4	
L-S teachers	208,802	224,840	243,208	262,543	280,943	295,056	306,067	310,620	
L-S P/T ratio	27.6	26.3	25.7	24.8	23.5	22.6	21.1	20.0	
U-S teachers	65,189	74,189	81,684	89,357	98,714	106,586	118,327	125,460	
U-S P/T ratio	30.3	29.7	28.6	27.5	26.5	26.3	25.2	24.8	
Votech teachers	9,565	10,189	9,327	10,247	11,121	13,937	14,230	14,540	
Votech P/T ratio	13.5	14.6	15.9	23.4	26.8	26.3	28.6	29.8	
College teachers	7,703	7,843	10,392	11,215	11,551	13,677	14,285	15,381	
College P/T ratio	17.3	19.0	16.1	14.8	15.9	13.7	16.9	17.2	
University teachers	22,606	24,362	25,546	27,393	28,434	33,969	34,294	38,137	
University P/T ratio	16.6	16.5	16.1	16.0	16.5	14.7	16.0	17.8	
Total regular State Budget expenditure [billion VND, calendar years]	10,356	12,649	16,906	18,625	27,830	35,007	45,595	55,240	

Note: Enrolment data in thousands, from the MOET website; GSO data [for December] are somewhat lower for enrolment, but the discrepancy is in the order of 1 to 2 per cent by 2006–07. P/T means Pupil/Teacher Ratio.

TABLE 3.3
Primary Sector Data

	1997–98 or 1998	1999–00 or 2000	2001–02 or 2002	2003–04 or 2004
Primary Pupils, number	10,250,214	9,751,431	8,841,004	8,350,191
Primary Schools, number	13,066	13,738	14,163	14,346
Primary Teachers, number	336,792	347,833	358,606	362,627
Estimated Primary GER, %	105.3	103.3	105.4	
Estimated Primary NER, %	91.0		90.1	
Estimated Primary NER, lowest HH expenditure quintile, %	81.9		84.5	
Estimated Primary NER, highest HH expenditure quintile, %	96.4		95.3	
Estimated Primary NER, urban, %	95.5		94.1	
Estimated Primary NER, rural, %	90.6		89.2	
Primary Share of MOET State Budget %	36.4	32.2	31.6	
Education share of GDP %	3.5	3.5	4.2	4.6
Education share of Public Expenditure %	17.4	15.1	16.9	17.1
Operational expenditure as % total, Primary	15	16	18	
Investment expenditure as % total, Primary	30	19	18	
Pupil/Teacher ratio, number	30.4	28.0	24.6	23.0
Pupil/Teacher ratio, highest Regional^ value, number			30.7	28.4
Pupil/Teacher ratio, lowest Regional^ value, number			21.3	17.9
Promotion rates, %, Grade 5 Primary to Lower Sec.	91.7	94.0	95.6	
Completion rates, %, Primary	69.6	74.4	80.5	
Failure rate %, 2003-4 Primary, Regional range				0.17–4.3
Dropout rate %, Primary, Regional range				0.52–6.68
Mathematics Grade 5 Attainment; range of Provincial mean scores*	16–73			65–95
Reading Grade 5 Attainment; range of Provincial mean scores*	20–79			39–74

Notes: Among the eight regions Red River, North-East, North-West, North Central, Central Coast, Central Highlands, South-East, and Mekong Delta; Highest value in Mekong Delta both years; lowest value in the North-West both years. GER = Gross Enrolment Ratio. NER = Net Enrolment Ratio.
* Not directly comparable between the two years or the two subjects.

Sources: *2004 Public Expenditure Review, Draft Annex [X], Education Sector* (World Bank Office in Vietnam, May 2004); and *Báo Cáo Đánh Giá Chi Tiêu Công 2004, Ngành Giáo dục và Đào tạo* (10 August 2004 draft) (the latter is preferred where the two are inconsistent).

Notes

1. This tends to be particularly the case with decisions and accounting of overhead and administrative costs. For example, in Vietnam, overall estimates place the proportion of the recurrent E&T budget accounted for by personal emoluments at 70 to 75 per cent in recent years, but at school level the ratio may be 90 to 95 per cent and in some cases allegedly higher.

2. Two apocryphal remarks allegedly made by Vietnamese civil servants in educational settings outside Hanoi illustrate some of the problems (I paraphrase and for obvious reasons do not provide more detail on the sources): first, when told answers were not consistent with a questionnaire completed and submitted earlier, "Oh yes, I remember that, you badgered us to complete it. But we did not keep a copy, so I don't know what numbers we gave you ..." Second, referring to an often-cited published study, "Don't believe the numbers in that; I helped prepare our submission, and we made up all the numbers over a weekend." My own experiences make me fully willing to accept these as reflecting reality.

3. Despite multiple and competing outside-funded efforts to develop and implement an EMIS system to cover the entire country, no satisfactory system is yet functioning. Efforts continue, but it is unclear when they will produce the kind of data often available in other countries, in part because some lower level units like what they now have.

4. The TFR (total fertility rate), is an estimate of the total number of children a woman would bear during her reproductive years, if in each five-year interval from ages 15–49, she gave birth to the same number of children as women of that age in the population as a whole did at the time of the estimate.

5. UN Population Division ranks Vietnam's 2005 urban population percentage as 159th in the world.

6. Anon. (2005), paragraph 20. The experience of this period still has real consequences more than twenty years later: throughout the government finance structures at all levels, meeting personal emoluments of established staff is the first priority for available funds. Only after those obligations are met can remaining funds be allocated to other operational expenses or capital improvements. This can be an important constraint on the quality of schooling in poorer provinces and districts because of the limits it puts on non-personnel operating expense.

7. The World Bank asserts that about a million primary-school-age children were not in school in 2005, although that is a higher estimate than government sources suggest (net enrolment of 88 per cent vs. 98 per cent from government sources).

8. An illustration is found at <http://english.vietnamnet.vn/educaton/2008/04/77 7327/>, showing that different authorities reported 14,000, 1,423, and 1,034

pupils dropping out in Khánh Hòa by the end of the first semester of the 2007–08 school year.

9. Lower secondary only covers four grades, six to nine, with entry to grade six guaranteed for all those completing primary school. Enrolment targets reflect a five year age group, however (99 per cent of eleven to fifteen year-olds in secondary school), while universalization targets (for meeting national certification standards) are couched in terms of transfer rates of primary graduates (99 per cent or 80 per cent in disadvantaged communes); reduced repetition and dropout to achieve completion rates of 90 per cent (75 per cent in disadvantaged communes); and 80 per cent (70 per cent in disadvantaged communes) of fifteen to eighteen year-olds having completed lower secondary school.

10. In Vietnam, Early Childhood Care and Education (ECCE) covers children from three months to three years (crèches) and three to five years (kindergartens). Over 10,000 kindergartens have between 2 and 2.5 million children attending, and well over half are non-public.

11. If we count only full-time students, the ratio has not exceeded twenty in the past decade; that number is exceeded at many U.S. State universities, including some research-oriented ones. Of course, the ratio varies substantially across institutions, faculties and programmes, and many programmes enrol large numbers of part-time students, students on upgrading and short-term programmes, and other activities that raise income for the institution and its staff, but do not increase full-time student numbers (MOET has not yet devised an operational measure of "full time equivalent" for either students or instructors in higher education, making all comparisons somewhat dubious). However, in aggregate, the student-instructor ratio at Vietnamese universities is much better than many think. Instructors do teach much more than is desirable, however. This is because of the remuneration structure, which typically defines expected teaching load in terms of class hours. Teaching staff therefore resist attempts to increase class size, and many lower level classes in Vietnamese universities are taught in inappropriately small sections, so that staff can obtain overloads (typically in other programmes in order to qualify for additional remuneration) often in reciprocal arrangements. Institutions with large enrolments may lack any lecture halls capable of holding more than a hundred students, and even when they do, they are often underutilized because of this reluctance on the part of instructional staff to reduce the collective wage bill by reducing instructional class hours.

12. The key issues are pupil time in class and teacher time in class, which often differ considerably; and the ratio of actual instructional time to class time. Both are notoriously difficult to collect data on with any reliability, because they require direct observation (which is costly) and direct observation

tends to alter behaviour. Anecdotally, teacher absenteeism and low ratios of instructional time to class time are often alleged for all levels of Vietnamese education.

13. For example, universities were not expected to select those whom they wished to add as academic staff until the final year of undergraduate study — but if they did select a student, that student was expected to comply.

14. The exception is funds in the National Target Programs (NTP), which are earmarked for clearly-defined purposes and must be spent on them. The education NTPs have been growing, partly because of donor funds channelled through them, and richer provinces have added their own funds to the centrally allocated amounts, but they amount to a very small fraction of total expenditure on education.

15. Cynics have been known to speculate that this situation is allowed to persist on purpose, the motivation being that, given the circumstances, any manager at provincial or district level who is actually doing his job will be breaking a norm. That means there are always grounds to discipline such a manager, should higher levels wish to for some reason.

16. Unrealistic in the sense that with current resources, only a tiny fraction of schools could possibly meet them.

17. Provinces are usually divided into "deficit" (those that "net-receive" funding from Hanoi) and "surplus" (those that net provide funding to the national budget) provinces, with respect to the taxes that are actually collected at the provincial level. There are only seven "surplus" provinces.

18. Provinces do have some influence over universities; for example, senior administrative appointments are normally subject to local Party approval.

19. MOET was instructed in January 2008 to adjust tuition fees in public schools "so that they do not exceed 6–8 per cent of each household's income", with actual rates to be determined by provincial authorities. No detail has been provided as to how this is to be done, since obviously tuition cannot be individually determined. See "Government expenditure on education to rise 10 per cent", <http://www.cpv.org.vn/english/scient_education/>, 10 January 2008.

20. I'm not aware of any serious discussion on abolishing tuition at lower-secondary level. As an aside, I was once told by a lower secondary headmaster that primary school heads were actually better off than he was because they could charge for full-day schooling and allocate the revenue as they saw fit, whereas the district took a lot of his tuition revenue and what was left had to be used according to strict guidelines.

21. In the state budget, "education" is general education, that is, pre-primary, primary, lower-secondary, and upper-secondary, schools; "training" is vocational/technical, and "professional secondary" schools, and colleges and universities

(higher education). Some training funds go to other line ministries than MOET for the institutions they control and run.

22. Technical assistance under the World Bank's Higher Education Development II project is intended to facilitate plans for reform of the universities, but contracts for that were only let during 2008 and extend over up to three years. The importance to continued economic growth of reform and quality improvement in higher education is emphasized by many analysts, notably in the Harvard study (Wilkinson 2008, p. 50), which under the heading "Revolutionize higher education" concludes (italics in the original) *"(T)hese reforms must be implemented with great urgency; if not, Vietnam will find it difficult to attain the level of development enjoyed even by Southeast Asian countries."*

23. This is a rather strong assertion, and it is obviously somewhat hard to document convincingly. I base it on both personal experience and observation, and the relatively frequent reports, even in the English-language press, of deviations from official policy at the local level; for example, "Part-time education comes up short", <http://english.vietnamnet.vn/education/2008/04/777921/> (11 April 2008), and "Apologies issued to students over late study loans, unapproved fees", <http://english.vietnamnet.vn/education/2008/04/776373/>, (2 April 2008).

24. It has been reported that in some districts, the District Finance Offices have allocated and disbursed funds to schools without even informing the district-level office of education. Treasury controls on spending are designed to ensure funds are spent in conformity with the allocation, so there is no reason for Treasury at the local level to alert local education and training agencies of deviations from the intentions at higher level, if the spending is in accordance with the actual allocations made at the lower level. In theory, Treasury data could permit disbursement unit comparison of expenditure against original intent, but it would be a herculean job to obtain, and then perform the necessary reaggregations on the detailed data that do not normally flow upward in a suitable form for that purpose.

25. Language is mentioned because schools always operate in Vietnamese, whereas this is not the home language of many ethnic minority pupils; there are also alleged to be difficulties arising from the attitudes displayed by majority Kinh teachers and administrators towards ethnic minorities. Economic causes arise not only from difference in family income, but also from differences in perceived opportunities as a result of success in school.

26. The best known are the World Bank's PEDC (Primary Education for Disadvantaged Children) project, and the elements of NTP funded by the Education For All implementation plan.

27. This is the reason it is sensible for government to always be a little sceptical of employer views on what the education system should be doing.

28. Both an official union and disciplinary organizations do exist, but it is almost unknown for them to disagree with the authorities.

References

Anon. "Education in Vietnam: Development History, Challenges and Solutions", <http://siteresources.worldbank.org/EDUCATION/Resources/278200-1121703274255/1439264-1153425508901/Education_Vietnam_Development.pdf, 2005>.

Anon. "Booming Online Trade in Fake Academic Degrees". Original source in Vietnamese *Tuổi trẻ Thanh Niên News*, 18 May 2008. <http://www.thanhniennews.com/print.php?catid=10&newsid=38610>.

Becker, Douglas L. "Private Sector Investment in Education — Welcome Ally or Unbidden Guest?" Presentation at the International Finance Corporation Forum, "Investing in the Future: Innovation in Private Education". Washington D.C., 14 May 2008, cited in Doug Lederman, "The Private Sector Role in Global Higher Education, <http://www.insidehighereducation.com/news/2008/05/15/private>.

Dapice, David O. "Vietnam's Economy: Success Story or Weird Dualism? A SWOT Analysis". A Special Report Prepared for the UNDP and Prime Minister's Research Commission. Hanoi: UNDP, June 2003.

Hanushek, Eric A. and Ludger Woessmann. "The Role of Cognitive Skills in Economic Development". *Journal of Economic Literature* 46, no. 3 (September 2008: 607–68).

Lin, Justin Yifu and Boris Pleskovic (eds). *Higher Education and Development*. Washington, D.C.: World Bank, 2008.

Lodhi, A. Haroon Akram. "Vietnam's Agriculture: Processes of Rich Peasant Accumulation and Mechanisms of Social Differentiation". *Journal of Agrarian Change 5*, no. 1 (2005): 73–116.

Ikeda, Miyako. "Formula Funding System for Vietnam Primary Education: Application of Needs-Based Resource Allocation". Paris: IIEP, UNESCO, May 2004.

Le, Van Hao. "General Trends of Higher Education and Models of Funding Development". Paper presented at the CIECER Conference on Comparative Education, 23 May 2008. CIECER, HCMC University of Pedagogy, <http://www.ciecer.org/joomla> (in Vietnamese).

London, Jonathan D. "Vietnam's Mass Education and Health Systems: A Regimes Perspective". *American Asian Review 21*, no. 2 (2003): 125–70.

Melbourne Development Institute (in association with Strategic Consulting Co.). *Final Report: Secondary Education Sector Master Plan 2006–2010*. Hanoi: Asian Development Bank and MOET, June 2006.

Nguyễn, Kim Hồng. "Some Thoughts about Finance Sources for University Education in Vietnam in the New Era". Manuscript, HCMC University of Pedagogy, 2008a.

———. "The Flow of Education in Vietnam in the Flat World". Manuscript, HCMC University of Pedagogy, 2008b.

Phạm Đỗ Nhật Tiến. "Vietnamese Education: Its Position on the World Map of Education and its Trends in Development". Paper presented at the CIECER Conference on Comparative Education, 23 May 2008. CIECER, HCMC University of Pedagogy, <http://www.ciecer.org/joomla> (in Vietnamese).

Socialist Republic of Vietnam, Education Publishing House. *The Education Development Strategic Plan for 2001–2010*. Hanoi: Education Publishing House, 2002.

Socialist Republic of Vietnam. *National Education for All (EFA) Action Plan, 2003–2015*. Hanoi, June 2003.

Socialist Republic of Vietnam, Inter-Ministerial Working Group of the CPRGS. *The Comprehensive Poverty Reduction and Growth Strategy [CPRGS]*. Hanoi, November 2004.

Trần Kiên. *Education in Vietnam: Current State and Issues*. Hanoi: Thế giới Publishers, 2002.

Hoàng Tụy. "Educational Crisis: Reasons and Solutions in Globalization Challenges". Paper presented at the CIECER Conference on Comparative Education, 23 May 2008. CIECER, HCMC University of Pedagogy, <http://www.ciecer.org/joomla>. (6 pp; translated from Vietnamese by Dang Tan Tin and Nguyen Viet).

United Nations Country Team Vietnam. *United Nations Common Country Assessment for Vietnam*. Hanoi: UNDP, November 2004.

Wagstaff, Adam. "Decomposing Changes in Income Inequality into Vertical and Horizontal Redistribution and Reranking, with Applications to China and Vietnam". Washington, D.C.: World Bank Policy Research Working Paper 3559, April 2005.

Weeks, John, Nguyen Thang, Rathin Roy, and Joseph Lim. "Seeking Equity within Growth" In *The Macroeconomic of Poverty Reduction: The Case Study of Vietnam*. UNDP, 2004.

Wilkinson, Ben (ed). *Choosing Success: The Lessons of East and Southeast Asia and Vietnam's Future*. Cambridge, MA: Harvard University, John F. Kennedy School of Government, Asia Programs, 2008.

World Bank. *Vietnam Development Report, 2004*. Hanoi: author.

4

MARKET-ORIENTED EDUCATION
Private (People-Founded)
Upper-Secondary Schools in Hanoi

Trần Thị Bích Liễu

This chapter concerns the private provision of education in Vietnam. Specifically, it examines the activities of private (people-founded) secondary schools in Hanoi as they strive to respond to and benefit from emerging market demand. People-founded schools refer to a particular type of "non-public" school permitted under Vietnam's law, while the term "market-oriented education" refers to education that operates under, and is responsive to, market rules — such as competition, price, and demand.

The chapter is in three sections. The first section discusses the liberalization of education that has accompanied Vietnam's transition from central planning to a "socialist-oriented market economy". It reports trends in the private provision of education at various levels, critically examines "New Education" (a buzzword that I use to refer to education that simultaneously meets the requirements of the market economy while remaining faithful to socialist ideals), and considers the challenges various kinds of "private" or "non-public" schools in Vietnam face in light of international experience and theoretical literature on organizations and adaptation in market economies. The second section reports results from case studies of two private secondary schools in Hanoi and their efforts to adapt school operations to changing demand. The final section draws lessons from these and other schools' experiences and suggests ways private schools may improve their adaptability to Vietnam's growing market economy.

In only a short period, the scale of private education has increased dramatically. However, the experience of private education providers has been mixed. Overall, I argue that many school principals in Vietnam are responding to market demands with increasing sophistication. After only a few years of operation, principals of some schools have devised new management arrangements, achieved notable success in overcoming people's poor view of private schools, and increased their ability to recruit students as well as improve the quality of teaching. Some private schools have proven especially effective in responding to the challenges and opportunities internationalization and globalization present, particularly as this affects the content of curricular and extra-curricular activities.

BACKGROUND

In 1986, Vietnam's leaders stated their commitment to developing a "socialist-oriented market economy". The country now has a regulated market economy that operates under market rules, but with a socialist orientation that emphasizes social and educational equity and the leadership role of Vietnam's Communist Party (VCP). The development of this hybrid system has impacted and stimulated changes in the educational system (Phúc and Châu 2000). In particular, the move towards a market economy has transformed arrangements governing education finance. The term "New Education" (*Giáo Dục Mới*) in Vietnam refers to education that matches the requirements of both the new market economy and the socialist features mentioned above. Indeed, the country's formal education system today incorporates both "market" and "state" elements, as shown in Figure 4.1.

Figure 4.1 shows that the education system in Vietnam operates under the leadership of the CPV, the management of the central government, and market rules. In principle, the involvement of the state and the CPV is to ensure rational management and the upholding of socialist principles.

Until the late 1980s, almost all formal education in Vietnam was provided by and financed by the state. However, since 1986, the government

FIGURE 4.1
Socialist and Market-oriented Features of Education in Vietnam

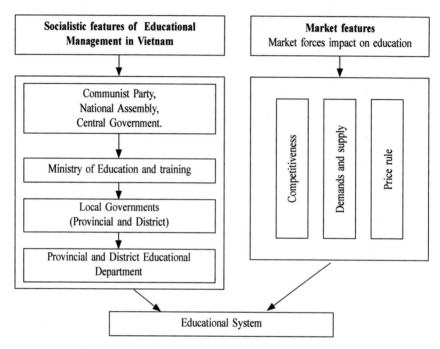

Source: Compiled by author.

began to permit private provision of education at the pre-primary, secondary, and tertiary levels. To adapt to the new market economy, the state has promoted a gradual shift from purely public education to a coexisting system of both public and non-public (private) schools. Public schools are schools founded and funded by the government. Non-public schools are schools that have private owners (private schools) or socio-economic organizations (people-funded schools) and that operate quasi-independently of the government. There are also semi-public schools (*bán công*). The government supports semi-public schools' physical infrastructure and pays the salary of half of their teaching staff. The schools have to find the funds for their operation and pay the salary for the rest of the teachers from different resources, including fees and tuition. Precise arrangments regarding the precise relation between the state and private and semi-public schools can vary across localities.

In total, the number of private schools in Vietnam is very small but growing, and private education is playing an increasingly important role in the overall education system. By 2007–08, 56.4 per cent of all children of preschool age were attending non-public kindergartens and crèches. By 2006 and 2008, private enrolment accounted for 6 per cent of all students enrolled in general (Grades 1–12) education, while private institutions accounted for nearly 13.3 per cent of all tertiary students. The percentage of students attending non-public kindergartens and crèches declined (over 62 per cent in the years before 2005, but dipped to 54.0 per cent in 2006–07 and to 56.4 per cent in 2007–08). The percentage of students in general (Grades 1–12) private education was small at around 6.0 per cent, but increased for tertiary education (from 11.8 per cent in 2006 to 13.3 per cent in 2008). The state has set an objective of 40 per cent of having students enrolled in higher or tertiary education by 2010 (Ministry of Education and Training, 2005*b*). Table 4.1 presents data on increases in the number of private schools and their students year on year over six years.

The most privatized level of education in Vietnam is preschool education, where over 50 per cent of participation is in non-public kindergartens and crèches, which are either private or people-founded. Although the percentage of non-public schools at this education level was reduced, the number was increased (from 8,976 schools in 2006 to 11,621 schools in 2008). For the general educational system, almost all primary schools are "public" as are the overhwhelming majority of lower-secondary schools. The highest proportion of non-public schools is in upper- secondary and tertiary education (See Table 4.1).

The liberalization of education has influenced the various levels of education differently. Urban education has been the most affected and is the most oriented to the market. Indeed, private schools are mostly concentrated in big cities such as Hanoi, Danang, and Ho Chi Minh City. The percentage of non-public schools in Hanoi in 2007–08 is: 60.9 per cent (467/767 schools) in preschool education; 3.2 per cent (21/653 schools) in primary education; 0.8 per cent (5/579 schools) in lower secondary; and 54.2 per cent (123/227 schools) in upper-secondary schools (Đại 7 March 2009). Danang, in the year 2007–08 (from Danang Department of Education), had 63.3 per cent (71/112 schools) of private kindergartens and crèches, and 8.3 per cent (6/72 schools) of private secondary schools. In Ho Chi Minh City, private schools make up 15.0 per cent overall of schools at all educational levels (236/1,575); of these, preschool education

TABLE 4.1
Number of Non-public Students and Schools

	2001-2002	2002-2003	2003-2004	2004-2005	2005-2006	2007-2008
Pre education (kindergartens, crèches and compounded both kindergartens and creches)						
Schools	7,707	7,952	8,368	8,587	8,976	11,621
Per cent	81.7	81.9	82.9	82.1	81.5	51.1
Students	1,542,606	1,583,189	1,585,538	1,603,984	1,0763,640	1,801,530
Per cent %	62.0	62.2	61.3	63.1	54.0	56.4
General Education (Primary and secondary)						
Schools	574	603	652	575	666	779
Per cent	2.3	2.3	2.5	2.1	2.5	2.9 Upper Secondary 651 (26.3%)
Students	984,373	992,616	1,000,891	893,565	1,053,783	939,756
Per cent	5.5	5.6	5.7	7.2	6.3	6.0 Upper Secondary 831,882 (27.1%)
Higher Education (Colleges and universities)						
Schools	23	23	27	29	34	64
Per cent	12.0	11.4	12.6	12.6	13.3	21.0
Students	100,990	111,856	137,122	137,760	160,420	188,838
Per cent	10.4	9.3	12.1	10.4	11.8	13.3

Source: Center of Information Technology — Vietnam's Ministry of Education and Training, <website: www.edu.net.vn>.

was 42.2 per cent (174/412) private; primary school was 5.5 per cent (25/458) private; lower-secondary schools were 1.29 per cent (3/234) private; and upper-secondary school were only 0.3 percent (2/72) private (Ho Chi Minh City Education Department statistics for 2006–07).

The shift from a centrally planned to a market economy presents important organizational challenges for education providers of all types. In Vietnam, some private schools founded after 1989 have had to adapt rapidly to the market by changing their strategies of development and implementing new management mechanisms. Almost all private schools in Hanoi and other large cities in Vietnam have developed their own market segment plans and each school has its target customers. Some schools focus on so-called "high potential" students, some on special students, and others on all sorts of students. Certain schools have gained a reputation for meeting the specialized needs of both students and parents. Among the top hundred upper-secondary schools that were ranked based on the number of students who earned a total score of between 27 and 30 in their grades in the three university entrance exam subjects in 2006, six were non-public secondary schools (four in Hanoi, one in Ho Chi Minh City and one in Vĩnh Phúc Province as reported on *VietnamNet*, 5 June 2007). In 2008 this number was three compared with 187 other public talented schools nationwide (at 31st place was Nguyen Khuyen Private Upper Secondary School in Ho Chi Minh City, at 36th was Luong The Vinh, and at 122nd was Dao Duy Tu Private Upper Secondary School in Hanoi, according to vnMedia.vn on 13 January 2009). Other evidence speaks of private schools' effectiveness in seeing their students graduate. In Ho Chi Minh City, only six private schools and five public schools had all their students pass the National High Secondary School Exams (Thời Báo 2007).

In many private schools, international education is an increasingly important curricular focus. Some secondary schools offer foreign curricula and have established connections with schools overseas to help students in education and culture exchange programmes. Hanoi's private schools have been working with Australian schools and universities in this endeavour, with interschool visits, and student/teacher exchanges, and Internet-based learning. They also have dialogues with Malaysian, U.K., Indonesian, and Korean schools. Almost all private schools in Hanoi and in Ho Chi Minh City have established a vision for their schools as a place to help students attain the knowledge, skills, and attitudes that would be similarly taught at international universities and schools. They focus on IT and the English or French languages, and orient students towards new professions that would enable them to work and live in a globalized world (Đại 7 March 2009 & Linh 4–7 December 2008).

International school establishment and management have been the focus of the management of Ho Chi Minh and Hanoi Education Departments where the number of this kind of schools has increased: from thirteen schools in 2006 to thirty schools in 2008 in Ho Chi Minh city (Linh, 4–7 December 2008); and forty schools in Hanoi in 2008 (Đại 7 March 2009). These schools provide international curricula and teach English or other foreign languages by foreign teachers, and are invested 100 per cent by foreign funds or Vietnamese funds. The number of students in a class in these schools is small — between sixteen and twenty students so that active teaching methods can be used effectively. The tuition fees of these schools are higher compared with other private schools in Vietnam (For example: in Ho Chi Minh City, tuition fee at the Parallel Linguistics School is between 5.900–6.900 USD/year for grades 9 to 12; at APU International School, it is nearly 1,000 USD per month, three to ten times higher than the fees of other non-public schools without international instruction).

The theoretical literature and international evidence suggest that organizations that fail to adapt to new institutional environments die. One can observe this tendency in Vietnam's private upper-secondary schools. Like private schools in developed countries, private schools in Vietnam have to face strong competition for their survival. Some private school operators can be very creative and active in finding and implementing new technologies, models, and strategies to help their schools develop. However, not all private school owners can do this as many obstacles still remain in private education, especially when owners lack a strategic vision for their schools' development.

While certain private schools have gained a sound reputation in the community, others still have difficulty finding their niche. Some are forced to close after a few years of operation. In 2000–01, the Hanoi Department of Education had to close seven private secondary schools because of low education quality (Hanoi Department of Education 2000–01). These schools could not recruit students because they lacked physical facilities and offered only small, dark, rented rooms for classes. Their principals also failed to hire adequately qualified teachers as they did not see the importance of teachers in student learning. Finally, school principals knew little about how markets work and did not invest in school infrastructure or in student learning. They opened schools as they thought they could earn money easily from tuition and fees.

Vietnam's 2005 Education Law recommends that all certificates and diplomas issued by private and public schools have the same value. But there remains significant bias against private education, some of which is justified, and some of which may not take into account recent developments. Much of the bias against private education stems from the circumstances in the development of private education in Vietnam in the early 1990s and the corresponding association of private education with substandard schools. Indeed, some private schools continue to face difficultires in recruiting students or qualified teachers, while others lack the physical infrastructure for teaching and learning. Many schools encounter difficulties in finding financial support for their future development. The government does not provide financial aid to private schools, leading some private school principals to feel that they cannot compete on an equal footing with public schools.

In the new amended Education Law of 2005, the government sought to improve conditions for private education. The measures included allowing private schools to rent land or premises with tax exemptions or reductions, and helping them to obtain low-interest bank loans to build schools. The government would support some private schools financially provided the schools implement certain policies and designated targets. The government would also provide funding to enable private schools to implement state policies (Article 68, Education Law 2005). Still, The Vietnamese Government and the Ministry of Education and Training (MOET) have not yet established a competitive environment for educational institutions. Perhaps the state's most fundamental concern with private education is the quality of education.

MOET from 2004 has set up standards to accredit universities (Bộ Giáo dục và Đào tạo 04 December 2004) and has also ranked upper-secondary schools according to students' graduation results (from 2006), as well as recommended the evaluation of the education quality of secondary schools from 2009 (Bộ Giáo dục và Đào tạo 12 May 2009). This is the first step in helping universities and secondary schools pay more attention to educational quality and so improve their competitiveness. But most private education providers in Vietnam have had to learn as they go along.

THE ADAPTIVITY OF PRIVATE PROVIDERS OF EDUCATION

Given the likelihood that private provision of education will increase, it is important to gain an understanding of the actual experience of Vietnamese schools in adapting to changing market conditions. It is also useful to have a clear understanding of what adaptability means. Theoretical literature on adaptability suggests that adaptation takes place on two levels: the structure of the subunit to fit its environment, and the organizational mode of integration and differentiation to meet the broader demands of the environment (Lawrence and Lorsch 1986 — as cited in Gumport and Sporn 1999). According to this definition, for an organization to adapt to a new environment, it has to change its overall structure as well that of its subunits. The most important thing for an organization undergoing change is to find the *strategies of equilibrium or fit* to survive in their new environment. The market economy requires that an organization or an individual be flexible, creative, and free in its operation (Watts 2004). Freedom for the development of an organization or an individual requires empowerment and acting according to market rules. Only when an organization meets these requirements can its production be of high quality. Quality is a crucial factor in enabling an organization to be accepted within the market economy.

To measure and evaluate the adaptive ability or market-orientedness of schools in Vietnam to a socialist-oriented market economy, ministerial-level research was carried out from 2004 to 2006 (Liễu 2004–06). Based on the features of Vietnam's socialist-oriented market economy and on the definitions of adaptation discussed earlier, our research developed eleven standards for measuring a school's adaptiveness. These standards and their corresponding criteria help to identify the market-orientation attributes of schools and the changes they have made for their development and management (see Table 4.2). If a school earned high scores on these adaptive standards, it means that the school is adapting well within its new environment and it is well-oriented to the new market economy.

Each standard has at least one criterion. Scores were assigned for each criterion where a score of five indicates an excellent level of adaptation; a four represents good adaptation; a score of three represents average, while non-adaptation and far below adaptation were given scores of two and one. This rubric is contained in Table 4.3. To complete the index of the

TABLE 4.2

Standards and Criteria for the Adaptive Ability of a School in Adjusting to the Socialist-oriented Market Economy in Vietnam

Features of a Socialist-oriented Market Economy	*Standards and Criteria relating to a Schools Adaptive Ability*
Market Features: Every production and business process occurs under market rules:	
• Follows the rules of supply and demand	1. Meet and satisfy the diverse demands and needs of customers in and outside the schools
• Price is a central focus	2. There is negotiation between school and parents on tuition fees, commensurate with market price and the income of parents
• Competition is important in producing high quality goods and services	3. Being competitive with other schools based on building a "school image"
• Production and service processes are operated by intervention of an "invisible hand"	4. Have a high quality of education to meet the demands and needs of its consumers. 5. Have a high quality service
• Decentralization, flexibility and change	6. Have autonomy and accountability to manage 7. Have flexible management and a good environment for teachers to develop and be creative 8. Have and operate a strategic plan. 9. Have a good flow of information between school officials and stakeholders
Socialist Features	
• Emphasize State and Communist Party leadership	10. Operating under control of state management and Communist Party leadership
• Ensure equality in income and social benefits	11. Ensuring educational equity for all children

Source: Liễu (2004–06).

TABLE 4.3
Case Studies Results

School	Grade	Adaptation Level
PF1(Private school)	4.5	High
PF2 (Private school)	4.4	Faily high
SP1 (Semi- public school)	3.8	Average
CL1 (Public school)	3.6	Average

Source: Liễu (2004–06).

adaptive ability of different schools, the researchers applied a coefficient for each standard according to their relative importance as determined by researchers. Admittedly, our understanding of adaptability is biased towards MOET's preferences and norms. The level of the adaptation was calculated as the sum score of criteria divided by the sum score of rating. The resulting index was organized into four levels of adaptation, ranging from a high of 5.0 to a low of 3.0 and below.

Additionally, case studies were carried out in four schools, including one semi-public school (*Bán Công* 1 or SP1), one public school (*Công Lập* 1 or P1) in Huế and two "private" people-founded (*Dân Lập*) schools (PF1 and PF2) in Hanoi, (Table 4.3). The principals of another 201 schools were asked to perform their own self-assessment.

CASE STUDIES

Two private senior secondary schools in Hanoi earned high levels of adaptation to the market economy. To provide insight into the market-oriented education of private schools, case studies of two schools are presented below.

Private School PF1

Private schools PF1 and PF2 were established in 1989. Both were among the first private schools in Vietnam in the *Đổi Mới* (renovation) period. The operators of these schools used their own money as well as money from parents to rent buildings to open the schools. Later, these investors built schools and the "owners" of each became the schools' principal.

The principals are responsible for hiring all the schools' teachers and staff for teaching and administration (public school principals have no power to hire teachers, but accept those sent to them by provincial or district educational departments).

Each school has its own mission and development strategy. The targeted students for school' PF1 are high-achieving students, while the target students for school PF2 are underachieving and special students, including students with learning difficulties and others with behavioural problems. ("Market segments" do not exist for public schools as most public schools accept all kinds of students). PF1 has focused on satisfying the needs of students wanting to enter university, while PF2 has focused on satisfying the needs of parents who want schools to correct their children's behaviour and help them find a suitable career. Both schools have created their own image and reputation. The way they have built their reputation is through marketing, enhancing their educational quality, and creating educational opportunties.

The Case of PF 1 suggests private schools can provide high quality education. The quality of PF1 has been enhanced every year, according to standardized measures.

In 2006, PF1 ranked 27th out of 100 nationally, and 36/200 in 2008 in terms of top upper-secondary school university entrance exam result. Although the top-ranked schools on this score are all long-established schools for "gifted" (that is, high-achieving) students, PF1 still outscored many other such schools. Additionally, PF1 is the only school in Hanoi in which all students passed the National High Secondary School Exams in 2006–07 (Thời Báo) and in 2007–08 (Thu Nguyễn 20 November 2008). During the 2003–04 school year, PF1 had three students who had the second highest scores in the university entrance exams. In 2008 50 per cent of PF1 students gained excellent (9.0 and 10) and good (8.0) scores in their graduation national exams compared with 14 per cent of the total number of Hanoi's students. Also in 2008, 98 per cent of PF1 students passed university entrance exams compared with 91 per cent in the previous years (Thu Nguyễn 20 November 2008).

The percentage of students and parents who are satisfied with the school is very high: a total of 97 per cent of parents reported some level of satisfaction; 32 per cent of parents were very satisfied, 65 per cent were fairly satisfied, and 71 per cent of students fairly satisfied. There were some dissatisfied students (29 per cent) and parents (3 per cent), mainly due to the school's lack of extracurricular activities for students (Liễu 2004–06).

To enhance the quality of education, PF1 has been implementing strategies such as instituting strict mechanisms to enhance quality education for students; promoting autonomy and accountability in management; and ensuring educational equity. PF1 has built its own strict set of mechanisms to ensure and enhance quality education for students. To ensure a high rate of students entering university, PF1 has been setting strict selection criteria that focused on students' abilities and their results from their primary and lower-secondary education. The school also provides extra tuition (extra study) to help slower students meet the requirements of the curriculum. The school provides elective subjects according to students' interest and their needs for university entrance exams (maths, physics, chemistry, for block A; literature, English, history, for block C). To help students perform well in the entrance exams, the school always sets mock exams for practice (Liễu 2004–06).

PF1 also hires highly qualified teachers. A total of 8.5 per cent of teachers have doctoral degrees and another 10–14 per cent have master degrees. The percentage of teachers with bachelor degrees exceeds 77 per cent. Teachers are assessed by both students and parents. Renewal of teacher contracts is contingent on student and parent assessment as well as students' performance. Teachers are paid based on an evaluation of the quality of their teaching, not on their work experience, academic qualifications, or rank. Professor Văn Như Cương, principal of PF1, expressed his philosophy following way:

> The secret of the high quality [of] our school is respect for educational quality … The school always provides truly quality teaching and learning, as well as an honest assessment of the (individual) student's learning results.

Professor Cương has built his school image and competed with other schools based on the educational quality of his programmes. According to Professor Cương, delivering quality is the best way for the school to gain a good reputation; better than any other kind of marketing. At first, PF1 became famous through parents' word of mouth and its reputation has since spread through the mass media. Indeed, PF1 has become almost famous in Vietnam. Professor Cương monitors students' performance in many ways: their attendence, their academic performance, and their home life (by liaising closely with parents). If a student is absent without a note from a parent, the school immediately calls the parents. The school uses 75 per cent of tuition fees to invest in student learning, new teaching equipment, and building a friendly learning environment for both students and teachers. Administrative costs take up only seven per cent of total expenditure because there are only six administrative staff members: three on the principal's board and three for administrative work and student services (Liễu 2004–06).

As a private school, PF1 has greater autonomy in its operation. The school has a very flexible management scheme, but one that emphasizes self-accountability among staff. The curricula are tailored to students' needs and abilities and while the content and standards of assessment exceed MOET norms. PF1 sets its own schedule for educational activities and sometimes devotes more time and energy to certain subjects. For example, MOET requires schools to allocate one 45-minute lesson period (*tiết*) to cover a famous poem by Nhuận Cầm. But because the poem is long, and to help students absorb its content and artistry, PF1 has allocated eight lessons to it and invited the poet himself to come and talk with the students. If students have difficulty in learning any given topic or skill, teachers will carry out further instruction, while in public schools teachers will only reexamine students without extensively revisiting the materials. The principal, teachers, and staff are constantly aware of market conditions, listen to parents' and students' needs, and negotiate with families to set appropriate tuition fees (Liễu 2004–06).

PF1 has simple but effective administrative procedures and structures. The school has no middle managers; teachers work directly with the principal as they are specialists in their subject areas. One teacher can act as head teacher for several classes. Teachers are invited to participate in planning courses and other activities. The school also encourages input from students, parents, and teachers concerning the running of the school. All students are treated equally and the school attempts to develop students according to their individual abilities. Professor Cương considers the principal's heart and vision as important factors for the success of any school in today's economic environment (Liễu 2004–06).

Private (People-Founded) School 2 (PF2) (Liễu 2004–06)

PF2, in contrast with PF1, educates a general student population, but caters to low-achieving students (17–18 per cent of the total students) and students with behavioural problems (20 per cent). With these students, PF2 has implemented some special strategies to enhance its education quality and help students improve their behaviour and orient them in choosing the right career for themselves.

The school sets placement tests, classifies students into different groups, and applies appropriate pedagogical methods to each group. It modifies the curriculum by spending extra time on subjects students find difficult. This has enabled students to achieve better academic results. Of forty students (in grade 12) who participated in the survey, two improved their overall performance from good to excellent and two others from average to good. According to the school's records, the percentage of good and fairly good students has increased year by year (from the school year 2002–03 to 2003–04 the percentage of good students increased from 0.9 per cent to 1.5 per cent; while the percentage of fairly good students increased from 22.9 per cent to 25.1 per cent, but slightly fell to 22.6 per cent in 2009 because of low inputs of students this year). The percentage of students with good ethics has increased from 36.5 per cent in 2002–03 to 43.4 per cent in 2003–04 and to 49.5 per cent in 2008–09 (Table 4.4).

TABLE 4.4
Quality of Student learning in PF2

	2002–03 (Total number of students: 790)	2003–04 (Total number of students: 867)	2008–09 (Total number of students: 1,258)	% Students Entering University
Learning Result				
Excellent	0.9%	1.5%	1.3%	10%
Good	22.9%	25.1%	22.6%	
Average	57.8%	55.0%	54.4%	
Bad	18.2%	17.6%	21.0%	
Ethics				
Good	36.5%	43.4%	49.5%	
Fairly good	44.1%	42.6%	39.0%	
Average	17.8%	10.8%	10.2%	
Bad	1.5%	3.5%	1.3%	

To help students with behavioural issues, the school has implemented diverse extra- and co-curricular activities that help students develop meaning to their lives and encourage them to spend more time in useful activities. The school invites famous speakers to talk to students to provide them with potential role models; builds a close relationship with parents; and carries out career guidance activities. It has implemented five basic principles for teachers in an effort to promote good behaviour among its students:

1. Accept the character and appreciate the challenges facing individual students;
2. Give a fair and objective assessment of all students;
3. Help students recognize their strengths and overcome their weaknesses;
4. Help students integrate into collective and community activties and appreciate the benefits of doing so;
5. Inspire students in a way that makes them adhere to educational rules and responsibilities.

The school credits these principles and school practices with reducing behavioural problems among its students. Ninety-eight per cent of parents and all students who took part in our survey were satisfied with the school. Like PF1, PF2 has very flexible and simple administrative procedures; there are no middle managers, and no delays in approving decisions or responding to students' needs and requests.

Discussion

The way PF1 and PF2 operate is very clearly market-oriented in nature; that is, both schools focus on and satisfy consumer needs; identify market segments; implement flexible management styles; compete through continuous enhancement of education quality; and build their school image. In addition, these schools have autonomy and greater internal accountability in their management; they have the right to hire teachers and pay them salaries based on the school's own budget; they can negotiate with parents on tuition fees; and use the entire school budget on school requirements. The principals are quite creative in their management strategies. Because these two schools target different students, they have different ways to meet the needs and demands of their clients. We can summarize the ways the two schools manage their activities according to market princples, as in Table 4.5.

TABLE 4.5
Market Management Mechanisms of PF1 and PF2 Schools

	Policies for Implementation of both PF1 +PF2	Other policies of PF1	Other policies of PF2
Quality	Real teaching, real learning, real assessment		
Students	Set assessment standards Classify students into groups Individualize students Set incentive policies to encourage students to learn Set strict control and high demands on their learning		Diversify student activities, inspire their ambitions
Teachers	Hire highly qualified teachers Enhance teachers' professionalism, especially develop professionalism of young teachers Pay salary based on teaching quality Build a good professional environment		Choose and develop warm hearted, patient, and compassionate teachers
Management	Autonomy in hiring teachers; using budget; setting tuition fees Flexible in implementing educational curricula Simple administrative procedures Carry out formative and summative assessment of student learning Good flow of information Building a strategic plan Implementing market segment and marketing	Have market sensibility, know and implement management based on law	Autonomy democracy humanity flexibility creativity
Parents	Involve parents in student learning and in school management		Involve parents in re-educating children

Source: Liễu (2004–06).

The new market-oriented trends in education that private schools have brought to Vietnam have contributed to new pedagogical developments; created different learning opportunities according to need; and helped education in Vietnam become more democratic and decentralized. Although the private system in Vietnam is still modest in scale, it has already created a competitive environment among public and private schools and among private schools themselves that help to enhance education quality. With the new government policies mentioned above, greater autonomy and freedom, private schools will firmly establish themselves in the educational system and may contribute to the development of the system as a whole.

The experiences of PF1 and PF2 and other schools suggest ways Vietnam's Government might assist all schools. Recommendations can be drawn from these case studies to help schools in the country to develop better. The government should grant greater autonomy to all schools in the education system and enhance schools' accountablity to help them operate creatively and effectively. The government should use market principles to enhance the functioning of the education system, especially higher and professional education, where responsiveness to labour markets is most important. The government should take measures to facilitate the adoption of international best practices (for example, develop teachers' and educational leaders' abilities, and apply ICT in teaching, learning, and administration). The government also needs to develop and implement further dedicated policies for private schools and evaluate their effectiveness regularly.

References

Bộ Giáo dục và Đào tạo (4 December 2004). *Quy định tạm thời về kiểm định chất lượng trường đại học* ban hành kèm theo Quyết định số 38/2004/QĐ-BGD&ĐT ngày 02 tháng 12 năm 2004 của Bộ trưởng Bộ Giáo dục và Đào tạo (Ministry of Education and Training [4 December 2004], *Temporary regulations of Higher Education Institution Accreditation* issued based on The Minister's Decision number38/2004/QĐ-BGD&ĐT, 2 December 2004).

———— (12 May 2009). *Ban hành Quy định về tiêu chuẩn đánh giá chất lượng giáo dục trường trung học cơ sở* (Ministry of Education and Training [12 May 2009], *Code of Criteria for evaluating education quality of secondary schools*).

Phạm Văn Đại (7 March 2009). Giáo dục Hà Nội: Đổi mới và hội nhập, *Hội thảo "Nhà trường Việt Nam trong nền kinh tế thị trường và trước bối cảnh hội nhập quốc tế"*, Hội đồng giáo dục quốc gia, Đề tài độc lập cấp Nhà nước "Phát triển giáo dục Việt Nam trong nền kinh tế thị trường và trước bối cảnh hội nhập quốc tế" 2008–09. (Pham Van Dai [7 March 2009]), Hanoi's Education: Renovation and Integration, Workshop proceedings *"Vietnam's schools in the market economy and in the context of globalization"*, in the scope of the Government Independent Research Project "Develop Vietnam's Education in the market economy and in the context of globalization", 2008–09, Vietnam's National Education Council).

Gumport P.J. and B. Sporn *Institutional Adaptation: Demands for Management Reform and University Administration.* Stanford University: National Center for Postsecondary Improvement, 1999.

Hanoi Department of Education. *Annual Education Report,* 2000–01.

Ho Chi Minh City Education Department. *Statistics for 2006–07,* <http://edu. hochiminhcity.gov.vn>.

In Tin Tức. *Da Nang chưa có trường THPT tư thục, dân lập chất lượng tốt,* (Da Nang has no high quality private schools), 13 December 2006.

Dương Kiều Linh (4–7 December 2008). Giáo dục phổ thông ngoài công lập Thành phố Hồ Chí Minh trong bối cảnh toàn cầu hóa, *Hội thảo Việt Nam học lần thứ III: "Việt Nam Hội nhập và Phát triển",* Hanoi. (Duong Kieu Linh [4–7 December 2008]; Non-Pubilic education in Ho Chi Minh City in the globalization, Third Conference on Vietnam Studies "Vietnam Integration and Development", Hanoi).

Trần Thị Bích Liễu. *Tìm hiểu khả năng thích ứng của các trường học vùng thành thị với cơ chế kinh tế thị trường định hướng xã hội chủ nghĩa ở Việt Nam và việc đưa nội dung kinh tế thị trường vào chương trình đào tạo hiệu trưởng trường học, Đề tài nghiên cứu khoa học cấp Bộ mã số* SP-0-101, 2006 (Study of the adaptive ability of urban schools to the market economy in Vietnam and how to incorporate the knowledge of market economy into training programmes for school principals, report to the Ministry of Education and Training, Vietnam, The Ministerial level research project] — code SP-0-101, 2006.

Ministry of Education and Training. *Education Law.* Hanoi: 2005*a.*

Ministry of Education and Training. *Quyết định của Bộ Giáo dục và Đào tạo số 20/2005/QĐ-BGD&ĐT ngày 24 tháng 6 năm 2005 về việc phê duyệt dự án quy hoạch phát triển xã hội giáo dục giai đoạn 2005–2010.* (Decision number 20/2005/QD-BGD&DT issued on 24 June 2005 on approval of the project for "Development of a Learning Society Period 2005–2010], 2005*b*).

Thời Báo Viet.com. "Ngôi trường có 100 per cent học sinh đỗ tốt nghiệp" (A school has 100 per cent of students pass the National High Secondary Exams), 17 June 2007, <www.danang.gov.vn/home>.

Tuoi tre online. THPT dân lập: Bao giờ hết nỗi lo "đầu vào"?! (People founded schools: When will the worries of the input students end?!) 31 July 2005, <www.tuoitre.com.vn>.

Thu Nguyễn (20 November 2008). *Lương Thế Vinh thương hiệu của niềm tin,* <http://luongthevinh.com.vn/>.

vnmedia. "*Xếp hạng 200 trường THPT điểm thi ĐH cao nhất 2008*" ("Ranking 200 upper-secondary schools of top university entrance exam scores in 2008"), 13 January 2009, <http://f.tin247.com/>.

Vietbao.com, "Trường phổ thông quốc tế, quốc tế đến đâu?" 19 May 2006, <http://vietbao.vn/Giao-duc/Truong-pho-thong-quoc-te-quoc-te-den-dau/>.

Vietnam Net. Máy chấm trắc nghiệm phát hiện nhầm 400 bài phạm qui (Test grade machine misrecognized 400 test answer sheets). 15 June 2007.

Vietnam Net. "Top 100 trường THPT có điểm thi ĐH cao" ("Top 100 of high gained entrance university exam high secondary schools").

Vũ Văn Phúc, Trịnh Minh Châu. *Một số vấn đề về kinh tế thị trường định hướng XHCN ở nước ta* (Some issues of the socialist-oriented market economy). NXB Chính trị Quốc gia, 2000.

Watts M. *What is a Market Economy?* Washington: US Department of State, 2004.

5

SCHOOL DROPOUT TRENDS IN VIETNAM FROM 1998 TO 2006

Bùi Thái Quyên

INTRODUCTION

After more than twenty years of *Đổi Mới* (*renovation*) which commenced in 1986, Vietnam has made remarkable achievements both socially and economically. Since 1991, Vietnam's annual GDP growth has averaged over seven per cent. Education and training have also undergone positive changes and the people's general knowledge has increased substantially. By the year 2000, the state had carried out literacy programmes and established "universal" (*phổ cập*) primary education (UPE) in all localities. (According to state standards, a province/city to be considered reaching UPE has more than 80 per cent of children in the area finishing Grade five by age fourteen. In the mountainous or difficult areas this rate is set at 70 per cent). By December of 2008, forty-seven out of sixty-three provinces and cities had universal enrolment in lower-secondary education (ULSE).[1] The government is now planning UPE and ULSE for all pupils reaching the requisite age for those particular levels of education, in addition to implementing universal upper-secondary education (UUSE) in some localities. Vietnam also plans to complete universal lower-secondary education (USE) for all provinces and cities in 2010.[2] However, ensuring the sustainability of UPE and USE remains a big challenge for Vietnamese education as the phenomenon of dropouts remains.

To help clarify the magnitude of dropouts, this chapter analyses dropout trends of Vietnamese pupils from 1998 to 2006, using the Vietnam Living Standards Survey (VNLSS) data. The analysis focuses on primary and lower-secondary levels of schooling, since universalizing education and retaining universal education at these two levels are stated goals of the Vietnamese Government. The analysis also attempts to analyse dropouts across regions, expenditure groups, sex, and age. Finally, the analysis examines reasons children drop out of school. A technical appendix provides details of the statistical methods employed in this analysis.

SCHOOL DROPOUT RATES FROM 1990 TO 2008: GENERAL TRENDS

It is important to emphasize that the term dropouts in Vietnam refers to students who cease attending school during the school year. Dropouts do not include students who discontinue their studies after a given school year. Data on dropouts are important, though they do not capture the full number of students who discontinue their studies. This said, dropout figures in Vietnam have fluctuated from year to year. At the three educational levels (primary school, lower-secondary school, and upper-secondary school), the highest dropout ratios are for upper-secondary school while the lowest figures are for primary school (see Figure 5.1). Since the 1999–2000, school year, dropout ratios for primary and lower-secondary school have declined markedly. By contrast, the ratio for the upper-secondary school level has grown. Reductions in dropouts have helped the government meet its development goals. For example, by the year 2000, more than 75 per cent of total pupils had completed the fifth grade by the requisite age of ten years.

In combination with data from the General Statistics Office (GSO), VNLSS data indicate that the primary dropout ratio has declined sharply, from nearly 12 per cent in 1990–91 to only three per cent by 2006–07; this includes a 1.63 percentage drop in 1999–2000. Dropout rates have also declined in lower-secondary education, from 8.51 per cent in 1999–2000 to 5.2 per cent 2004–05. These reductions are in line with Vietnam's education policies and strategies[3] and its international commitments.[4]

FIGURE 5.1
Dropout Rate According to Educatinal Level, 2000–07

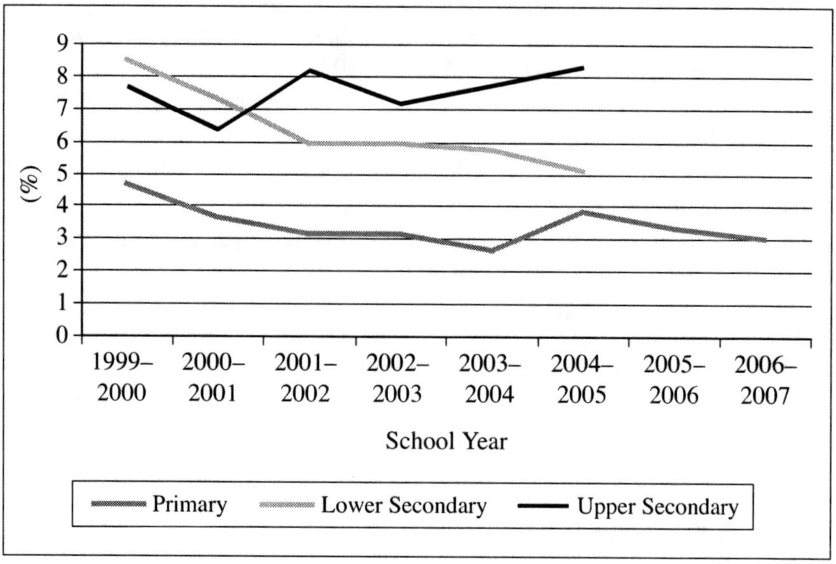

Source: Ministry of Education and Training (MOET) <http://www.moet.gov.vn/ ?page=11.10&view=9264>.

Since the second half of 2007, Vietnam has faced increasingly difficult macroeconomic conditions. The increasing price of oil, food, and other materials on world and local markets combined with an overheated domestic economy to produce rampant inflation. Natural disasters, livestock epidemics (notably "blue ear" swine disease) and plant blights have greatly affected the agricultural sector. Daily life is affected as well, and hence the dropout situation is also affected. But how great has the impact been on dropouts? According to GSO data, in 2007–08, over 215,000 students dropped out, accounting for nearly 1.4 per cent of all Vietnam's pupils; this includes 32,000 (or 0.5 per cent of primary pupils); 105,000 lower-secondary education (accounting for 1.8 per cent), and 78,000 upper-secondary school students (or 2.6 per cent of upper-secondary school students).[5] In the first semester of 2008–09 , 86,000 out of 15.3 million students in primary and secondary education had dropped out of school.[6] These dropout rates are consistent with previous years, suggesting that while price increases may have affected household expenditures on education, they have not resulted in dramatic waves of dropouts. Whether or not price increases associated with global economic shocks lead to future declines in enrolments requires further investigation. Our discussion now shifts to a more detailed consideration of dropout trends across different socio-economic indicators.

SCHOOL DROPOUTS BY REGION

Over the last ten years the percentage of primary dropouts declined significantly from 11.6 per cent (1990–91) to 0.5 per cent (2007–08). Declines have been significant in most regions. Dropout rates in 2003 in the Red River delta were an eighth of that recorded in 1990. In north-central and south-central Vietnam, 2003 dropout rates were one seventh of that recorded in 1990. Other regions' primary dropout ratio for this period fell by three times on average. However, the regional variation is significant.

FIGURE 5.2
Primary School Dropout Rate by Region

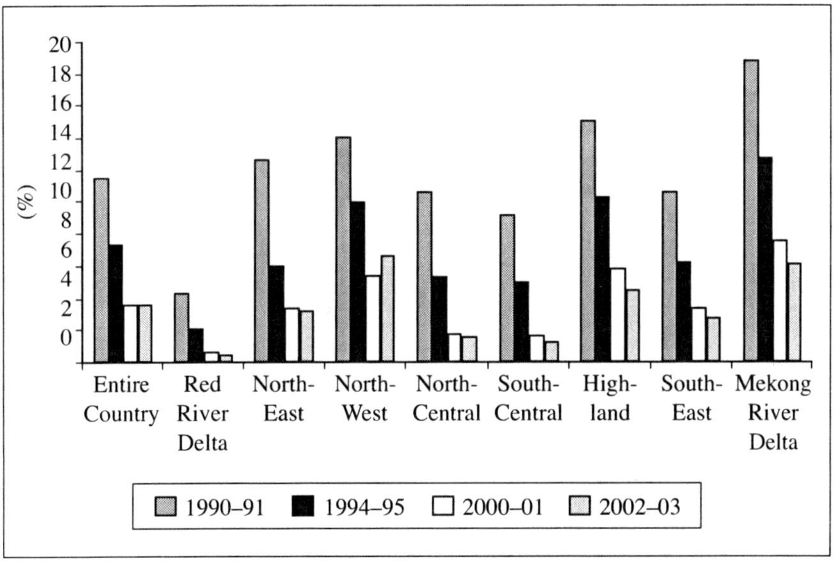

Source: Vietnam Social Development Data in the 1990s and Early Twenty-first Century, Statistical Publishing House, Hanoi.

The Red River delta has the lowest ratio of primary dropouts. In 2000–01, the region's primary dropout rate was 0.72 per cent, compared with the national rate of 3.67 per cent. In 2002–03, the Red River delta's primary dropout rate was an eighth of that recorded in 1990–91. By contrast, the dropout ratio in the Mekong River delta was the highest. In 2000–01, the primary dropout rate in the Mekong delta was twice the national average and ten times higher than that of the Red River delta region. In 2002–03, this ratio was 6.22 per cent, whereas the ratio for the entire country fell to 3.66 per cent. Poor transport links is usually cited as the most significant reason for primary dropouts, as the canals and ditches that link communities to schools are subject to frequent flooding. In the absence of significant new infrastructural upgrades, forecasts of rising water levels in the coming years suggest transport problems may well worsen.

As in primary education, the Mekong River delta has the highest lower-secondary dropout ratio, whereas the Red River delta has the lowest. In the period 1999–2003, the north-west region's dropout ratio declined markedly, by more than 2.1 times, whereas the ratios in other regions declined between 1.3 times and 1.6 times.

FIGURE 5.3
Lower Secondary School Dropout Rate by Region

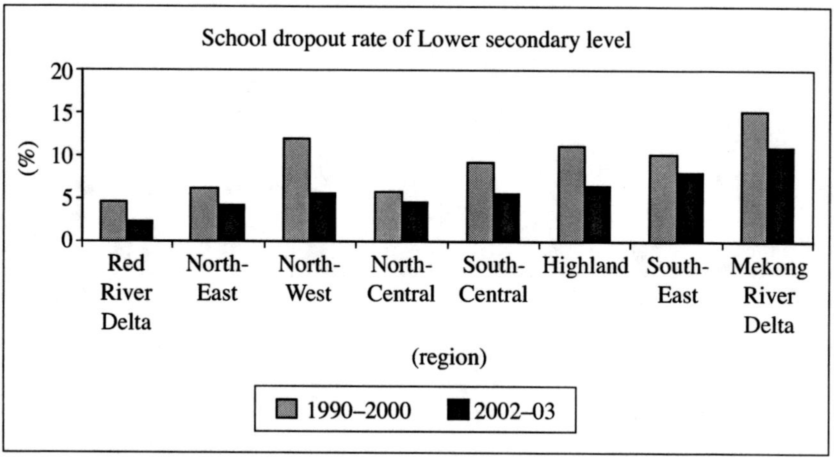

Source: Vietnam Social Development Data in the 1990s and Early Twenty-first Century, Statistical Publishing House, Hanoi.

SCHOOL DROPOUTS BY AGE GROUP

Generally, from 2002 onwards, the dropout ratio has fallen quite markedly for all age groups. However, the ratio differs between each group. The highest dropout ratio was in the 15–16 age group and the lowest in the 8–10 age group. Household circumstances and the development of children affect the dynamics of dropouts. In the youngest age groups, families dictate school attendance. In the third, fourth, and fifth grades of primary school, children tend to become more interested in learning and attending school, therefore, the ratio is quite low and stable. At the same time, primary education is the least costly level of education as it is not subject to fees, although there are other expenses. After primary schooling, the costliness of education tends to increase with grade level. Whether or not this is a principal reason for dropouts is addressed below. Nevertheless, from the age of eleven onward (lower-secondary school), the dropout ratio steadily increases as the child gets older, with the highest ratio being for the aged sixteen group; 40 per cent in 2002, and 28.8 per cent in 2006.

FIGURE 5.4
School Dropout Rate by Age

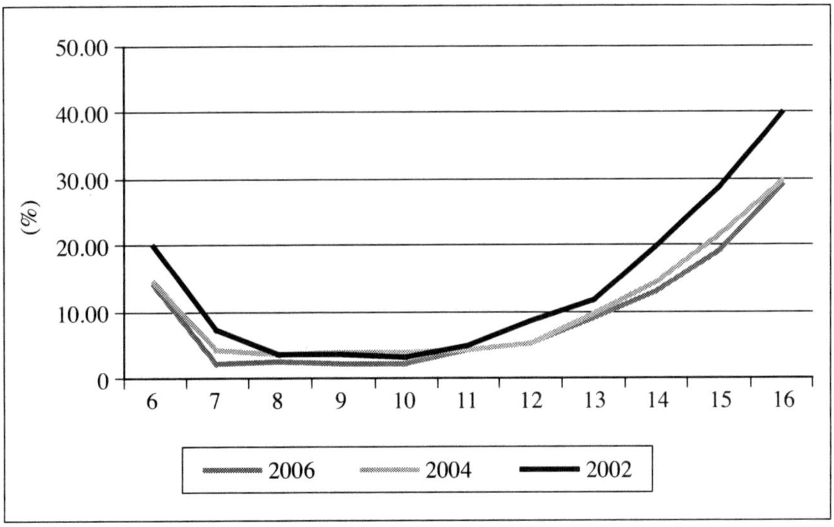

Source: Writer's analysis of VNLSS 2002, 2004, 2006 data.

SCHOOL DROPOUT RATIO BY EXPENDITURE QUINTILE

Income has a strong association with dropouts. The poorest quintile households have the highest dropout ratios. Dropout ratios decline as household income increases. In the 6–10 age group (primary level), the dropout ratio of pupils in poor households was 5.7 times higher than that of rich households. For the 15–17 age group (upper-secondary level), this ratio is 3.2 times higher (see Figure 5.5).

In the period 2002–06, the odds ratio differed by age and expenditure group. Nonetheless, dropout ratios among pupils from poor households has declined across all age levels. For instance, between 2002 and 2006, dropouts in this group fell (roughly) from 12 to 9 per cent for the 6–10 age group; 20 to 16 per cent for the 11–14 age group; and 58 to 51 per cent for the 15–17 age group. Declining dropout rates among poor household no doubt reflect great efforts put forth by parents in low-income households. On the other hand, the high dropout rate (over 50 per cent) in the 15-17 age groups is suggestive of financial and other obstacles such households face. At the other end of the continuum, one observes moderate fluctuations across age groups of pupils from rich households. For the 15–17 age group dropouts rose from 13 per cent in 2002 to 16 per cent in 2006 (see Table 5.1).

FIGURE 5.5
School Dropout Rate in 2006 by Quintile and Age

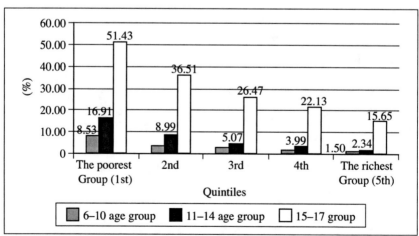

Source: Writer's analysis of VNLSS 2002, 2004, 2006 data.

TABLE 5.1
Proportion of School Dropouts by Age Group, Quintiles and Year

| | Age groups | | | | | |
| | 6–10 | | 11–14 | | 15–17 | |
	Poorest Households (1st)	Richest Households (5th)	Poorest Households (1st)	Richest Households (5th)	Poorest Households (1st)	Richest Households (5th)
2002	12.32	2.18	20.27	2.59	58.01	13.22
2004	11.58	2.31	17.52	3.46	51.90	13.14
2006	8.53	1.50	16.91	2.34	51.43	15.65

Source: Writer's analysis of VNLSS' 2002, 2004, 2006 data.

TABLE 5.2
Proportion of School Dropouts by Year and Gender

	2002		2004		2006	
	Boy	Girl	Boy	Girl	Boy	Girl
Primary School	6.92	6.97	5.80	6.23	5.47	4.26
Lower Secondary School	9.67	12.42	8.45	9.92	9.49	8.32
Upper Secondary School	34.64	41.76	30.75	34.50	33.21	30.35

Source: Writer's analysis of VNLSS' 2002, 2004, 2006 data.

SCHOOL DROPOUT RATIO BY GENDER

It is widely assumed that girls are more likely to be asked by their families to withdraw from school. Does this mean higher dropout rates for girls? Table 5.2 shows that in 2002 and 2004, the proportion of girls dropping out was higher than boys at all levels of education. However, 2006 data show sharper declines in the dropout ratio for girls than for boys, bringing dropout rates for girls lower than those for boys (Table 5.2).

At the primary level, the dropout ratio for girls fell from nearly 7 per cent in 2002 to 4 per cent in 2006, whereas boys' dropout rates declined less significantly, but from a lower base. At the upper-secondary level, the dropout ratio for girls declined a remarkable 11.42 per cent in the period 2002–06, whereas the ratio for boys fell only slightly, by 1.4 per cent. What accounts for these declines? State officials would no doubt point to the efforts of government agencies and ministries in implementing various new laws aimed at promoting the education and protection of children, and girls in particular. A causal link between policies and outcomes would require analysis beyond the scope of this chapter.

SCHOOL DROPOUT RATIO BY AREA
(RURAL/URBAN)

The differences between urban and rural areas strongly influenced the ratio of dropouts at all levels of education. Generally speaking, pupils in rural areas drop out more than the ones in urban areas. This trend is reflected in Figure 5.6. As the level of education increases, so does the

FIGURE 5.6
School Dropout Ratio by Area

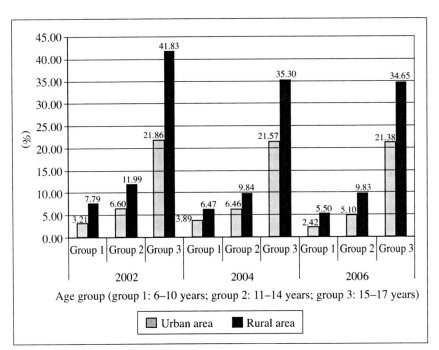

Age group (group 1: 6–10 years; group 2: 11–14 years; group 3: 15–17 years)

☐ Urban area   ■ Rural area

Source: Writer's analysis of VNLSS' 2002, 2004, 2006 data.

gap between the two areas. At different levels of education, the ratio of dropouts in urban and rural areas has declined. For instance, the ratio fell from 4.58 per cent in 2002 to 3 per cent in 2006 at the primary school level (6–10 age group), and from roughly 20 per cent to 13 per cent for the upper-secondary school level (15–17 age group) during the same period. In both urban and rural areas, the dropout ratios at all levels of education have fallen quite significantly. In urban areas, the ratio fell from 3.21 per cent (2002) to 2.42 per cent (2006) for primary school level (6–10 age group), and from 6.6 per cent (2002) to 5.10 per cent (2006) for lower-secondary school level (11–14 age group). In rural areas, the downward trend was notable, from 7.79 per cent (2002) to 5.5 per cent (2006) for primary school level, and from 11.99 per cent (2002) to 9.83 per cent (2006) for lower-secondary school level (see Figure 5.6).

REASONS FOR DROPPING OUT OF SCHOOL

The above analysis has suggested some reasons dropouts occur at the primary and lower-secondary levels. These factors include the natural environment and socio-economic conditions in different regions/areas; income level of households; and the different priorities assigned to learning for girls and boys. The following section will explore these suspected causes using a Probit model and the "Vietnam Living Standard Surveys" dataset.[7] In the model, the factors influencing dropouts are divided into two separate groups. Group 1 includes pupil characteristics (age, sex, school level); Group 2 includes household characteristics (households' average expenditure, households' expenditure on education, parents' education). Additionally, dropout rates are also influenced by region[8] and area (urban/rural), as well as public expenditure on education.

The likelihood of dropping out of school is influenced by many factors. This study just focuses on two: (1) the characteristics of each pupil: sex, age, school level; (2) the characteristics of households: size (number of members), average annual expenditure (expenditure quintiles[9]), the educational level of households and parents, and the regions/areas where pupils live (urban/rural, eight regions). The choices for these variables are in line with the theoretical assumptions and the available data.

Regression Results

The estimation was calculated by inserting the variables one by one into the models to estimate how the explanatory variables influence the independent variables. In all, this analysis constructed six models. Tabulated results are presented, in Tables 5.3 and 5.4.

Table 5.3 shows that if other elements do not change, the "sex" variable has an inverse ratio to the probability of dropping out of school. In the other words, if the value of sex variable rises (from 1 = male to 2 = female), the probability of dropping out of school is reduced by four per cent in Model 1. This suggests that in 2006, girls were less likely to drop out than boys. Regression results indicate that the age of pupils is positively associated with dropouts. As children get older, the likelihood of them dropping out of school increases by 20 per cent in all models. Results suggest the size of households affects the probability of dropping out, even as dropout rates are falling in large households. Model 2

TABLE 5.3
Variables Affecting the Probability of Dropping Out

	Independent Variables: Dropout Probability					
	1	2	3	4	5	6
Sex	-0.040 (0.055)	-0.050 (0.055)	-0.145* (0.074)	-0.142 (0.074)	-0.136** (0.074)	-0.146** (0.074)
Age	0.204*** (0.012)	0.204*** (0.011)	0.210*** (0.016)	0.212 (0.016)	0.211 (0.016)	0.212 (0.016)
Primary school	-3.066*** (0.093)	-3.064*** (0.094)	-2.707*** (0.163)	-2.709 (0.164)	-2.718 (0.164)	-2.712 (0.166)
Lower secondary school	-3.469*** (0.081)	-3.457*** (0.081)	-2.951*** (0.104)	-2.956 (0.103)	-2.964 (0.103)	-2.962 (0.104)
Upper secondary school	-3.662*** (0.101)	-3.639*** (0.1025)	-3.164*** (0.123)	-3.142 (0.123)	-3.143 (0.123)	-3.147 (0.125)
Household size		0.034** (0.015)	0.046* (0.027)	0.029 (0.028)	0.031 (0.028)	0.032 (0.029)
Household education			-0.064* (0.044)	-0.045 (0.045)	-0.042 (0.046)	-0.041 (0.046)
Spouse's education			-0.0648 (0.054)	-0.055 (0.055)	-0.052 (0.056)	-0.048 (0.058)
Log (annual average expenditure)				-0.170* (0.082)	-0.136 (0.091)	-0.175* (0.096)
Urban/rural					0.128 (0.117)	0.118 (0.117)

TABLE 5.3   *(continued)*

	Independent Variables: Dropout Probability					
	1	*2*	*3*	*4*	*5*	*6*
Red River delta						0.333 (0.214)
North-east						0.124 (0.222)
North-west					−0.259 (0.201)	
North-central						0.274 (0.215)
South-central						0.164 (0.235)
Highlands						0.158 (0.241)
South-east						0.403* (0.239)
Mekong River delta						0.334 (0.225)
Data	9,880	9,880	5,487	5,487	5,487	5,487
Pseudo R2	0.7212	0.7217	0.6343	0.6356	0.6364	0.638

Note: *** p<0.01, ** p<0.05, * p<0.1.
Source: All the regressions based on VNLSS 2006 data are robust.
Table 5.3 used the Probit model. All the models provide a Pseudo R2 that is very high, from 0.6 to 0.7.

TABLE 5.4
Statistic Index Summary

Variable	Obs	Mean	Std. Dev.	Min	Max
School dropouts	9,880	0.1475709	0.3546920	0	1
Sex	9,880	1.4908910	0.4999423	1	2
Age	9,880	12.2511100	3.3055730	6	17
Educational level					
Primary	9,880	0.3297571	0.4701486	0	1
Lower-secondary	9,880	0.3511134	0.4773425	0	1
Upper-secondary	9,880	0.1712551	0.3767508	0	1
Household characteristics					
Household size	9,880	5.17409	1.64598	2	17
Household education	7,246	1.99255	1.40096	0	6
Spouse's education	6,003	1.89855	1.32537	0	6
Annual average expenditure	9,880	4895.682	3559.485	685	67,656
Area					
Urban/rural	9,880	1.797976	0.4015306	1	2
Region					
Red River delta	9,880	0.1658907	0.3720013	0	1
North-east	9,880	0.1419028	0.3489681	0	1
North-west	9,880	0.0623482	0.2417991	0	1
North-central	9,880	0.1275304	0.3335830	0	1
South-central	9,880	0.0973684	0.2964738	0	1
Highlands	9,880	0.0968623	0.2957852	0	1
South-east	9,880	0.1283401	0.3344850	0	1
Mekong River delta	9,880	0.1797571	0.3840044	0	1

Source: Writer's VNLSS 2006 data-based calculation.

indicates that whenever households increase in size by one member, the chance of a child dropping out of school increases by 3.4 per cent.

Not surprisingly, the regression shows a negative relation between households' head (and spouse's) education and the probability of dropping out of school. If the households' head and spouse have a higher education level, the chances that their children will drop out of school are lower. For instance, as the education of households' head (and spouse) increases by one level, the likelihood that their child will drop out will be reduced to 6.4 per cent (see Model 3). Nor is it surprising to find a relation between average annual household income (measured by expenditure data) and dropout rates. Results from Table 5.3 suggest that the probability of a child dropping out of school is reduced when household expenditure increases. Results of Model 5 suggests that if the households' annual average expenditures increase by one per cent, the dropout ratio of their children will be reduced by 13 per cent. Models 5 and 6 show children in rural areas have a higher probability of dropping out of school than do children in urban areas. In these models, "rural" pupils are 12 per cent more likely to drop out.

Perhaps the most interesting finding concerns dropout ratio by sex, as there have been obvious and positive changes. We can see from Table 5.3 that the estimative coefficient shows that the sex variable had an inverse relation with the dropout probability, meaning that whenever the value of gender variable increases from 1 (for boys) to 2 (for girls), the dropout probability declines. The regression results in Table 5.3 are relatively good, as all models have a high value of Pseudo R2 from 0.6 to 0.7.

CONCLUSION

School dropouts refer to students that discontinue their studies during the academic year. The issue of school dropouts is an important one in Vietnam as its prevalence negatively influences the quality of the nation's human resources. From 1999–2000 onward, Vietnam's dropout ratio has sharply declined, especially at the primary and lower-secondary school levels. In the years 1999–2000 and 2002–03, the Red River delta had the lowest dropout ratio whereas the Mekong River delta had the highest ratio at all three levels of education. By age, the 7–10 group is quite stable and the dropout ratio is the lowest, but as pupils get older, the dropout ratio climbs. This is because age has a positive relation with the ability to work. Household income is one of the most important factors affecting the likelihood of pupils dropping out of school. In Model 6, the coefficient of the variable is (–0.17), whereas the influence of other variables is extremely small, for instance, the household size coefficient is (0.032). This mean, if household annual expenditure increases one per cent, the likelihood of a child dropping out will decline 17 per cent, while if the number of household members increases by one, the likelihood of a child dropping out would increase by only 3.2 per cent. Thus, households with higher average expenditure will have fewer dropouts.

Perhaps the most interesting finding concerns dropout ratio by sex as there have been obvious and positive changes. In 2002 and 2004, the ratio of girls at all levels dropping out was higher than that for boys, whereas 2006 data show that the ratio has declined faster for girls than for boys. Overall, because of time limits, this study has not evaluated the impact of some variables such as households' expenditure on education and the government's expenditure on education. More needs to be done on the variables affecting educational achievement. Identifying the reasons for pupils dropping out of school requires further investigation.

Notes

1. Socio-Economics situation 2008 of Vietnam, GSO, <http://www.gso.gov.vn/default.aspx?tabid=413&thangtk=12/2008>.
2. Socio-economics development plan for five years, 2006–10.
3. At the "International Conference on Education for All" in Jomtien, Thailand, in 1990, Vietnam signed the "World Declaration on Education for All" and the "Action Plan to Meet Basic Learning Needs". Following this, Vietnam organized a national conference on "Education for All" in October 1992 and set out objectives to be achieved by the year 2000. One of the objectives was to reach UPE, and reduce the dropout rate from 12 per cent to below 6 per cent by the year 2000.
4. Since the1990s, the Vietnamese Government has promulgated a number of laws on education and training sector development, specifically: The Universal Primary Education Law promulgated by the National Assembly, 12 August 1991; Constitution of the Socialist Republic of Vietnam September 1992; the Education and Training Law, 2 December 1998 and amended, 14 June 2005; National Assembly Resolution 40/2000/QH10, 9 December

2000 on curriculum reform for general education; National Assembly Resolution 41/2000/QH10, 9 December 2000 on implementing ULSE; National Assembly Resolution 37/2004/QH11, 3 December 2004 on Education; Decision of the Government 73/2005/QĐ-TTg, 6 April 2005, promulgating the action plan of the government in implementing Resolution 37/2004/QH11 and others.

5. <http://www.gso.gov.vn/default.aspx?tabid=413&thangtk=12/2008>.

6. <http://www.vtc.vn/xahoi/giaoduc/gan-90-ngan-hoc-sinh-bo-hoc/209122/index. htm>.

7. The Probit model is a model of standard probability, and it uses a dummy variable which represents dropout trends. The dummy variable equals 1 or 0, based on actual dropouts at a particular time. The decision for attending or dropping out of school depends on the latent variable. This latent variable cannot be observed directly and is influenced by explanatory variables (such as age, gender, education level, average household expenditure, expenditure on education, educational level of parents, and regions/areas). The bigger the latent variable, the higher the probability that a child will drop out of school. The data used for regression are VNLSS 2006 data. All observations in the data are for all those in the population ranging in age from six to seventeen, at the time of survey who do not attend school (these figures do not include those on summer vacation at the time of the survey).

8. Eight regions: north-east, north-west, Red River delta, north central, south central, highlands, south-east, Mekong River delta.

9. In the VHLSS, there are five quintiles, the first quintile is 20 per cent of the poorest households that have the lowest expenditure level, and the fifth quintile is 20 per cent of the richest households that have the highest expenditure level.

References

Behrman, Jere R. and James C. Knowles. "Household Income and Child Schooling in Vietnam". *The World Bank Economic Review* 13 (1999): 211–56.

Bray, M. *Counting the Full Cost: Parental and Community Financing of Education in East Asia, A Collaborative Report between WB and UN Children Fund*. World Bank, 1996.

Choi, G.S. *An Analysis of Economic Returns to Investment in Education* (in Korean). 2001.

Đặng Bá Lâm. *Giáo dục Việt Nam trong thập kỷ đầu của thế kỷ 21 — Một chiến lược phát triển* [Vietnamese Education in the First Decade of the 21st Century — A Development Strategy]. Hanoi: Educational Publishing House, 2003.

Glewwe, P. and H.A. Patrinos. "The Role of the Private Sector in Education in Vietnam: Evidence from the Vietnam Living Standard Survey, 1992–93". Background Paper on the Vietnam Education Finance Sector study (VEFSS). Washington D.C.: The World Bank, Policy Research Department and Human Development Department, 1996.

Glewwe, P. and H.G. Jacoby. "Economic Growth and the Demand for Education: Is there any wealth effect?" Forthcoming, *Journal of Development Economics*, 2000.

Ministry of Education and Training. *Thống kê giáo dục 1945–1995* [Educational statistics, 1945–1995]. Hanoi: Educational Communication Central, Ministry of Education and Training (MOET), 1995.

————. *Đánh giá 10 năm Đổi Mới giáo dục 1986–1996* [Evaluation of 10-year educational renovation, 1986–96]. Hanoi: Ministry of Education and Training (MOET), 1997.

————. *Chiến lược phát triển giáo dục 2001–2010*, [Educational Development Strategy, 2001–2010], Hanoi: Ministry of Education and Training (MOET), 2001.

Pham Minh Hac. *Giáo dục Việt Nam trước ngưỡng cửa thế kỷ XXI*. [Vietnamese Education on its Way to Reaching the 21st Century]. Hanoi: National Politics Publishing House, 1999.

Socialist Republic of Vietnam. *Chương trình mục tiêu quốc gia về giáo dục và đào tạo đến năm 2005. Quyết định số 26/2003/QĐ-TTg, 17 tháng 2* [National Education and Training Goals Towards 2005. No. 26/2003/QD-TTg Decision, 17 February], 2003.

————. *Vietnam: Managing Public Expenditure for Poverty Reduction and Growth — Vol. I: Cross-sectoral Issues*. Hanoi: Financial Publishing House, 2005a.

————. *Vietnam: Managing Public Expenditure for Poverty Reduction and Growth — Vol. II: Sectoral Issues*. Hanoi: Financial Publishing House, 2005b.

General Statistics Office. *Điều tra mức sống dân cư 1992–1993*. [Household living standards survey, 1992–1993]. Hanoi, 1993.

————. *Điều tra mức sống dân cư 1997–1998* [Household living standards survey, 1997–1998], Hanoi, 1998.

————. *Điều tra mức sống dân cư 2002–2004* [Household living standards survey, 2002–2004]. Hanoi, 2004.

————. *Điều tra mức sống dân cư 2006* [Household living standards survey 2006]. Hanoi, 2007.

————. *Niên giám thống kê các năm* [Statistical yearbook].

United Nations Country Team Vietnam. *MDGs and Vietnam's Socio-Economic Development Plan 2006–2010*. Hanoi, November 2005.

Vo Tri Thanh and Trinh Quang Long. "Can Vietnam Achieve One of its Millennium Development Goals? An Analysis of Schooling Dropouts of Children". William Davidson Institute (WDI) Working Papers, 2005.

World Bank. *Vietnam Poverty Assessment and Strategy, Country Report*. Washington D.C., 1995*a*.

———. *Priorities and Strategies for Education*. Washington, D.C., 1995*b*.

———. *Priorities and Strategies for Education: A World Bank Review* (*Development in Practice*). Washington, DC: World Bank, 1995*c*.

———. *Vietnam: Education Financing Sector Study*. Human Resources Operations Division, Country Department I, East Asia and Pacific Region, 1996.

6

"THEY THINK WE DON'T VALUE SCHOOLING"
Paradoxes of Education in the Multi-Ethnic Central Highlands of Vietnam

Trương Huyền Chi

Based on a sociological survey and ethnographic field research conducted in 2005 in Đắk Nông Province,[1] this chapter places education at the intersection of ethnicity and class in Vietnam's Central Highlands, a region that not only integrates with national and global markets, but also hosts intensified interaction between indigenous peoples and multi-ethnic migrants. Examination of two prime agents in education — teachers and parents — and their views of education and of one another — reveals that instead of being a site of cultural transmission or a meritocratic springboard for upward mobility, schools in this multi-ethnic setting reproduce existing structural inequalities among ethnic groups.

Following a brief introduction to Đắk Nông province and its education system, I detail the ways in which teachers and parents there perceive and talk about themselves and each other and the kinds of expectations parents have for their children. By identifying areas of convergence as well as disagreement among the concerns *of* and *about* teachers, I suggest that parents and educators are not communicating effectively and, in fact, are not engaged in a genuine dialogue. The missing dialogue between these two groups of education agents, I contend, stems from a more fundamental distance between indigenous residents and migrants that is in turn rooted in the recent history of the local political economy.

This chapter also links M'Nông's schooling outcomes with their social mobility, or lack thereof.[2] As discussed by M'Nông parents and observed through ethnographic fieldwork, the paradox of centralized examinations and diploma-based recruiting policy of local enterprises is complicated by on-site ethnic tensions. I argue that the existing mode of education not only fails to transform interlocking ethnic class divisions, but breeds exclusion, as is seen in the failures of schools to produce M'Nông graduates to fill a wide range of jobs that are increasingly available in the fast industrializing local economy. The chapter shows how ethnic and class relations shape schooling outcomes and how education is a social field in which differences and inequalities are lived and felt.

Overall, however, this chapter does not presume that Kinh and the M'Nông teachers are totally indifferent and that M'Nông students just react passively. Instead, by presenting the unmediated perceptions and voices of both the practitioners and supposed beneficiaries, as well as a broad range of life aspirations that give meaning to their pursuits, I hope to make visible their intentionality in the education endeavour. This agency of intention, or "people's project in the world and their ability to both formulate and enact them" (Ortner 2001, pp. 78–79), proves a fruitful way to explore the alternative spaces of upbringing for M'Nông youths. I provide examples of spaces towards the end of the chapter, including Protestant house churches, some of which appear to offer a place that helps prepare the M'Nông to become the kind of people they want to be.

EDUCATION AT THE INTERSECTION OF THE STATE, ETHNICITY, AND CLASS

The state's role in education and the role of education in nation building are long-established themes in Southeast Asian studies, easily preceding Anderson's famous recognition that national curricula and the use of national languages in instruction are powerful instruments of nation building (Anderson 1991). While the arguments developed in these studies are diverse, they share a tendency to complicate schematic and deterministic models of the omnipotent state in which the latter seems to exert an unchallenged power over its subjects and its devices (cf. Levinson and Holland 1996).

In her 1982 monograph examining Franco-indigenous schools in French Indo-China between 1918 and 1938, Gail Kelly challenges the assumption of a coherent and unified school system under colonialism and questions interpretations of the relation of colonial schools to national integration that emphasize either horizontal (cross-regional) or vertical (across social strata) integration. Observing the diversity of school systems in colonial Vietnam, Kelly argues that instead of fostering national integration, schooling exacerbated regional and class tensions within Vietnamese society (Kelly 1982, p. 52). Gerald Hickey, in his ethno-historical study of the Central Highlands, provides detailed accounts of a network of Montagnard elites who were the first to graduate from Franco-indigenous schools in the highlands in the first few decades of the twentieth century. Modern schooling, Hickey seems to suggest, and its alumni network fortified via inter-ethnic marriages, contributed significantly to creating a new identity that would eventually turn into a driving force in Montagnard politics (Hickey 1982). Alexander Woodside, in an attempt to assess the achievements and failures of mass education in post-revolutionary Vietnam, renders "a notion of a simple, secular upward progress in the promotion of schooling" unwarranted (Woodside 1983, p. 408). He identifies a number of paradoxes that stem from the pre-revolution culture of learning, characterized by mandarinism, the revolutionary legacy of egalitarianism, and the rising pragmatic utilitarianism of a bureaucratic state. With a similar regard for pre- and coexisting patterns and purposes of learning, Charles Keyes and other contributors in the 1991 volume on rural education and cultural change in Southeast Asia point to the importance of understanding local specificities, religious schools, and traditional social hierarchies as they come into contact with modern schooling systems introduced by the state (Dulyakasem 1991; Keyes et al. 1991). This chapter builds on the premise of the recognition of a complex intertwining of competing state and local forces in education enterprise embraced by the previous scholarship.

Education and schooling are also instrumental in the creation of ethnicity and ethnic structures of domination. By presenting minority groups as children or having child-like intellects and therefore both inferior and educable, it is justifiable for the state to bring social progress to them (Harrell 1995, p. 13). This children-ethnic minority analogy constructed by the state is in turn inculcated in the consciousness of the masses as one of the conceptual devices that helps to make sense of the differences between peoples of multi-ethnic countries. Furthermore, the introduction of formal schooling with standardized curricula and examinations using the national language inevitably entails varied performance among students of different ethnic groups. For the first time, and directly contradicting the promotion of national solidarity in multi-ethnic Vietnam, students of disadvantaged ethnic groups become aware of, or are made to believe in their comparative backwardness (Woodside 1983, p. 421).

This chapter delves into the process in which ethnicity is formed as schools have become a site where differences and inequalities are felt and lived. It takes schooling as one of the arenas of contestations of identities, examples of which are the ethnic identification project (Evans 1992; Keyes 1997a; Salemink 1999), a short-lived and unsuccessful attempt to construct a new socialist type of person in Vietnam's Central Highlands (Evans 1992), and a more recent state agenda of selective preservation of ethnic cultures (Salemink 2001).

Alongside ethnicity, class is another dimension that no research on the impact of education on a differentiated population can or should ignore. Indeed, class and class conflict mysteriously disappear from public discourse in a country such as Vietnam, where political authorities claim adherence to socialism while promoting prosperity for its people through state-sanctioned market forces. Without tackling class in a classic Marxist sense, it is nevertheless unavoidable to factor in the social relations shaping the outcomes of schooling as it produces, or fails to produce, competent graduates for different kinds of work for a changing local economy. Following Bourdieu and Passeron (1977) and Willis (1981), it also becomes necessary to ask how a sense of one's social position and social limits is developed, internalized, and resisted against through everyday interaction at school. In the Central Highlands, where many classrooms are internally differentiated across ethnic groups, it also becomes necessary to identify the specific ways in which schools prepare certain kinds of students to become certain kinds of citizens.

Inasmuch as ethnicity takes shape through sharing common experience of "suffering in the hands of others" (Keyes 1997b, p. 153) I hope to illustrate the process whereby M'Nông youths and their parents come to recognize their common conditioning in the local political economy and find ways to give meanings to their positioning (Thompson 1966). Whether or not and in which way the ongoing structural inequality within and beyond the classroom is challenged is an entirely different matter, one that requires another set of conceptual tools, that is, a focus on education subjects and their intentionality, to which we now turn briefly.

SCHOOLING AND CONTESTED INTENTIONALITIES

Studies of education and the state in post-colonial settings have been instrumental in moving the field beyond simple "reproduction theory" to more nuanced perspectives that are cognizant of the ways class, ethnicity, gender, and age can figure in the determination of education and stratification outcomes. The salience of these factors becomes particularly clear along the geographic, class, and ethnic peripheries of state building projects. There is also a shift away from simplistic models of the state and its supposed use of schools as instruments of control and subject making (Levinson and Holland 1996, p. 7).

One way of advancing from the above criticism is through a focus on the relationship between schooling and various education agents. Students, for example, may be viewed not as "passive bearers of ideology, but active appropriators who reproduce existing structures", and do so "through struggle, contestations and a partial penetration of those structures" (Willis 1981, p. 75). Teachers, educators, administrators, parents, and community members are also important education agents who actively take part in shaping the trajectories and outcomes of educational endeavour.

Correspondingly, I attempt to uncover the subjectivity of two major groups of education agents, teachers and M'Nông parents, as they engage education discourse in their daily life.

To give voice to local subjects necessarily requires good ethnography. But, an ethnographic scrutiny of everyday interactions, practices, and discourse should not be privileged at the cost of a clear insight into the structure of the local political economy. As this analysis demonstrates, the political economy particular to the Central Highlands of Vietnam over the past two decades is not simply a backdrop for the stories to be told. Rather, local political and economic structures have been powerfully internalized and (perhaps, equally strongly) resisted in the daily life of students in Đắk Nông, as narrated by their teachers and parents. The resultant agency of intentions — of projects or desires — may neither entail heroic acts of resistance nor routine everyday practices, yet it powerfully infuses life with meaning and purpose, even when the latter, in the case of M'Nông youths, can only take form in alternative spaces of socialization. Moreover, since no agency is free of structural power, looking into this particular form of subjectivity or intentionality is particularly helpful in revealing structurally defined differences — those between ethnic groups, professions, life prospects, and so forth — and differentials of power within and beyond schools. Looking at the range of intentionalities produced by the structure of social relations in present-day Đắk Nông, and the ways in which these intentionalities contest one another, reveals spaces both within and beyond schools where changes may take form.

THE CENTRAL HIGHLANDS AND A NEW PROVINCE

The five provinces of Vietnam's Central Highlands account for 16.5 per cent of the country's total area, and for 5.7 per cent of its population. It is the homeland of Malayo-Polynesian and Austronesian-speaking ethnic groups known in the literature on Indo-China as the Montagnards. The area has experienced dramatic changes in demography and ethnic composition throughout the twentieth century, but the pace and scale of change have increased over the past three decades, particularly after the introduction in the early 1980s of the New Economic Policy. This was followed by what is (misleadingly) referred to in official literature as "spontaneous migration", that is, the large scale migration of Viet lowlanders and minorities from the northern mountains to the region in the 1990s. From 1.2 million in 1976, the Central Highlands' population had doubled just a decade later (2.1 million in 1985) and had quadrupled by 2007 (4.7 million).

The massive influx of new population has transformed the political economy of the Central Highlands (Salemink 2010; Hardy 2003). In addition to the surging demand for land, state policies and local initiatives have propelled the highlands into global markets for coffee, rubber, cashews, pepper, and other cash crops. The total foreign direct investment for this area came up to more than US$1 billion between 1988 and 2005 (General Statistics Office 2005). By measures of income, expenditure, and other indicators, living standards in the Central Highlands have improved considerably in recent decades. On the other hand, the pace of improvements in living standards has been highly uneven. And the rapid influxes of population and capital have destabilized long-existing social institutions and heightened and ignited long-standing social tensions. For example, newly arrived settlers are often accused by locals of being a major cause of rapid deforestation in the province and the region at large (Huỳnh Thị Xuân 1999; UBKHXHVN 1990).

Đắk Lắk (including what is now Đắk Nông) was the homeland of the Rhade and M'Nông peoples before 1975, and shares many of the attributes of highland provinces. State-commissioned research published in 1990 found that its population increased 2.5 times between 1975 and 1990, but also saw a decline in the proportion of local indigenous people, from approximately 50 per cent after 1975, to 24 per cent in 1988. By 1998, indigenous minorities represented only 20 per cent (Huỳnh Thị Xuân 1999), and we can expect this figure to have declined further over the last decade. As mentioned, the inflow of population to the Central Highlands comprised a mixture of Viet and other ethnic minority groups (such as the Tày, Nùng, Dao, and H'mong) (Huỳnh Thị Xuân). Most new settlers arrived on their own with the help of their kin and villagers, but without support from local authorities at either the sending or receiving sites.

The province of Đắk Nông was established in January 2004 based on six southern districts of Đắk Lắk.[3] Its borders largely overlap with those of the former Republic of Vietnam provinces of Quảng Đức and parts of Tuyên Đức. Gia Nghĩa, the new province's capital, was one of the most important commercial and administrative centres of the highland foothills before 1975. Of all five highland provinces, Đắk Nông has the smallest area (6,514.5 square kilometres) and stands second lowest in population density (61 persons/square kilometre) (General Statistics Office 2005). Of its more than 400,000 inhabitants, 34 per cent come from thirty-one non-Viet ethnic groups, among which the M'Nông represent more than ten per cent of the total population (Hội đồng Nhân dân tỉnh Đắk Nông).[4] Instead of restoring the pre-1975 name that was apparently subsumed by the coastal Viet-centred rubric, the new province is named as the homeland of the M'Nông. Despite an explicit call to preserve and promote the M'Nông culture, however, the predominant presence of Viet coming from coastal provinces in key positions of provincial offices would complicate any suggestion of an indigenous political revival.

While a provincial breakdown of many socio-economic statistics is not available, Đắk Nông inhabitants may share an economic status with those living in the Central Highlands: their monthly average income per capita at current prices in 2004 was VND390,200, standing fourth from the bottom of eight regions of the country (General Statistics Office 2005).[5] Nevertheless, the region is considered to be strategic as its targets of development are as Prime Minister Nguyễn Tấn Dũng stated in his speech in July 2006 at a conference on socio-economic development of the Central Highlands for the years 2006–10 — cash crops, forestry, hydroelectricity, and bauxite mining.[6]

As a new province, Đắk Nông's political leaders are eager to seize such initiatives. By 2005, the province had hosted and granted licenses to five foreign direct investment projects amounting to US$8.4 million (General Statistics Office 2005). The Tâm Thắng industrial zone alone hosts twenty-two different projects, foreign and national, with a total investment exceeding VND850 billion, or roughly US$53 million. As some of its districts sit squarely on bauxite reserves, in the years 2004 and 2005 the province hosted teams from China, Australia, Japan, and the United States to explore and draft investment proposals.[7] In 2009, a multibillion-dollar plan to exploit these reserves boiled over into a national controversy, as a diverse group of opponents has challenged the project on environmental grounds.

The rapid development of the newly established province can be seen in the dramatic changes in Gia Nghĩa. On my first visit in 2004, it was a small rural town that functioned only as a stopover station along a busy traffic route northward to Buôn Ma Thuột. By the time of my return in 2007, there was fresh construction everywhere, roads were expanded and paved and street names and new traffic signs had been put up. The transformation continues. An official master plan aims at, in the words of its advocates, transforming the small sleepy town of Gia Nghĩa into a city as grand as Buôn Ma Thuột and as charming as Đà Lạt. In the meantime, the construction of two new workshops — a paper mill and a rubber factory — started in Đắk Glong and Đắk Mil districts in locations that are readily accessible by provincial roads.

The transformation is, however, most strongly felt among town dwellers and those living alongside its roads and at its intersections, most of whom are Viet migrants — farm owners, merchants, and state officials. The frenzy of development has not yet had a visible impact on more rural and poorer areas. A representative sample of 485 households surveyed in spring 2005[8] found roughly 80 per cent living below the national poverty line and 86 per cent deriving their income from agriculture.[9] The situation and stories reported in this chapter largely concern this rural population of the M'Nông and, to a lesser extent, their interaction with the Việt, within and beyond the school setting.

ĐẮK NÔNG K-12 EDUCATION: AN OVERVIEW

As of September 2005, the province of Đắk Nông had a total of forty-six kindergartens and 168 schools of general education of all types and combinations, 4,980 teachers, and 102,715 students of all grades (Table 6.1).[10] These figures imply that Đắk Nông has the lowest student population ratio in the Central Highlands: for every hundred people, only twenty-five attend schools.[11] However, the province stands second in the highlands with respect to teacher-student ratios: on average, 4.8 teachers attend to every 100 local students. Đắk Nông has the second lowest per centage of minority teachers in general education of the highlands (5 per cent), and it stands at the bottom regarding the percentage of students coming from minority groups (23.4 per cent).

Consistent with trends in the central highlands and nationally, minority enrolment tends to be sharply lower at higher educational levels. In Đắk Nông, minority enrolment in 2005 stood at 27 per cent at the primary level, 19 per cent at the lower-secondary level, and less than 7 per cent at the upper-secondary level (Table 6.2).[12] As the vice principal of a primary school in one Đắk Nông district related: "Local [M'Nông] students enter the school in large numbers and exit in small numbers."[13]

Results of the survey provide additional observations of M'Nông literacy for those of working age. Over 35 per cent of respondents state that they have never been to school of any kind, including informal literacy

TABLE 6.1
Number of Schools, Teachers, and Students in Kindergarten and General Schools in 2005

	Kindergarten			General Education			Total		
	School	Teacher	Student	School	Teacher	Student	School	Teacher	Student
Central Highlands	635	7,318	171,303	1,808	51,935	120,2873	2,443	59,253	1,374,176
Kon Tum	87	1,284	20,444	205	5,940	102,037	292	7,224	122,481
Gia Lai	153	1,856	46,278	418	11,754	276,564	571	13,610	322,842
Đắk Lắk	189	2,146	51,522	594	17,923	462,587	783	20,069	514,109
Đắk Nông	46	313	12,163	168	4,667	90,552	214	4,980	102,715
Lâm Đồng	160	1,719	40,896	423	11,651	271,133	583	13,370	312,029

Source: Statistical Yearbook of Viet Nam (2005).

TABLE 6.2
Percentage of Students from Minority Groups in General Education in 2005

| Central Highlands | Total | Students of Minority Groups | | |
| | | *In which* | | |
		Primary	Lower-Secondary	Upper-Secondary
Total	**28.73%**	**35.60%**	**24.43%**	**14.64%**
Kon Tum	na	na	na	na
Gia Lai	39.53%	50.22%	30.25%	16.65%
Đăk Lăk	32.29%	39.73%	28.83%	17.87%
Đăk Nông	23.41%	27.14%	19.05%	6.94%
Lâm Đồng	24.23%	30.04%	21.78%	13.07%

Source: Statistics of the Ministry of Education and Training.

classes, and therefore can be classified as being unable to read or write in the national language Figure 6.1).[14] Another 43.9 per cent claim to have completed primary school. Nevertheless, being unable to read or write in the national language does not mean being unable to communicate in daily life or access national media. Indeed, 60 per cent of respondents converse in Vietnamese fluently, while another 37 per cent can communicate to a lesser extent (Figure 6.2).

FIGURE 6.1
The Highest School Completed by Respondents

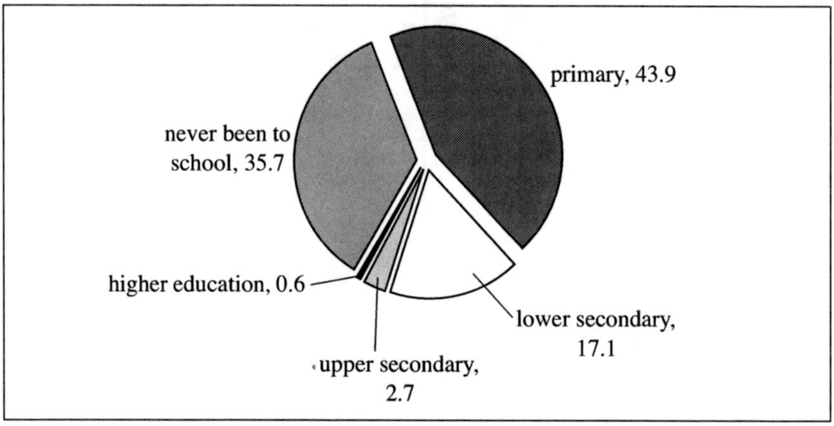

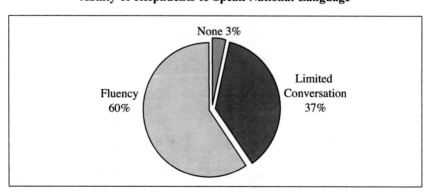

Source: Survey results compiled by author.

FIGURE 6.2
Ability of Respndents to Speak National Language

Source: Survey results compiled by author.

In discussion groups and individual interviews in five research sites throughout the province, teachers and parents provided their own views on K–12 education for M'Nông in Đắk Nông.[15] These views tended to cluster around two themes: material constraints — including the geographical proximity of the school and expenses pertaining to children's schooling — and language barriers, in particular classroom problems surrounding the language of instruction. These themes of resource constraints and language barriers resonate with evidence from earlier studies. For example, a 2003 report relates the plight of one student in Ea'Hiao commune who had to drop out of school because her parents could not contribute to school construction and pay other fees (Action Aid Vietnam 2003, p. 26).[16] The same report conveys parents' complaint of the difficulty in communication between teachers and students as well as teachers' expertise and attitude, a topic that we will return to discuss at length in the later sections of this chapter.

What makes these findings particularly interesting and alarming is the reality that provincial authorities have been quite aware of these issues and have taken significant, if not yet effective, steps to address them. Between 1999 and 2002, for example, Đắk Lắk Province (including now Đắk Nông) increased its budget for education from VND24 billion to VND38 billion (Action Aid Vietnam 2003, p. 24), and education continues to represent a significant proportion in the Đắk Nông provincial budget.[17] In 2006, 42.3 per cent of Đắk Nông's VND30 billion from the 168 Program budget went to educational expenses, including assistance for school construction, purchase of student health insurance, and the provision of textbooks and notebooks to students at no charge.[18] Efforts were also apparent with respect to language problems. Within two years of its establishment, the new province also approved a VND700 million project to refine the M'Nông written language and complete its M'Nông–Việt dictionary, supervised by the Department of Education and Training.[19] Starting from the academic year 2004–05, M'Nông language has been taught as a subject from Grade 3 to Grade 12. By 2004, a state report announced that some 2,000 students in six boarding schools were able to study their language as a subject from two to five times a week.[20]

An overview of the situation of K-12 education in Đắk Nông suggests limited progress in the face of widely recognized and persistent problems concerning resources and language. Although authorities in Đắk Lắk and (now) Đắk Nông appeared willing to take significant measures to address these problems, the problems persist.

A MISSING DIALOGUE

Discussions with Việt and M'Nông teachers and with M'Nông parents revealed a host of shared concerns, but also a stark absence of an effective dialogue. Issues surrounding language of instruction, attitudes and behaviour of students and teachers, quality of teaching and learning, learning motivation, and school outcomes are indeed salient in everyday discourse. Both teachers and parents had their own explanations of problems they confronted and the apparent limited scope of progress in education. These problems and the missing dialogue between these two groups of education agents, I would suggest, stem from a more fundamental distance between indigenous and migrants that is, in turn, rooted in the recent history of the local political economy.

Language of Instruction

In Đắk Nông, teachers' and parents' views on education and of each other only occasionally converge. One exception concerns language, or to put it more precisely, the use of Vietnamese as the sole language of instruction in early grades of primary school. Both teachers and parents see it as a major problem, if often for different reasons. A Việt teacher acknowledges that at the middle and even later stages of primary school, many M'Nông students still do not understand simple classroom commands such as "open your book" or "class dismissed" in Vietnamese.[21] When one learns about teaching practices in Đắk Nông, the lack of effective communication becomes easier to understand. As it happens, many Việt teachers do not communicate with individual students at all, but only teach using a "mass approach" (referred to, oddly, as *dạy tập trung*), understood as addressing the classroom as a single homogenous block. This approach to teaching has many known deficiencies, but it is particularly problematic when teachers make little or no effort to accommodate ethnic and linguistic minorities who become, in effect, doubly neglected. Such practices are a disappointment for many M'Nông parents. As one mother lamented: "[Việt] teachers only talk to their own [Việt] pupils while ignoring the children of their compatriots (*con em đồng bào,* [sic]). Even when my children understand [the national language] in daily life," she elaborates, "they could not, in fact would not dare, interrupt the teacher to ask a question."[22]

Having instruction in M'Nông at the entry level would help, but the socio-economic context of many M'Nông households often means language is not the only barrier to more effective schooling. The difficulty is complicated by the lack of pre-school preparation, as one M'Nông first grade teacher describes:

> In a lucky year I would host pupils who have gone through kindergarten, who would by then be able to recognize the alphabet. Likewise, it would be extremely difficult to introduce the alphabet from the start. Yet, I am lucky indeed to be a M'Nông so I can explain difficult words in our own language. I love my pupils as my own kids; I even fetch water to wash their hands every morning before class begins. You ask how my effort pays off, don't you? Last year 29 kids enrolled in my class in the beginning, only 25 made it through. The other four did not even complete the first grade.[23]

The current linguistic difficulties become more interesting when one puts them in historical perspective. A senior M'Nông teacher who started his career in 1973 recalled the differences between the two educational systems of pre- and post-1975 regimes. Before 1975, M'Nông teachers dominated both the pre-school and the first two or three grades of primary school and used the local language in their instruction. Vietnamese was introduced only from the second grade onward and would become the principal medium from grades three or four. He recalled that both pre-school and first grade textbooks were bilingual and that M'Nông children enjoyed learning from them.[24] Another major historical difference concerns teacher training policies. Until the mid-1980s, M'Nông youths who graduated from secondary school could enrol to be trained as pre-school and primary school teachers. The professionalization of teachers training since the early 1990s has ironically undermined the effectiveness of teaching in Đắk Nông. In particular, the requirement of a high school diploma for entry to pedagogical college has effectively disqualified many M'Nông youths who would otherwise be enthusiastic about becoming local teachers (see also UBKHXHVN 1990).[25]

One of the most fascinating issues concerning these language problems concerned a discrepancy in the Vietnamese M'Nông who were exposed to the mass media and which language they used in their daily lives and in the formal education of their children. Many teachers employed in Đắk Nông came from parts of Vietnam with speech virtually incomprehensible

to locals. A teacher from Hà Tĩnh Province acknowledged this issue,
quipping that his distinctive and "heavy" Hà Tĩnh accent would be tough
even for most Việt teachers, let alone students. M'Nông locals, young
learners included, who would have been acquainted with the standardized
spoken Vietnamese of the national media, find it difficult to comprehend
the distinctive dialects of Việt teachers coming from coastal provinces. In
an interview one parent put it rather bluntly:

> — If the teachers speak as clearly and beautifully as you do, my kids
>   wouldn't have any problem following [their lectures].
> — What do you mean by saying I speak clearly?
> — Well, you speak the VTV [Vietnam Television] language. Your speech
>   sounds exactly like that of a television newswoman. Our teachers
>   speak in a completely different accent that sounds almost like a
>   foreign language to us![26]

Even so, none of the parents would raise this issue at the parental meetings
because they do not want, as they explained, to be misunderstood as
ridiculing the provincial dialect or background of the teachers.

Compounding the linguistic problems is the reality of changes in Đắk
Nông's ethnic composition and the increasingly multi-ethnic composition
of classes in particular. While the linguistic concerns of the M'Nông need
to be addressed, the M'Nông are no longer the large majority they once
were. In fact, today in Đắk Nông, a multi-ethnic classroom is far more
common than a single or bi-ethnic one. Hằng, a Việt teacher and principal
who has been married to an M'Nông for about twenty years, states it
succinctly

> I do speak the M'Nông language; yes, they say I am as fluent as a local.
> But looking at the pupils of my school, which language should I speak?
> I can't use the M'Nông, indeed. We have kids from 11 ethnic groups,
> not just the Kinh and the M'Nông.[27]

It is then understandable that M'Nông teachers or those such as Hằng
hesitate to use the vernacular language in a classroom where Tày, Nùng,
Dao, and H'Mông students are also present.

Attitudes and Behaviour

Another aspect where teachers' and parents' views converge and differ
are the teachers' attitudes or behaviour towards students. Virtually all

the teachers interviewed upheld an ideal of the teacher as an intellectual whose mission was to enlighten the masses. To meet this ideal, teachers were expected to sacrifice their self-interests, tolerate material and physical hardships, and conduct their lives as moral exemplars for their students. Teachers' accounts of their efforts to reach out to more remote settlements in the local population were often impressive. These included long hikes through the forest to reach remote huts. Often it was necessary to visit such areas during the farming season to convince parents to resend their children to school. Some teachers interviewed for this research reported spending days in M'Nông villages, knocking on every (proverbial) door to persuade villagers to enrol their children. Small gestures were sometimes used to encourage desired outcomes. Lê Hoàng Sơn, for example, bought a white shirt for a bright M'Nông student because the latter was going to quit school as he was embarrassed about not having a proper school outfit.[28]

Despite these tales of the good deeds of many teachers, group discussions of M'Nông parents were invariably also interspersed with broken stories of abuse and conflict at school. Parents in one of our selected sites reported that every year there would be in their commune at least one pupil who quit school after being scolded. A mother described how humiliated her daughter became after being publicly criticized and punished for not handing in her homework. It took almost a month for her to be convinced to return to school. More common cases of dropouts were reported of students who did not do well in class and were alienated further by rarely being called on by teachers to answer a question. They eventually found no motivation to remain in the classroom.[29]

M'Nông parents went to great lengths to explain the difference between M'Nông and Kinh parenting practices:

> Kinh parents may scold their children harshly, or even beat them every now and then. We never raise our voice when speaking to ours. If they do something wrong, the old people in the house often talk it out with them in a gradual and discreet manner. When they genuinely feel sorry, they would never repeat the mistake. Just look at the adults, while the Kinh curse and fight each other to a broken end, we only talk to heal.[30]

Although this account may tend towards idealism and exaggeration, differences between the attributes of interpersonal communication

among the M'Nông and in the schoolroom indeed contrast. While
the frequency and intensity may be in question, the public criticism
and punishment employed by Việt teachers is a great concern among
M'Nông parents.

Are Việt teachers aware of this concern? Perhaps they are in
principle. "Of course, we must talk to them especially sweetly to sway
them," Nga agreed, as she described her colleagues' sensitivity and her
own towards the local populace.[31] Despite their recognition of cultural
difference, our observation of classrooms leaves some reason for doubt.
In these sessions, the teachers seemed to "administer" rather than teach,
with their authority reinforced through a series of verbal commands,
aided by a wooden ruler that would regularly hit the table surface or
the blackboard. Such practices conveyed a tense ambience that could
quickly degenerate into frustration and intimidation. On the other hand,
no teacher in the communities researched had ever been directly criticized
by parents, nor had the local community had ever been approached for
consultation in culturally sensitive matters. While discourse on education
is indeed salient in both the school setting and local community, teachers
and M'Nông parents seem to talk *past* one another. A genuine dialogue
between them is missing.

Motivation

There is an aspect of which teachers and M'Nông parents most clearly
disagree, even though this disagreement has never been voiced directly
to each other. Teachers and provincial officials, Việt and M'Nông alike,
all attribute the unsatisfactory performance and early dropping out of
minority students to their lack of interest and motivation, and especially
that of their parents and the adult community at large. In Mr Sơn's
the words of teacher, "no matter how hard you try to mobilize (*vận
động*) [the parents], they just don't see it. They do not see the value
of schooling. For them it would be fine if their kids can just grow
up to be farmers working in dried fields (*rẫy*). They would not ask
for more than that."[32] Echoing this reasoning, one high rank official
states that:

> The lack of an awareness of the benefits of schooling lies at the heart of
> the problem of education for the minorities in our province. Their [the
> M'Nông's] understanding is very low and limited (*nhận thức rất thấp và*

hạn chế). Parents do not take pride in sending their children to school; they do not see the importance of being cultured.[33]

This in turn is believed to be reflected in the lack of motivation among students in the classroom. Another teacher, Hằng, described her students as "not knowing what learning is for. They do not have a sense of purpose or aim. Once they could not solve a [math or science] problem or complete an assignment and get criticized by the teacher, they would easily drop [out of school]".[34]

Both data from our survey and interview materials directly challenge this view. Ninety-eight per cent of respondents agree, very strongly or strongly, with statements that "the aim of study is to have a more prosperous life" and 94 per cent agree that "it is for one's self to achieve social progress" (Figure 6.3). In all the parents' discussions, participants were starkly aware of their expectations for their children and their schooling. Among the most frequently listed occupations were government post, factory job, followed by medical doctor and teacher. Some M'Nông parents were especially specific about their children's prospects:

FIGURE 6.3
To have schooling is to ...

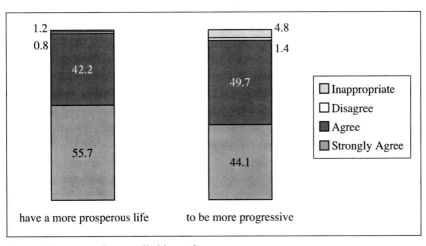

Source: Survey results compiled by author.

> We've heard that electricity will come everywhere. Supporting pillars will have to be erected and cables will have to be connected. If only my son can get a job as a cable worker in an electric company, we would be glad.[35]

One M'Nông mother's expectations of her children's learning are verbalized as follows:

> Whichever job [my children would get], I just want them to be smart and savvy. They must know how to apply what they learned to operate the home economy (*hoạch toán kinh tế gia đình*), how to be thrifty and how to calculate the profits.[36]

We will see in the next section to what extent the high school diploma is essential for the future prospects of M'Nông youths. Suffice it to note here that in contrast with the predominant view of teachers and officials, M'Nông parents do clearly understand the value of education in the most general terms. In other words, in the present day highlands, education is one of the sources of aspiration of social mobility for the M'Nông as much as for the Kinh. When asked which level of education they wish their children to complete, over 50 per cent of respondents who have school-attending children in state schools expressed a desire for them to complete at least an upper-secondary education (55.2 per cent for daughters and 60 per cent for sons).

Assuming a mediator role between the two prime parties of the education dialogue, we conveyed a message of M'Nông understanding of the aims of education to the teachers participating in our research in one of our follow-up trips. All but one Việt teachers kept silent; the only vocal one objected by questioning me on whether I knew the difference between what was said and what would be done. Two young M'Nông teachers gave me a blank look, while the senior, a charged stare: "There're many things your survey cannot obtain; neither your interviews."[37] Following this hint, I turned to look outside the school setting and eventually found the root of the above reported miscommunication.

I have found that the lack of a genuine dialogue between teachers and M'Nông parents is due to an absence of interaction between M'Nông parents and teachers in their daily lives in the first place.[38] Except for two teachers of a provincial boarding school who lived in the school campus in Gia Nghĩa, all the Việt teachers who talked to us had their homes by a road or at major intersections; some kept a small convenience shop. This is also true for most of the Việt and other non-local teachers, including the Tày and the Nùng who recently settled in the region. Apart from their salaries, teachers and their families also receive income from other activities, such as producing cash crops for later sale. Some owned farms and hired farmers, mostly Việt or of minority groups from the north, to work. In terms of both geographical location and livelihood, Việt teachers have little, if any, connection with the M'Nông. That is perhaps the reason any trip to a M'Nông village is often highlighted in their narrative as an extraordinary record of their dedication: they would have to go out of their way to reach their critical masses. M'Nông parents, likewise, hardly come into contact with their children's teachers. Except for parental meetings held twice a year, M'Nông parents do not take the initiative to visit teachers' homes on Teachers' Day and the Việt New Year Day unlike their Việt counterparts.

The distance between teachers and M'Nông communities is rooted in a more profound transformation of the local political economy over the past two decades, with special reference to the teaching profession. The highest waves of spontaneous migration from the coastal lowlands and northern uplands in the early 1990s followed shortly after what was termed the "crisis in education" in then Đắk Lắk.[39] This alarming situation was reported as follows:

> Teachers' dedication has fallen; many of them do not put their mind to teaching, of which quality [sic] has decreased as if the lecturer has left his or her profession while s/he is still in the teaching platform. The number of those who actually have left the profession tend to increase: there are tens of applications to change the location or to change profession every year. During the academic year of 1987–1988, 101 teachers left their job, making the total number of the resigned reach 300 in the year 1988–1989 (UBKHXHVN 1990, p. 219).

The 1990s witnessed a major transformation of the teaching workforce in the Central Highlands. A vast majority of teachers who were originally assigned to their posts in the uplands have now left and joined their families in registering in the same or different province as migrants, and by extension, joined the non-state workforce. To fill this gap, which has since widened, new recruits for quick-fix training were locals, who were mostly coastal Việt or from northern ethnic groups. In addition, some teachers who left their job in the homeland to join their families to migrate would reclaim a post in the new settlement. I heard complaints about the quality of the newly recruited teachers. While these complaints may or may not reflect their actual abilities, I suspect they implicitly hint at an intricate connection between teachers and the livelihood-driven migration movements that was largely unapproved by the locals.[40] The comment on the provincial dialect of a teacher reported above, therefore, may not be as naive as it sounds. In my interpretation, it could well allude to a broader criticism of the M'Nông aimed at their newly settled compatriots.

Not only are teachers (most of whom are migrants) and local students and their families geographically and socially apart in the Đắk Nông landscape, but the school is also disconnected from the community. Some of the manifestations of this disconnection is experienced bodily by local students. Every school has a similar architecture: a U-shaped annex of buildings surrounding a square or rectangular open courtyard is laid out on flattened ground. The shape and colour of doors and windows resemble either Soviet-style blocks of flats or the post-colonial style recently revived in the major cities. Variations, adaptations, considerations of topographical and climatic conditions, not to mention cultural features specific to each locale, are virtually absent. It seems to us visitors that schools are built to comfort youths of second and third generations of migrants, who understandably outnumber natives in the classroom, and remind them of the social landscape once familiar to their forebears.

This suspicion of ours seems warranted by a brief survey of school names. Except for one school named after a M'Nông figure, N'Trang Long[41] and schools that take location as their names, the vast majority of schools are given names of Việt figures that are completely alien to local history and memories. School names such as Chu Văn An, Nguyễn Tất Thành, Lê Đình Chinh, and Lê Văn Tám, often found their way to the provincial and national media. Three of the four newest schools built in the year 2005–06 are named Hùng Vương, Quang Trung, and Phan Bội Châu. We can recall that while it must be good sense to name the new province Đắk Nông instead of Quảng Đức, it must indeed make perfect sense to name new schools after the legendary founder of today's Vietnam and two Việt historical figures regarded as national heroes. A similar naming practice applies to streets and locations that are recently mapped. Naming and architecture, at best in their capacity of symbolic violation, attest to the power of ongoing efforts to write the national history in one of the most distant parts of its sovereignty (Bourdieu and Passeron 1977; Pelley 2002).[42]

THE POLITICAL ECONOMY OF MISSED OPPORTUNITIES

While omissions and miscommunications must be common in daily exchange, the way in which they are negated does indeed say something about the social relations between the parties involved. The more I learn of the ongoing socio-economic transformation of the highlands, especially of the increased economic differentiation and social distance between settlers and the indigenous, the majority and the minorities, the more I am convinced that not only teachers and M'Nông parents talk *past* each other, there is also a void space between them that is engulfed by something unspoken. Some of the sources of this unspoken barrier eventually opened up to us when we probed further about one of the supposed outcomes of schooling: the ability to join the workforce. We now look at the occupation choices that are available to M'Nông youths, the kind of access they have to these opportunities, and their actual ability to get them.

Rapid economic development has undoubtedly brought about new job opportunities in Đắk Nông. Civil construction and electricity workers are in immediate demand, while new factories, workshops, and mixed enterprises are getting prepared to recruit workers on a regular or seasonal basis. In the meantime, former state owned forest and agricultural enterprises have transformed themselves into state owned or mix owned companies. This transformation helps open up enterprises that once exclusively served migrants and now offer jobs to the locals. For the first six months of 2006, the Department of Labour, Invalids, and Social Welfare claims to have created 5,800 new jobs in the province or 48.5 per cent of its target and aims at creating another 6,000 jobs for the second half of the year. Đắk Nông even sends its labourers abroad: 168 workers have been contracted to work in Malaysia and Taiwan during the first half of 2006. Vocational schools offer short-term training to over 1,500 students during the same period.[43]

Unfortunately, I could not obtain the exact breakdown of the above statistics of employment and vocational training by ethnic groups. Our conversations with M'Nông parents, however, clearly suggested that not only are they well aware of the availability of these opportunities, but they also want their children to get one of these jobs. Some of them even compare and contrast specific jobs — construction workers versus electric workers — for instance. Others show particular knowledge of the prospects of becoming a state cadre at the commune or district level or a primary school teacher, and express details of the salary and benefits one can get in these posts. That the M'Nông are content growing up to be farmers is a myth in official narratives.

Becoming state officials or working for the government is the most frequently mentioned in the job preference list in our survey. This aspiration is not without foundation: the local M'Nông may look up to 288 M'Nông men and women who are currently working in administrative offices of various levels, representing 46 per cent of the total posts held by non-Việt. While we do not know the current proportion of the officials of minority backgrounds out of the total number of state officials in Đắk Nông, the provincial authority has set a target to bring it up to twenty per cent by the year 2010.[44]

The considerable desire of some parents for their children to work in non-agricultural jobs seems to contradict the survey data. When asked "Which level of education would you prefer your child(ren) to complete?", a significantly high percentage of respondents chose "Inappropriate": 30 per cent for daughters and 26 per cent for sons (Figure 6.4). We brought this "inappropriateness" to parents' group discussions, hoping for a clarification. What encountered us was far beyond our expectations: a frustration, at times anger, at the injustice reported to dominate schools and especially examinations. The most vociferous mother in a group described an exam her son recently attended:

> In the exam rooms, Kinh students hid cheat-sheets on their bodies under clothes. Some teachers even brought them the solutions or answers; all they had to do was to copy them down and submit. Our children had always been diligent at school but failed. As they failed, they were upset and gave up.[45]

A similar situation is reported in all the sites of our research. A father of a daughter who made it through twelfth grade yet ended up without a diploma voiced his frustration:

> My daughter has high self respect. She would rather drop out than cheat. For all her schooling years, she never cheated once. But she was not alone. All of her [M'Nông] friends did not know how to cheat. We never teach our children to lie. How can I tell her to bring and use the cheat-sheets in the exam? She left without the diploma.[46]

FIGURE 6.4
Desired Schooling Level for Children

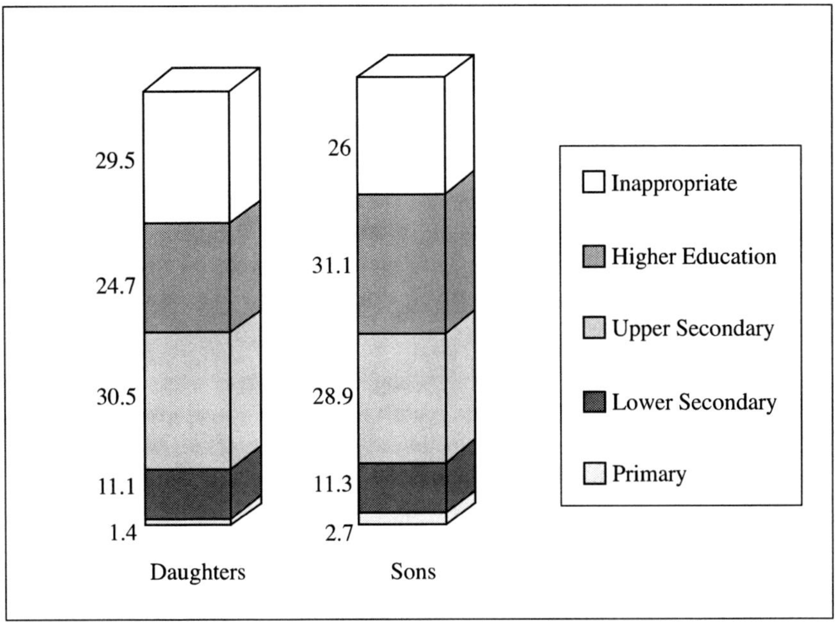

29.5	26
24.7	31.1
30.5	28.9
11.1	11.3
1.4	2.7
Daughters	Sons

☐ Inappropriate

▨ Higher Education

▨ Upper Secondary

▨ Lower Secondary

☐ Primary

Source: Survey results compiled by author.

Other parents added:

> We are unlike those [the Kinh parents] who would visit teachers at home
> every now and then. We never bring gifts to the teachers. Bribing (*lo
> lót*) or lobbying (*chạy chọt*) is unthinkable for us. Our children are left
> with whichever mark they get. We would not do anything to change the
> mark. Nor we have the money [to buy good marks]. No wonder teachers
> never support our [M'Nông] children.[47]

It was not until the summer 2006 that the national media picked up
serious fraud in the examination administration, brought up by a teacher
in Hà Tây Province, Đỗ Việt Khoa.[48] This was followed a year later by
the release of an outrageous video clip, shot by cellular phone of chaotic
exam rooms in Quảng Bình and Nghệ An Provinces.[49] These and other
events unleashed a wave of criticism of the administration of exams and

education quality. What was reported by Khoa and shown on the video clip were indeed more or less similar to the ongoing situation described by M'Nông parents of their children's exam experience. As most of them are shyer than their non-M'Nông classmates, M'Nông youths often keep silent as reprehensible acts take place in front of their eyes. Nowhere is the discrimination against minority students, or to put it more precisely, an explicit favouritism towards Kinh ones, stronger than in the exam halls. Some M'Nông youths share their frustration with their parents, while others keep quiet. Demoralized and disillusioned, very few, if any, would take a second test to obtain the high school diploma.

The irony is that the diploma itself is the key to jobs of which M'Nông parents, and perhaps youths themselves, dream about. All companies require a high school diploma as a prerequisite.

— Every time my son prepares a job application, he is asked to include a photocopy of the diploma. He doesn't have it. His school even refuses to issue a paper saying he completed the twelfth grade; he just did not pass the final exam. Without the diploma or this certificate, he is never able to apply for a worker's job.
— But you don't need a high school diploma to work in a restaurant, a beauty salon, a mechanic or electronics shop, or any shop — I protested, pointing out that numerous restaurants and shops have recently opened in Gia Nghĩa.
— You haven't talked to a restaurant girl, have you? They are not locals, but come from Buôn Ma Thuột or Bình Phước, or all the way from Hồ Chí Minh City. And they even have weekend leave just like the officials![50]

I have come to realize that Gia Nghĩa is, above all, a bureaucratic town. Its service sector caters to officials and cadres who commute from Buôn Ma Thuột on a weekly basis. On the weekends when people return home, most of the restaurants and shops are closed. Answering my query on why he does not employ locals, M'Nông in particular, the owner of one of the restaurants we frequented smiled: "You must be joking. They [the M'Nông] do not have a sense of time or work discipline, not even the service spirit. You surely do not want to go out of business by putting them to work."[51] Perhaps to help ease a tense expression on my face, he added with a curious blink: "Plus, all the [M'Nông] prettiest [women] have already enrolled in performance troupes. They wouldn't want to wait tables in our restaurants or hotels."

This pejorative judgment about the M'Nông and their lack of the modern work ethic is quite common among the Việt. It is also likely to persist for a long time, as it is rooted in the conceptualization of the indigenous highlanders put forth in the late 1980s by Vietnamese ethnologists, guided by Marxist-Stalinist evolutionist thinking (Evans 1985). While this is not the place to detail multiple manifestations of this perception in daily life in Đắk Nông, suffice it to say that the M'Nông and minorities in general are portrayed as backward and at an inferior stage of development.

This view of backwardness and inferiority is typically presented in state commissioned studies of the late 1980s and 1990s. "[T]he minorities [are]," a research describes, "in the process to slowly dissolve its traditional community while entering a transition to socialism" (UBKHXHVN 1990, p. 28). Before 1975, the research finds, "[the indigenous] were fundamentally in the transition between the last stage of primitive communal society to a class society, distorted by the turmoil of the French old colonialism and the new American colonialism" (UBKHXHVN 1990, p. 22). It goes on to propose affirmative action in education policy for the minorities. "Between now [1990] and the year 2000 and 2005, primary education can be made compulsory for a more limited target including *children of schooling age, adults of adolescence and middle age,* and especially the *managers and the workforce.* From this platform, approximately twenty per cent of the primary school graduates would proceed to secondary school, and five per cent would continue to high school" (UBKHXHVN 1990, p. 51, original italics). The same logic of levelling down to match the development stage specific to minorities, summarized in a phrase "aiming to fit their level", applies in every arena of socio-economic policy.

Imbued with the image of minorities lacking the modern industrial work ethic, employers in present day Đắk Nông, mostly Việt, hesitate to hire them. A requirement of high school diploma effectively bars the M'Nông from the job market. Schooling proves the opposite of a meritocratic springboard for social mobility for M'Nông, regardless of their aspirations for education and a progressive future. With its internal structure of inequality, the schools fail to foster national integration across ethnic groups, and instead breed exclusion. To be sure, it does produce young citizens, but those of different projections of their future, who in turn are supposed to be ethnically differentiated to fit what the state deems appropriate.

Class is, in this sense, intrinsically linked to ethnicity. In the multiethnic setting of Đắk Nông, the class-ethnicity interlocking is reproduced precisely at the site where the nation building project administers through its most visible and experiential device: the school. As stories collected from the field attest, schools only prepare certain kinds of youths for certain kinds of jobs. At school, the majority of young M'Nông, instead of learning to become workers in a rapidly industrializing country, first and foremost acquire a sense of their social position and limits. This is what schooling means for them; and they learn it the hard way. Schooling, with this specific meaning of *social positioning*, is visually and bodily experienced. From early schooling days, M'Nông youths would learn precisely in which particular way they would eventually miss out on the opportunities their classmates and cohorts elsewhere may grasp. Whether or not M'Nông youths accept what is in store for them is yet an entirely different matter. As we will now see in the last section, it is exactly the reverse.

CONTESTED INTENTIONALITIES AND
ALTERNATIVE SPACES OF POSITIONING

The accounts above of the paradoxes of education in Đắk Nông should not be taken as an attempt to frame the M'Nông's difficulties in terms of victimization or self-victimization. None of the M'Nông I met talked of themselves as victims of progress or blamed themselves for turning their back away from opportunity of the new economy. Neither are the accounts presented above meant to charge teachers of their wrong intentions or misconduct. On the contrary, by presenting unmediated voices from each side I hope to make clear the genuine intentions of each party, expressed in good faith. Inasmuch as teachers see themselves as contributing to the enlightenment of local youths, local parents do have their own aspirations for their children, and by extension, a project for their lives. What parents have described of their children's experience at schools hints that the M'Nông youths are by no means docile bodies to be inculcated with dominant ideology that justifies their subordination. By contrast, we can infer from both teachers' and parents' accounts the extent to which the students themselves are critical about schooling, and at times resist in their own ways against the experience of being schooled, that is, being socially and ethnically positioned.

Recalling the very first example a Việt teacher gives to demonstrate the language incompetence of M'Nông fourth or fifth graders, anyone who has once taken or taught a second language class would immediately spot something unusual. In the particular context of speech, one does not need to understand literally the words spoken to follow the specific commands. Moreover, "book opening" and "class dismissed" are in fact all too common to miss. We can only speculate that by citing certain incidents, exaggerated as they may be, the teacher seems to emphasize perhaps not simply the students' inability, but also a non-collaborating attitude. On the students' part, if it does happen, it may signify a lack of willingness to comply. Even the most innocuous incident can be a contested site of contrasting intentions.

It is nothing new to suggest that numerous cases of school absence or dropouts reported for more or less similar reasons — not being able to pay school fees, or failing to hand in homework, or consequently, being criticized or punished in public — can also be seen as acts of resistance. However, instead of seeing these more or less self-detrimental moves as weapons of the weak (Scott 1987), I tend to see them as having a message to convey, a message about discrimination and school abuse, of unsatisfactory exchanges at school, and of frustrated hopes. Instead of seeing the reactions of M'Nông students as negative, as something that shows their passivity, I tend to see them as communicating tokens as they articulate the unspoken.

None of the parents participating in our research heard directly from teacher Hằng or her colleagues that "they don't have a sense of purpose or aim". But everything they said in group discussions and our follow up conversations showed the reverse. It powerfully attests to their right to have purpose and desire, or a project, in life, precisely the right goals consistently rejected by teachers and officials. By upholding a make-believe image of the minorities as simple, honest, modest, and peaceful peoples, educators and officials alike refuse them the right to be sophisticated and capable of competing for better jobs, a better life, and meaningful pursuits. By articulating their aspirations and desires, the M'Nông parents forcefully assert their intentionality, and by extension, that of their children. It is indeed true that when intentionalities are contested, their contestation compellingly reveals the structurally defined differences and differentials of power at schools (Ortner 2001).

Even though in this research we rarely had direct access to school students, our discussions with young adults confirm the agency of M'Nông students in particular and of M'Nông youths at large. This can be seen in their intended rejection of the social positioning imposed on them, as reported below:

> At the time my third sister started primary school. My brother and I were in secondary school. School construction and other fees of three of us came close to half a million. We could request an exemption had we obtained a "poor household" status. My father talked to my mother of getting the certificate [of poor household]. One morning I saw a classmate handing a copy of it to the teacher. It was written "stupid" (*ngu*) as the status, not poor (*nghèo*), in M'Nông language. Actually, it read "stupid and insane" (*khùng*) to our [M'Nông] eyes. Back home I told my parents: "I'd rather leave school than have our family labelled such." They kept silent. The next day, they went to borrow some cash to cover the fees for my siblings. I started helping my uncle renting water pumps apart from working in our fields.[52]

A certificate of a "poor household" status, granted by the local authority, is the key to obtaining numerous material benefits: exemption from school and other fees, guaranteed access to collateral-free loans, and many other free services. It is part of multiple state funded strategic programmes pouring down hundreds of millions of *đồng* aimed at poverty eradication in the remote areas and among the minorities. It could be a genuine mistake on the part of the M'Nông cadre in choosing the translation of the term "poor" to include in the subtitle of the certificate in an attempt to convey the meaning of "the neediest". How "the neediest" turns into "idiot" may just be a matter of individual interpretation; but the forthright rejection on the part of the student and his family in the above narrative conveys a strong sense of their conscious choice. Instead of passively accepting their constraints, some M'Nông deliberately refuses to internalize the socio-economic structure that powerfully shapes their life (Willis 1981; Bourgois 2002).

As mentioned earlier, very few or none of the M'Nông youths we met saw themselves as victims or losers. Instead, a strong sense of purposeful choice is reaffirmed many times in our discussion of jobs and occupations. A bright M'Nông woman recalls:

> When I was younger I wanted to be a primary school or pre-school teacher working in our own commune. I was not bad in learning; my notebooks were often selected for exhibitions of neat handwriting. I once won the district math contest and served as the team leader of the Youth League for three years. By the time I completed secondary school, the

policy that allowed secondary school graduates to be trained as teachers was abolished. Three or five more years of high school, then pedagogical college seemed unbearably long for me. So I left. Some suggested that I enrol in a singing contest to join a performance troupe; but I did not want to become a performer because I did not want to live far away from home. If we were allowed to go on from there [to pedagogical training], there could have been more M'Nông teachers now.[53]

The confidence the woman exudes attests to her rightness of choice: happily married, she now owns three hectares of coffee and hundreds of pepper poles, and one of her two children goes to district boarding school. She expresses no regret at not becoming a professional singer, for having a happy family fulfils her life. She is now the soloist in the choir of her church.

A similar sense of purpose guiding other activities of M'Nông youths in their quest of a fulfilling life can be best seen elsewhere. In the search for M'Nông alternative spaces of positioning, I once entered the house of an evangelist. It was a brick house built on the ground and the interior was arranged more or less like that of a Kinh house. From the central living area where I was offered an iced tea, I could see an adjustable compartment with a blackboard on the wall at the far end. Our host explained that the living area can be turned into a classroom that can accommodate thirty to forty learners who could come and study the Bible. I walked to the board to have a closer view of neat M'Nông handwriting in Latin letters. My field notes detail how my host described his weekly schedule:

The three consecutive days in the middle of the week — Wednesday, Thursday, and Friday — are used for gatherings according to age and gender. Wednesday is for children of primary school age who would come to pray and listen to Bible stories before practising singing. Thursday is for teenagers and youths who come to play games and join a competition on their knowledge of the Bible, in between singing practice. Friday is exclusively for women of all ages. They would exchange information about crops and prices on the market or share what they know about loan or land certificate procedure, or anything that would interest others, before taking turns to recite selected Bible passages. Because these women gatherings are a lot of fun, the evangelist asks some unmarried girls to come to both the youth and women's groups and thus present at his house on two consecutive days. This schedule keeps the evangelist especially busy preparing the content of teaching as well as inventing new fun activities. The choir would take care of the practice themselves and sometimes organize an additional evening at the home of one of the members.[54]

Readers who are familiar with the structure and operation of the Motherland's Front and its mass organizations in Vietnam would be stunned to recognize a striking parallel between the former and that of a house church described here. When asked the significance and benefits of participating in these activities, comments from the youth and women who attend these gatherings sound astonishingly similar to those from members of the Communist League or Women's Union elsewhere in the lowland. "It is not only joyous," a young woman states, "we also learn a lot and receive support from each other. The teacher [evangelist] gives us guidance that assures us. The more you take part, the more you want to contribute, not money, but with what you can do, like singing or storytelling."[55]

> It's not just for fun, indeed, it is not ultimately about having fun. We gather to tell each other many things helpful for us: How to estimate the volume of water you need to buy for your coffee during the dry season, for example, or how to dry the pepper seeds properly, when and how to spray the chemicals to the cashew, so on and so forth. But it is not like in extension service trainings where they always want you to buy varieties or products from them. We go there [the house church] for what we really need.[56]
>
> I learned this pattern [of weaving] from a friend when we were listening to a [Bible] story. The story was at times quite moving that my friend stopped showing me the steps. In the end we did finish a stretched palm length [of cloth]. Many of my friends in the neighbourhood became skilful craft makers from those Bible nights."[57]

These Protestant house churches, as these accounts suggest, serve as places where recreational activities and vocational training are offered, interspersed with Bible teaching, which is thought of as storytelling for many participants. The vocational training is by no means systematic or exhaustive; rather it is *ad hoc* and pragmatic and timely in attending to the needs of daily life. Participants attend these gatherings not only to be enriched with knowledge and skills, but also and perhaps most importantly, to be assured of themselves and their actions, be it a livelihood or an emotional matter. Moreover, the Bible night I attended had an unmistakable familiar ambience: it resembled nights when the elderly would recite legendary epics, interspersed with fun stories and moral fables, in such a charming way that would make listeners return for more. Instead of a fireplace on a bamboo floor as is often romantically represented by popular media, the participants would gather around a large screen television set from where they would watch beautiful scenes of faraway places and learn of stories of people who are so different from them and yet share miraculously similar feelings. The house churches indeed offer an alternative space where the M'Nông can choose and shape their own positioning through sharing not suffering, but aspirations and hopes, and an assured sense of a purpose, or a sense of project in life, and actively engage themselves in the materialization of their projects. It is an alternative space, or one among other spaces, that helps prepare the M'Nông to become a certain kinds of people, the kind they would want for themselves. It is, in short, where their intentionality was fulfilled.

CONCLUSION

Within a relatively short time since its establishment, the province of Đắk Nông has received and planned a large budget for cultural matters. A total budget of VND182.2 billion from multiple sources has been allocated for the period from 2004 to 2010 for the construction of 129 cultural houses in villages and a number of cultural centres in some districts or regions, to develop a library network; train local cadres in the preservation and promotion of culture; collect and restore oral tradition; compile historical annals and epics of the minority groups; devise M'Nông language textbooks and a dictionary; and erect monuments and preserve historical sites.[58] From 2005 to 2007, forty *gong* (a musical instrument) classes have been organized, training approximately 600 M'Nông youths. The funding comes from the United Nations Educational, Scientific and Cultural Organization (UNESCO) — US$91,000 — aided by an additional US$43,000 from the state.[59] From 2005 to 2009, the province is supposed to carry out a VND5 billion project to restore traditional festivals, decorative patterns, the art of playing *gong* and other folk musical instruments.[60] In 2006, the province is reported to have successfully restored twenty traditional festivals and rituals, completed the construction of 117 cultural houses in villages, bought fourteen sets of *gong* to performance troupes, and organized seven training courses of traditional weaving for a hundred participants.[61] In October 2007, a historical site commemorating

N'Trang Long received a national certificate from the Ministry of Culture, Information, and Tourism, the construction of which is estimated to cost about VND30 billion.[62]

In July 2005, it is reported that more than 37,000 Protestants in Đắk Nông received VND102 billion in aid from the provincial authority.[63] A year later, in July 2006, the number of Protestants increased to 40,000; these go to six "branches" (churches) and fifty-two "points of praying" (house churches) across the province.[64] The Evangelical Divinity Institute of the Evangelistic Association of Vietnam (Southern part) granted its certificate to thirty-two local evangelists who were the first graduates from its training courses. Nine graduates later became ordained ministers, and another thirty-seven evangelists obtained their certificates from the second training course offered by the institute.[65] Within a year from July 2006, the number of Protestant churches and registered points of praying doubled, thirteen for the former and 105 for the latter; the number of evangelists came up to 200, and the number of ordained ministers, fourteen.[66]

The exchange, or lack thereof, between teachers and parents regarding education, as I hope this chapter has made clear, is not simply a matter of miscommunication or unintended misunderstanding. The predicaments of education in Đắk Nông are in fact rooted in the majority/migrant and minority/indigenous relationship that is powerfully shaped by state policy and local practices. Furthermore, due to the centralized examination system and diploma-based recruiting policy of local enterprises, complicated by in-class ethnic tensions, a vast majority of M'Nông youths find themselves disqualified from mainstream job opportunities created in their own homeland. Nevertheless, as this chapter has elaborated, M'Nông youths have probably never assumed a passive role in accepting the social positioning prepared for them at schools. Instead, they turn away in search of alternative spaces, among those house churches of Protestantism, to fulfil their ambitions. Consequently, whether or not the paradoxes of formal education in multi-ethnic Đắk Nông can be solved by promoting local language and culture remains to be seen.

Notes

The research used in this chapter was part of a project commissioned by the Đắk Nông Department of Culture and Information in 2004–06. Additional in-depth interviews and ethnographic observation were conducted during research funded by the Southeast Asian Studies Regional Exchange Program (grant number

2006-EC-16). I would like to thank David Marr, Jonathan London, and the participants of Vietnam Update, Canberra, November 2007, as well as Charles F. Keyes, Hy V. Luong, and the participants of the International Conference of the Anthropology of Vietnam, Bình Châu, December 2007, for their comments on earlier drafts.

1. Fieldwork was carried out in 2005, with return trips in 2008.

2. The M'Nông is a Mon-Khmer-speaking ethnic group living in the southern part of the Central Highlands in Vietnam and north-eastern Cambodia, most notably Mondulkiri Province. The work of renowned French ethnologist George Condominas features an ethnographic study of a village of the M'Nông Gar, a local group living north of the Nông plateau (Condominas 1977).

3. Vietnam's Communist Party Online. *"Đắk Nông: Những bước phát triển lớn sau khi thành lập tỉnh"* [Đắk Nông Province: Huge Developments After Setting Up], <http://www.cpv.org.vn/details.asp?id=BT680785389> (accessed 7 August 2007).

4. Ethnic composition in the Central Highlands increased from approximately twenty indigenous groups before 1975 to forty-seven minority groups living in the area (See Vietnam: Vietnamese Academy of Social Sciences 1990; General Statistics Office 2005).

5. Exchange rate in 2004 was US$1 = VND 16,060; in 2007 US$1 = VND16,060.

6. Nhan Dan Online, *"Ngày 17-7 tại TP Hồ Chí Minh, Thủ tướng Nguyễn Tấn Dũng tiếp tục chủ trì Hội nghị phát triển kinh tế — xã hội Tây Nguyên giai đoạn 2006–2010"* [PM Nguyễn Tấn Dũng chaired conference on Central Highlands' socio-economic development in the 2006–2010 period], Hồ Chí Minh City, 17 July 2006 (accessed 7 August 2007).

7. The People's Committee of Đắk Nông Province, *"Báo cáo tình hình thực hiện kế hoạch phát triển kinh tế xã hội và đảm bảo an ninh quốc phòng 6 tháng đầu năm và nhiệm vụ 6 tháng cuối năm"* [Report on implementing socio-economic development plan and defence work for the first six months and task for the last six months], Gia Nghĩa, 7 July 2006.

8. Sampling was drawn taking into consideration the geographical distribution of various local groups of the M'Nông, as well as the proximity to urban and industrial centres and major roads.

9. The national poverty line is defined as an income of VND124,000 per person per month (General Statistics Office 2005).

10. There is a noticeable discrepancy between state and provincial statistics. In an official 2006 report of the Provincial People's Committee, the total number of schools in Đắk Nông in the same academic year is 234 and total number of students is 126,705 (UBND Đắk Nông 2006). The difference of twenty schools and 23,990 students can be explained by additional schools that were built to accommodate new students who reach school age.

11. Compare, for example, 30 per cent of the population of the province of Đắk Lắk attended school as provided by the Vietnam's Committee of Social Sciences (UB KHXH VN 1990, p. 221).

12. Interview with Đào Thị Nga (Mrs), Đắk Song District, March 2005. All names in this chapter are pseudonyms and some locations have been swapped among the research sites. The total enrolment for general education of Đắk Lắk Province (now including Đắk Nông), nevertheless, increased steadily from 142,500 in 1985 to 337,300 (more than doubled) in 1995 and 553,139 (almost quadrupled) in 2005 (General Statistical Office 1985, 1995 and 2005). Unfortunately, we cannot track the proportion of ethnic minority students in these numbers throughout these years.

13. This too, is, in a stark contrast with the provincial report stating that the illiteracy rate is as minimal as 2.6 per cent (UBND Đắk Nông 2006). Nevertheless, our result corresponds to an estimation by Action Aid Vietnam that approximately 60 per cent of the local population between fifteen and forty years old can read and write Vietnamese (AAV 2003, p. 29).

14. We conducted a total of twelve in-depth interviews with teachers and educators from five research sites and the capital town of Gia Nghĩa, three of whom were M'Nông ethnic and one was married to a M'Nông and fluent in the local language. At each site we organized one group discussion group of M'Nông parents who had one or more school-attending children, another discussion of M'Nông youths aged from eighteen to twenty-five, married or single, members or non-members of the Communist League, Women's Union, or other organizations.

15. The report makes clear that even though Decree 35 and Decision 186 sanction an exemption of school fees for minority students, in reality they still have to pay fees ranging from VND50,000 to VND70,000 per year for primary school, and from VND150,000 to VND200,000 per year for secondary school. This would be a burden for families who have more than one child attending school, especially if they also live below the poverty line.

16. The number of students of general education in Đắk Lắk Province in 1999 was 484,367.

17. *Vietnam's Communist Party Online*, *"Đầu tư hơn 30 tỷ đồng cho đồng bào dân tộc thiểu số ở Đắk Nông"* (Funding over VND30 billion [US$1.8 million] as support to ethnic people of Đắk Nông) <http://www.cpv.org.vn/details. asp?id=BT590760813> (11 October 2006) (accessed 7 August 2007).

18. It is a conspicuous budget allocation, given that the M'Nông make up only around ten per cent of the province's population. *Vietnam News Agency*, 28 December 2005, *"Hoàn thiện chữ viết và biên soạn từ điển M'Nông"* (Complete the M'Nông alphabet and produce the first Vietnamese-M'Nông

and M'Nông–Vietnamese dictionary) <http://vovnews.vn/Home/Hoan-thien-chu-viet-va-bien-soan-tu-dien-tieng-M039039Nong/200512/21100.vov>.

19. *Vietnam's Communist Party Online*, "*Đắk Nông, Hà Giang quan tâm dạy tiếng dân tộc thiểu số*" [Đắk Nông and Hà Giang provinces focus on teaching ethnic language], 25 August 2004, <http://www.cpv.org.vn/details. asp?id=BT2580460772> (accessed 7 August 2007). The same piece of news adds that apart from language, students can study M'Nông history and culture. It also states that there are still another 30,000 ethnic minority students who do not take M'Nông language as a subject. Comparing this with the total number of students of all ethnic minorities in Đắk Nông in 2005 — 21,202 it is unclear whether it is meant that *all*, minorities, and perhaps some Việt also, should take it as a subject. Enrolment at boarding schools for the minorities is limited to children of invalids or those who contributed to the revolution or wars, and in many cases in Đắk Nông and elsewhere, children of civil servants who currently serve local offices. The rest of the children go to regular schools.

20. Interview with Trần Văn Hừng (Mr), Đắk Song District, May 2005.

21. Focus discussion groups with parents, Đắk Nông District, March 2005.

22. Interview with H'Glang (Ms), Đắk R'Lấp District, May 2005.

23. Interview with Y'Roan (Mr), Đắk Song District, May 2005.

24. Ibid. and casual conversation with H'Mai (Mrs), Đắk Mil District, September 2005.

25. Parents' discussion in Đắk Song District, May 2005.

26. Ibid.

27. Interview with Nguyễn Thu Hằng (Mrs), Đắk Mil District, September 2005.

28. Interview with Lê Hoàng Sơn (Mr), Đắk Song District, May 2005.

29. Interview with Đào Thị Nga (op. cit.).

30. Parents' discussion in Đắk Mil District, September 2005.

31. Interview with Lê Hoàng Sơn (op. cit.).

32. Interview with Đỗ Văn Nguyên (Mr), Department of Education and Training, September 2005.

33. Interview with Nguyễn Thu Hằng (op. cit.).

34. Parents' discussion in Đắk R'Lấp District, May 2005.

35. Ibid.

36. Parents' discussion in Đắk Song District (op. cit.).

37. Interview with Y'Roan (op. cit.).

38. Action Aid Vietnam also observes the same lack of information exchange between teachers, parents, and community (AAV 2003, pp. 24–25).

39. Over 60 per cent of the total spontaneous migrants from 1986 to 1996 arrived in Đắk Lắk during the five years between 1991–95 (Đỗ Văn Hòa 1999, p. 91).

40. Space limitations prevent me from elaborating on this field observation at length. It suffices here to say that the M'Nông we met were both critical of the settlers and vocal in their criticism.

41. Andrew Hardy, "Introduction to the Vietnamese Translation of Henri Maitre's *Les Jungle du Moi*", In *Rùng Nguòi Thượng*, edited by Andrew Hardy and Nguyen Ngoc (Hanoi: Thế Giói Publishers, 2008).

42. Giving schools Vietnamese names is, however, not only a practice of the Socialist Republic of Vietnam. Also in 1955 when the Central Highlands had officially become a part of the national territory of the Republic of Vietnam, Collège Sebatier was renamed the Nguyễn Du School and the curriculum became Vietnamese (Hickey 1982, p. 10).

43. The People's Committee of Đắk Nông Province, op. cit.

44. Vietnam's Communist Party Online. "*Thực trạng đội ngũ cán bộ dân tộc thiểu số hiện nay ở Đắk Nông*" [Actual situation of ethnic minority cadres in Đắk Nông province], 5 September 2007, <http://www.cpv.org.vn/details. asp?id=BT590760813> (accessed 7 August 2007).

45. Parents' discussion in Đắk Song (op. cit.).

46. Parents' discussion in Đắk Mil (op. cit.).

47. Ibid.

48. "Gặp "giám thị tố cáo tiêu cực thi cử" ở Hà Tây" [Meet the rector who exposed examination fraud in Hà Tây province] Tienphong Online, 22 June 2006, <http://www.tienphongonline.com.vn/Tianyon/Index.aspx?ArticleID=51 060&ChannelID=71> (accessed 7 August 2007).

49. "Những đoạn phim gây sốc về tiêu cực thi cử" [Shock video on examination fraud] Thanh Nien Online, 9 November 2007, <http://www2.thanhnien.com. vn/Giaoduc/2006/9/3/161181.tno> (accessed 7 August 2007).

50. Parents' interview in Đắk Mil (op. cit.).

51. Casual conversation with Dinh in Gia Nghĩa, May 2005.

52. Youth discussion in Đắk R'Lấp, May 2005. We have verified this incident with a number of M'Nông cadres. For an unknown reason, the M'Nông word *r'nak t'rơi*, in which *t'rơi* means "insane" was mistakenly typed in place of *r'nẽ r'ơi*, meaning "poor".

53. Casual conversation with H'Mai (op. cit.).

54. Field notes of a visit to an evangelist, Dieu Bang (Mr), Đắk Song District, March 2005.

55. Youth discussion in Đắk Song District, March 2005.

56. Ibid.

57. Ibid.

58. "*Đắk Nông: đầu tư phát triển văn hóa cơ sở*" [Đắk Nông: Investing to develop local culture], Vietnam Communist Party Online 5 June 2005, <http://www. cpv.org.vn/details.asp?id=BT540032347> (accessed 7 August 2007).

59. "*Đắk Nông tổ chức 40 lớp truyền dạy cồng chiêng*" [Đắk Nông province has held 40 courses on gongs] Vietnam's Communist Party Online, 12 October 2007, <http://www.cpv.org.vn/details.asp?id=BT1290757640> (accessed 7 August 2007).

60. "*Đắk Nông bảo tồn truyền thống văn hóa dân tộc M'Nông*" [Đắk Nông preserves the traditional culture of the M'Nông ethnic minority], Vietnam's Communist Party Online, 5 January 2005, <http://www.cpv.org.vn/details.asp?id=BT410585305> (accessed 7 August 2007).

61. "*Đắk Nông: Bảo tồn văn hóa cho đồng bào dân tộc thiểu số*" [Đắk Nông: preserves ethnic minority groups' culture], according to Vietnam's Communist Party Online 17 January 2007, <http://www.cpv.org.vn/details.asp?id=BT1710734931> (accessed 7 August 2007).

62. "*Đắk Nông: Phục dựng khu di tích lịch sử Anh hùng dân tộc N'Trang Lơng*" [Đắk Nông: Recover historical vestiges of national hero N'Trang Lơng], VOV, 8 October 2007, <http://www.vietnamtourism-info.com/tindulich/tinvan/article_15789.shtml> (accessed 7 August 2007).

63. The number of both Catholics and Protestants was reported in December 2005 was 140,000, Vietnam's Communist Party Online, 2 July 2005, <http://www.cpv.org.vn/details.asp?id=BT270540259> (accessed 7 August 2007).

64. "*Đắk Nông: Hoàn thành lớp bồi dưỡng thần học đầu tiên*" [Đắk Nông: has completed first training course on theology], Vietnam's Communist Party Online, 16 July 2006, <http://www.cpv.org.vn/details.asp?id=BT1670678841> (accessed 7 August 2007).

65. "*Đắk Nông bồi dưỡng kiến thức cho truyền đạo viên Tin lành*" [Đắk Nông held training course for Protestants"], Vietnam's Communist Party Online, 3 July 2007, <http://www.cpv.org.vn/details.asp?id=BT280737350> (accessed 7 August 2007).

66. "*Đắk Nông: Thành lập 13 chi hội Tin lành*" [Đắk Nông sets up thirteen Protestant branches], Vietnam's Communist Party Online, 6 July 2007, <http://www.cpv.org.vn/details.asp?id=BT570769445> (accessed 7 August 2007).

References

Action Aid Vietnam. *Đánh giá nghèo có sự tham gia của cộng đồng tại Đắk Lắk* (insert English), 2003.

Anderson, Benedict. *The Imagined Communities* (rev. and extended edition). London and New York: Verso, 1991.

Bourdieu, Pierre and Jean Claude Passeron. *Reproduction in Education, Society, and Culture*. London and Beverly Hills: Sage Publications, 1977.

Bourgois, Philippe. *In Search of Respect: Selling Crack in el Barrio*. Cambridge: Cambridge University Press, 2002 (org. 1995).

Condominas, George. *We Have Eaten the Forest*. New York: Hill and Wang, 1977 [1957].

Đỗ Văn Hòa and Trịnh Khắc Thẩm (eds). *Nghiên cứu di dân ở Việt Nam* [Research on immigration in Vietnam]. Hanoi: Nông nghiệp, 1999.

Dulyakasem, Uthai. "Education and Ethnic Nationalism: the Case of the Muslim-Malays in Southern Thailand". In *Reshaping Local Worlds: Formal Education and Cultural Change in Rural Southeast Asia*, edited by C.F. Keyes, pp. 131–52. New Haven, Conn.: Yale Southeast Asia Studies Yale Center for International and Area Studies, 1991.

Evans, Grant. "Vietnamese Communist Anthropology". *Canberra Anthropology* 8, no. 1 (1985): 116–47.

―――."Internal Colonialism in the Central Highlands of Vietnam". *Sojourn* 7 (1992): 274–304.

General Statistics Office. *Statistical Yearbook of Vietnam*. Hanoi: Statistical Publishing House, 2005.

Hardy, Andrew. *Red Hills: Migrants and the State in the Highlands of Vietnam*. Honolulu: University of Hawai'i Press, 2003.

―――. "Introduction to the Vietnamese Translation of Henri Maitre's *Les Jungle du Moi*". In *Rung Nguoi Thuong*, edited by Andrew Hardy and Nguyen Ngoc. Hanoi: Thế Giới Publishers, 2008.

Harrell, Stevan. *Cultural Encounters on China's Ethnic Frontiers. Studies on Ethnic Groups in China*. Seattle: University of Washington Press, 1995.

Hickey, Gerald Cannon. *Sons of the Mountains: Ethnohistory of the Vietnamese Central Highlands to 1954*. New Haven: Yale University Press, 1982.

Huỳnh Thị Xuân. "Report on the Impact of Rural-rural Migration to Resettlement Areas in Đăk Lăk Province". Hanoi (unpublished paper), 1999, pp. 88–104.

Kelly, Gail Paradise. "Franco-Vietnamese Schools, 1918–1938: Regional Development and Implications for National Integration". Wisconsin Papers on Southeast Asia; no. 6. Madison, WI: Center for Southeast Asian Studies University of Wisconsin-Madison, 1982.

Keyes, Charles F. "The People of Asia" — Science and Politics in the Classification of Ethnic Groups in Thailand, China, and Vietnam. *The Journal of Asian Studies* 61: (1997a): 1163–1203.

―――. "Ethnicity, Ethnic Group". In *The Dictionary of Anthropology*, edited by Thomas J. Barfield, pp. 152-54. Oxford: Blackwell, (1997b).

Keyes, Charles F., Jane E. Keyes, and Nancy D. Donnelly (Joint Committee on Southeast Asia and American Council of Learned Societies). *Reshaping Local Worlds: Formal Education and Cultural Change in Rural Southeast Asia*. New Haven, Conn.: Yale Southeast Asia Studies Yale Center for International and Area Studies, 1991.

Levinson, Bradley A. and Dorothy C. Holland. "The Cultural Production of the Educated Person: An Introduction". In *The Cultural Production of the Educated Person: Critical Ethnographies of Schooling and Local Practice, SUNY Series, Power, Social Identity, and Education*, edited by B.A. Levinson, E.F. Douglas, and D. Holland. Albany, NY: State University of New York Press, 1996.

Ortner, Sherry B. "Specifying Agency: The Comarroffs and Their Critics". *Interventions* 13 (2001): 76–84.

Pelley, Patricia. *Postcolonial Vietnam: New Histories of the National Past*. Durham and London: Duke University Press, 2002.

Salemink, Oscar. "Ethnography as Martial Arts: Ethnicizing Vietnam's Montagnards, 1930–1945". In *Colonial Subjects: Essays on the Practical History of Anthropology*, edited by P. Pels and O. Salemink. Michigan: Ann Arbor, 1999.

———. "Who Decides Who Preserves What? Cultural Preservation and Cultural Representation". In *Vietnam's Cultural Diversity: Approaches to Preservation*, edited by O. Salemink. Paris: UNESCO, 2001.

———. "Creating a Dega Homeland: Vietnam's Central Highlanders". In *Political Fragmentation in Southeast Asia: Alternative Nations in the Making*, edited by V. Wee. London and New York: Routledge, 2010.

Scott, James. *Weapons of the Weak: Everyday Form of Peasant Resistance*. New Haven: Yale University Press, 1987.

Thompson, E.P. *The Making of the English Working Class*. London: Vintage, 1966.

Ủy ban Khoa học Xã hội Việt Nam (UBKHXHVN), Tỉnh ủy Ủy ban nhân dân Tỉnh Đắk Lắk, Vietnam Academy of Social Sciences, Party Committee and The People's Committee of Đắk Lắk Province. *Vấn đề phát triển kinh tế xã hội các dân tộc thiểu số ở Đắc Lắc* (Socio-economic development of ethnic minority groups in Đắk Lắk province). Hanoi: Khoa học Xã hội, 1990.

Willis, Paul. *Learning to Labor: How Working Class Kids Get Working Class Jobs*. New York: Columbia University Press, 1981 [1977].

Woodside, Alexander. "The Triumphs and Failures of Mass Education in Vietnam". *Pacific Affairs* 56 (1983): 401–27.

7

HIGHER EDUCATION REFORM IN VIETNAM
Boundaries of Autonomy

Elizabeth St. George

In 2005, the Government of Vietnam issued Resolution 14, on Higher Education Reform, specifying the means by which the state would achieve a "fundamental and complete renovation" of higher education by 2020. The resolution emphasized the need for "renovating the thinking and system of higher education", the "clarification of the roles and responsibilities of state administration" and also "the protection of the right to autonomy, increased social responsibility, and the transparency of tertiary education institutions".[1] The resolution set clear targets for the expansion of the higher education sector, and recognized the need for clearer boundaries between the respective roles and responsibilities of the state and universities.

This chapter examines the relationship between universities and the state in Vietnam's education policy since the introduction of *đổi mới* (renovation) in 1986. The first section deals with the decade immediately following the introduction of *đổi mới*, and examines how a variety of different experiments in areas such as the private funding of higher education, the restructuring of administrative responsibility, and changes to the curriculum, shaped the relationship between universities and the state. The following two sections examine the period from 1998 to the present. The second section highlights key changes to the legislative framework for higher education, while the third section examines in more depth the limits of autonomy for a private university and for the curriculum. They show that where the first decade of *đổi mới* in higher education was one of searching for an appropriate direction, the last decade has been one of consolidating and refining the existing direction. In the final analysis this chapter considers the extent to which Resolution 14 foreshadows greater autonomy for universities and whether sufficient attention is paid to the role of the faculties directly responsible for actual teaching and course delivery. It questions whether, in the light of past experience, Resolution 14 is likely to bring about the "fundamental and complete renovation" it promises.

EXPERIMENTS IN AUTONOMY IN THE 1990S

Prior to 1986, it was difficult to distinguish between the state administrative apparatus and higher education institutions. Pre-eminent academics who oversaw research activities and the development of university curriculum were invariably also senior Communist Party of Vietnam officials. Universities for the most part were the training arms of central government ministries and graduates were allocated to state enterprises or government offices.[2] In the 1980s, however, the state became unable to meet basic educational outlays such as teacher salaries and university infrastructure costs and this unitary structure was placed under enormous stress. The economic crisis across the country provided some important opportunities to rethink the system of higher education in Vietnam, and the role of universities in relation to the state.

The policy of renovation, or *đổi mới*, which allowed for market transactions was announced at the Sixth Party Congress in 1986. The following year education officials responded by announcing that higher education institutions would now have to seek funding from outside the state sector and produce graduates to meet the needs of the wider society (Trần Hồng Quân 1991, p. 3). This announcement aimed to shift the higher education system from one focused on meeting the labour needs of a planned socialist economy, to one that could also meet the as yet undefined needs of a market economy, and address broader social objectives.

A number of *ad hoc* and state sponsored experiments emerged in different parts of the country to meet the needs of renovation and resolve immediate problems brought about by the economic crisis. The experiments quickly highlighted the parameters within which change was possible and desirable.

Enrolment

One of the most important early reforms concerned enrolment. In order to generate increased income for universities a system of "open enrolment" was introduced in the south of the country in late 1986. University lecturers at the University of Hồ Chí Minh City experimented with a system of enrolling fee paying students who had failed to obtain the marks needed for a state funded place, which also guaranteed employment at the end of their degree. The open enrolment system was already familiar to the university prior to 1975, and provided both a source of income to supplement teachers' salaries and a means of addressing high levels of unmet student demand. It was given low-key permission to proceed as a pilot by the state and proved highly successful in attracting students and providing an extra source of income for lecturers. By the start of the 1988–89 academic year, the first publicly sanctioned year for open enrolment, thirty universities were enrolling 4,489 students, and by 1992/3, at the peak of open enrolment, 28,731 students were categorized as open enrolment students.[3]

The rapid expansion of open enrolment was a direct reflection of the desperate need for universities to earn alternative income and provide lecturers with a minimum standard of living, as well as the pent-up demand for higher education among students who would have been refused a place in a system focused exclusively on meeting the needs of the state. It rapidly became apparent, however, that such rapid expansion in the number of students was having a detrimental effect on the quality of graduates. In 1993, the government cancelled the open enrolment option for all but two universities, which were given a mandate to provide distance education to poorer, rural students. The experiment had highlighted the possible trade-offs between the quality and quantity of graduates.

In another experiment, also given initial tentative sanction by the government, the first fully private institution in the Socialist Republic of Vietnam was opened in the north of the country. Thăng Long Tertiary Education Centre was established by a group of foreign educated mathematicians and computer scientists in 1987, and, given its early success, was officially allowed to operate as a university from 1990. A second private institution then followed rapidly. Hồ Chí Minh City Semi-Public Open University (Đại học Mở Bán Công TpHCM) opened in the south in 1990, on the basis of an existing institution. As with open enrolment, "private" university education was rapidly taken up by both universities and students. Over the eight years to 1998, eighteen "people-founded" and "semi-public" universities were opened, enrolling over 69,000 students or more than 12 per cent of the total higher education population.[4] In 1998, however, recognition of any new non-state institutions was suspended. As with open universities, there was significant public outcry over the rapid and unchecked expansion of such institutions which was perceived to have led to a significant lowering of the quality of the graduates they were producing.

The ability of universities to find their own funding and manage their enrolments were clearly important steps in the separation of responsibilities between the state and universities, but these experiments also highlighted the risks associated with allowing universities to expand rapidly with very limited oversight. Predictably, universities suffering economic hardship were keen to increase their income as rapidly as possible, but government officials appear to have little anticipated possible trade-offs between rapid expansion and the quality of graduates. Key concerns of ministry officials at the time focused on whether graduates would be able to find employment on graduation and on possible inequalities for poor students unable to afford a paid place. Universities were given far greater autonomy over enrolment and funding, with very little official oversight. The need for public oversight only become apparent when the situation reached crisis point.

Reforms of University Structure and Curriculum

A second area of innovation during the 1990s concerned the reorganization of the university structure and curricula. The experiments began in earnest in 1993. In contrast to the university-led experiments in private funding, these innovations were directed by the Ministry of Education based on detailed research and policy analysis, which were then implemented through a series of ministerial decrees and regulations. Key elements included the introduction of a split degree system, the amalgamation of existing small, specialized institutions, and courses based on a credit system.[5]

The most significant of the innovations both in terms of its scope and its impact on the structure of the university system as a whole was the introduction of the split degree system, or "two-phase" system. The two-phase system was largely inspired by the U.S. and Canadian models of higher education, and underwent a number of adaptations over time. Initially it required students to undertake a broad range of foundation studies courses in their first two years of study, and weaker students were required to pass an exam before continuing. Students would receive a foundation studies award at the end of the first two years that would enable them to continue in their preferred specialization, seek employment, or transfer to another university. The two-phase system was intended to address a number of stated concerns of the ministry, such as the passivity of students who were guaranteed a degree once they had been admitted to university, the narrow knowledge and skills base of graduates, and the perceived inequities in higher education for rural students who were unable to afford four or five years of study in a major city. The two-phase system was also intended to enable students to complete their first two years of study near their home at new community colleges, before moving to the more prestigious, degree awarding universities. At the same time, courses became more flexible from annual courses with an examination at the end of each year, to semester-length courses that students could repeat if they failed one semester (St George 2003, pp. 282–92).

The reforms were adopted in a piecemeal fashion across the country. The two national universities in Hanoi and Hồ Chí Minh City, as well as some regional universities, introduced a separate "Foundation Studies School" (Đại học Đại Cương) to teach the first two years of generalist studies. Others simply opened an administrative office to handle the extra paperwork required for what they viewed as a two-stage enrolment process. While some universities required the majority of their students to sit for the examination at the end of the first phase of study, and faced a parental outcry if their children failed the exam, others instituted the examination in name only. Very few prestigious universities were willing to admit students from other universities into their own second phase of studies. Students complained that teachers of second-phase studies retaught the first-phase curriculum, believing that students did not yet have a firm grounding in the subject. For their part, teachers complained that they no longer had enough time in the shortened, specialized phase of the degree programme to impart the knowledge required in the discipline.

The greatest difficulty, however, was faced in overcoming the entrenched authority of individual, highly specialized faculties within universities. Under the old system, faculties had become autonomous enclaves within universities, responsible for students' entire programme of study, as well as their ability to graduate and find a job on graduation. The two-phase system required courses to be delivered in separate components, managed by different parts of the university. Not only did it undermine the closely guarded autonomy of the faculty, it also meant that different faculties had to work together in the delivery of the students' course. The content of the course also had to be hierarchically divided between teaching the less prestigious foundation studies courses, and teaching the more advanced specializations in the final years of study (St George 2003, pp. 282–92). Such divisions were further reinforced by the planned introduction of a credit system (Decision 59/DH c.1994), in which subjects were allocated credits according to the amount of study considered to be required in order to complete the course. The credit system was first experimented with at the University of Đà Lạt in 1993/94. By 2000 it had been abandoned, with university officials citing a "lack of understanding on the part of the university's staff".[6] Experimentation with the two-phase and credit systems highlighted both the extent to which the government assumed responsibility for structuring training in higher education, and brought into question the idea of the university as a unified entity.

A thorough review of the two-phase higher education system was undertaken in 1998 amidst strident calls for its abandonment by the public and by university educators who felt that their autonomy was being undermined. At the annual rectors' conference in 1998, the minister for Education pre-empted criticisms of the system by announcing the abandonment of the cornerstones of the two-phase system, namely the examination between the two phases, and an end to separate foundation schools for teaching the first-phase programme, at both national and regional universities (Decision 67/1998/NĐ-CP 1 September 1998). The comments by educators at the 1998 conference show that they were particularly sceptical of the two-phase system at the outset, although those who had perceived a direct benefit to their institution gradually became more positive during its implementation. The Education Law, promulgated the same year, abandoned all mention of the two-phase system, although the concept of a division between generalist studies in foundation years and more specialist studies in later years, has now become an institutionalized feature of Vietnamese higher education.

Despite its shortcomings, the two-phase system was significant in two other respects. First, it was one of the most significant top-down attempts to restructure the university system since the reunification of the country. Second, it illustrated the limitations of top-down "rational" reforms. It was introduced according to the well-rehearsed method in Vietnam whereby the ministry issues a decree for universities to follow, which is then refined and re-issued in the light of subsequent experience. The introduction of the two-phase system made sound policy sense. It introduced a structure with the potential to tackle some of the biggest problems in Vietnamese higher education: the need for greater flexibility, equality of access, and a broader curriculum. It did not, however, have strong support from within universities. In his analysis of the reasons for abandoning the two-phase system, the Minister concluded that perhaps the most important of the problems faced by the decree was that the policymakers had not asked widely enough for the opinion of those directly involved in implementing the system. This had led to a situation in which teachers resented the imposition of the programme and became unwilling to support it.[7] The two-phase system did not involve a redistribution of authority between the state and universities, but rather redistributed authority within the universities themselves. This redistribution directly impacted on faculties with their strong tradition of academic autonomy (St. George 2003, pp. 303–04). This is an important lesson to consider in the light of the new round of reforms proposed in 2005.

Curriculum Reform

Finally, the issue of curriculum content and the ideological direction of education was of fundamental concern in the new environment. As early as December 1988, the then Ministry of Higher, Technical and Professional Education issued an instruction to reduce the number of prescribed hours in a university degree for Marxist-Leninist studies (which included subjects such as Hồ Chí Minh Thought, History of the Communist Party, Marxist-Leninist Political Economy, and Scientific Socialism).[8] This was in recognition of the fact that such studies, sometimes comprising up to a quarter of the total programme (that is, equivalent to a full year of study in a four-year programme) were no longer as relevant in the new environment. Despite the instruction and overt student protests against the requirement to study these subjects, universities such as the School of Economics at the Hồ Chí Minh City National University continued to teach them as a significant part of their programme for a number of years, arguing that such subjects and the teachers teaching them could not be quickly replaced. The ministry was forced to accede to a more limited reduction in the number of hours these subjects were taught in the interim. This issue has not been resolved and is revisited in the final section of this chapter.

The 1998 Education Law

The achievements and ambiguities of the 1990s were brought together concisely in the Socialist Republic of Vietnam's first Law on Education promulgated in 1998. The law provided a general basis for the principles and general conduct of educational institutions but it almost completely sidestepped contentious issues highlighted above, and left many gaps in separating the responsibilities of the state and education institutions. On the issue of private funding, for example, while the law acknowledged the existence of public, semi-public, people-founded, and private higher education institutions (Article 44), it did not clarify the differences between these different types of institutions, or their relationship to the state. The law left the founding of all such institutions to individual government decisions, which allowed the government the flexibility to adjust its approach on a case by case basis.[9] Mention of the two-phase system and community colleges was also removed from the final law, but the importance of Marxism-Leninism and Hồ Chí Minh thought as the foundations of the education programme were strongly emphasised. As stated in Article 3: "Vietnamese education is socialist education that is popular, national, scientific, modern and laid on a foundation of Marxism-Leninism and Hồ Chí Minh Thought".

The country's first Education Law replaced a system of multiple decrees and regulations, and formed the basis for an integrated education system intended to meet the needs of an emerging market economy. It provided for universities to operate in accordance with the law, an independent mechanism external to the state, but the state was still able to intervene in any university matters where it might deem necessary. The law showed a number of unresolved tensions and contradictions facing the Vietnamese higher education system, regarding the appropriate division of responsibility between the state, universities, and the wider community — a direct result of the experiments in alternative governance arrangements for universities conducted during the 1990s. The decade of the late 1980s to late 1990s was a decade in which almost the entire system of thinking around higher education in Vietnam was questioned, from the role of education in society through to the ideological foundations of Marxism-Leninism and Hồ Chí Minh Thought, however there was little consensus on the nature of the relationship between higher education institutions and the state.

THE REFORM AGENDA AND AUTONOMY IN THE NEW MILLENNIUM, 1998–2008

If the period 1986–98 was one of searching for direction, experimentation, and trial and error to meet the needs of a rapidly changing environment, by contrast, the subsequent decade was largely one of consolidation and refinement. Although the higher education system has continued to evolve, the changes have been in line with the overarching directions and ambiguities evident prior to 1998. Since 1998, important developments have included the rapid increase in the budget allocated to education, and the appointment of the Minister for Education Nguyễn Thiện Nhân as deputy prime minister, giving him greater authority to resolve the numerous cross-ministerial education issues. The decade has also seen the founding of a large number of new universities.[10] In general, the division of responsibility between universities, the state, and other actors is gradually becoming clearer, and Vietnamese higher education is looking to the future. Nowhere is this more evident than in the revised Education Law and the Higher Education Reform Agenda, both promulgated in 2005.

The Revised Education Law of 2005

The revised Education Law of 2005, which still stands, clarified a number of the issues that had been left out of the original law in 1998, and provided a renewed basis for higher education reform to move forward. As with the original law in 1998, it should not be seen so much as a watershed in the development of higher education, but as a document that brings together the diverse regulations, policy documents, and experience of the preceding years.

Of greatest note in the revised law is the much greater recognition of private funding for higher education. In the revised law, out of a total of ten new articles, four are dedicated to clarifying the set-up and responsibilities of private institutions. The revised law continues to acknowledge "people-founded" and "private" institutions in higher education, in addition to state public institutions, and they are recognized as equivalent to public institutions in terms of their organization, responsibilities, and the recognition given for the degrees they offer (Article 65). The category of "open" university, however, has been abandoned, reflecting that many regular universities are now providing distance education and more flexible programmes of study, which were the two key features of a specialist open university. Investing in education for profit is no longer stigmatized to the same extent as previously. Private investors are supported with the acknowledgement that those who have invested in the schools are permitted to make a profit on their investment once costs associated with running the school have been met (Article 66). Article 67 recognizes the property and finance of non-public institutions as belonging to those investing in these institutions, in accordance with the law, while Article 68 prioritizes private universities in the allocation of state land. All these additions to the law serve to give private education a much clearer position and basis for operation within the education sector compared with previously.

The revisions to the education law in 2005 go much further than strengthening the foundations of private education in Vietnam, however. The Ministry of Education and Training emphasized that the ten new articles and 86 revised articles focused not only on the issue of private funding, but also on four further key areas: ensuring quality; improving administrative clarity; ensuring equity; and lifelong learning and vocational education (Hà Anh 2005).

In terms of the first two closely associated issues of quality and administrative clarity, MOET has developed a number of mechanisms to ensure quality in higher education in recent years and many of the changes to the law suggest a revised understanding of the role that the law itself is intended to play. From being an instrument principally designed to codify the state's discretionary power to intervene, the revised law moves further towards an education system that is managed under a system of law operating independently of the state administrative apparatus. It creates a more robust system of checks and balances among different actors within the education sector, recognizing the importance of non-state mechanisms, and the allocation of clearly defined responsibilities to ensure the quality of education.

An example of these changes is found in Article 53, which requires all educational institutions to establish a school board with "deciding responsibility for the activities, mobilisation and oversight of the institution, bringing the institution closer to the community and society and ensuring that educational aims are met". For universities, the school boards are established in accordance with regulations governing the operation of each institution, as promulgated by the prime minister. Such a board was already envisaged in the University Regulations issued in 2003. These regulations cover everything from the steps to be taken to found a new institution, through to the responsibility of different administrative units and office holders within a university (Chính Phủ 2003). They were followed by separate, but very similar regulations governing private higher education institutions in early 2005 (Chính Phủ 2005a). In other areas, Article 58 assigns senior administrators of the educational institution (nhà trường) responsibility for the quality of infrastructure and the quality of educational outcomes, where before this responsibility was not allocated. In doing so, it addresses two of the areas of greatest perceived weakness that were not addressed in the 1998 law.

Central and local MOET offices (at the municipal or provincial level and below) now also have their responsibilities and powers more clearly defined. In particular, they are now responsible for monitoring whether institutions are operating according to the law (Article 111.1), fighting corruption (Article 111.2), and rectifying problems found during inspections, a process which is significantly simplified under the new law (Article 112). Nevertheless, some issues are still left subject to discretionary intervention. In a new clause, and a statement more reminiscent of the 1998 law, the law states that "the Government will define the penalties relating to administrative violations in the education sector" (Article 118). In other words, penalties remain subject to ad hoc decision making.

While the revised law goes a long way towards clarifying responsibilities in many areas that were left vague in 1998, the most widely discussed issue around the administration of higher education over the last decade has been the issue of institutional autonomy. Article 14 of the revised law, emphasizes that the role of the state is to "increase the autonomy, and raise the sense of responsibility of educational institutions". What this autonomy means in practice, however, remains the subject of subordinate regulations, in particular the founding regulations for each university. The revised law gives more recognition to the importance of non-state actors in the education system as a whole, and their roles and responsibilities. Students themselves are now recognized as actors in the education system, with an article outlining the responsibilities of students and defining illegal activities such as: damaging the reputation of teachers, cheating, smoking, drinking alcohol, and disturbing the peace (Article 88). While such activities were becoming of increasing concern during the 1990s, and not only among students, the government's approach to overcome them at that time was through a variety of campaigns to raise moral consciousness. The revised law recognizes that it is now appropriate for them to be addressed by legal means, but more fundamentally, as with the recognition of private investors, in so doing, it recognizes the interaction of actors outside of the state-institution dichotomy, which also has wider implications for a discussion of university autonomy.

The revisions to the Education Law, particularly those defining the parameters for the non-state funding of education, were fundamental changes to enable the reforms announced under Resolution 14.

Resolution 14 — Higher Education Reform Agenda

The overarching aim of the Higher Education Reform Agenda is for Vietnamese higher education institutions to be among the leaders in the region, and to be on a par with the advanced countries of the world, by 2020. It sets the challenge of greatly increasing the size of higher education while also raising its quality. The development of such a comprehensive road map for higher education in Vietnam and the achievement of its targets rely heavily on the greater recognition of private higher education in the 2005 Education Law.

The resolution recognizes that the key weaknesses in the higher education system include the need to produce more graduates, weak administration, poor linkages between institutions, the inefficient use of resources, and ongoing corruption in examinations and the awarding of degrees (Chính Phủ 2005b, Introduction). In order to overcome the weaknesses of the system and achieve its aims by 2020, the resolution proposes to overhaul teaching methods and training programmes in universities completely, to link the different branches of study within universities, and to ensure greater coordination between tertiary education and secondary and vocational education. It also proposes to modernize the administration of higher education, clarify the separation of roles and responsibilities between the state and universities, and, furthering the theme developed in the Education Law, to clarify both the autonomy (*tự chủ*) of higher education institutions, and the community involvement in their activities (Chính Phủ 2005, Part 1).

As part of this strategy, Resolution 14 envisages that "public higher education institutions will move towards greater autonomy, with sufficient legal rights and the deciding power and responsibility for training, research, organisation, personnel and finance". (Chính Phủ 2005, Art 3.e). The resolution further provides specific targets for student enrolment, teacher qualifications, and private funding for both 2010 and 2020,[11] confirming the targets already announced in the strategic development plan for 2001–10 (Socialist Republic of Vietnam 2001). Overall responsibility for implementing the resolution is given to MOET, under the leadership of a committee, including a number of vice-ministers and government officials with responsibilities relating to education.[12]

In large part, the resolution does not represent a radical reshaping of higher education. Much of the resolution develops, in more concrete form, the direction already evident in higher education policy since the late 1990s. Of great significance, however, is the abolition of line ministry control over higher education institutions. With the resolution, MOET becomes the sole ministry responsible for higher education institutions. Historically, the majority of higher education institutions were directly administered by individual government ministries, and were responsible for providing targeted training to their staff. Line ministry control meant that institutions offered very different standards of training in higher education, and often very narrowly focused programmes of study. Two cross-ministry training institutions, the Hồ Chí Minh National Political Institute and the National Institute for Public Administration, the two leading institutions for the training of government officials, have also been brought under the Ministry of Education and Training, and are now subject to the education law. This decision was made amidst concerns that the standard of the specialist training being offered at the institutions was insufficient, and that there was a lack of breadth in the teaching, hindering the ability of officials to make informed decisions (Nguyễn Trọng Điều 2002).

The decision to abolish direct line ministry control over higher education institutions reflects a clear recognition both of the need to treat the provision of education as a specialized field in its own right, and on the other hand, of the increasing power of MOET within the government system. The abolition of line ministry control will go some way in ensuring a unified higher education system, and be an important step towards meeting the expressed goals of greater linkages between institutions and training programmes of all types and levels. The abolition of line ministry control is replaced by a "system of state ownership representation" on administrative boards for all public institutions. It is likely that line ministries will continue to exercise significant influence through these boards, but it remains to be seen how this measure will work in practice.

How successful is the implementation of Resolution 14 likely to be? Khanh Van Dao and Martin Hayden (2008) suggest that Resolution 14 is likely to encounter significant difficulties overcoming entrenched interests. Line ministries have enjoyed important benefits in their management of higher education institutions, including opportunities for promotion and recommendation, not to mention easy access to training for the ministry's staff, and are unlikely to give these up easily. Khanh and Hayden further argue that the trend demonstrated in the resolution is one of moving away from direct state control, and towards a more indirect state supervisory model. Based on international experience, they argue that this is likely to require a significant degree of capacity building in university audit bodies and among community members who will provide alternative accountability mechanisms. The success of such innovations will be substantially dependent on the level of state funding provided for such training. Furthermore, they also note the difficulty of creating an "infrastructure of institutional self-governance", the system of regulations needed to clarify responsibilities and relationships of accountability if the state control model of higher education is to be genuinely left behind.

The experience of the previous decade suggests a number of further weaknesses in the resolution's ability to meet its proposed aims. The resolution is written largely as a template of actions for MOET to undertake over the coming ten years. It pays only limited attention to the actions required by universities, and omits any mention of the role of sub-university level units. Furthermore, while the resolution foreshadows the clarification of responsibilities between the state and universities, and the increased transparency of universities, it again omits to address the lack of transparency within faculties, where the core university work takes place. The experience of the 1990s, however, suggests that the ability to achieve real qualitative improvement in educational outcomes rests with individual faculties, which are the units responsible for the actual delivery of courses and the graduation of students.

Regulations introduced over the last decade have, in fact, tended to reinforce the authority of faculties within universities, and their lack of accountability. The 2003 University Regulations, and the related private university regulations promulgated in 2005, for example, both confirm the faculty as the foundation stone for teaching in Vietnamese universities, with responsibility for the development, publication, and quality of teaching programmes, as well as enrolment, research activities, international relations, production activities, and the social and moral life of their students and teachers (Chính Phủ 2003, 2005a). This last in particular is most evocative of the way in which faculties continue to exist as communities within communities, as substantively autonomous units within universities. Legislation has gone some way to demanding greater transparency from universities. The University Regulations, for example, require universities to publicize the university plan for the coming year, including the number of students being enrolled, the methods of examination, and university regulations and responsibilities (Article 23), but there is little requirement for greater openness at the subuniversity level. In reality, the overarching university structure has tended to be used more as an administrative shell that interfaces between the ministry and the academic work of the faculty, which is jealously guarded. The autonomy of the faculty within the university remains intact, even with the development of officially sanctioned curricula, as discussed below.

In comparison to the 1990s, the division of responsibilities in the higher education sector has now been greatly clarified, particularly through the setting up of a legal framework which limits the discretionary power of the state, and clarifies the rules under which public and private institutions can operate. The recent period has also seen a strong recentralization of government power in higher education into the hands of MOET, which is likely to standardize the environment in which all higher education institutions are operating, and, in the longer term, ensure a relative comparability of standards across institutions, and more transparency in the sector as a whole. There remains, however, an appropriate balance to be struck between offering the flexibility for institutions to operate, and ensuring that minimum national quality standards are met. Compared with the 1990s, the arena for debate no longer centres around whether there should be a separation between universities and the state, but on where the limits of institutional autonomy and state intervention should lie for both public and private institutions.

AUTONOMY IN PRACTICE — CASE STUDIES

Several years after the promulgation of Resolution 14, progress appears to be slow. The vice-ministerial committee announced to oversee the reforms was not formed until almost a year later, in October 2006 (Chính Phủ 2006), although a number of regulations have been developed relating to the quality of higher education. The issue of autonomy remains confused. It is not yet clear how much autonomy universities will be given in practice in a "socialist-oriented market economy", and nowhere is the issue more confused than in relation to curriculum. Two case studies of educational autonomy illustrate these points.

Higher Education Curriculum Frameworks

While government policy has overall been strongly supportive of university autonomy, particularly in the interest of making educational institutions responsible for their own results, this autonomy has been least welcome in the area of curriculum. As discussed above, in both the original and revised education laws, Article 3 specifies that "Vietnamese education is socialist education that is popular, national, scientific, modern and founded on Marxism-Leninism and Hồ Chí Minh Thought." While higher education in Vietnam has changed fundamentally in many areas, and the content of many subjects has changed significantly, the requirement to study Marxism-Leninism and the state oversight of the curriculum remain non-negotiable.

A Vietnamese higher education system that is based on Marxism-Leninism and Hồ Chí Minh Thought, in practice, is one in which the study of these subjects is compulsory. While the number of hours required for the study of Marxist-Leninist subjects was standardized and largely reduced in the immediate aftermath of đổi mới (Instruction 12, 1 December 1988), the 1990s saw a reaffirmation in official circles of the importance of Marxist-Leninist studies. This has been further reinforced since 1998. Following the promulgation of the law in 1998, MOET has steadily been building a "framework" curriculum for higher education, which leads to important questions around the extent to which universities and individual faculties really have autonomy in what they teach.

In 1999, following many years of experimentation with the best structure for a university course, and the investigation into the two-phase higher education system, Decision No. 4 (04/1999/QĐ–BGDĐT, 11 February 1999)[13] provided for all higher education courses to consist of two parts: foundation studies (*đại cương*), and specialist studies (*chuyên ngành*), without the requirement for an examination between the two phases. The programme of studies also comprises compulsory subjects (*bắt buộc*) and electives *(tự chọn)*. According to this decision (again, following on from pilot experimentation conducted in the 1990s), courses are divided into credits (*đơn vị học trình*) where one credit point is equivalent to 15 lessons of theory teaching, or 30–45 lessons of discussions or experiments, or 45–90 lessons of practical application, or 40–60 hours associated with the preparation of a final thesis or for examinations (each lesson being 45 minutes in length).

While the first experiments into a credit system and foundation studies programme established a common standard of credits for all programmes of study (Decision No. 2677 and 2678/GD-ĐT, 3 December 1993), this revised decision allows for variations in the total number of credit points and for the balance between compulsory and elective credit points required to complete a degree, depending on the area of study. The compulsory foundation studies component is comprised of around 90 credits, or about one-and-a-half years of study, with courses determined by MOET, while responsibility for subject specialization is given to universities. In order to graduate, students must prepare a final paper or project, or pass an examination in their chosen specialization (as decided by the university rector), and pass a national examination in Marxism-Leninism and Hồ Chí Minh Thought, in accordance with MOET instructions (Decision No. 25/2006/QĐ-BGDĐT, 26 June 2006, Article 14). In other words, decisions regarding Marxist-Leninist studies remain in the hands of the state, and Marxist-Leninist studies remain a compulsory part of the university curriculum across the country.

In general, Marxist-Leninist studies are undertaken as part of the foundational studies programme for students, in the first two years of study, while the examination is taken in the fourth or final year of study. Consequently, students must not only study the compulsory subjects to pass their foundation studies exam, but must revise their knowledge and understanding a considerable time after they were actually studied to obtain their final degree. Each of the compulsory Marxist-Leninist studies components has a detailed study programme attached to it, prescribed by MOET, including the specific number of hours for lectures, discussion time, and the prescribed reading.[14] Of particular note is the greater emphasis placed on Marxist-Leninist studies for those studying for an economics or business administration degree. For example, a business degree requires a total of 25 credits (or approximately 375 contact hours) of Marxist-Leninist studies, while an economics degree requires 28 credits (or 420 hours). By contrast, a degree in literature requires a relatively modest 22 credits in these subjects (or 330 contact hours). The study of Marxist-Leninist Political Economy is an area of particular note for economics-related degrees. While study for all other degrees requires a compulsory five credits in Marxist-Leninist Political Economy (75 contact hours), an economics or business administration degree requires a compulsory eight credit points in the same subject (120 contact hours). Under state-central planning, Marxism-Leninism studies constituted the core of all economics-related degrees and such courses have continued to have the highest number of compulsory subjects under the new curriculum frameworks. A closer look at the subject matter of Marxist-Leninist Political Economy shows that half is historical, largely focusing on explaining Marxist-Leninist concepts of capitalism and socialism, while the second half presents the government's development policy under *đổi mới* (Decision No. 45/2002/QĐ-BGDĐ& ĐT, 29 October 2002).

The framework for non-compulsory specialist studies can also be highly prescriptive. In 2005, for example, MOET established eight possible differ-ent branches of university study in the social sciences,[15] and commissioned a group of eminent academics to develop the detailed framework for each specialist course of study within these (Decision No. 01/2005/QĐ-BGDĐT, 12 January 2005). A similar process was followed for the humanities and economics. Of the curriculum frameworks that were available for comparison, in economics, social sciences and humanities, the law programme contained the greatest number of prescribed hours of study (139 credits out of a total of 190 credits required — 73 per cent), while subjects such as politics and accounting had 83 credits (43 per cent of the total programme) and 101 credits (56 per cent of the total program) prescribed by such eminent specialists, respectively. Only a limited proportion of a degree programme can be determined by a university faculty teaching the subject. This suggests a high degree of state intervention in university curriculum but the picture is complicated by the fact that the ministry-prescribed "frameworks" are developed by prominent university academics, who are themselves usually Communist Party of Vietnam members from the leading Hanoi universities in each subject field. This picture highlights the blurring of boundaries between the state and universities, but also highlights a very real example of the division within the university sector between the leading universities with close links to the central government, and the less prestigious universities which may or may not be more independent in their teaching.

MOET officials argue that universities have often not been sufficiently confident to develop a curriculum of study on their own and often seek guidance on designing an appropriate programme of teaching. At the same time, a common complaint of younger teachers, who have frequently studied abroad, has been that they are not supported in developing new programmes of study. One former teacher from Thăng Long University complained that on taking up her teaching post she was keen to introduce her own teaching materials, but these had to pass through a university academic board for approval. Both the development of the materials and the approval process were so time consuming, with no recognition or reward for the amount of effort required, that it was not in her best interests to go through the process again.[16] Some universities have also recognized that there is a lack of competent senior university staff following the rapid expansion of the higher education sector. Senior staff would normally be the ones expected to contribute to developing new courses and curricula. Some universities have taken a proactive role in addressing this problem by offering special incentives to their most talented students to remain with the university and teach (Nguyễn Văn Mẫu 2004).

The seriousness of the consideration given to the curriculum in Vietnam is perhaps nowhere more evident than in the debates that surrounded the passing of the revised Education Law in 2005. While the draft law was put to the National Assembly several times in 2004 and 2005 to seek direction, the final discussion concerning the law included vigorous debate around whether to allow for more than one textbook for a subject, in other words, whether students would be offered competing versions for study. The issue was put to the National Assembly by the Standing Committee on Education. The Committee was in favour of making more than one textbook available, and for educational institutions to be able to choose their preferred text. However, in the final vote, 61.14 per cent (203) members voted in favour of one textbook per course, 36.45 per cent voted in favour of several textbooks being allocated for one programme, and two members voted for teachers to be able to choose their own textbooks for one programme (Văn Tiến 2005). The National Assembly argued that while in the future having several textbooks might be appropriate, there needed to be a greater pool of expertise available for writing the textbooks before this was system was adopted.

The paradox of the curriculum is that while universities and the faculties within them are given responsibility for the development and delivery of courses according to both the Education Law and the University Regulations, the requirement that these courses be in accordance with the "framework curriculum" provided by MOET, means that in practice, faculties have little leeway to develop substantively new courses, and teachers face many difficulties within their faculties if they wish to introduce new teaching materials. Equally paradoxically, prominent academics within the leading institutions of Vietnam, are usually also senior members of the Communist Party of Vietnam, who maintain a monopoly on curriculum textbooks for use throughout the country, with almost non-existent academic or other oversight to ensure they are of high quality.

FPT University

A second case study in university autonomy is that of the establishment of the private FPT University in 2006. FPT university specializes in IT courses for the FPT Company, and was the first corporately owned university to be established in Vietnam. It is the type of institution that is at the core of the government's vision for higher education in 2020, as outlined in the Higher Education Reform Agenda.

Despite clear official support for greater institutional autonomy for higher education institutions, the university encountered a number of difficulties in setting up. The process of its establishment was followed closely on the news website VietNamNet,[17] which has run a very active discussion forum on the issue of education, and higher education in particular, with regular question and answer sessions with MOET officials (including the minister), senior academics, and students. The issue of institutional autonomy is a frequent topic of debate.

The university was given official permission to open by MOET in August 2006, but was not given permission to begin enrolling students at this time. The two key sticking points were the lack of a specified curriculum in the papers it had submitted for approval, and the lack of clarity it was providing around intended enrolment numbers. The university argued that MOET itself had not yet established a model curriculum in the IT sector for them to follow, and that, even if it did, the university would be upgrading its curriculum every six months because of the speed with which the IT industry was changing. In terms of enrolment, it argued that its own board of directors was best placed to understand the skill requirements of the industry and to ensure quality graduates, not MOET. The university insisted that these were two areas where the university must have autonomy.

MOET, for its part, argued that it was the ministry's responsibility to ensure that basic standards were being met before allowing a university to operate, and the university needed to prove first that it had sufficient facilities and teachers to enrol the proposed number of students. In addition, MOET noted that enrolment quotas across universities for 2006 had already been assigned by the Ministry for Planning and Investment, and therefore they would need special approval from that ministry before being able to enrol students in addition to the national planning quotas. It argued that even private education had a wider social responsibility and that MOET needed to ensure that responsibility was being met, a clear reference to the public outcry that followed rapid student expansion during the 1990s (Hoàng Lê 2006a, 2006b; Le Cam Le 2006; Trường Giang 2006). The dispute even prompted the Minister for Education to address the National Assembly on 7 November 2006, to explain the problems of devolving autonomy to universities too fast, because they often had poor administrative practices (*Vietnam Economic Times Online* 2006)

The exchange between the university and the ministry highlights the large divergence of opinion around how the issue of autonomy should play out in practice and who is best placed to make decisions on individual issues to ensure both the quality of education and national development needs are met. On 15 November 2006, the university was finally given permission to enrol its first students, despite concerns about whether the proposed teachers had sufficient teaching qualifications (Hoàng Lê 2006d).

This private institution rejected perceived government interference in its curriculum. For public universities, the issue of autonomy is further complicated by their limited ability to seek outside funding. The rector of the University for Foreign Trade (*Đại học Ngoại Thương*) argued that his university had long wished for greater independence in the areas of training and research, staffing, administrative responsibilities, finance, and international relations, but if they were not allowed to raise student fees, then they did not have the capacity to undertake these activities independently and their quality suffered (Hoàng Lê 2006*b*).

CONCLUSION

Higher education policy in Vietnam has progressed greatly in complexity and understanding since 1986 and a discussion on university autonomy is no longer merely a theoretical exercise. Assessing the extent to which universities are able to, and should be able to, manage their own affairs, remains problematic however.

Education policy since 1986, and particularly since 1998, has confirmed two distinct trends in university autonomy. The first is one of progressively greater financial autonomy. This is particularly true of private universities, which, under the revised Education Law of 2005, are now able to return a profit to investors, but is also true to a lesser extent of public universities which can enrol fee-paying students under strict guidelines. The picture is much less clear with regards to autonomy in the curriculum, however. On the one hand the MOET curriculum frameworks prescribe in great detail a significant proportion of the curriculum for degree courses, including detailed requirements for the study of Marxism-Leninism and Hồ Chí Minh thought. On the other hand, this curriculum has been developed by university academics, albeit with close links to the government.

What are the implications of this state of affairs for the achievement of the Higher Education Reform Agenda? Resolution 14 lays out impressive goals both for increasing the size of the higher education system in Vietnam, and improving its quality. Past experience suggests that in order to meet these goals, it will be essential for MOET to move beyond detailed plans of action, which are the current focus of Resolution 14, and address in more detail, not only the duties and responsibilities of universities, but also the role of the faculties at the sub-university level.

Notes

1. Resolution No. 14 — On the fundamental and complete renovation of higher education in Vietnam in the period 2006–20, "*Trên cơ sở đổi mới tư duy và cơ chế quản lý giáo dục đại học, kết hợp hợp lý và hiệu quả giữa việc phân định rõ chức năng, nhiệm vụ quản lý Nhà nước và việc đảm bảo quyền tự chủ, tăng cường trách nhiệm xã hội, tính minh bạch của các cơ sở giáo dục*

đại học." Government Resolution No.14/2005/NQ-CP "*Nghị Quyết về đổi mới cơ bản và toàn diện giáo dục đại học Việt Nam giai đoạn 2006–20.* Author's translation.

2. Two notable exceptions to this were the two national universities in Hanoi and Hồ Chí Minh City.

3. Figures supplied by the Centre for Administrative Information, MOET, 1998 and 2000.

4. Figures from Government Statistics Office, 2007.

5. The key decree in this regard was Decision 90/CP (24 November 1993) "Defining the structural framework of the national education system, educational awards and certificates for education and training in the Socialist Republic of Vietnam". [Nghị Định 90/CP (24 November 1993) *Quy định chương trình khung của hệ thống giáo dục quốc dân, hệ thống văn bằng chứng chỉ về giáo dục và đào tạo của Nước Cộng hòa Xã hội Chủ nghĩa Việt Nam*] Interview with Nguyễn Hữu Đức, rector, University of Đà Lạt 1 June 1998 and senior MOET official, 25 April 2000.

6. Đại Đoàn Kết, 13 April 1998, p. 3.

7. According to Instruction No. 12, 1 December 1988.

8. For more detail concerning discussions in the lead-up to the finalization of the 1998 Education Law, see St. George, 2005.

9. Five universities were given permission to operate in 2005, twelve in 2006, one in 2007, and four in 2008 to September, according to the foundation decrees listed on the MOET official website. These include "sub-universities" within the two national universities.

10. The resolution foresees 200 higher education students per 10,000 population by 2010, and 450 students per 10,000 population by 2020; 40 per cent of teachers with a Masters degree and 25 per cent with a PhD by 2010, 60 per cent with a Masters degree and 35 per cent with a PhD by 2020; 15 per cent of income from productive or service enterprises by 2010, and 25 per cent by 2020.

11. Vice-ministers include those from the Ministry of Planning and Investment, Ministry for Science and Technology, Ministry of the Resources and the Environment, Ministry of Finance and Ministry of the Interior.

12. The details described here were repeated more recently in Decisions No. 25/2006/QĐ-BGDĐT, 26 June 2006, No. 43/2007/QĐ-BGDĐT, 15 August 2007, which better integrate college (*cao đẳng*) courses into the higher education curriculum framework.

13. For decisions relating to the different programmes of study, see QĐ45/2002/QĐ-BGDĐ&ĐT, 29 October 2002 (Marxist-Leninist Philosophy), QĐ 45/2002/QĐ-BGDĐT, 29 October 2002 (Marxist-Leninist Political Economy); QĐ 34/2003/QĐ-BGDĐT, 31 July 2003 (Scientific Socialism); QĐ 41/2003/QĐ-

BGDĐT, 27 August 2003 (History of the Communist Party); and QĐ 35/2003/
QĐ-BGDĐT, 31 July 2003 (Hồ Chí Minh Thought).

14. The eight branches were: Philosophy; Linguistics; Literature; Hán Nôm Studies;
History; Việt Nam Studies; Southeast Asian Studies; International Studies.

15. Interview with former Thang Long University staff member, Canberra, July
2007.

16. <www.vietnamnet.vn>.

17. The website ran a special forum on the issue of higher education autonomy
during October 2006, in which both the minister for education and the head of
the department for higher education in MOET participated, <www.vietnamnet.
vn>.

REFERENCES

Chính Phủ. *Quyết định số* 153/2003/QĐ-TTg, 30/7/2003 — *Điều lệ trường đại học*
(Decision No. 153/2003/QD-TTg, 30 July 2003 — University regulations), 2003.

————. *Quyết định số* 14/2005/QĐ-TTg (17/01/2005) *Quy chế tổ chức và
hoạt động của trường đại học tư thục* (Decision No. 14/2005/QĐ-TTg
[17 January] Regulation on the organization and activities of private
universities), 2005a.

————. *Nghị quyết về đổi mới cơ bản và toàn diện giáo dục đại học Việt Nam
giai đoạn 2006–20.* (Resolution on the fundamental and complete renovation
of higher education in Vietnam 2006–20), 2005b.

————. *Quyết định* 1362/QĐ-TTg (18/10/06). *Quyết định về việc tổ chức và hoạt
động của ban chi đạo đổi mới giáo dục đại học* (Decision 1362/QD-TTg
[18 October], Decision on the organization and activities of the Committee
for the renovation of higher education), 2006.

Dung, Hue Doan. "Moral Education or Political Education in the Vietnamese
Educational System?" *Journal of Moral Education* 34, no. 4 (2005): 451–63.

Hà, Anh. "*Luật giáo dục: Các khoản đóng góp được góp chung*", *VietNamNet*,
<http://vietnamnet.vn>, 2005 (accessed 11 July 2007).

Hoàng, Lê. "FPT University Receives Licence". VietNam Net Bridge, <http://
english.vietnamnet.vn>, 2006a.

————. "*Cần thực hiện ngay tự chủ tài chính!*". *VietNam Net*, <http://vietnamnet.
vn>, 2006b.

————. "*Đại học FPT và Bộ GD-ĐT: Tiến 0 bước!*". *VietNam Net*, <http://
vietnamnet.vn>, 2006b.

————. "*Đại học FPT đã được phép tuyển sinh*". *VietNam Net*, <http://vietnamnet.
vn>, 2006c.

Khanh, Van Dao and M. Hayden. "Modernising the Governance of Higher
Education in Vietnam". In *Modernising Higher Education in Vietnam*, edited
by M. Hayden and G. Harman. Forthcoming.

Le Cam Le (2006). "FPT University". Mimeo. No date. Published in *VN Economy*.

Lưu, Hà Vĩ. *"Niềm tin khoa học — điều kiện tiên quyết đối với đội ngũ giảng viên Mác — Lênin"*. *Tạp chí cộng sản 20* (2005): 27–30.

Nghiêm, Đình Vỹ. *"Quan điểm đánh giá chất lượng giáo dục"*. *Tạp chí cộng sản 22* (2004): 30–34.

———. *"Giáo dục Việt Nam khi gia nhập Tổ chức thương mại thế giới"* [Education in Vietnam on accession to the World Trade Organization]. *Tạp chí cộng sản 22* (2006): 28–32.

Nguyễn, Phú Trọng. *"Về cuộc đấu tranh tư tưởng trong tình hình hiện nay* [On the ideological struggle in today's situation]." *Tạp chí cộng sản 21* (2005): 3–8.

———. *"Thách thức của sự phát triển và quá trình đào tạo cử nhân tài năng ở Trường Đại học Khoa học Tự nhiên"*. *Tạp chí cộng sản 17* (2004): 62–65.

Nguyễn Trọng Điều. *"Về quy trình và phương thức đào tạo, bồi dưỡng cán bộ lãnh đạo"*. *Tạp chí cộng sản 16* (2002).

Socialist Republic of Vietnam. Decision of the prime minister on the approval of "The Education Development Strategic Plan for 2001–10", No. 201/2001/QĐ-TTG, 28 December. Hanoi: The Government of Vietnam, 2001.

St. George, E. "Government Policy and Changes to Higher Education in Vietnam 1986–1998: Education in Transition for Development?". Canberra: Department of Political and Social Change, RSPAS, Australian National University, 2003.

Trường, Giang. *"Cần xóa bỏ lô cốt bảo thủ trong quản lý giáo dục"*. *VietNam Net*, <http://vietnamnet.vn>, 2006.

Văn, Tiến. *"Quốc hội thông qua Luật Giáo Dục (sửa đổi)"*. *VietNam Net*, <http://vietnamnet.vn>, 2005.

8

CHALLENGES TO HIGHER EDUCATION REFORM
A University Management Perspective

Nguyễn Minh Hồng

Vietnam's higher education system was designed to generate and circulate knowledge under prescient central management. In practice, these arrangements produced poor results. In the face of urgent new challenges — such as economic globalization — the Vietnamese Government has decided (once again) to reform higher education. While the current round of higher education reform resembles previous reforms in some respects (such as calls for increased autonomy), other aspects of the reforms are novel and even promising. One such example is a Dutch-sponsored project on the development of professional higher education — the Vietnam–Netherlands project on Professionally Oriented Higher Education (PROFED, March 2005– March 2009). Commencing in 2005, eight universities were chosen to participate in this project which, in agreement with Ministry of Education and Training (MOET), provided the participating universities with increased managerial autonomy, so they could develop curriculum following competency-based principles.

Researchers at Hưng Yên University of Technical Teacher Education (HYU) — one of the eight universities chosen — used this opportunity to develop a curriculum responsive to the needs of regional employers. Specifically, researchers undertook a survey of employers in sixty-two representatively selected enterprises in the Red River delta, including interviews with nearly two hundred managers and engineers. Based on the data, graduate competency profiles were developed and used as the basis for development of two curricula for undergraduates majoring in Electrical Engineering and Information Technology. For these curricula to be implemented successfully at the university level, a new learner-centred pedagogy would also be required, as would a new learning environment. Unfortunately, the absence of such conditions at the university undermined the implementation of the new curricula.

The analysis suggests tremendous challenges remain in Vietnam's higher education system. If innovative programmes such as the Dutch programme are to yield results, higher education reforms will have to address outstanding rigidities and pathologies in the organizational management of higher education more effectively. Doing so will enhance the prospects for more innovative reforms and help improve the quality of graduates. Specifically, we conclude that the reform process in higher education requires a faculty level (bottom-up) change from teacher-centred to learner-centred principles, and at the university level, a change from commanding administration to supportive and quality-responsive management, but such reforms can only be successful in concurrence with changes at the system level.

ECONOMIC CHANGE AND THE IMPORTANCE OF PROFESSIONAL EDUCATION

It is widely appreciated that Vietnam's movement to a market economy and its associated process of integration with the regional and world economy has spurred economic growth and permitted certain improvements in the availability and quality of education. There is also considerable awareness of some of the challenges facing higher education. What is not frequently recognized is that the country has seen equally profound cultural changes regarding education. Among other things, the movement to a market economy has freed individual initiative and created a society in which innovations are increasingly valued and even rewarded. But herein lies a paradox: while there is tremendous vitality in Vietnam's population — the spirit of individual initiative and innovation is visible to any visitor — and while there is a tremendous thirst and need for skills, the country's higher education institutions have been slow to accommodate this energy. Indeed, there is wide recognition that Vietnam's institutions of higher education are not meeting the country's needs and that meeting these needs would require urgent action.

As was noted in the introduction to this volume, the present round of higher education reforms in Vietnam is not the first round. Previous efforts were aimed at partial aspects of the whole system (such as changes in style of writing letters, school textbooks, "two stage" higher education), but neglected basic issues such as educational philosophy and mission of the education system. As a result, the reforms' effectiveness was doomed. But now there is a greater sense of urgency. Perhaps most basically, there is a huge bottleneck emerging: Vietnam today has a young population. Over 28 per cent of eighty five million inhabitants are below the age of fifteen, while only ten per cent of the relevant age group participates in higher education.[1]

The Government of Vietnam and individual universities have attempted to respond to the mounting social demands by rapidly expanding the higher education system. During the last decade (1998–2008), MOET allowed seventy-eight new universities to be established, almost equal to the whole higher education development during the previous half century (in total, only eighty-two universities were established in the period 1953–98). And just in the recent two years (2006–07), half of that number, that is, thirty-nine new universities, came into existence. This hurried development, although addressing the enrolment demands of learners, reflects the lack of strategic planning, because many of these universities turn out to have insufficient manpower in terms of both quantity, quality, and infrastructure to provide adequate education quality as MOET itself concluded at a recent workshop on "Development and Operation of Universities and Colleges established in 1998–08".[2] There is, in short, a general gap between will and skill, and a general shortage of students with professional skills suited to Vietnam's needs.

At the institutional level, universities are centrally controlled by MOET on almost every aspect of education, from curriculum (content, organization of teaching, testing, and examining) to enrolment, finance, and senior university personnel. This rigidity makes it hard for universities to react more responsibly to society needs. In an official evaluation,[3] beside modest praise for achievements, certain weaknesses were pointed out: poor quality of training; inadequate educational/training scale; inappropriate system and institutional structures; limited resources; rigid/inflexible training programmes; lack of lecturers and managers in terms of both quantity and qualification; heavily subsidized, bureaucratic, and controlled macromanagement; and inefficient national investment due to the lack of a national strategic plan for higher education development.

For example, many universities have greatly expanded the number of courses (and therefore graduates) in various degree and non-degree programmes, particularly in areas that do not require great investment (for example, economics, accounting, simple IT training, and foreign languages). But they have done so with flimsy resources, excessively big enrolment, overloaded staff and infrastructure, and no serious quality assurance. The results have been poor programmes and poor students.

Recognizing these and other inadequacies, the Vietnamese Government has issued Resolution No. 14/2005/NQ-CP, which lays out an ambitious Higher Education Reform Agenda.[4] This agenda includes two fundamental reforms: the division of higher education into two streams, research-oriented and professionally oriented streams, and increasing universities' autonomy.

A POLICY EXPERIMENT: CURRICULAR DEVELOPMENT AT HƯNG YÊN UNIVERSITY

In March 2005, the Netherlands Association for Universities of Applied Sciences (HBO–raad) and MOET embarked on a joint four-year project aimed at developing professionally oriented higher education (POHE). This project (hereafter referred to as PROFED) was designed with two main objectives in mind: to improve students' career options by developing professional education programmes in an experimental form that would emphasize responsiveness to the labour market; and to develop a model for professionally oriented higher education policy with a new policy implementation role for MOET.[5] A key component of this project was that MOET would grant chosen universities the freedom to go beyond existing curriculum regulations and to develop instead competency-based learning curricula informed by the needs of "the world of work" (that is, labour markets) and consistent with international practices in the area of professional education. Universities would then be allowed to implement these new curricula, subject to the approval of university boards, not MOET. In agreeing to these terms it was clear MOET had taken an important step towards decentralized management.

Hưng Yên University of Technical Teacher Education (HYU), located 40 km east of Hanoi in Hưng Yên Province — just at the centre of the Red River delta — was established in 2003 by a MOET decision to upgrade the former College of Technical Teacher Education No.1, whose history traces back to the Hưng Yên Industrial Vocational School founded in 1966. Thus HYU has a rather long tradition as a technical skills training centre. In the summer of 2007, the first rector retired after twenty years of service. The new rector, formerly head of a chemistry research laboratory at another university, was unknown to most HYU staff prior to his appointment by MOET in July 2007.

HYU's facilities and teaching staff qualifications were adequate for technical education at a junior college level, but not for university education. Until the upgrading decision was made in 2003, there was no research laboratory, and there had been only two staff with PhD degrees, one in theoretical physics and the other in mechanical engineering. As of 2007, the university had seven faculties: mechanical engineering, automotive mechanics, electronic and electrical engineering, textile and fashion, information technology, technical pedagogy and basic sciences (for teaching subjects such as mathematics, physics, and chemistry).

Naturally, for its new mission, this university needs more investment in infrastructure and manpower. However, until 2007, the infrastructure upgrading process had been slow. Some facilities have been obtained through existing foreign projects (mostly from various German technical support projects and some from this PROFED project). A number of new classrooms were built from the so-called *vốn tự có*, on "capital raised" from tuition fees. Still, and despite these fundamental difficulties, the university has grown fast, especially since 2007 under the regime of the new rector, in terms of staff and enrolment. In 2003, HYU had about 120 teaching staff, in addition to about sixty administrative staff, and around 3,000 students. By 2008 the teaching staff numbered 370 (out of a total 460 staff) and enrolment rose up to well above 10,000.[6] Almost all new staff are new graduates from other advanced universities, such as the Hà Nội University of Technology or Hà Nội National University.

The rapid growth of HYU is not uncommon and illustrates the huge need for higher education, as well as the pressure existing on the whole higher education system, both in terms of opportunity (to develop new and expand existing educational institutions) and threat (to maintain education quality). Realizing its weaknesses (in staff and infrastructure) as well as its strengths, especially in technical skills training, HYU originally found in the PROFED project an opportunity to build itself along the professional higher education stream. The author was assigned to lead the university PROFED team.

In the PROFED project, participating universities were to develop one curriculum in collaboration with a Dutch University. But HYU decided to develop two curricula, Electrical Engineering (EE) and Information Communication Technology (ICT), within the budget limited for only one curriculum. The two Dutch partners were Fontys University of Applied Sciences and Saxion University of Applied Sciences. In what follows, I describe the conduct and outcomes of one of the project's core tasks: curricular development on the basis of an empirical survey of employers and their technical staff — the so-called "world of work" (WoW).

To carry out this project, the HYU project team designed and conducted a survey of employers using questionnaire and interview surveying techniques provided by the Dutch experts. During a ten-day period in January 2006, four groups of three lecturers visited sixty-two representatively selected enterprises. The teams went to the Red River delta and interviewed 200 managers and engineers, and at least one manager and two engineers per enterprise. In terms of ownership, 58 per cent were state owned, 22 per cent were joint ventures with foreign ownership, and 20 per cent were private (including totally foreign-owned companies). Questionnaires were prepared, but after a trial survey it was recognized that direct dialogue with closed-response and open-ended questions were much more informative. In addition to information on the company's organization and scope of activities, three main kinds of information were obtained: (1) the company's demand for university graduates given their short- and long-term vision; (2) the quality of newly graduated engineers and the company's policy on additional training; and (3) the company's proposal on revising engineering curricula and their vision of the relationship between the company and universities. An open invitation was also given to employers interested in bridging the existing gap between university and the company by taking part in a WoW committee to be established at the university.

Analysis of the obtained results allowed us to formulate job descriptions and skills and competency requirements for a range of specific EE and ICT jobs.[7] The significance of the survey and curricular development projects in Hưng Yên and the other seven participating universities should be underscored: This is the first time in Vietnam that higher education curricula have been developed on the basis of job competency profiles. While competency standards and skill profiles are available in the United States[8] and in Europe,[9] they are totally new to Vietnamese higher education. The establishment of a WoW committee integrated into the universities' organization was also new and exciting for the project participants.

The Hưng Yên surveys and interviews yielded interesting and useful insights. According to employers, newly hired engineers lacked both practical knowledge and skills, and 85 per cent of the newly hired required anywhere from six months to 24 months to perform his or her job satisfactorily.[10] Correspondingly, some 53 per cent of enterprises surveyed provide on-the-job training, whereas the other 30 per cent, most of which are joint ventures with foreign partners or foreign-owned companies, provide short-course training, either on site by foreign experts, or at their mother company facilities abroad. Almost all employers shared the view that new employees lack problem solving/work planning skills, communication/presentation skills, and teamwork skills. These observations are in general agreement with conclusions drawn by a U.S.-sponsored survey of the four most prestige universities located in Hanoi and Hồ Chí Minh City and published in the summer of 2006.[11]

As university outreach programmes have been largely unknown in Vietnam, one of our major questions concerned the interest in industry-university collaboration. Interestingly, 93 per cent of companies had positive reactions concerning mutually beneficial university-enterprise relationships. In the surveys and interviews, employers stressed that university training programmes need to follow enterprise production technology closely and that any internship would need to be sufficiently long for employers to train the students effectively. For example, 66 per cent of employers surveyed proposed periods of six months or more, whereas present internships are usually shorter than two months. Employers also emphasized the need to train employees in "soft skills", as well as the English language. For the long-term development of university-enterprise relations, employers suggested the need to upgrade every aspect of university education, for universities to provide retraining for companies' technical staff, and for applied research to help solve companies' technical problems. Some employers even suggested that universities play a role in the installation and maintenance of companies' facilities and machinery.

The WoW survey conducted was successful, not only in the sense that it provided information to analyse required knowledge, skills, and values, but it also convinced our project team of the urgency of change, thus helping to facilitate the growth of support for the initiative, from just a few people at the beginning, to most of the university's two faculties after just two and half years of activity (from March 2005 to October 2007). Based on our surveys and international experience, it is clear that Vietnam requires engineering graduates with both better basic and specialized competencies, as well as broad professional training in skills and values, such as English and teamwork. Producing such graduates will require a new curriculum, which was precisely the aim of the PROFED project.

Until today, curricula in Vietnam universities are rigidly and centrally designed — with so-called "curriculum frameworks" or "standard curriculum" approved by MOET that universities have to adopt with only minor space for modification. The content is overwhelmingly theoretical and abstract. Students are asked to learn everything by rote, while little attention is paid to project assignments that could help them to integrate their subject knowledge and to develop their problem solving and teamwork skills. Learning is still a one-way process where teachers are expected to deliver a lecture, standing in front of the class while students take notes. At the end of the course, students will take an exam usually comprised of questions that they could answer by repeating, rather than understanding what they have memorized.[12] It is this learning approach that makes Vietnam higher education a failure in delivering graduates qualified to meet WoW demands. According to the modern theory of education, knowledge and comprehension are only the lowest levels on the hierarchy of cognitive skills,[13] whereas research indicates that students need to develop their skills to apply, analyse, synthesize, and evaluate in order to acquire the highest degree of cognition. New educational philosophy, particularly in the field of professional education, suggests education needs to emphasize competency-based learning.

Developing new curricula on principles of competency-based learning was totally new to all eight universities, and to a large extent, to the Vietnam higher education system. The process of developing the new curricula proved exciting. For the first time, university staff were allowed to design, and thus own, "their" curricula. The new curricula at HYU included such subjects and modules as "Job Orientation" and "Communication Skills" that are not available in the MOET standard curriculum. The curricula for both EE and ICT offered longer internships (of up to a full semester's length). Problem-based learning was integrated into the curricula through a series of projects starting from the first to the fourth year of study. These projects were to be designed to be performed by groups of students. Overall, the practical/theoretical studying load ratio in the curricula has increased from about 30/70 to 60/40. We found that not only will we be able to train students to achieve designed levels of competencies, but that our designed curricula would allow a logical articulation from a college level degree to a university one — a problem that the Vietnam education system has not been able to solve appropriately until today.[14] It implies, however, that curricula at the college level would have to be redesigned on the same competency-based principles. Thus only by reorganizing the education system on the basis of competency-based-training, can the Vietnam education system be able to provide Vietnamese citizens with an appropriate educational environment for lifelong learning.

With this new approach in higher education, it also becomes possible to address the most critical challenge of the current Vietnam higher education system — the quality of graduates. By developing close linkages with the labour market and building curricula addressing its needs, we are able to bring graduates' competencies closer to the needs of the labour market. However, in order to implement these curricula successfully from the organizational management point of view, tremendous challenges need to be overcome which I will discuss in the next section. However, actually implementing these curricula presents tremendous challenges in its own right.

IMPLEMENTATION CHALLENGES

At the HYU, we have started to implement the two curricula to freshmen in October 2007, with the participation of 400 students from the Information Technology (IT) and Electrical Engineering (EE) faculties. But implementing the new curricula has encountered large obstacles, in large part because the systemic policy reforms designed for achievement at the system level (MOET) within the PROFED framework were still not implemented after two years. However useful, interesting and productive the surveys, interviews, and curriculum development activities were, they were not accompanied by the reforms to facilitate the implementation process.[15] In particular, attention needs to be given to lecturers' competencies, the organization and management of higher education, funding, and students' learning habits.

In the following discussion, I will concentrate on issues related to interactions among major stakeholders within the education system. These include lecturer competencies, organizational management system, and students' learning habits.

Lecturers' Attitude and Competences

At first it was believed that it would not be easy for HYU lecturers to adapt quickly to the new way of teaching, especially in a culture such as the Vietnamese where there is a deep tradition of respect for teachers and a distance between teachers and students. However, after some initial hesitation, young Vietnamese lecturers became excited about the new teaching philosophy. They have been actively participating in the curriculum-development process and the practice of a student-centred teaching methodology. They were so devoted that in the first week of November 2007, one month after learning that the management of this university was considering a reduction in the scale of implementation to only one quarter of total freshmen due to cost reasons, the staff of the IT faculty managed to persuade university management to allow all IT students to continue studying with the new ICT curriculum. For the EE curriculum, however, the situation is not as positive as will be explained later in this chapter.

The major problem regarding lecturers is the lack of those with practical skills, knowledge, and time. Selection for university employment has not been based on industry experience, but on previous academic performance and degrees held. As mentioned previously, to increase university income, many universities increase enrolments (for degree as well as non-degree programmes), exceeding their education resource capacity. Lecturers are paid according to time spent lecturing and thus try to lecture more,[16] and have little time for anything else, even for research.[17]

Guest lecturers from companies are crucial to profession-oriented programmes. However, it is not a common practice in Vietnam for universities to invite experienced engineers to participate in university education. A policy needs to be developed to encourage universities to exploit this important resource.

University Organization and Management System

In the PROFED project, a bottom-up process of educational change, starting from lecturers and faculties, achieved a certain momentum. However, organization and management rigidities at the level of university administration have jeopardized and continue to jeopardize the PROFED project and its prospects of success.

Unlike elsewhere in the world where academic professional experts (professors) are the foundation of universities, Vietnam's universities are based on an administrative hierarchy,[18] comprising in many cases of non-academic officers performing defined roles to keep the university in line with numerous MOET and related (finance, labour) ministries' regulations. The regulations cover everything from personnel, decisions on investment and expenditure, to enrolment, curriculum, learning methodology, and assessment methods. In addition, social and political organizations also take part in university administration.[19] In this hierarchical system, lecturers who play no role in administration are, in practice, at the lowest position. Therefore it is not surprising that the dean of a faculty is not considered as important as the head of an administrative department with regard to the decision making process within universities. Moreover, the system has come to function in a more or less impersonal manner in the sense that any lecturer can be replaced without much affecting the whole education enterprise. Education becomes less a creative approach than a routine procedure that every educator has to follow. This bureaucratic administration, together with the fact that university heads are appointed by a higher administrative body (MOET), and not through election,[20] results in a phenomenon that certain university heads become "very afraid of responsibility".[21] In fact, a person promoted to rector could hold this position until retirement, or be promoted to an even higher position in the hierarchy, provided he does nothing wrong. Thus fear of responsibility mentioned above is reflective of a person who is simply trying to avoid making mistakes by taking no personal initiatives.[22]

On the other hand, it is very easy for a rector to misuse his power, because under the current regulations, the rector has the full right to decide every university activity, including personnel promotion, and there is practically no effective internal regulatory mechanism for a democratic decision making process.[23]

Within the PROFED project, frustration to a certain degree about indifferent university leadership from time to time could be seen among project teams. Careful university leaders naturally listen to MOET before deciding to implement anything new at the university. Reforms developed by PROFED teams have sometimes been considered too radical or too progressive and treated with scepticism because another part of the PROFED project — to work with MOET to develop a framework for a profession-oriented higher education policy — failed.[24]

Another problem encountered was discontinuity in university policy that occurred with changes in university leadership. As a matter of fact, the lack of a comprehensive long-term strategic plan built in conjunction with university staff is a common problem for the Vietnamese higher education system. Every leader has his or her own personal vision and subjective ambition and a change in leadership naturally leads to university policy change, either for the better or worse, depending on the leader's personal quality and education background.[25] Indeed, this has happened at HYU. Under the former rector who was conscious of improving university education quality, the university had rather moderate enrolment increases, with an objective attain 10,000 students by 2010, and the PROFED project had been fully supported. Starting from September 2007, the new rector decided the university should develop very fast in terms of staff and enrolment. The result is that the enrolment for the academic year 2008–09, including informal/part-time students, reached 13,000.[26] In December 2007, the new rector decided that HYU should pursue a research-oriented rather than a profession-oriented direction, irrespective of its lack of research manpower and infrastructure. The rector accused the PROFED project team of violating MOET's regulation on curricula and ordered the two PROFED curricula to be revised to follow the standard MOET curricula closely. The ordered revisions were made from December 2007–January 2008 and implemented from February 2008. To facilitate this university policy change, in December 2007, the new rector took control of the PROFED project team and in January 2008, replaced the deans of both ICT and EE faculties, regardless of their reputations.

It will be hard to change an administrative system that had a commanding role in every step of the education process into one accepting new roles relating to support, services, and quality assurance. This will be a change not only in habits, but also in the social system of values, and thus culture. And in the long term, organizational management change will be the greatest challenge for the Vietnam higher education system. This is true even of the top national universities, which were supposed to have greater autonomy, but which remain dependent on MOET, and locked in an ineffective management mode.

If the higher education management system does not change, rapid improvements in research and education quality will not materialize.[27]

Educational Expenditure

It is clear that making curricula more competency based can improve the quality of graduates. However, quality cannot be attained for nothing; it has a price, which is both countable and uncountable. The first is concerns lecturers' time and effort. As mentioned above, under the current salary system, lecturers are paid based on their time spent actually lecturing, whereas coaching and supervising require more time and responsibility that cannot always be measured. Thus education expenses per student increase. Furthermore, the new curricula require students to do more practical work in projects and internships. These activities elevate education expenses even further. Seeing the cost of education cost escalate in the first month, October 2007, the university administration considered a 75 percent reduction in the number of students using these new curricula, that is, forcing 300 students back to using the old curricula. During the first two weeks of November 2007, educators of the two faculties, Electrical Engineering and Information Technology, had tried to persuade the administration to continue using the new curricula. For ICT it was possible because extra expenses of the new curriculum did not cost much. For EE which is more costly, the faculty and students decided that those who wanted to continue with the new curriculum would have to pay an extra amount for their studies. This situation would last for one year, as the Vietnam Government allows the university to adjust the tuition fee.[28] The advent of state loans for student studies in September 2007 enabled a compromise solution so that all EE students could afford this tuition fee.[29]

However, in December 2007, the new rector ordered the project team to revise the two curricula so that it would follow closely the existing MOET standard curricula (also called the "curriculum frameworks"). The ordered revisions had been made from December 2007 to January 2008 when the rector effectively took over the PROFED project. Six months of general education that had been eliminated were reinstituted. Thanks to the efforts of the new dean of the ICT faculty, the ICT curriculum is still structurally that of a PROFED curriculum, albeit with six months of general education! By contrast while the EE curriculum is now simply a standard curriculum with some PROFED elements, such as longer internship and additional practice assignments. Thus there was a reversal taking place at this university in 2008 even as the education expenditure problem discussed above is no longer a relevant issue. Fortunately, this move at HYU only seems to reflect the individual vision of its new rector, not MOET policy. In fact, PROFED has gradually gained important support from senior MOET staff. In a PROFED meeting in May of 2008, MOET vice-minister, Prof. Dr Bành Tiến Long, highlighted the positive contributions of this project to higher education reform and proposed prolonging the PROFED project into a second phase after March 2009.[30] In a meeting on 9 August 2008, he concluded:

> For MOET, the experiments at these pilot study programmes are of utmost importance; it will create a foundation for developing a national policy framework on POHE (professional-oriented higher education) and provides support for the realization of one of the most important policy objectives of the Higher Education Reform Agenda: "in 2020, 70 – 80 percent of all HE students should be enrolled in professionally oriented programmes".[31]

As far as national education expenditure is concerned, Vietnam now spends about twenty per cent of national expenditure (about 8.5 per cent of GDP) on education. More careful study of the efficacy of budgeting is in order, as it is apparent that university budgets could be allocated more effectively without increasing tuition fees.[32]

Students' Learning Habits and Awareness

Vietnamese students arrive at university unprepared for active learning due to the passive learning reinforced earlier in their school years. Furthermore, the division of university entrance exams into branches A (mathematics, physics, chemistry), B (biology, chemistry, mathematics), C (literature, history, geography), and D (mathematics, literature, foreign languages) creates unidimensional graduates who are also often short on the skills they require. Improving social awareness of professionally oriented higher education will be important for the development of this type of education. This type of education is part of a worldwide tendency to bridge education and the labour market. It has been effective not only in developing countries, but also in Western countries over a dozen years ago. Its mission is to prepare a well educated workforce for the country's future socio-economic development, and its programmes aim at the bulk of students, up to 80 per cent by 2020 in the Vietnamese context. For Vietnamese society, emphasis on achieving the highest degree of education possible is the wish of millions of families. But professionally oriented higher education, by bringing graduates closer to employment, is the best assurance of having a job relevant to one's choice and thus the shorter route to achieving individual lifelong learning objectives.

CONCLUSION

"The shift from teaching-based to learning-based is much more than a simple semantic change, it is a dramatic shift in the basic way we think about the educational enterprise."[33] The PROFED project, as an experiment for university autonomy in curriculum development, has given the eight participating universities a great opportunity to design a new approach to education. During the course of curriculum development, at each university, the project teams developed into energetic coalitions leading important change processes. Rigid management and an indifferent managerial mentality within universities remain major obstacles. Policy development at the system (MOET) level, which has been designed into the PROFED project, has not kept pace with university team activities and thus has been inefficient to reform university management in appropriate ways. The coexistence of the new curriculum, designed according to the modern philosophy of education, and the traditional bureaucratic management structure, already regarded as one of the main reasons for the education quality problem, makes it difficult for new curriculum implementation and will certainly limit the project's success differently at different universities. At HYU, the change in university management unexpectedly changed the PROFED project's course of development. Fortunately, due largely to the strong commitment of the PROFED team, professionally oriented higher education (POHE) features are still present in the two developed curricula, especially in the ICT curriculum.

Contributions of the PROFED project at the eight universities and the rising need for management policy reform have been acknowledged by

MOET in an official evaluation given to more than a hundred university rectors and management staff at the MOET Conference on Professionally Oriented Higher Education in September 2008:

> After three years running the PROFED project the first clear signs of transfer of the POHE concept and approach to other study programmes in Vietnam are becoming visible. As the POHE concept becomes reality in Vietnam, it raises a need for a national policy framework and guiding principles on that concept. This framework would support the realization of one of the most important policy objectives of the Vietnamese government stated in Resolution 14/2005/NQ-CP "*to enroll a majority of the students in career application [profession-oriented] programmes by 2020*".[34]

In February 2007, in coordination with PROFED project, MOET organized a first large stakeholder conference, called "National Conference on Education based on Society's Needs" in Hồ Chí Minh city.[35] A number of PROFED universities participated with important contributions. It was encouraging because for the first time, the mission of higher education to address society needs has been seriously considered, although with some confusion.[36] In October 2007, tremendous changes occurred in MOET's awareness and policy towards professionally oriented higher education. Under the chairmanship of Deputy Prime Minister and Minister of Education and Training, Dr Nguyễn Thiện Nhân, MOET organized a two-part "National Conference on Manpower Training and Scientific Research for the Needs of Enterprises", in Hồ Chí Minh City on 28 October and in Hanoi on 10 November 2007. A breakthrough is Dr Nhân's decision to offer a 2–3 per cent tax reduction for enterprises that take part in education,[37] a proposal discussed earlier within PROFED project teams.[38] Other decisions such as state investment to improve university infrastructure, policies to facilitate university-enterprise relationship development, have also been proposed at the conference in Hanoi (see note 36). It is now a matter of formulation of details and implementing new policies. In September 2008, a National Committee on Education based on Society's Needs (*Ban chỉ đạo quốc gia về đào tạo theo nhu cầu xã hội*) was established and held its first meeting.[39]

The autonomy in PROFED allowed in the area of curriculum development shows that partially granted autonomy can bring about limited improvements in higher education institutions.

Higher education reform at the faculty level (bottom-up change, from teacher-centred to learner-centred principles) can only be successful when it takes place in concurrence with reforms in university administration (from controlling and commanding to supportive and quality-conscious and responsive management) and reforms at the system level (from learning-process to learning-output management).

With Resolution No. 14/2005/NQ-CP, universities in Vietnam will be granted greater autonomy. From our analysis, one cannot deny that quality improvement requires the right kind of investments. But education quality can easily be compromised if university management fails to develop its "quality consciousness".[40] University autonomy should go hand in hand with university social responsibility. It requires universities to be restructured with a new organization philosophy, where lecturers are of pivotal importance within the university hierarchy and education quality is among the university's core values. University leaders should be chosen through a transparent selection process to promote competent reformers (or at least reform supporters) who, in turn, would lead or assist change at universities. Internal regulatory mechanisms need to be set up to keep university leaders accountable and encourage active participation of lecturers in university effective management, which will in turn improve university performance and thus its social accountability.

Therefore the best university organizational management is expected to be built on the basis of intellectual excellence.

Notes and References

The author is grateful to the PROFED project which provided him with the opportunity to take an in-depth look at Vietnam's higher education problems. Special thanks are due to Dr Pieter Bon of the Business School of Fontys University of Applied Sciences in Eindhoven, the Netherlands, and to Phạm Thanh Tùng and Nguyễn Đình Hân of HYU for their shared vision and close cooperation. Last, but not least, the support of the retired rector, Dr Võ Thanh Bình, in the period 2003–07 had been crucial for the project team's achievements that are at the root of profound changes still taking place today in the two faculties, Electronics and Electrical Engineering and Information Technology.

1. Arian van Staa and Nguyễn Thị Liên Hương, paper for the UKFIET conference, Oxford, United Kingdom, 11–13 September 2007, <www.cfbt.com/ukfiet>, "Increasing Responsiveness of Higher Education: First Experiences of a Vietnam-Netherlands Cooperation Project".

2. MOET statistics and conclusions reported at the workshop "Development and Operation of Universities and Colleges Established in 1998–2008", Hanoi 30 August 2008, see <http://vietnamnet.vn/giaoduc/2008/08/801447/>.

3. MOET, Vietnam Higher Education Reform Agenda, 2006–20, English circulation version, pp. 12–14.

4. See Ngo Doan Dai, for proceedings of the workshop's, "Higher Education Development in Vietnam by 2010: Goals, Strategic Measures, Implementation and Challenges".

5. See Vietnam-Netherlands Higher Education Project, <www.vietnethhep. edu.vn>; The eight universities participating in PROFED are: Hanoi National Economics University in Hanoi Agricultural University No. 1 in Hanoi, Thái Nguyên University Of Agriculture and Forestry, Thái Nguyên University of Education, Huế University of Agriculture and Forestry, Hưng Yên University of Technical Teacher Education, Vinh University, Hồ Chí Minh Nông Lâm University (Hồ Chí Minh University Of Agriculture and Forestry).

6. The statistics are on the university's website, <www.utehy.edu.vn>, and data for 2008 were given by Nguyen Quoc Thin, head of HYU's department for academic affairs, in September 2008 in a private communication with the author.

7. For readers who are not familiar with this concept, professional competency are qualifications that an engineer possesses in order to perform in a satisfactorily manner his assigned tasks in an industrial context. Professional competency can be defined as knowledge, skills, and attitudes. Furthermore, engineers are also expected to possess common/social soft skills. See, for example, Michael Eraut, *Developing Professional Knowledge and Competence* (London: Routledge/Falmer, 2006).

8. See for example, <www.abet.org>.

9. See for example, <www.jointquality.nl>.

10. This is a clear indication of the low quality of Vietnamese higher education. As a matter of fact, in 2007, of 2,000 interviewees, Intel Vietnam could select only forty candidates for their US$1/- billion factory being built in Hồ Chí Minh City (see *"Nhà máy Intel VN đang thiếu nhân lực trầm trọng"* [Intel Vietnam facing critical manpower shortage], *Vietnam Net*, 9 June 2008, <http://vietnamnet.vn/cntt/2008/06/787464>.

11. See <www.vef.gov>, "Observations on Undergraduate Education in Computer Science, Electrical Engineering, and Physics at Select Universities in Vietnam".

12. Extensive descriptions of university education situations can be found in Note 11.

13. Benjamin S. Bloom, *Taxonomy of Education Objectives* (Allyn and Bacon, MA: Pearson Education, 1984).

14. On 26 October 2004, MOET issued Guidance No. 6147/QĐ-BGD&ĐT-ĐH&SĐH on temporary regulation of articulation training. Starting from that date, there has been an ongoing debate about current articulations from lower degrees to university. These articulations are artificial because training programmes are designed from a knowledge base. See for example "*Đào tạo liên thông: Chưa thông đã vội mở rộng*" [Articulation training: open widely when curricula are not articulated as yet], *Vietnam Net*, 3 January 2006, republished from the newspaper *Sài Gòn Giải Phóng*, <http://VietNamnet.vn/giaoduc/tuyensinh/2006/01/528836/>.

15. In mid-2007, the learning objective at the level of the Higher Education Department (HED) of MOET had not been realized adequately. The creation of the subcommittee referred to in Resolution 14/2005/NQ-CP stagnated and, as a result, the proposed link between PROFED and the implementation of national policy was not realized. ... Doubts arose about the necessity of an active approach within a project whose aim was to experiment with decentralized government management. ... Nevertheless, little progress has been made with regard to the concrete implementation of what MOET understands by profession-oriented higher education in Vietnam and how it sees its policy implementation role with regard to realizing the objectives set out in the Resolution, namely to offer 70 per cent of the students this type of education within twelve years.

 This evaluation was made in September 2007 by Arian van Staa and Nguyễn Thị Liên Hương, as quoted in Note 2.

16. A teacher's salary is composed of two parts, a fixed part largely dependent on his/her time serving in education, and a flexible part, paid in proportional to the number of teaching hours performed in a month. This system encourages teachers to spend all their time only for teaching.

17. In our university and elsewhere, there are lecturers who teach twice the standard amount of teaching hours regulated by MOET. See also Hanh Van *Người Lao Động* (Worker), 22 December 2006; ("Sad reality for university staff: lecturing too much, forgetting research) or Thanh Hà, *Khi các giảng viên chỉ còn là "thợ dạy"* ... [Research in universities: When staff become merely lecturing workers], *Tuổi Trẻ Online*, 24 June 2005, <http://www.tuoitre.com.vn/Tianyon/Index.aspx?ArticleID=84834&ChannelID=13>. A fixed salary, independent of teaching duties, would enable lecturers to devote themselves more to improving education quality and would resolve this problem, but it would take the Vietnamese Government a long time to accomplish.

18. Hoàng Ngọc Vinh, "*Cần sớm triển khai 6 công việc trong tầm ngắn hạn và 4 công việc tầm xa để tăng dần quyền tự chủ cho các trường, xóa bỏ cơ chế bộ chủ quản*" [University autonomy: 6 short term, 4 long term issues

to be done], *Vietnam Net*, 11 November 2006, <http://VietNamnet.vn/kinhte/vieclam/2006/11/632347/>.

19. In fact, Vietnamese universities are overwhelmingly politicized, in the sense that the Communist Party system is established parallel with the university administration system and plays the leading role in all decisions making processes at every level of the system. Senior administration staff, such as the rector, have to be party members.

20. In fact, almost twenty years ago, MOET (the Ministry of Higher Education at that time) allowed the University of Hanoi (part of present-day Hanoi National University) to experiment with electing its own rector. It had been an exciting phenomenon. However, the author does not know why by the end of this elected rector's term of service, MOET decided to resume its right to appoint university leader. That election was the first and was unique for Vietnam higher education.

21. Huỳnh Hữu Tuệ, a former Canadian professor shared his observation after working a few years at the College of Engineering, Hanoi National University: *"Tôi thấy rất rõ về cách làm việc kỳ cục: Lãnh đạo rất sợ trách nhiệm"*. [I see very clearly a strange way of working: leaders are very afraid of responsibility]. <http://www.gel.ulaval.ca/~huynh/Huynh_en.htm>; *"Giáo sư Canada gốc Việt Huỳnh Hữu Tuệ: Giáo dục Việt Nam: Quá "kỳ dị" và "dị kỳ" quá!"* [Vietnamese-Canadian professor Huỳnh Hữu Tuệ: Vietnam education: too "bizarre", and too "strange!"] *VieTimes Online*, 22 October 2007, <http://www.vietimes.com.vn/vn/doithoaiviet/3866/index.viet>.

22. The phenomenon that "a fraction of party cadres try to avoid conflicts, do not dare to take responsibility" (*"bộ phận cán bộ càng né tránh, ngại va chạm, không dám chịu trách nhiệm"*) has been so widely spreading among the party cadres who occupy positions in the administration hierarchic ladder that the secretary of Communist Party Committee of Hanoi, Nguyễn Quang Nghị, has made this criticism on 6 July 2009: "One has to say frankly that such behaviour is an unfair way for self protection, not for common/social benefit" (*"Phải nói một cách thẳng thắn rằng, đó là cách "giữ mình", không chính đáng, không xuất phát từ lợi ích chung"*). He further elaborated that emphasized selecting Party cadres for administration positions, "we need to appoint and select non corrupted cadres and party members to participate into various levels of Party committee, not the one who chooses easy tasks for himself, leaving difficult tasks for others and wants the chair (position) but avoid responsibility". (*"Chúng ta cần giới thiệu, lựa chọn những cán bộ, đảng viên không tham ô, tham nhũng tham gia cấp uỷ các cấp, chứ không lựa chọn những người luôn giành việc dễ cho mình, nhường việc khó cho người khác, chức vụ thì muốn nhận, nhưng trách nhiệm thì né tránh"*.) As will be seen in our analysis presented in this work, unless the selection of leader is made

in a transparent manner and based on merit, and a mechanism is available to regulate the leader's use of power, and keep him accountable, this kind of social sickness will still linger and become an obstacle, preventing the society from development. See: <http://www.vietnamnet.vn/chinhtri/2009/07/856775/>.

23. An example is the rector of Quy Nhơn University, Dr Trần Tín Kiệt, and the mismanagement scandal which surfaced in March 2008. See, *Thanh Niên* <www. thanhnien.com.vn/Giaoduc/2008/4/12/234181.tno>. In August 2008, there was a forum on at <www.dantri.com.vn> addressing the fate of young university lecturers. It is interesting to observe that internal university democracy and autonomy are addressed as conditions for a healthy teaching staff personal advancement and university development (see for example, "*Cơ chế thiếu dân chủ, khó có thầy giỏi*" [with a lack of democracy, retaining good teachers is difficult) *DanTri Online*, 13 August 2008, <http://dantri.com.vn/diendandantri/ Co-che-thieu-dan-chu-kho-co-thay-gioi/2008/8/246114.vip>.

24. PROFED project, mid-term evaluation, unpublished; see also Note 2.

25. There is in Vietnam a phrase "*New mandarin, new policy*", reflecting its leadership-dependent tradition — a result of the traditional autocratic culture of a hierarchic society.

26. Private communication with HYU's head of academic affairs, Nguyen Quoc Thin, in September 2008.

27. This perhaps explains why the Vietnam Government has put its effort in building an internationally recognized university with special organizational management principles, not on one of these two national universities, but on the Vietnam Academy of Sciences, where many of the staff are recognized scientists, and the administrative hierarchy is less heavy. See e.g. Vũ Quốc Phóng, *VietNamNet*, 12 September 2007, <http://vietnamnet.vn/giaoduc/ vande/2007/09/739869/>, "A sketch of a regional level university"

28. Tuition fees would increase in 2008, see interview with Deputy Prime Minister Dr Nguyễn Thiện Nhân, see Kiều Oanh, *VietNamNet*, 30/8/2007, <http://www2. VietNamnet.vn/giaoduc/2007/08/735768/>.

29. Studies loan: Prime Minister's order No. 21/2007/CT-TTg, 4 September 2007.

30. See <http://www.vietnethhep.edu.vn/index.php?option=com_content&task=bl ogcategory&id=16&Itemid=46>.

31. Deputy Minister Bành Tiến Long's keynote speech at the National Workshop: "Profession-Oriented Higher Education in Vietnam", 9 August 2008, Hạ Long, see <http://www.vietnethhep.edu.vn/index.php?option=com_content&task=blo gcategory&id=16&Itemid=46>.

32. According to Dr Phạm Minh Hạc, former minister of MOET, in a statement made at a live TV forum on education, VTC1, 17 November 2007.

33. See <http://www.eng.iastate.edu/muses/spring98/cover1.htm>.

34. Ministry of Education and Training, Vietnam-Netherlands Higher Education Project, "Key characteristics of Profession-oriented Higher Education (POHE) and Conditions for Implementation", document for discussion at the "Workshop on Profession-Oriented Higher Education in Vietnam", Hạ Long City, 9 August 2008.

35. National Conference on Education based on Society's Needs, Hồ Chí Minh City, 1–2 February 2007.

36. In an interview in February 2007, Minister of Education Dr Nguyễn Thiện Nhân said he regarded the professional oriented higher education as an education approach suitable for a poor country only, while in practice its development had been initiated in developed countries. See Hà Anh, *Vietnam Net*, 2 February 2007, "*Đào tạo theo nhu cầu: Làm giáo dục kiểu nước nghèo*" (Education on demand: an education approach for poor countries), <http://VietNamnet.vn/giaoduc/vande/2007/02/660459>.

37. Interview with Deputy Prime Minister and MOET Minister Nguyễn Thiện Nhân. See Kiều Oanh, *Vietnam Net*, 12 November 2007, "Special tax treatment to enterprises participating to education", <http://VietNamnet.vn/giaoduc/2007/11/754278>.

38. Nguyễn Minh Hồng. Presentation at PROFED project Workshop on World of Work Survey, Hanoi, 18–19 July 2006, unpublished; also Nguyễn Minh Hồng, "Foundations of Professional Oriented Higher Education, Applied to Engineering Training" in the *Proceedings of the National Conference on Higher Education for Social Needs*, pp. 30–43; Nguyễn Minh Hồng, "Manpower Training and Applied Research for the Needs of Enterprises: Awareness and Proposals", thesis submitted to Dr Hoàng Ngọc Vinh, MOET's chairman of Vocational Training.

39. The announcement was made on 24 September 2008. See website of Vietnam's Communist Party, <http://www.cpv.org.vn/tiengviet/khoagiao/details.asp?topic=9&subtopic=32&ID=BT2890840556>.

40. Interview with Professor Vũ Minh Giang, a member of the National Education Council. See "*Đổi mới giáo dục đại học bắt đầu từ giảng viên*" [Renovation of the education system begins with teachers], *Vietnam Net*, 9 August 2006, <http://VietNamnet.vn/giaoduc/vande/2006/08/600207/>.

9

MARKET-LED GLOBALIZATION AND HIGHER EDUCATION
The Case of Đà Nẵng University

Hồ Vũ Khuê Ngọc

This chapter explores impacts of globalization on higher education in Vietnam through a case study of Da Nang University (hereafter Da Nang University, or DU). Informed by literature on globalization and based on a survey of 240 DU academic and administrative staff, as well as in-depth interviews, the study aims to clarify DU's responses to globalization and how globalization processes are affecting the university's lecturers', researchers', and administrators' attitudes towards, and understanding of, higher education. The analysis finds DU operating within two institutional responses to globalization; a top-down response that emanates from the central government authority; and a bottom-up response, which has developed within DU itself. Top-down responses to the globalization of higher education in Vietnam include the emergence of a new framework for the governance of higher education that promotes greater reliance on and responsiveness to market forces among universities and greater institutional autonomy, within certain limits. DU's own response to globalization has been characterized by efforts to improve the educational quality of the institution through a more commercial model of higher education that makes use of spin-off enterprises and specialized programmes oriented to the globalizing local economy.

This study focuses on only one university, but is suggestive of how universities and colleges across Vietnam are conducting their own reform and development plans, with varying degrees of autonomy from the Ministry of Education and Training (MOET). The analysis highlights some opportunities and risks pertaining to economic, cultural, and political processes underway at DU that are associated with globalization.

GLOBALIZATION OF HIGHER EDUCATION

Globalization may be defined as the intensification of social ties across borders. Globalization is surely not new, but it is undeniable that globalization has intensified in recent decades owing to political and economic reasons, as well as certain technological advances. Contemporary globalization can be understood as "market-led" to the extent that market institutions are driving global integration. On the other hand, "market-led" globalization has emerged within a specific and competitive interstate system — and is therefore political. There is wide agreement that globalization is transforming higher education, though the sheer diversity of higher education and of globalization processes resists generalization. One generalization that can be made is that the relation between higher education and globalization is interdependent: globalization processes affect higher education, but higher education can also shape the character of globalization and its local and extralocal outcomes.

How is higher educational global? There are different ways to address this. Without examining the content of higher education, it can be observed that higher education has become a global enterprise. In wealthy countries and in many lower-income ones, higher education plays an important role in shaping economic growth and social development, though the way in which it does this varies across countries (Damme 2001, p. 2). Indeed, it is widely assumed that for nations to be successful in the global era, they must have strong higher education systems than can produce an increasing number of highly skilled and high-mobile workers who can "thrive in a constantly changing environment" (Seltzer 1996, p. 2). In a short chapter centred on the analysis of a single university, it is not possible to review the tremendous complexity of globalization and its significance to higher education. On the other hand, it will be useful to underscore how basic political, economic, and cultural aspects of globalization are relevant to higher education.

In political terms, globalization entails a redefinition in the global and local relations between the state, economy, and education, but there is tremendous cross-national variation. Almost all states have an interest in higher education, as higher education involves the development (and/or underdevelopment) of a country's human resources. In economic terms, market-led globalization has contributed to the commercialization of higher education, which has now become a significant "export" earner for comparatively "advanced" economies, such as Australia, the United States, and Singapore. As Hirsch and Weber (1999) show, globalization is driving and structuring demand for higher education's products and services, and therefore directly and indirectly affecting what higher education institutions do. Cultural dimensions of globalized higher education refer not only to transmission of ideas and values across borders (or the illusory "borderless" world). Cultural globalization also involves the spread of certain normative principles. The use of global standards of quality assurance is only one example as are globalized normative debates concerning the governance of higher education (Wagner 2004).

To be sure, the nature of globalized higher education is changing. By the year 2000, there were already an estimated 16 million students studying outside their home countries. But the globalization of higher education is no longer simply seen as being specialized international programmes and student exchanges. It has moved into the mainstream of the curricula and administrative structures at many universities (Altbach 2002; Scott 1998; Sedgwick 1999; Brown 2000). In other words, the globalization of higher education includes, in addition to student mobility, curricular reform, staff training and development, and administrative functions.

TOP-DOWN GLOBALIZATION AND HIGHER EDUCATION IN VIETNAM

Theorists of globalization have observed that globalization can result in either or both transnational homogenization and localized differentiation (Roberson 1995). Higher education institutions around the world have had to change to cope with the challenges of market-led globalization and the opportunities and risks it presents. But the way in which they do so depends much on local contexts and circumstances, including features of the national and local political economy, and the interests and capacities of those heading tertiary education institutions. The globalization of higher education can be examined on many different levels as globalization affects different actors differently. One useful, if perhaps simple, way of thinking about globalization within a given country is to examine it from the perspective of national and local actors and authorities.

As in many developing countries, Vietnam's is currently facing pressing issues on how to modernize and internationalize the economy rapidly. In Vietnam, the state's current efforts at higher education reform are subordinate to a national project: to develop a multisector commodity economy under market mechanisms with state control. From the perspective of the central state, the function of higher education is fundamentally different from that in the past. Under state-socialism, the idealized function of higher education was to provide a foundation for centrally planned socialist industrialization. Although state-socialist Vietnam was internationally isolated, higher education still had globalized attributes, the prime example of which were the tens of thousands of Vietnamese who received academic training overseas, and in Eastern Europe and the Soviet Union in particular. Ironically, many of these people — trained in command economies — are leading Vietnamese universities in a marketized climate.

In the context of market reforms, the Vietnamese Government has sought to globalize higher education in a much different way. The state now sees higher education as a means to improve Vietnam's competitiveness in regional and world markets, and to promote economic growth and welfare improvements within the country. The World Bank and other experts, especially those from the United States, have been invited to the country to recommend changes. These rather top-down efforts identify and promote higher education policy changes that will ostensibly promote Vietnam's socio-economic development. One of these is to make higher education institutions more responsive to market forces. And yet these efforts also reveal certain tensions, not only between Vietnam's political leadership and foreign actors, but also within Vietnam's education system itself. Vietnam's leaders (including its education leaders) approach promoting the globalization of higher education in a way that not only fosters economic growth, but also sustains and maintains local identity and culture and, presumably, preferred political alignments. Efforts by the state to reform and steer the globalization of higher education in Vietnam can be understood as an instance of "glocalisation" — "think global, act local" (Barnevik, cited in Dirlik 1996, p. 31). The purpose of this chapter is to shed light on "glocalisation" processes within a single university, the University of Da Nang (UD).

BOTTOM-UP GLOBALIZATION: THE CASE OF THE UNIVERSITY OF ĐÀ NẴNG (UD)

UD is a regional, multidisciplinary university established by the government in 1994. It is a public (that is, state run) university and the only major university in Đà Nẵng, Central Vietnam's largest city. UD does not intend to serve only Da Nang. Vietnam's government has designated it as the main centre for training and research for the country's Central and Central Highlands regions. UD was created through the amalgamation of universities and colleges that had previously existed independently for thirty years. The university has 1,600 staff divided among six units, including an administrative division and five separate academic units, as shown in Table 9.1. As a result, UD is spatially dispersed, with parts of the school scattered across different areas of the city. There are plans for one major campus, to be located in the city's more spacious and rural Hòa Vang district, though this is several years away.

TABLE 9.1
University of Đà Nẵng's Five Member Universities and Colleges

Institutes of UD	Abbreviation	Number of staff	Ratio
University of Engineering	U.Eng	389	24%
College of Education	C.Ed	311	19%
College of Economics	C.Ec	231	14%
College of Foreign Languages	C.FL	220	14%
Junior College of Technology	C.Te	160	10%
Đà Nẵng University Administration Division	UD.Ad	289	18%
TOTAL		**1,600**	**100%**

Source: University of Danang website.

To explore issues pertaining to globalization, the author conducted a survey of 240 lecturers and administrators. This sample was drawn from each of the five different UD academic units. Sample size chosen from each unit was proportionate to the unit's share of UD's total staff as given in Table 9.2:

TABLE 9.2
Number of Participants of Each Member of the University of Đà Nẵng in the Study

Institute	% of each Institute/UD	Percent of Staff taking part in the study
University of Engineering	24%	58
College of Education	19%	47
College of Economics	14%	35
College of Foreign Languages	14%	33
Junior College of Technology	10%	24
Đà Nẵng University Administration Division	18%	43
Total	100	240

Source: Author's own compilation.

Among the 240 surveyed, 108 were women, who accounted for 45 per cent of the sample. Gender and age breakdowns were broadly representative of the university, though not of the individual academics units. The dominant range of faculty age, from 34 to 43 years, accounted for 51 per cent of the sample. The age groups 24–33 and 44–53 accounted for 16 per cent each. Staff under age 24 accounted for 9.2 per cent while those above age 54 represented 8.3 per cent. With respect to staff qualifications, there were forty with doctoral degrees, 180 with masters degrees, and twenty with bachelor's degrees, making up 17 per cent, 75 per cent and 8 per cent of the sample respectively. Most of these degrees (70 per cent) were earned from Vietnamese universities. In what follows, survey results pertaining to economic, cultural, and political aspects of globalization and higher education are discussed in turn.

ECONOMIC GLOBALIZATION AND THE COMMERCIALIZATION OF HIGHER EDUCATION

Throughout the world, universities have become enterprise-oriented and businesslike (Odin and Manicas 2004; Slaughter and Larry 1997). This phenomenon is partly the result of economic globalization, as higher education is increasingly subject to market rules. Universities and other higher education providers are competing locally and globally for resources, including students. Increasingly, students can choose which institutions, which forms of education, or which courses to pursue. Whether intended or not, the introduction of new tuition schemes, scholarships, cross-border higher education programmes, and educational services has led to the formation of entrepreneurial universities and students. In one way or another, universities have had to accept the reality that under globalization the production and transmission of knowledge has been commoditized, which means it can be manufactured, bought, and sold (Orr 1997, p. 46).[1] On the other hand, the commercialization of higher education associated with globalization stands in tension with two idealized functions of university: teaching and research. However, as the trend has become more pronounced, higher education institutions in all countries have had to recognize, cope, with and make specific plans for their future development.

Commercialization

Item 17 of the current (2005) Education Law states that, "no form of commercialization of education is accepted". Yet Vietnam's higher education institutions are now developing within a market economy and the commercialization of higher education in Vietnam is in some respects already a reality. Not only is the country's government promoting the development of "people-founded" institutions, whose funding relies almost completely on students' tuition fees, but it also recognizes that higher education institutions must be attentive to global and local economic conditions and is encouraging universities to develop with the human resources needs of the country in mind. Still, the "commercialization of higher education" is hotly debated by both Vietnamese educators and the public. If there is no "commercialization" (*thương mại hóa*), there is certainly "commodification". Whether or under what conditions these outcomes are acceptable depends on whom you talk to.

The ideas are diverse, but can be divided into two main groups. The first group argues that Vietnam's Confucian heritage and ideals forbid the selling and buying of "words". Commercialized education will mean that those who have money will have access to knowledge, while those who do not will not. This group considers teaching to be the noblest of careers and teachers to be more important than parents. Consequently, commercialization of higher education is totally rejected because it is thought to bring social inequality and disorder. They believe that a modern higher education system is definitely needed in Vietnam, but that this system must have nothing to do with commercialization.

A second group strongly supports the concept of market principles in higher education. They point out that this is unquestionably the direction of higher education under the impact of the globalization. It is only when the economic benefits to students are considered in the provision of higher education that quality higher education is assured. They point out that foreign and foreign-partnered higher education providers have successfully and increasingly recruited Vietnamese students, narrowing the market share of wholly Vietnamese non-public universities. They emphasize the need for a legal framework to guide competition between both domestic and international institutions in Vietnam. Without this framework, Vietnam will face more challenges on its way to globalizing its higher education system.

Some 80 per cent of sampled staff supported the view that the commercialization of higher education in Vietnam is an urgent need. These respondents came mostly from the College of Foreign Languages, the College of Economics, and the University of Engineering. It is notable that staff from these colleges have had more chances to go abroad for postgraduate degrees and training courses and their opinions are more economically oriented than those of staff from the College of Education. At DU, there appears to be a difference between the mindsets of those whose degrees were obtained from foreign universities, and those whose degrees were not.

Regarding the meaning of "commercialization of higher education", over 90 per cent of UD staff thinks that it means considering higher education as a profitable business; and that it implies the disappearance of the subsidized system, giving way for higher education to develop in compliance with the law of supply and demand. Also in their opinion, UD

FIGURE 9.1
UD's Definitions of the "Commercialization of Higher Education"

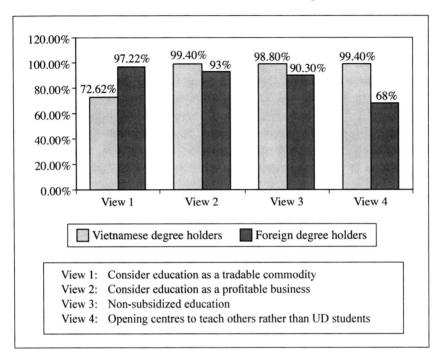

View 1: Consider education as a tradable commodity
View 2: Consider education as a profitable business
View 3: Non-subsidized education
View 4: Opening centres to teach others rather than UD students

Source: Author's own compilation.

has already been commercialized because there have been centres opened within UD for the purpose of gaining profit. For example, 82 per cent of participants agree that currently, UD's centres are not aimed at UD students, but at the public in general. This is correct. UD is making a good profit from expanding its teaching activities to meet market demands. So far, UD centres have been established and operated successfully in Đà Nẵng City and other central and highland provinces, providing both UD and its staff with many chances to increase their revenue and income through the provision of training to the public, companies, and the government. These programmes are actively promoted through advertising. Through these activities, UD will be exposed to higher standards of teaching and management. It may enhance future competitiveness with other universities in Vietnam and the Southeast Asian region.

However, it is worth arguing that the core value of the commercialization of higher education is to consider students as customers, and courses and educational services as products of a university. Of course, every customer wants to have good products at competitive prices. It is proposed in this chapter that UD centres should have concrete cooperation policies with departments in UD's five member institutions to recruit students. As it turns out, there is a need for UD students to improve their computer skills and English competency because usually these courses are not satisfactorily taught in their undergraduate programmes. Paradoxically, students there also have to attend extra courses in the evening at private computer and English centres in the city, whereas UD's commercial centres spend money on advertising their programmes to the public, looking for learners from companies, government departments, and even secondary schools.

Private Provision

Since 1986, higher education has been expected to change from being a subsidized system to a market-oriented one under socialist supervision. The state is no longer capable of funding all higher education activities. Recently, the ex-prime minister Phan Văn Khải confirmed to the National Assembly that education is one of the five social fields being changed into services. This is to say that the private provision of education is to be permitted.

Many academics and others believe that higher education in Vietnam will develop more and the quality will improve if there is a private sector in the higher education field. Institutions would have to find ways to improve teaching and research to meet the demands of the public and society. It is assumed that the old, socialist higher education ideology and the subsidization policy have dragged down Vietnamese higher education. The subsidy policy, with its bureaucracy and corruption, has led to poor management, troublesome paperwork, waste, and low quality in higher education. Many academics and those in the public argue that the private provision of higher education will bring about many opportunities and challenges for Vietnamese universities and that private higher education will give universities the impetus to forge ahead. But how is the private provision of higher education viewed by staff at UD, one of Vietnam's "public" universities?

To survey attitudes at UD, this study considered four aspects of private higher education. These include the establishment and management of private universities, profit orientation, decentralization, and private fees-paying students. Eighty-five per cent of the sample responded that besides maintaining public universities, the state should encourage individuals to open private universities. If students cannot get into public universities, they could go to a private one of a good quality. Interestingly, this viewpoint is most strongly expressed by UD administrators. The administrators argue that private provision is crucial for Vietnamese universities to catch up with current trends in the region and the world, but that it is also necessary to maintain public universities. A key point is not whether Vietnamese universities should be privatized, but what is the ideal proportion of private universities in the system. Decree 05/2005/NQ-CP set the target at 40 per cent by 2010, which is roughly the proportion indicated by surveyed staff.

Viewed internationally, however, this is a high percentage. In the United States, the country famous for having the most successful private universities in the world, only 23 per cent of students are in private universities (Vũ Quang Việt 2004). But, private universities in America are not working for profit, which is not properly understood in Vietnam. In Vietnam private provision of higher education is thought of as being a good solution, but it will be extremely dangerous if the concept is interpreted wrongly.

THE CULTURAL DIMENSION

There are many well known cultural aspects of globalization. But cultural globalization can also be found in higher education. The credit system is a particularly interesting example. The credit system has proved to be successful in many countries because it focuses on the interests of students, which is the basis of most learner-centred education theories. This system encourages students not only to be active in choosing courses, schedules, and lecturers, but also to do research and self-study. Students become more flexible and adapted to the working world.

Although MOET decided to apply the credit system in colleges and universities as of 2001, there were only six institutions nationwide applying this system (Hanoi Construction University; Thăng Long people-founded University in the north; Nha Trang Marine University, Đà Lạt University,

University of Natural Sciences-National University, and the University of Technology in the south). The system is new to most Vietnamese students and their parents. For them, the idea that students can choose what to study, whom to study with, when, and where to study is exciting, but they do not know clearly how the system will be applied. For lecturers and administrators, using the credit system is a good move towards open-minded higher education in Vietnam.

However, how to apply it successfully is still a difficult question because the requirements of the system have not been met by Vietnamese universities. Most of them do not have enough facilities for students to do experiments or work on assignments or carry out discussions required in the syllabus. To make matter worse, Vietnamese students are not familiar with research and learning on their own. They may choose the easiest courses taught by the least demanding lecturers in the hope that their grade will be high, making it easier to them to look for a good job.

At UD, 70 per cent of the respondents support the application of the credit system. UD has applied the system since 2005, although it is too early to say whether the system is successful. In January 2005, Professor Bùi Văn Ga, president of Đà Nẵng University invited Professor Hà Dương Tường from Compiègne University of Technology (UTC), France, to talk about the credit system of UTC. The discussions provided useful insights into the application of the credit system in UD. Although this system is undoubtedly an appropriate step towards improving teaching and learning at UD, it can create confusion for both students and lecturers/administrators. There are a lot of challenges ahead and UD should be careful in evaluating the suitability and success of the system.

POLITICAL GLOBALIZATION

Political globalization includes not only the expansion of international and supranational institutions, but the diffusion of governance arrangements across numerous spheres of "public management". In Vietnam's higher education system, university autonomy has emerged as a key by-product of the state's broader movement towards decentralization. Globally, British and American universities have the most autonomy; other European universities are average, and Asian universities have the least autonomy (Cummings and Altbach 1997). But the seemingly global move towards decentralization is now affecting higher education in Vietnam.

Institutional Autonomy

Under the old subsidy system, universities could operate smoothly without autonomy because they were simply expected to fulfil the tasks set by MOET and the state. However, marketization and globalization now require Vietnamese universities to make wise and timely decisions to deal with unexpected challenges, as well as to exploit unplanned opportunities. To survive, universities need to catch up with regional and global standards in teaching and research. If universities have to wait for instructions from MOET in every single case, they will definitely fall behind in all aspects. Nor will MOET be able to offer good supervision to all universities in the country because they are so different in their terms of conditions and objectives. There is indeed an urgent need for Vietnam to apply a new governance mechanism in which universities are given more autonomy.

On 12 September 2006, the Minister of Education and Training Nguyễn Thiện Nhân claimed that henceforth each university would be able to form an academic board which would be permitted to design and assess its own courses, and this way, universities would be academically autonomous. However, most academic activities of most higher education institutions are still closely controlled by MOET, including university entrance examinations, courses and curriculum design, degree granting, personnel recruiting and promoting, etc. In short, Vietnamese universities still do not have the authority to make decisions on key academic, personnel, financial, or development issues. This has slowed down, if not prevented Vietnamese universities from moving ahead, or meeting the increasing demand for quality higher education from the public, thus failing to serve the country's industrialization and modernization goals. In the UD survey, 95 per cent of those in the sample strongly agreed that UD would develop more quickly and stably if it received more autonomy from the state and MOET.

Institutional Accountability

In addition to autonomy, the push for accountability is another manifestation of political globalization and it is also evident in Vietnam's higher education system. Institutional accountability refers to the responsibilities of the university to ensure good educational quality, efficient use of resources, transparent policies, and satisfactory reporting to students, the state, and the public (Peterson and West 2003). This is to ensure that once the university is given autonomy, it has to follow certain rules of operation.

According to globally prevailing notions of accountability in higher education, the university needs to have a university board which includes students and representatives from both the university and the public. This is to make sure that the university is working for the benefit of the whole community, and not for any single individual or group. This is a new idea in the Vietnamese context as so far, actors outside the state education apparatus have never had a voice in the operation of universities. In a survey conducted in twenty-eight Australian universities in 2000, public representatives make up 50 to 60 per cent of the university board. These numbers indicate the significance of having different voices in a university to help it fulfil its accountability to the state and the public, especially the students. According to the "Bologna process" signed in Berlin in June 2003 by 33 European countries, the proportion of students on boards should be between 10 and 30 per cent.

At the UD, there was wide agreement among respondents concerning the members of the university board. These members should include representatives from MOET, the UD president, UD administrators, representatives from the People's Committee of Đà Nẵng City, UD lecturers, professors, and students. These are the key personnel who will be influential in UD development in the future, and thus they are expected to sit on the university board, increasing UD's accountability. The percentage of the members in order of importance is shown in Figure 9.2. An admitted weakness in the survey is that it did not ask about the importance or roles of other important actors, such as both state and non-state employers that might hire university graduates.

FIGURE 9.2
Expected Percentage of Members on University Board to Ensure the University of Đà Nẵng's Accountability

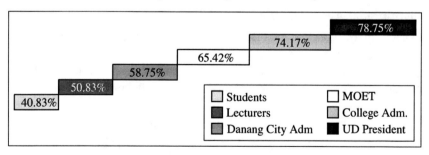

Source: Author's own compilation.

CONCLUSION

This chapter argues that globalization has exerted new pressures on Vietnamese higher education, making reforms in its systems, mechanism, and universities an absolute necessity. Three dimensions of globalization namely economy, politics, and culture are analysed in the context of Vietnamese higher education through the case of Danang University, the biggest university in Central Vietnam. The chapter illustrates dimensions of "glocalization" processes in higher education.

There have been many and major changes in Danang University. Future changes must be supported by well organized personnel who understand the nature of globalization and its implications for higher education and local political economies. In terms of economic globalization, commercialization at UD should be harnessed to offer higher quality courses and services to UD students. In other words, it is advisable for UD centres to focus primarily on teaching UD students, rather than cashing in on external activities. In so doing, these centres can still make a profit and UD students can improve their academic levels, fulfilling the mission of UD as the regional university for Central Vietnam.

In terms of cultural globalization, applying the credit system and other globalized higher education practices must go hand in hand with steps to address long-standing problems at the system level. Otherwise, time, energy, and money DU invests in such initiatives will sooner or later be rejected by higher authorities. The credit system is needed by Vietnamese universities; however, it has to be carried out with great care. The best way is to implement pilot programmes is at chosen universities and then draw the necessary lessons. It would be damaging if the credit system was applied in Vietnamese institutions without sufficient planning and consideration.

In terms of political globalization, my closing remarks will focus on the issue of autonomy. Almost all UD staff strongly support the idea of having more autonomy from MOET and they also support the formation of a quasi-independent university board. This is unfortunate. For although this survey did not ask about the relation between DU and state and non-state employers, it is clear that in Vietnam, the higher education system still operates according to planned instructions from MOET, rather than the demands of industries, markets, and civil society.

Note

1. An alternative perspective is that students are not consumers and that higher education institutions can transform knowledge and social value systems (see the work of Karelis, Thomas, Garnier, and Delanty).

References

Altbach, P.G. "Perspectives on Internationalizing Higher Education". *International Higher Education*, 2002 at <http: //www.bc.edu/bc_org/avp/soe/cihe/iheframe. html> (accessed 20 April 2007).

Altbach, P.G. and D.C Levy. *Private Higher Education: A Global Revolution.* Program for Research on Private Higher Education (PROPHE), School of Education, University at Albany, 2005.

Baldwin, P. "Higher Education: Quality and Diversity in the 1990s". Policy statement by the Hon. Peter Baldwin, minister of Higher Education and Employment Services. Canberra: Australian Government Publishing Service, 1991.

Brown, L. *People Flows and Knowledge Flows: International Students and Public Policy* 2000. <www.ma.hw.ac.uk/RSE/meetings_ect/ordmtgs/2000/people.htm> (assessed 20 April 2007).

Cam, L. "President Clinton's Talk about Challenges Facing Vietnam in the new Century". *The Saigon Economist*, 17 November 2000.

Cummings, W.K. and P.G. Altbach (eds). *The Challenge of Eastern Asian Education: Implications for America*. New York: State University of New York Press, 1997.

Damme, D.V. "Higher Education in the Age of Globalization: The Need for a New Regulatory Framework for Recognition, Quality Assurance and Accreditation". Introductory paper for the UNESCO Expert meeting, 2001.

Dirlik, A. "The Global in the Local". In *Global/Local: Cultural Production and the Transnational Imaginary*, edited by R. Wilson and W. Dissanayake. Durham: Duke University, 1996.

Do, Minh. "A Look at the Vietnamese Higher Education System from the Perspective of Globalisation". *Sunday Youth*, 26 (2000): 6–7.

Dore, R. *The Diploma Disease: Education, Qualification and Development*. London: Institute of Education, University of London, 1997.

Education Laws. Vietnam: National Publishing House of Politics, 1998.

Hirsch, W.Z. and E.L. Weber. *Challenges Facing Higher Education at the Millennium*. American Council on Education: Oryx Press, 1999.

Huisman, J.P. Maassen and G. Neave. *Higher Education and the Nation State: The International Dimension of Higher Education.* Tokyo: Pergamon, 2001.

Kellner, D. "Globalisation and Nnew Social Movements: Lessons for Critical Theory and Pedagogy". In *Globalisation and Education: Critical Perspectives*, edited by N. Burbules and C. Torres. New York: Routledge, 2000.

Le, T.C. *Higher Education Reform in Vietnam, Laos and Cambodia*. New York Press, 1991.

Le Van, J.H. "Vietnam: Revolution of Postcolonial Consolidation". In *Revolutions of the Late Twentieth Century*, edited by T.R.G. Goldstone and M. Farrokh. Boulder: Westview Press, 1991.

Lingard, R. "It Is and It Is Not: Vernacular Globalisation, Education Policy and Restructuring". In *Globalisation and Education: Critical Perspectives*, edited by N. Burbules and C. Torres. New York: Routledge, 2000.

Luke, A. and C. Luke. "A Situated Perspective on Globalisation". In *Globalisation and Education: Critical Perspectives*, edited by N. Burbules and C. Toress. New York: Routledge, 2000.

Luke, C. "Globalisation and Education – Learning Guide". *The School of Education Policy* 14 no. 1 (2000): 19–31.

Nguyễn, X.T. "Higher Education in Vietnam: Key Areas Need Assistance". *Higher Education Policy* 10, No. 2 (1997).

Odin, J.K. and P.T. Manicas (eds). *Globalisation and Higher Education*. Honolulu: University of Hawai'i Press, 2004.

Pennycook, Alastair. "English Universities, and Struggles over Culture and Knowledge". In *East-West Dialogue in Knowledge and Higher Education*, edited by Ruth Hayhoe and Julia Pan, pp. 64–80. New York: M.E. Sharpe, 1996.

Peterson, P.E. and M.R. West. *No Child Left Behind? The Politics and Practice of School Accountability*. Washington, D.C.: Brookings Institution Press, 2003.

Phạm, M.H. *Vietnam's Education: The Current Position and Future Prospects*. Hanoi: Thế Giới Publishers, 1998.

Pieterse, J.N. *Globalisation as Hybridization*. In *Global Modernity*, edited by M. Featherstone, S. Lash, and R. Robertson. London: TCS/Sage, 1995.

Roberson, R. *Globalisation: Social Theory and Global Culture*. London: Sage, 1992.

Scott, Peter. "Magnification, Internationalization and Globalisation". In *The Globalisation of Higher Education*, edited by Peter Scott. Buckingham: Open University Press, 1998.

Sedgwick, R. Book Review: *The Globalisation of Higher Education*. *WENR 12* No. 6 (1999): 1–3.

Seltzer, K. "A Whole New Way of Learning". *New Statesman* 44, no. 56 (1999): 128–31.

Silverstone, R. "What's New about New Media?" *New Media and Society 1*, No. 1 (1999): 10–12.

Slaughter, S. and L.L. Larry. *Academic Capitalism: Politics, Policies and the Entrepreneurial University.* Baltimore: Johns Hopkins University Press, 1997.

Thái, D.T. "Understanding Methods in Doing Research in the Education Field. *Vietnamese Higher Education Journal 3* (2000).

UNESCO. "International Conference on Autonomy and Accountability in Higher Education", reported by Prof. Vũ Văn Tảo, 1998.

Vu, Q.V. "Comparing Higher Education in America and Vietnam" at <www.ncst. ac.vn/HVGD/>, 2005.

Wagner, P. "Higher Education in an Era of Globalization: What Is at Stake?". In *Globalization and Higher Education*, edited by J.K. Odin and T.P. Manicas. Honolulu: University of Hawai'i Press, 2004.

10

RESEARCH-INDUSTRY COOPERATION AND SUSTAINABLE DEVELOPMENT

Marea Fatseas

INTRODUCTION

The twenty-first century presents the world with unprecedented challenges that could either threaten the survival of human societies as we know them or, if addressed in time, lay the foundations for sustainable societies on this planet for centuries to come.

What are these challenges? In this century, we will see the world's population grow from the current 6.7 billion to 9 billion (Chamie 2003). We will see crises in energy and water security, the catastrophic impacts of global warming, environmental degradation and species extinctions on a massive scale. We will see global economic integration of a kind never experienced before, with all its implications for growing interdependency and competitiveness between countries.

The challenges of the twenty-first century will affect all of humanity, and the solutions will have to be crafted at a global level. The solutions will need to draw on the skills and capacities of all sectors of societies. They will need to be based on sound evidence that is translated into effective responses. How do these challenges relate to Vietnam and to this chapter?

Vietnam will face these global challenges with its own unique set of circumstances. It has been transforming itself from a command economy to a market economy, and is now on a rapid growth path. It is changing from an insulated, to a gradually more globally integrated economy. But its geography and population distribution make it one of the most vulnerable countries in the world to the impacts of climate change.

For some time, developed countries have considered science, technology, and innovation (STI) as central to their strategies for addressing twenty-first century challenges. They have regarded increased collaboration between researchers and industry as fundamental for maximizing the application of research outcomes, and for ensuring that industry and broader societal needs can help to drive research. What is becoming clearer from the scale of the challenges facing the world in the twenty-first century is that investment in science, technology, and innovation will also have a critical role to play in helping developing countries to respond to these challenges. In that context, collaboration between universities and research institutes and industry in Vietnam will become ever more important in developing responses to national challenges.

In this chapter, I will consider these issues from my perspective as a consultant and former government official in Australia, with experience in developing and implementing policies and programmes aimed at fostering research and innovation, and in promoting collaboration between the providers and users of research. I will also look at them from my perspective of having lived and worked in Vietnam for several years over the past two decades and being familiar with Vietnam's development path in that timeframe.

Specifically, I will consider:

- current thinking in international circles on the role of cooperation between research institutions and industry in supporting development, including sustainable development;
- some of the specific sustainability challenges Vietnam faces;
- the Vietnamese Government's policies to address these challenges, particularly, those relating to science and technology and sustainable development;
- evidence of industry needs for science and technology and how they view the capacity of universities and research institutes to meet their needs; and

- evidence of policies and actions taken by universities and research institutes in response to the needs of industry.

CURRENT THINKING IN INTERNATIONAL CIRCLES ON THE ROLE OF RESEARCH-INDUSTRY COOPERATION IN DEVELOPMENT

There is wide recognition of the importance of innovation and of research-industry cooperation to economic growth and development. Evidence suggests, additionally, that strong linkages between public research organizations and industry are essential for ensuring that research conducted in the public sector can meet the needs of industry and facilitate knowledge and technology transfer between them (OECD 2006, p. 70).

Many countries have established programmes to encourage research-industry cooperation. Typical goals of such programmes include the support of science and technology research that contributes to achieving national objectives in the social and economic spheres; efforts to facilitate the practical application and benefits of such research by involving users through cooperative programmes and cooperative research centres; and ongoing training initiatives — particularly at the graduate level — that include active involvement of researchers outside the higher education system and involving students in major applied research programmes.[1]

There has also been significant international policy focus on the role of research-industry cooperation in the context of sustainable development. The United Nations' seminal report, *Our Common Future*, defined sustainable development as "the development that satisfies the needs of the current generations without compromising the capacity of future generations to satisfy their own needs" (UNWCED 1987). The report called for the consideration of environmental impact to be at the heart of government policymaking by central agencies, not those at the periphery. It recognized the important roles to be played by scientists, and of industry, including through cooperation with each other and with other segments of society, in support of sustainable development.

The subsequent Agenda 21, which developed out of the 1992 UN Earth Summit on Environment and Development in Rio de Janeiro, has a significant focus on technology transfer, cooperation, and capacity building. As part of capacity building strategies, particularly in developing countries, it highlights the importance of promoting long-term technological partnerships between the holders and potential users of environmentally-sound technologies (United Nations 1992).

A world authority on theories of competitive advantage, Michael Porter, has also highlighted the importance of linkages between different entities, such as universities and firms, in contributing to national innovative capacity. He does not see any conflict between sustainable development and efforts by countries to remain globally competitive. Indeed, he sees environmental improvement as an economic and competitive opportunity, not as an annoying cost or an inevitable threat:

> Increasingly, the nations and companies that are most competitive are not those with access to the lowest-cost inputs but those that employ the most advanced technology and methods in using their inputs. Because technology is constantly changing, the new paradigm of global competitiveness requires the ability to innovate rapidly.
>
> Developing countries that stick with resource-wasting methods and forgo environmental standards because they are "too expensive" will remain uncompetitive, relegating themselves to poverty. (Porter and van der Linde 1995)

More recently, the World Bank has started to focus on the importance of innovation and research-industry cooperation in shaping its policy on loan assistance to developing countries. In February 2007, the Bank hosted a Global STI Forum in Washington, D.C. in the United States to promote discussion on the importance of science, technology, and innovation in promoting sustainable development and poverty reduction in developing countries (World Bank 2007). One of the issues generating significant discussion was initiatives in different countries aimed at bringing together researchers and industry, and there was also discussion on how that may apply in addressing challenges such as energy security and water conservation.

VIETNAM'S CHALLENGES IN THE TWENTY-FIRST CENTURY

Vietnam has come a long way in the past twenty years. From a situation of economic crisis in the middle-to-late 1980s, the country has entered the twenty-first century with a rapidly growing economy.

Internationally isolated as recently as the early 1990s, Vietnam today is an outward-looking economy, which was admitted to the World Trade Organization in early 2007. While Vietnam still has major strengths in primary industries, with rice, marine products, and wood all being key exports, its top export by 2005 was textile products. This reflects the massive expansion of its manufacturing sector.

However, Vietnam's rapid economic growth of 7–8 per cent per year is now facing potential roadblocks in the form of some supply-side constraints such as power-generation insufficiency.

While the workforce is growing rapidly, and the workforce age profile is quite young, there is a lack of sufficient skilled workers, and hence major human resource challenges for industry.

Rapid economic development has led to increased degradation of the environment such as overflowing waste in urban landfill sites, and polluted air and water nationwide.

A World Bank report released early in 2007 (Dasgupta et al. 2007) concluded that Vietnam would be one of the ten countries in the world most adversely affected by climate change. According to the report, rising sea levels are projected to severely impact highly populated regions where much of the country's agriculture and manufacturing industries are located.

In the context of these challenges, what roles does the Vietnamese Government see for science, technology, and innovation in helping it to address these challenges? And in these roles, does it see the need for greater research-industry cooperation?

RELEVANT VIETNAMESE GOVERNMENT LAWS, POLICIES, AND STRATEGIES

The Vietnamese Government has stated its intent to make science and technology the driver of its development in the twenty-first century. This has been made clear in pronouncements by the Vietnam Communist Party, and in government laws, policies, and strategies. The government has also sought to increase incentives for greater cooperation between researchers and industry.

At the Ninth Congress of the Vietnam Communist Party in 2001, the Party affirmed that Vietnam would aim to become an industrial country by 2020 and that science and technology would help it to achieve that objective. The Party also declared its commitment to sustainable development, stating that, "Fast, effective and sustainable development, economic growth should occur in parallel with the implementation of social progress and equality and environmental protection."[2] Nor was this mere rhetoric. In the same year, the Law on Science and Technology was enacted to give effect to this intention, and to encourage specifically the practical application of research outcomes. In 2004, the government issued Vietnam Agenda 21, its roadmap for ensuring sustainable development.

Law on Science and Technology

The Vietnamese Government's 2001 Law on Science and Technology stipulates that state organizations and cadres engaged in scientific and technological activities have a responsibility to transfer and apply the outcomes of those activities. To promote this, the Law established a suite of tax and credit incentives, and a fund to supply low- or no-interest loans for technology transfer activities.[3]

To facilitate the development of science and technology, the Law confirmed the government's policy of building high technology parks to underpin new high technology industries (as indicated in the section below on technology parks).

The Law also contained provisions to develop a technological market, whose exact form was not defined, but whose presumed functions would be to facilitate the sale of technologies developed through scientific and technological activities. Specific measures to promote this outcome include: policies and legislation on industrial property ownership (intellectual property); preferential policies for testing of new technologies, for promoting S&T consultancy activities, and boosting technology exports; rewards for organizations and individuals that file patents, make innovations, and apply new technologies; and permission for S&T organizations to set up enterprises, enter into joint ventures, and conduct technology transfer activities.[4]

Since the Law was enacted, additional strategies have been developed, and regulations and supporting structures have been put in place, as will be explained later on.

S&T Development Strategy and Supporting Structural Reforms

The Science and Technology Development Strategy issued in 2003 states unequivocally the role of science and technology in supporting national development. Science and technology are seen as a means of enhancing the quality of economic growth, improving efficiency, and competing with global and regional economies.[5]

The strategy identifies a number of priority fields for receiving government support. Given Vietnam's strengths in information and communication technology, it is not surprising that this field is one of the stated priorities. Other prioritized fields include biotechnology, advanced materials, automation, atomic and alternative energies, and machinery technologies.

In accordance with a decision (in September 2004) of the prime minister, the Ministry of Science and Technology was to implement the reforms in coordination with relevant ministries, ministerial-level agencies, government-attached agencies, and provincial and city People's Committees.[6] A document issued alongside the prime minister's decision established how the government proposed to encourage increased research and training links with industry, namely, by transforming applied research and development organizations into enterprises.

A special subgroup of those enterprises, known as Science and High-Technology Enterprises, would be eligible for support similar to that provided to high-technology enterprises in high-technology zones, and would be eligible for support for training and retraining staff, including overseas training and the means to ensure the efficient use of such trained staff on their return.

The document announced incentives to attract prestigious foreign research institutes and universities to establish branches or S&T training programmes in Vietnam. Finally, the document indicated that new organizations would be developed to act as intermediaries between researchers and industry and to consult on technology transfer. State agencies from all economic sectors would be encouraged to provide intermediary services to the technology market.

Sustainable Development Policy and the Role of Research/Industry Cooperation

Vietnam has had a longstanding interest in sustainable development. As far back as 1991 it developed and implemented the "National Plan on Environment and Development in the Period 1991–2000" (Decision No 187-CT of 12 June 1991), which established a foundation for sustainable development in the country. This was followed by Politburo

Directive No. 36-CT/Tw of 25 June 1998 that stressed the importance of strengthening environmental protection during the period of industrialization and modernization. The Vietnamese Government has also been active in international forums on sustainable development. It sent high-level delegations to the Earth Summit on Environment and Development in 1992 in Rio de Janeiro (Brazil) and to the World Summit on Sustainable Development in 2002 in Johannesburg, South Africa.

The key outcome of the Rio summit was the Declaration on Environment and Development by the 179 participating countries, which committed those countries to Agenda 21 on global solutions for sustainable development in the twenty-first century. The Johannesburg summit led to commitment to full implementation of Agenda 21.

To give effect to this commitment and to the Ninth Vietnam Communist Party Congress Resolution on Sustainable Development, the Vietnamese Government in 2004 issued its own Agenda 21, called "The Strategic Orientation for Sustainable Development in Vietnam (VN 21)". This agenda sets out a very comprehensive strategy for embedding a sustainable development policy within the country's economic, social, and environmental plans. It identifies priority areas for attention, and specific actions to be taken in each of these areas.[7] Amongst the eight key principles VN 21 enunciates is the principle that science and technology is the foundation for the country's industrialization, modernization, and sustainable development, and that priority should be given to the wide application of modern, clean, and environmentally friendly technology in production industries.

Consistent with VN 21, Vietnam's Five-Year Socio-Economic Development Plan for 2006–10 identifies a role for the application of science and technology in support of sustainable development. The Plan sets out a number of ambitious targets to be achieved by 2010 including:

- 100 per cent of new production establishments to apply clean technology or be equipped with pollution control facilities;
- 50 per cent of production and business establishments to have been awarded certificates for meeting environmental standards or ISO14001 certificates;
- 40 per cent of urban areas and 70 per cent of industrial and export processing zones to have installed centralized waste water treatment systems that satisfy environmental standards;

- 80 per cent of toxic waste and 100 per cent of medical waste to be treated.

However, the Plan is much less specific about the policies to be introduced to achieve these targets. It refers only in general terms to completing the system of relevant laws and policies, capacity building in state agencies, the conduct of baseline surveys, and making polluters pay for pollution they cause (Ministry of Planning and Investment 2006). It is clear then that both the government's broad socioeconomic development plan and its sustainable development strategy stress the importance of industry uptake of science and technology to reduce and mitigate the impact of environmental problems, but frequently do so in very general terms.

The Challenges of Translating Government Policy into Action

Anyone living and working in Vietnam knows there can be large gaps between formal structures and what actually happens. A basic question is whether and how government laws and policies will actually be enforced.

The treatment of industrial waste water is a case in point.

In September 2007, inspectors from the Ministry of Public Security and the Ministry of Natural Resources and Environment found that Taiwanese Vedan Company was discharging 105.6 million litres of untreated waste water into Thị Vải River each month and had been doing so for fourteen years. In September of 2008, the company faced potential closure. Four thousand petitions from local people in Đồng Nai were lodged against Vedan Vietnam Company's polluting activities, and environmental officials were criticized for inaction. Eventually, the Government fined the company several million dollars in backlogged environmental protection fees from previous years (newspaper reports differ in their estimate of the fines), and the environmental officials were censured. By the end of 2009, the company was still operating and the farmers' petitions for compensation had not been resolved.[8]

Many obstacles Vietnam faces in implementing its research-industry collaboration laws and regulatory remits stem from legacies of a centrally planned economy and the country's tradition of a narrowly based and highly theoretical higher education and research system.[9] Getting the higher education and research system where it needs to be will require overcoming major hurdles.

A major issue in Vietnam is whether or how best to train the layers of officials and other stakeholders in the science and innovation system, including in universities, who are tasked to implement the Science and Technology Law and the Science and Technology Development Strategy. A massive upgrading of the physical infrastructure within Vietnamese universities and research institutes will be required to support quality improvements in research. Fortunately, these are areas in which the Vietnamese Government has been taking action, supported by the World Bank's first and second higher education loan projects. A final issue concerns industry demand for the research and technology transfer services of universities and research institutes, to which our discussion now turns.

Industry Needs and Perceptions of Universities and Research Institutes

In examining research-industry cooperation in Vietnam, it is critical to consider demand-side issues, particularly, the extent of demand by small and medium-sized Vietnamese firms for new technologies, innovations, and skilled workers.

In the command economy that preceded market reforms, state-owned enterprises that reported to line ministries dominated the economic landscape, and even today they play a key role. It is only in the past decade or so that private companies have begun to play a significant role in Vietnam, and almost all of them are still small and medium-sized enterprises.[10] In essence, Vietnamese firms — state or privately owned — are not accustomed to operating in a competitive environment, and certainly not in an internationally competitive environment.

Vietnam only joined the World Trade Organization in early 2007 and many of its companies are grappling with the challenge of bringing their operations, infrastructure, and skills base up to international standards. Many firms have only begun to contemplate collaborating with research institutions to boost their research and development to promote their performance and competitiveness. Such cooperation is difficult enough to encourage in a developed country, let alone in a developing country such as Vietnam, which is simultaneously seeking to address so many other challenges. Cooperation between industry and research institutions in the environmental field is likely to be even more problematic, as the environment is often a major casualty in the rush for rapid economic development.

Nonetheless, existing research identifies some Vietnamese industry needs for new technologies, innovations and the underpinning labour force skills and obstacles they face in addressing those needs. A 2005 survey by the Agency for Small and Medium Sized Enterprises (SMEs) Development and the Technical Assistance Centre in Hanoi found that only 8 per cent of 63,760 enterprises used advanced technology and many of these were foreign-invested enterprises. While foreign-invested companies were always looking for new technology and engineering information, domestic companies paid little attention to technology and the development of new products to improve their competitiveness. The director of the Technical Assistance Centre, Tạ Đình Xuyên, admitted, "innovation of technology and equipment is an emergency issue but very difficult at present".[11]

A range of obstacles prevents innovation in SMEs. There are inadequate resources for long-term investment, including capital and highly skilled labour and appropriate equipment. There is a lack of information about available technologies, and there are also market barriers such as a lack of awareness of product requirements and distribution channels (Tran 2007). Other impediments to innovation in industry more broadly, including in large enterprises, are weaknesses in the capacity of enterprises in Vietnam to design products and to cooperate with other enterprises within and between industries. There are also unwieldy management practices in the majority of state-owned enterprises and a lack of modern business management skills that is hindering capacity to deal with the challenges of global integration (Phùng 2007, p. 121).

The 2005 survey found that only 11.55 per cent of the companies surveyed in the north of Vietnam had a computer or used local area networks, and only 2.16 per cent had their own websites. The level of education attainment of company owners was low, with 43.3 per cent of enterprise owners having only a primary education. In the context of these weaknesses, is there any evidence of cooperation between industry and universities and research institutions to address their technology and skills needs?

Evidence of Industry Cooperation with Research Institutes and Universities

The evidence suggests very little such cooperation. Even in the minority of Vietnamese companies that are interested in introducing innovations, they rarely turn to research institutes and universities for assistance, with as little as 10 per cent sourcing ideas for innovation from such organizations.[12] Indeed, an innovation survey conducted in 2004 in the mechanics and food processing industries found that most small firms gained ideas for innovation from their own activities (82.4 per cent) and from customers' suggestions (58.8 per cent). These innovations tended to be minor and incremental in nature.

For larger companies such as state-owned enterprises, cooperation with domestic, foreign, and Foreign Direct Investment partners were considered more important channels for addressing challenges in the innovation process than universities and research institutes. The survey found that 71 per cent of SMEs and 93 per cent of non-SMEs in the mechanics sector reported having relationships with foreign/foreign direct investment firms (Tran 2006, pp. 7–8).

Collaboration between public research institutes and industry may lead to research institutes benefiting from knowledge and technology transfer, but there is little evidence of such flows as yet. In his research, Tran (2002) examined foreign companies in Vietnam and the extent to which there was knowledge and technology transfer to Vietnamese partners or institutions. He found that research institutes and universities did not benefit much from spillovers from the business activities of multinational companies.[13] This may change, however, in response to the rapid growth in demand by foreign companies for highly skilled personnel. For example, as a member of the U.S. — Vietnam Education Taskforce, Intel Vietnam is reported to be working closely with the Vietnamese Government to support, amongst other things, more joint programmes between universities and industry to give students the opportunity to apply theory to practical problems in a modern business environment.[14]

Even when firms desire it, there are numerous barriers to industrial cooperation with Vietnamese universities and research institutes. Tran (2006) found that firms widely express a desire for greater cooperation with universities and research institutes, but that this demand is rarely met. He cites problems such as a lack of capabilities for firms and universities to negotiate with each other, for learning and sharing information and for absorbing new knowledge. He said that rarely are institutional mechanisms in place to facilitate such interactions and so collaboration often occurs as a result of informal and personal relationships. Finally, he cites the overall structure and dynamism of markets as a barrier to innovation, as there is not enough "pull" for university staff to pay more attention to innovation and to serving industry needs (Tran 2006, p. 29).

There are signs, however, of increasing instances of companies working proactively with universities and research institutions to address business needs, including in fields relevant to sustainable development. For example, Green Energy, Vietnam produces biofuel feedstocks and refines and sells biodiesel. It has cooperated with the University of Adelaide's Department of Chemical Engineering to build a modular and mobile refinery.[15]

As noted earlier, such barriers are found in developed countries as well. Therefore, it is not at all surprising to find similar problems in Vietnam. Might high technology parks be a means to overcoming such barriers?

THE ROLE OF HIGH TECHNOLOGY PARKS

The Vietnamese Government views the establishment of high technology parks as a key plank of its strategy for encouraging research-industry interaction, and technology transfer and commercialization. In the 1990s, the Government planned for high technology parks that would be co-located with new campuses of research-intensive national universities. These research-intensive universities were to be formed through amalgamations of smaller, less viable universities in the north and south to create the comprehensive, multidisciplinary Vietnam National University–Hanoi and Vietnam National University–Ho Chí Minh City. They were to receive priority attention and resources and report to the prime minister rather than the minister for education and training.

The government's Decree 99 on the regulation of high-tech parks, issued in August 2003, stated that one of the objectives of the parks would be:

> To create favourable conditions for linking high-tech training, research and development with production and services, step up technological renovation, nursery of high-tech enterprises and commercialization of high technologies. [16]

Decree 99 specified several fields as being eligible for investment in the high-tech parks, including information, communication, and informatics software technologies; biotechnology, new materials; and environmental technologies. A follow-up decree from the Ministry of Science and Technology in late 2006 was more specific about the kinds of projects that would be priorities within each of these fields (Ministry of Science and Technology 2006).

Both these decrees have been issued relatively recently and so it is too soon to determine the success of efforts to bring together researchers and industry within the context of such hi-tech parks, let alone see whether they have been successful in generating cooperation in specific fields such as environmental and energy technologies. This is a very ambitious goal for any country to achieve. Nevertheless, it is instructive to examine what progress may have been made to date in establishing research-industry cooperative ventures in the two national hi-tech parks — Hoa Lac Hi-Tech Park near Hanoi and the Saigon Hi-Tech Park near Ho Chí Minh City. Their success will rely to a significant degree on industry demand and pull as much as the government's supply of infrastructure.

Saigon Hi-Tech Park is better developed than Hoa Lac, having been established in late 2002. It is located 15 km northeast of Ho Chí Minh City and adjacent to Ho Chí Minh City National University, which has more than 15,000 students studying science and technology. At the time of writing, it had granted investment licences for twenty-five projects with total committed capital of US$1,366 billion. An examination of its tenant profile indicated that its primary focus was on microelectronics, information and telecommunications industries.[17] Tenants included Intel, which had made an investment pledge of US$1 billion for an assembly-and-test house at the Park that would be the company's largest back-end plant of this kind in the world.[18]

The Saigon Hi-Tech Park provides services aimed at encouraging research-industry interaction and research commercialization. For example, the Neptech Centre there advertises its role as being one of assisting companies to design and manufacture new technology in cooperation with institutes and specialized research centres.[19]

So far, there does not seem to be much activity at the Park in relation to environmental and energy technologies.

The Hoa Lac Hi-Tech Park is at a far earlier stage of development. Located 30 km west of Hanoi, it is still in the stage of land clearing and construction of infrastructure facilities. Environmental technologies are one of the stated priorities for the Park,[20] but at the time of writing, only one tenant in this field was listed on the Park's website, namely Always Positive Solar Silicon Limited, which appears to be planning to manufacture solar panels. The majority of listed tenants are in the information and communication technology sector. For instance, U.S. company V-CAPS is reported to be investing US$155 million in a project to build a chipset packaging factory and the Thuận Phát Joint Stock Company is investing US$70 million in a project to build an electronic card and mobile phone plant (VietNamNetBridge 2007).

Hoa Lac High-Tech Park has not developed as expeditiously as the government would have liked. On 8 March 2007, the government terminated the responsibility of the Vietnam Construction and Import-Export Corporation (VINACONEX) as the main building contractor of the park, and appointed FPT, a leading Vietnamese technology solution and telecommunications service provider, to take over responsibility for park development.[21] Early in 2008, the deputy minister of science and technology attributed slow progress at Hòa Lạc to delays in ground clearing, only modest funding devoted to improving the park's infrastructure, and the disadvantage of being located 30 kms from Hanoi and 152 kms from Hải Phòng port (*Thanh Niên News* 2008).

In the case of both high-tech parks, it will be important to monitor their development to assess whether they make a significant difference to Vietnam's capacity to bring together researchers and industry to address national challenges. From their attraction of major multinationals in the ICT sector, it does appear that there may be sufficient industry pull to support further development of the tech parks.

Local Government Efforts to Encourage Research-Industry Links

At local levels, there has been significant activity in several parts of the country to encourage greater interaction between the research and industry sectors and to promote technology transfer. Specifically, the Hồ Chí Minh City authorities have created a university council with participation of research institutes, companies, and universities to advise on the promotion of training and innovation, and to link these more closely to urban development needs. They established the Neptech Centre,[22] referred to above under high-tech parks, to design and manufacture new technology for firms, in cooperation with institutes and specialized research centres. Their action plan Program 04 is aimed at developing new technologies appropriate for the city's needs at reasonable cost, mainly relying on the efforts of domestic research and innovation organizations (Tran 2006, pp. 23–24). Authorities approved the establishment of a Fund for Science and Technology Development (FOSTED) to help apply research results nationwide,[23] and agreed to set up a research group to undertake a feasibility study into the establishment of a "Science City" in the northeast of the city. One of their most interesting initiatives was their role in the development of Techmart.[24]

Techmart aims to support technological innovation and promote commercialization of technological and industrial products. It also aims to sharpen the competitive edge of the national economy in the face of international integration. Techmart Vietnam 2007 was co-organized by the Ministry of Science and Technology and related departments and people's committees in Ho Chí Minh City, Hanoi and Đanang. As many as 235 memoranda of understanding and technological transfer contracts, worth a combined value of VND700 billion, were reported to have been signed during the four-day event. This performance far exceeded that of national Techmarts in 2003 and 2005.[25] (Media reports on the Techmart Ha Noi event in September 2008 indicated that it led to 100 contracts and memoranda of understanding worth a total of VND500 billion (US$30 million) being signed.[26] Technologies relevant to public transport, energy saving and environmental solutions were displayed. There is also a national online Techmart that includes environmental technologies amongst its categories of technologies being promoted.[27]

Techmart events are now organized by local governments across the country. The Hồ Chí Minh City Department of Science and Technology had a key role in pioneering Techmart in Hồ Chí Minh City. Its Centre for Science and Technology Information (CESTI), acts as a bridge between technology providers and users. It runs Techmart events and a daily Techmart exhibition on its premises.

TO WHAT EXTENT DO UNIVERSITIES AND RESEARCH INSTITUTES IN VIETNAM COOPERATE WITH INDUSTRY IN RESEARCH, AND TECHNOLOGY TRANSFER AND COMMERCIALIZATION?

To what extent do universities and research institutions appear to be actually engaging in cooperation with industry? On the surface, there are indications such collaboration is on the rise.

Phùng Xuân Nhạ's research indicates that by 2002, for example, universities had established 167 campuses for undertaking scientific research in cooperation with industry. These campuses included 20 applied research institutes and 147 executive research centres and consulting firms. Yet cooperation between universities and industry was still not the norm and cooperative projects tend to be ad hoc arrangements based mainly on informal relationships (Phùng 2007, p. 19).

One of the difficulties was that many Vietnamese universities did not trust cooperation with enterprises, with intellectual property being one of the bones of contention. This is an issue in Australian universities as well, but the incidence of intellectual property breaches is far greater in Vietnam (Office of U.S. Trade Representative 2005). As stated by Nhạ:

> Enterprises don't pay copyright to the inventor when they exploit new technologies. This not only reduces the confidence of researchers in their relationship with enterprises, but ultimately discourages researchers and universities from investing time and money in new innovations (office of U.S. Trade Representative 2005, p. 21).

Research by Tran Ngoc Ca provides further insight into possible barriers to greater research-industry collaboration. He found that while the number of people who claimed to be involved in R&D is quite high, there are serious quality issues, as many of these personnel were trained under a theoretical and Soviet-oriented learning system, and gained little practical and technological experience. The research infrastructure in most public institutions is well below regional and international standards; government R&D funding is very modest in scale; and research continues to be supply-driven with few connections to the needs of industry (Tran 2002, p. 5).

Ca concluded "the role of Vietnamese universities in research is much weaker than teaching and that their contribution to the socioeconomic development of the country is limited to the production of an educated labor force rather than innovation" (Tran 2006, p. 1). Even on the level of developing skilled workers, however, there are indications that universities are not really meeting the needs of industry (Tran 2006, p. 19).

The government's objective, stated in its Higher Education Reform Agenda, is to increase university revenue from science and technology activities to 15 per cent of total university revenue by 2010, and to 25 per cent by 2020 (World Bank 2007, p. 2). On current indications, the 2010 target in particular looks very unrealistic.

CONCLUSION

From my examination of current and proposed strategies for increasing cooperation between research institutions and industry in Vietnam, I have concluded that the Vietnamese Government is very serious about boosting such collaboration. Indeed, it views such cooperation as critical to the uptake of science and technology outcomes that it hopes will drive Vietnam's future economic development. Complementing its science and technology strategy, the Government also seems committed to a set of policies that will ensure that Vietnam's rapid economic development will be environmentally sustainable. Yet despite these comprehensive legal and policy frameworks, like many developed and developing countries, Vietnam is facing a range of obstacles in implementing them.

Some of these obstacles are specific to Vietnam's own situation as a developing country still throwing off the shackles of a centrally planned economy, and trying to catch up with other countries in its education and research capacity and infrastructure. Vietnam is also seeking to build its science and technology capability from a very low base. Its universities and research institutes still have very poor infrastructure and the quality of the research undertaken in those institutions is still low by international standards. The level of R&D funding by government is very low, and only a small proportion of personnel in universities and research institutes are highly qualified compared with their international counterparts.

On the other hand, there are some challenges that the Vietnamese universities and research institutes share with their counterparts in developed countries. These include the need for more intermediaries to help bridge the gap between universities and industry, better institutional mechanisms to facilitate research-industry interactions, and more market pull and incentives to encourage researchers to respond better to industry needs. Other common challenges are sustaining initiatives aimed at promoting research-industry interaction after their original novelty and funding ends, and providing for effective evaluation of the effectiveness of such initiatives to ensure that lessons can be learnt for the future.

These challenges are no doubt even greater in the emerging area of sustainable development, given that a lot of the issues to be addressed in this area, especially in relation to climate change and environmental degradation, are just now becoming clear.

The whole world is grappling at the moment with clearly defining sustainable development and climate change issues and identifying what needs to be done. All countries have to race against time to understand fully the issues and develop responses. To be effective, these responses have to be informed by good science and research, and they need to be rolled out with the support of government and industry and all sectors of our societies.

Notes

1. Ralph Slatyer, "Cooperative Research Centres: The Concept and its Implementation", in *Research Grants: Management and Funding: Symposium Proceedings* (from a symposium held on 23–25 July 1993), edited by Fiona Wood and V. Flynn-Meek. The author managed the CRC Programme from 2002–05. More information about the Programme is at <www.crc.gov.au>.
2. Vietnamese Government, *Strategic Orientation for Sustainable Development in Vietnam (Vietnam Agenda 21) — Introduction.* Available at time of writing at <http://www.va21.org/eng/va21/VA21_stratergy_introduc.htm>.
3. Vietnamese Government, *Law on Science and Technology*, Articles 39, 42, and 43.
4. Vietnamese Government, *Law on Science and Technology*, Section 2, Article 33.
5. Vietnamese Government, *Vietnam Science and Technology Development Strategy by 2010*, 2003.
6. Vietnamese Government, Decision No. 171/2004/qd-ttg, 28 September 2004, *Approving the Scheme on Renewal of Science and Technology Management Mechanism.* The accompanying document from the Ministry of Science and Technology was the Proposal on the Reform of the Science and Technology Management Mechanism, 2004.
7. Vietnamese Government, *The Strategic Orientation for Sustainable Development in Vietnam (Vietnam Agenda 21) — Introduction.*
8. Based on information compiled from the following sources: *The Saigon Times Daily*, "Vedan Vietnam faces doomsday", by Hanh Lien, 18 September 2008; *Laodong.com.vn*, "Hội nông dân sẽ cử đại diện kiện Vedan VN", by Ngo Son, 26 February 2009, *VietNamNet Bridge*, "Nearly 4,000 complaints against Vedan Vietnam unsolved", 11 February 2009 and "It's official: Vedan killed the Thi Vai River", by Vinh Minh, 8 December 2009; *ThanhnienNews.com*, "Dong Nai Rebukes Officials in Vedan Pollution Scandal", by Hoang Tuan, 17 February 2009.
9. For example, the World Bank refers to this legacy in its Project Appraisal Document on a Proposed Credit in the Amount of SDR39.0 Million (US\$59.4 million equivalent) to the Socialist Republic of Vietnam for a Second Higher Education Project, 16 May 2007, p. 1.

10. Ministry of Planning and Investment, *The Five-Year Socio-Economic Development Plan 2006–10*, Hanoi, March 2006, p. 31. This Plan indicates that 96 per cent of private enterprises are small and medium ones, and that the number of newly established enterprises from 2001 to 2005 (160,000) was 2.6 times higher than that in the ten-year period from 1991 to 2000, and their registered capital was 6.1 times higher.

11. "SMEs Need Finance, Technology", 30 November 2005, in *Vietnam News.*

12. Nguyễn, Võ Hùng, 2004, cited in Tran, Ngoc Ca, 2007, p. 122.

13. Tran, Ngoc Ca, *Learning Technological Capability for Vietnam's Industrial Upgrading: Challenges of the Globalisation*, December 2002, p. 24. First in a series of papers presenting outcomes of the SIDA-SAREC III project: Strengthening Vietnam's Technological Capabilities in the Context of Globalisation and Economic Liberalisation.

14. U.S. Department of State and Vietnam Ministry of Education and Training, *U.S.-Vietnam Education Task Force — Final Report*, 30 September 2009.

15. See website of Green Energy, Vietnam, available at time of writing at <www.greenenergy.com.vn>.

16. Vietnamese Government, Decree no. 99/2003/nd-cp, *Promulgating the Regulation on High-Tech Parks*, August 28, 2003.

17. Saigon Hi-Tech Park website, available at time of writing at <http://www.shtp.hochiminhcity.gov.vn>.

18. Drew Wilson, *"Vietnam Continues to Draw Investors; Is It the Next China?"*, Electronic Business, 13 September 2007. Reproduced on the website EDN: Electronics Design, Strategy, News available at time of writing at <http://www.edn.com/article/CA6477011.html>.

19. See the website of the Saigon Hi-Tech Park at <http://www.shtp.hochiminhcity.gov.vn>.

20. See the website of the Hoa Lac Hi-Tech Park at <http://www.hhtp.gov.vn> and Decision No. 27/2007/QD-BKHCN of the Vietnamese Minister for Science and Technology, "Promulgating the Regulation on criteria for identifying projects on production of hi-tech products".

21. *VietNamNet Bridge*, "FPT Corporation assigned to develop Hoa Lac High-tech Park", 11 March 2007.

22. See the website of the Saigon Hi-Tech Park at <http://www.shtp.hochiminhcity.gov.vn>.

23. News item on HCMC People's Committee website: "City to establish local fund for science and technology development", 12 June 2007.

24. The author was briefed on Techmart and other local initiatives by the director of the Centre for Science and Technology Information in Ho Chí Minh City, Ms Trần Thị Thu Thủy, during a visit to the Centre on 19 September 2008.

25. *VietNamNet Bridge*, "235 MoUs and contracts signed at Techmart 2007", 10 September 2007.
26. *Báo Vietnam*, "Over 100 Contracts Signed at Techmart Ha Noi 2008", 21 September 2008.
27. <www.techmartvietnam.com.vn>.

References

Chamie, Joseph. *World Population to 2300*. New York: UN Population Division, 2004.

Dasgupta, S., B. Laplante, C. Meisner, D. Wheeler and Yan Jianping. "The Impact of Sea Level Rise on Developing Countries: A Comparative Analysis". World Bank Policy Research Working Paper 4136, February 2007.

Hargroves, Karlson "Charlie" and Michael H. Smith (co-authors and editors). *The Natural Advantage of Nations*. London: Earthscan, 2006.

Ministry of Planning and Investment. *The Five-Year Socio-Economic Development Plan 2006–10*. Hanoi, March 2006.

Ministry of Science and Technology. Decree No. 27/2007/QD-BKHCN. "Promulgating the Regulation on Criteria for Identifying Projects on Production of Hi-tech Products". 18 December 2006.

MultiActor Program (MAP) Thematic Network. *RoadMAP: Good Practices for the Management of MultiActors and MultiMeasures Programmes (MAPS) in RTDI Policy*. Vienna, 2004.

National Legal Database, Vietnam. Decree no. 99/2003/nd-cp. "Promulgating the Regulation on High-Tech Parks". 28 August 2003.

OECD. *Economic Policy Reforms: Going for Growth*, 2006.

Office of the U.S. Trade Representative. *2005 Special 301 Report*.

Phùng, Xuân Nhạ. "A Perspective on Industrial Development and Industry-University Cooperation in Vietnam". VNU *Journal of Science, Economics-Law XXIII*, no. 1 (2007).

Porter, Michael and C. van der Linde. "Green and Competitive: Ending the Stalemate". *Harvard Business Review*, September–October (1995): 121–34.

Slatyer, Ralph. "Cooperative Research Centres: The Concept and its Implementation". In *Research Grants: Management and Funding: Symposium Proceedings* (from a symposium held 23–25 July), edited by Fiona Wood and V. Flynn-Meek, 2003.

Tran Ngoc Ca. "Learning Technological Capability for Vietnam's Industrial Upgrading: Challenges of the Globalisation". European Institute of Japanese Studies Working Paper series, no. 126, December 2002.

———. "Universities as Drivers of the Urban Economies in Asia: The Case of Vietnam". World Bank Policy Research Paper 3949, June 2006.

————. "Innovation Systems in Vietnam: Toward an Innovation Policy for Competitiveness and Sustainable Development". *Journal of Science Policy and Research Management* 22, no. 2 (2007).

United Nations World Commission on Environment and Development (UNWCED). *Our Common Future.* 1987.

United Nations, *Agenda 21.* <http://www.un.org/esa/sustdev/documents/agenda21/english/agenda21chapter34.htm>, 1992.

Vietnamese Government. Law on Science and Technology, 2001.

————. *Decision No. 171/2004/qd-ttg, 28 September 2004,* Approving the Scheme on Renewal of Science and Technology Management Mechanism.

————. Proposal on the Reform of the Science and Technology Management Mechanism. Ministry of Science and Technology, 2004.

————. "The Strategic Orientation for Sustainable Development in Vietnam (Vietnam Agenda 21)", Introduction (2004). Available at <http://www.va21.org/eng/va21/VA21_stratergy_introduc.htm>.

VietNamNet Bridge. "US$500 Million Ready to Flow into Hoa Lac Hi-Tech Park", 4 September 2007<http://english.vietnamnet.vn/tech/2007/09/737064/>.

Vietnam National University — Ho Chi Minh City. *Strategic Plan 01–05.*

Wilson, Drew. "Vietnam Continues to Draw Investors; Is It the Next China?". Electronic Business, 13 September 2007. Reproduced on the website EDN: Electronics Design, Strategy, News, <http://www.edn.com/article/CA6477011.html>.

World Bank. *STI Global Forum,* February 2007, <www.worldbank.org/STIGlobalForum>.

11

WTO ACCESSION, SOCIO-ECONOMIC TRANSFORMATION, AND SKILLS DEVELOPMENT STRATEGIES IN VIETNAM

Alexandre Dormeier Freire

In January 2007 — following ten years of negotiations — Vietnam became the 150th member of the World Trade Organization (WTO). To further achievements made since 1986 and meet challenges imposed by current economic reforms such as the WTO accession, Vietnam does not only need "20,000 PhDs" as stated by the government, but it also needs a basic skilled labour force. As of 2008, roughly eighty per cent of Vietnam's workforce was unskilled. But skilling will be essential if Vietnam is to sustain the industrialization process and the quality of skilling in Vietnam will have wide-ranging effects on the quality of industrialization the country will experience. This chapter examines the evolution of the national skills development system in Vietnam and discusses some of the initial consequences of the WTO accession on skilling in Vietnam.

Although frequently overshadowed by discussions of higher education, the general issue of skills provision is nevertheless a crucial issue in the development and industrial strategy of any developing country. Education sector reform cannot omit attention to skills and the importance of skills development is stressed not only by educationists but also by many in Vietnam's industrial sector. As a recent United Nations Development Programme (UNDP) report on the Top 200 enterprises in Vietnam clearly demonstrates, large enterprises in Vietnam see the question of skills development as essential. The report states: "Without a large and sufficiently skilled workforce attempts to upgrade and achieve economies of scale would be fruitless" (Cheshier and Penrose 2007, p. 31).

Recent research by Dormeier-Freire and Vũ (2006) found problems affecting the skills development system (and the whole education and training sector) include poor quality of training, weak links to the labour market, inequalities of access across different regions and population segments, and corruption. Although political leaders[1] have shown an increasing awareness of these problems, there remain large gaps between current skills development strategies and policies, on the one hand, and the needs of a modern economy and labour market on the other.

VIETNAM'S NATIONAL SKILLS DEVELOPMENT SYSTEM

Historically, the prevailing notion of "skills development" in Vietnam has been primarily related to professional skills. The roots of the national skills development system can be traced back to the planned economy, in which socio-economic plans (embodied in the five-year plans) "commanded" the development of necessary skills for the economic system. This was largely to take place through the technical and vocational education and training (TVET) system. In interviews, however, several government officials noted that in the context of *đổi mới* (renovation) there has been a trend towards the adoption of a broader perspective on skills development (Dormeier-Freire and Vũ 2006). This broader notion of skills development often includes not only professional and "elite" skills, but also "life skills" (with a strong social component), soft skills, technical and vocational skills, as well as non-technical and vocational skills.

The renovation policy has profoundly transformed Vietnam in economic and social terms. Among the numerous *đổi mới* factors affecting skills development and their perception in Vietnam, two can be identified as being especially important. The first factor is the transition from a centrally planned system to a "market economy". This shift has revealed serious shortages of skills required for the reformed economy, both in the public and private sectors (Dormeier-Freire and Vũ 2006). The second factor is normalization with advanced industrial countries and international organizations, as well as with bilateral cooperation agencies. Beyond financial assistance, these actors have influenced skills development strategies in Vietnam through cooperation projects and technical assistance, bringing into the country new practices and different conceptions of skills development.

The scale of the skills development challenge that Vietnam faces is large. In 2006, the country was estimated to have a labour force of about 48 million, representing about half of the population (48.7 per cent). Annual growth of the labour force was calculated at 2.7 per cent in the years 1996–2000, or more than a million newcomers each year. As of 2006, 60 per cent of the labour force was aged between fifteen and thirty-four years. But Vietnam's trained labour force is still extremely small, only about 15 per cent.

The structure of professional skills reveals that a large part of the labour force is not integrated in the skills development system: 85 per cent of the workforce has had no formal skills training; of those trained, technical workers comprised 6.77 per cent; those with secondary professional education, 4.84 per cent; and those with higher education, 3.9 per cent. The structure of skills development continues to be weak and informal. For instance, human resources employed in the primary sector (agriculture, forestry, and fishing) represent three quarters of the total labour force, but only 7 per cent of trained labour (Dormeier-Freire and Vũ 2006). One of the consequences is that some companies (especially large ones), train even the workers building their schools (such as FPT, or Vinashin). All enterprises with expansion strategies need to consider skills development though many see it as a "risk". The reason is that a well-trained worker can easily find another position due to the existing shortages (Cheshier and Penrose 2007).

All those shortages raise one simple but critical question: where is skills development supposed to occur in the education and training system? According to the decree 90/CP on 24 November 1993 on the structure of national education system, and the Education Law of 1998, there are four layers of education and training: pre-school, basic education, secondary education (including vocational and professional training), and higher education. In this formal system, the provision of skills is located at the two highest levels, the secondary and tertiary levels.[2] Decree 02/2001/ND-CP issued in 2001 provided a boost to vocational training centres after their sharp decline during the early stages of the transition period. By 2003, there were 214 vocational schools and 221 vocational training centres under the authority of Ministry of Labour Invalid and Social Affairs (MOLISA), as well as 268 secondary technical and vocational education schools, and 132 post-secondary technical and vocational education colleges. To these figures, it is necessary to add the non-formal education centres (part of the National Education for All Action Plan adopted in 2003 and oriented on adult education, life skills, and lifelong learning) such as Community Learning Centres, Permanent Education Centres, which were estimated to more than 1,000 in 2003. A number of actors are active in non-formal education which provides various programmes. As of 2006–07, Vietnam had 299 universities and colleges and over 2,100 vocational and training centres of various kinds, demonstrating the quantitative boost to these centres.

In Vietnam, the historical legacies of central planning, as well as the corresponding absence of long-term market-regarding strategies and effective management have limited the development of a coherent skills provision system. As stressed by authors such as Duggan, the whole system was fragmented during the 1990s. The government then attempted to rationalize it but somehow at the expense of skills development (Duggan 2001, p. 194):

> The system was highly fragmented with general education consisting of primary, lower secondary and upper secondary education and vocational education with streams of secondary vocational and technical (lower and upper) education. This structure has since been revised to enable significant growth in general secondary education at the expense of rationalizing and reducing structures in vocational education.

Most of the centres of the formal education and training system have provided short-term training programmes responding to immediate needs, with a low level of quality services due to untrained staff and other quality shortages (such as infrastructure, budget, and allocation per student). Nonetheless, despite difficult conditions, the number of skilled workers rose from 13.4 per cent in 1998, to 16.8 per cent in 2006. This reflects the efforts of the authorities. But the increases were still slower than economic growth, and there continues to be questions raised about the "quality" of the skilled workers.

These few examples show that changes taking place following đổi mới have affected the skills development system. The level of qualifications of the workforce remains low, but the need for skills has emerged as a national issue. What are the reasons? The nature of skills development strategies expressed in education and training sector strategies reflects a formal and classical vision of skills development among political and economic leaders in Vietnam, one that is largely limited to a supply-driven technical and vocational education and training (TVET) system and higher education. An analysis of the evolution of skills development strategies during đổi mới will help us to understand why.

EVOLUTION OF SKILLS STRATEGIES DURING ĐỔI MỚI

There's no doubt that Vietnam's Government considers education and training a national priority and views the development of human resources as crucial for the economic growth of the country. But what about skills development? An earlier historical analysis by Dormeier-Freire and Vũ (2006) suggests there were three key periods during đổi mới showing different trends in skills development. These three periods are broadly reflected through three indicators: enrolment rates of TVET and higher education (as a simple indicator for skills development), and comparisons with ODA inflows, and economic growth rate over the period. The graph below shows three distinctive periods in the evolution of skills development: a first from 1986 to 1992, "overcoming" the crisis created by the launching of the renovation policy; a second, from 1993 to 1997, which witnessed a fast growth or a "miracle"; and a third, from 1997 to 2006, which can be considered a "consolidation" phase. The year 2007 marks the beginning of a new phase with Vietnam's accession to the WTO and the acceleration of economic reforms.

The first period (1986–92) was marked by low economic growth, low enrolment rates in higher education and TVET, and low ODA inflows. The number of students remained stable at the college and university level during this period, but in the TVET it declined from 139,700 in 1986 to 92,500 in 1989. Skills development remained largely based on the modality of formal professional education and training and was ill adapted to the thrust of the renovation policies and the requirements of market-based industrialization,

FIGURE 11.1

Evolution of Growth (GDP %), Higher Education and TVET (enrolment rates), and ODA (in millions USD), 1986–2006 (index number: 1986 = 100)

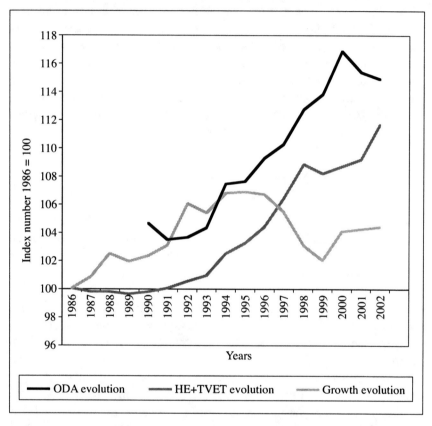

Note: This graph represents a rhythm of evolution and expansion of the three selected factors.

Source: Alexandre Dormeier Freire, Vũ Bích Thùy (2006, p. 24).

in particular. Rather than a multifaceted education strategy, education and training policies were dominated by the drive to universalize primary education and improve enrolment rates at the secondary levels, mainly in cities and industrial provinces. Leaders have paid constant attention to basic education indicators, but little was done for other layers of the educational system, including skills development. Indeed, skills development was relegated to second-class status, a peripheral concern of the Ministry of Higher Education and Vocational Education and Training.

Although the period 1986 to 1992 saw few changes in the area of skills development, there were important policy developments that occurred in 1991 and 1992 that would lay the foundations for important changes. Specifically, three events in 1991–92 warrant attention. These were the merger of the Ministry of Higher Education and VET with the Ministry of Education, creating a single and unified Ministry of Education and Training, with responsibility for education and training activities throughout the country; the launching of a UNDP and UNESCO-sponsored national project entitled "Education Sector Review and Human Resources Analysis" in 1991–92, which injected the concept of "human resources" into Vietnamese policymaking and replaced the more narrow conception of "cadres" that was restricted to personnel in the public sector; and, the identification of education and training as "top national policy".[3] During that period, the whole of society was struggling to adapt itself to new rules and principles based on a profit-driven economy. The socialization policy (*xã hội hóa*) launched in the middle of the 1990s is a good illustration of the new role individuals have to play in a renovated society. It was argued that sharing the costs in social sectors became necessary for the country to continue to sustain a rapid growth and transform society. It was also a response to demographic change and new financial constraints in the public sector (UNDP 2006, p. 39). New types of "non-public" institutions were created in the education and training system. But the implementation of user fees in the social sectors also created or widened disparities.

In the period that followed (1993–97), major changes occurred. The country experienced high levels of economic growth (eight per cent) and the normalization of the relations with Western countries (including the United States) also allowed important inflows of ODA.[4] As mentioned earlier, this period was marked by increased emphasis on education and training as a national priority. For example, the Central Party Committee adopted the first independent resolution on education and training, which followed the most comprehensive review of the sector since 1945. The resolution claimed the importance of "human resources" development in the continuing renovation of education and training. In considering education and training as an "investment good", the party emphasized that education and training would be the driving forces for the achievement of socio-economic development objectives.

Apart from the investment in basic education and the goal of universalization, the focus in other education and training layers was more on "talented human resources" and advanced skills professions. This explains the rapid expansion of enrolment in higher education compared with those in TVET. Vocational Education and Training was recovering after the crisis prior to 1986, but without a significant augmentation of schools and students. Broadly, higher education was accorded greater prestige compared with the TVET layers. This tendency is shown in the in Figure 11.2.

Despite a decline in economic growth in 1997–98 (down from 9 per cent to less than 6 per cent), the period from 1997 to 2006 was characterized

FIGURE 11.2
Evolution of HE and TVET 1986–2006

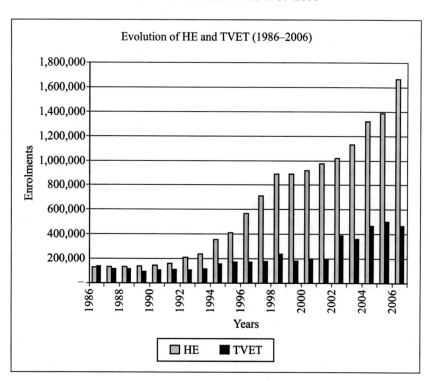

Source: Alexandre Dormeier Freire and Vũ Bích Thùy (2006, p. 29) and the GSO of Vietnam.

by a strong ODA level inflow and steady economic growth. In order to adapt the education and training system continuously to the fast changing environment, the government issued several strategic papers providing general guidelines for the development of the country, including its human resources.[5] Of particular note was Decision 500/TTg signed by Prime Minister Võ Văn Kiệt in 1995 which resulted in the paper, "Education and Training Development Strategy 2001–2010" in 2000 (ETDS). The ETDS's main aim is to provide general objectives for education and training in concordance with the socio-economic development plan. The strategy has six core components. With respect to skills development, it proposes the following quantitative targets:

TABLE 11.1
Skills Development-linked Strategies for 2010 (by Level of Skills)

Level of skills	2000	2005	2010
Percentage of secondary professional education in age cohort	0.05	0.1	0.15
Percentage of VET in the age cohort	0.06	0.1	0.15
Percentage of high school graduates in high skills training programmes		0.05	0.1

Source: Alexandre Dormeier Freire and Vũ Bích Thủy (2006, p. 30).

The elaboration of this strategic paper was remarkable in two other respects. First, that for the first time, the General Department for Vocational Training (GDVT) actively participated in this project as a member organization within MOET. Second, although the ETDS was prepared in parallel to other sectoral strategies, its preparation was not based on deliberate assessments of human resources identified by key sectors (such as technology, agriculture, industry, commerce, banking, and insurance). Key actors from many sectors were not consulted in drafting the strategy (Alexandre Dormeier Freire and Vũ 2006, p. 30).

Indeed, the design of the ETDS and its targets reflect again a certain disconnection between the labour market, the economy, and the provision of skills. In addition to the non-inclusion of other sectoral strategies, several key actors were left out of the process. Members of the implementation

TVET evaluation team pointed out additional shortcomings which made it difficult to translate the strategy into effective and concrete actions (Dormeier-Freire and Vũ 2006). A new law was also issued in 2006 (76/2006/QH11). Besides defining the structure of professional and vocational training, it emphasized the role of informal training and lifelong learning as key dimensions in skills provision.

According to a researcher at NIESAC (National Institute for Education Strategy and Curriculum Development), the main characteristic of *đổi mới* is to favour informal education and training in answering both social and labour market needs (Dormeire Freire and Vũ 2006, p. 33):

> Non-formal programmes have been flourishing in various forms such as Technical and Permanent Education Centres (TPEC). In Vietnam, the distinction between formal and non-formal skills development resides in the fact that the first, aiming at a diploma after taking regular or in-service training programmes, is managed by MOET, GDVT, specialized ministries, or provincial authorities, while the second is principally created and funded by social actors and associations such as YU (Youth Union), WU (Women Union), LU (Labour Union).

Whether and how a non-degree training programme can effectively respond to labour market needs remains in doubt. For the moment, enrolment in colleges and universities continue to attract the large majority of students who seek post-secondary education. In contrast to many other countries, skilled workers who have received formal training in Vietnam are fewer than university graduates. Despite efforts to develop non-degree education and training and thereby gain some flexibility and enhance adaptability to the new needs of the industrialization process, the demand for university education remains stronger and more stable.

In conclusion, there are several gaps regarding skills development policies and strategies and the economic challenges in Vietnam today. First, it seems that skills strategies are not clearly aligned with the national and provincial development goals. As a consequence, Vietnam's abundant workforce remains largely unskilled (in 2006, 83.2 per cent of the total workforce of 44 million people) and the lack of prioritization of skills development at both central and provincial level is a problem. Second, some actors such as business and entrepreneurship associations are left outside the design and conception of both policies and strategies. Third, skills development strategies engender tensions between a social approach to skills development and a more "technical" vision. Some actors strongly believe that skills development strategies have to be linked to market and labour questions, whereas others consider them as being limited to only social issues (such as working with women, maternal health training). Fourth, skills development is still more supply-driven than demand driven. Many reasons could be found to explain this: two among these would be the remaining vestiges of central planning practices, and labour market segmentation across regions, gender, and industries.

CURRENT SOCIO-ECONOMIC CHALLENGES: THE WTO ACCESSION AND ITS IMPACTS ON EDUCATION

At a recent international conference on twenty years of *đổi mới* in Vietnam, CIEM (Central Institute for Economic Management, Hanoi) experts pointed out some of the major challenges regarding Vietnam's WTO accession. These included the need for institutional reforms so as to achieve broader integration and secure foreign direct investment (FDI), and the need to adapt the country's human resource development to the reforms by undertaking fundamental changes in the education and training system. Without such changes, the numerous adjustments that the government will have to make to fulfil its commitment to the WTO may well jeopardize the stability of the economic growth that the country is enjoying. But WTO accession is also likely to affect and the training system itself. To appreciate how, it is useful to examine the place of education in the WTO agenda. Thus adapting its industries to a gradually open market may affect certain industrial sectors, which are far from being able to cope with international competitors. More broadly, changes in the global economy dictate that developing countries such as Vietnam will need to adjust continuously its economic structure (Cheshier, Penrose, and Pincus 2006, p. 21).

With this in mind, we then ask what would then be the consequences of this new context for the skills development system and human resources in general? First, before looking into the Vietnamese case, it is useful to relocate education in the WTO agenda. Education is one of the twelve sectors covered by the GATS (General Agreement on Trade and Services) part of the WTO. Some authors have emphasized that education services did not draw as much attention as other sectors. As a result little progress has been made towards market access and national treatment and liberalization in education sectors by contracting members at the WTO (Saner and Fasel 2003, p. 277). Therefore, the modes of education supply such as defined by the GATS depend on the contracting member parties' negotiations and may vary from one country to another. Table 11.2 shows the modalities available for contracting members of the WTO.

As a general comment, these modes of supply can be considered as a deregulatory package. Obviously, this kind of reforms should not be implemented without an existing regulatory framework to ensure that the local environment can face the competition driven system implemented through this deregulation. Any member of the WTO would also benefit from a clear strategy for all the service sectors affected by this contracting member agreement. Additionally, some level of quality should already exist, and the state must maintain clear and transparent policies; in other words, the service sector should be strengthened to be able to cope with new competitors.

It is also the case that different WTO members have made different levels of commitments and it is widely known that in its bid for WTO accession, Vietnam was pressured to accept commitments that went well beyond those for countries such as China or Cambodia.

Regarding educational services, the nature of Vietnam's commitment remains lower than in other sectors, and appears to stem from the smaller degree of attention given to education compared with other sectors (such as telecommunications or tourism) and also because the Vietnamese delegation succeeded in partly protecting its education sector. Thus, the unbounded education modes of supply (see Table 1.4) remains, therefore, "off limits" for certain rules, giving the possibility to the government to introduce regulations, rules, and laws which could limit market access, without causing any violation of the WTO agreement.

Notably, as indicated Table 11.3, on most modes of supply, Vietnam's commitment remains unbounded. Compared with Cambodia's accession conditions, for instance, Vietnam's educational services continue to be largely under the scrutiny of the government. In Cambodia, there are virtually no limitations on market access or national treatment for educational services.

Nevertheless, in Vietnam's the accession to the WTO, the regulations on the second and third mode of supply, namely "consumption abroad" and

TABLE 11.2
Mode of Supply in GATS, Education Services

Mode of Supply	Explanation	Example of Education Services
1. Cross-Border Supply (Mode 1)	The provision of a service where the service crosses the border (does not require the physical movement of the consumer).	Distance education; virtual education institutions; education software; corporate training through ICT delivery
2. Consumption Abroad (Mode 2)	Provision of service involving the movement of the consumer to the country of the supplier.	Students who go to another country to study.
3. Commercial Presence (Mode 3)	The service provider establishes or has a presence in commercial facilities in another country in order to render service.	Local university or satellite campuses; language training companies; private training companies, e.g., Microsoft, CISCO
4. Presence of Natural Persons (Mode 4)	Persons travelling to another country on a temporary basis to provide service.	Professors, teachers, researchers working abroad

Source: Saner and Fasel (2003, p. 279).

TABLE 11.3

Working Party on the Accession of Vietnam to WTO, the Educational Services

VIETNAM'S GATS ON EDUCATIONAL SERVICES

Only in technical, natural sciences and technology, business administration and business studies, economics, accounting, international law and language training fields.

With regard to points (C), (D), and (E) below: The education content must be approved by Vietnam's Ministry of Education and Training.

Sectors and Subsectors	Limitations on Market Access	Limitations on National Treatment	Additional Commitments
B. Secondary education services (CPC 922)	(1) Unbound. (2) None. (3) Unbound. (4) Unbound, except as indicated in the above section.	(1) Unbound. (2) None. (3) Unbound. (4) Unbound, except as indicated in the above section.	
C. Higher education services (CPC 923) D. Adult education (CPC 924) E. Other education services (CPC 929 including foreign language training)	(1) Unbound. (2) None. (3) None, except: Upon accession, only in the form of joint-ventures. Majority foreign ownership of such joint-ventures is allowed. As of 1 January 2009, 100 per cent foreign-invested education entities are permitted. After 3 years from the date of accession: none. (4) Unbound, except as indicated in the horizontal section.	(1) Unbound. (2) None. (3) Foreign teachers who wish to work in foreign-invested schools shall have at least 5 years of teaching experience, and their qualifications shall be recognized by the competent authority. (4) Unbound, except as indicated in the horizontal section.	

Source: Working Party on the Accession of Vietnam to the WTO (2006, p. 34).

"commercial presence", are much less restrictive. The scope of limitations only concerns foreign shares in higher education joint ventures (to be passed in 2009), adult education, and other education services. Secondary education services will remain more protected.

Indeed, conditions and negotiations of Vietnam's WTO accession serve the interest of some large educational services providers (such as Australia or the United States) to gain guaranteed access to a new education market (particularly in higher education and training) and ensure the mobility of Vietnamese students (consumers) abroad. Some see GATS as an opportunity for large education providing countries to reduce barriers to gain better access to foreign educational markets (Van der Wende 2003, p. 196).

VIETNAM, SKILLS DEVELOPMENT, AND THE WTO: NEW CHALLENGES, OLD PROBLEMS?

The terms of Vietnam's accession to the WTO are done in some respects complementary to the country's broad educational and human resource strategy. In particular, Vietnam's WTO commitments may be viewed as consistent with the aim of promoting gross and net enrolment in higher education by relying on diverse forms including state, private, cross-border, and joint venture forms (Varghese 2007). All these different measures should then ensure an increasing number of skilled workers.

However, the targeted enrolment increases can only be reached through a certain level of liberalization of education. From this perspective, private actors could contribute to providing the upper secondary, higher education, and vocational training the country needs to meet its skills requirements. The current policies already allow "non-public" or private institutions to run higher education programmes. WTO accession will foster the diversification of educational suppliers. There are many reasons to expect such an outcome, though the main reason is robust demand for higher education. The sector is already attracting private investors. The prestige of certain international private educational institutions, notably among young generations, is making the education market in Vietnam more dynamic. As an example, one thinks in particular of all the programmes related to "business"; while in 1990 the non-public faculties and institutions of economy and business were only two out of twenty, in 2000, they were twenty out of fifty.

At the beginning of 2000, private universities only accounted for 11 per cent, of total enrolment, and the government targeted 30 per cent by 2007. With accession to the WTO, the presence of foreign education and training providers is likely to expand quickly. Obviously, one expected result of the simultaneous diversification of supply and demand for educational services is the creation further opportunities for all the actors involved. Through transnational education, or private institutions providers, it is hoped that the supply will better meet the demand.

On the TVET side, it seems that all key actors are now emphasizing the importance of the provision of skills below higher education in order to reverse the tendency that has been described earlier in this chapter. Recently, the Ministry of Labour and Social Affairs has announced that it would grant licences to individuals and organizations to run vocational schools, provided certain criteria and standards are met. The government's objective is to reduce the proportion of university students in higher education gradually from 78.4 per cent at present to 56 per cent by 2020 while raising the ratio of college students from 21.6 per cent to 44 per cent, respectively. At the same time, more technical secondary schools and technical training programmes would be established. Currently, Vietnam has nearly 1,600 public vocational training centres and schools attended by 1.1 million students annually. Yet the differences in the quality of these institutions are so great that the numbers themselves are not terribly meaningful. The government also expressed its intention to allocate US$1 billion[6] into the vocational and training system over the next years, whereas for the time being, the sector only receives US$125,000 per year. All actors seem to be mobilized in that direction. Enterprises are now being encouraged to spend some proscribed percentages of their expenses to train or retrain workers. The Ministry of Education also expressed its wish to establish better collaboration between enterprises, universities, and training centres (see Nguyễn Minh Hồng, this volume) in order to avoid certain gaps existing between what is offered and what is needed, without mentioning the question of quality.

All this suggests the possible benefits of WTO accession and corresponding moves by the Vietnamese Government. There are, however, a number of uncertainties and hazards that appear on the horizon, and it is to these that the discussion now turns.

UNCERTAINTIES: INEQUALITY, QUALITY, LABOUR MARKETS, AND COSTS

First, the education and training systems in Vietnam suffer from some recurring problems. Those have been widely discussed in the literature on this issue and in the introduction to this volume, and include the question of social inequalities, the quality of education, gender disparities, academic corruption, and, as a transversal issue, the undesirable effects of liberalization and privatization. Many of these issues raise special problems in connection with skills development and the WTO accession. To see how, consider the following list of impacts associated with WTO accession (based on Van der Wende 2003; Saner and Fasel 2003):

1. new role of coordination and certification for the government (not only education supplier);
2. impacts for student access (inequalities);
3. compensation mechanisms (education stipends);
4. quality and accreditation;
5. academic corruption;
6. research and intellectual property rights;
7. mobility of professionals and labour force;
8. linkages and adequacy with labour market;
9. institutional autonomy, academic freedom, etc.

1. Inequalities.

Social inequality in Vietnam's education and training sector is well documented.[7] Many of the dimensions of inequality have been discussed in the introduction to this volume.

If we divide skills development into three main areas, higher education, TVET, and non-degree vocational education, the effects of the accession on inequalities can be contrasted. First, higher education has already a very competitive and even a certain "elitist" face with the "specialized schools" (*trường chuyên*), or the "selection classes" (*lớp chọn*) in the regular universities (122 classes in 2006) designed for students with putative talents in certain fields such as mathematics.

Data indicate that 70–75 per cent of the students come from the richest quintile of the population (VLSS 1998; VLSS 2002).

Given the association with educational achievement and income, and the ongoing development of the non-state form, it is reasonable to expect that accession will not only reinforce the existing privatization and liberalization policies, but intensify tendencies towards a two-tiered system in higher education as noted by the UNDP. One could easily imagine the education and training system would then be composed of three levels of higher education institutions: a first level with joint venture or completely owned by foreign institutions (such as RMIT, Asian Institute of Technology Center in Vietnam, Centre Franco-Vietnamien de Gestion, Victoria University, HSB-Hawaii.) mainly attracting better-off and talented students; a second level with national universities, and a third level with provincial universities with lower levels of quality and less talented students. Besides the income discriminant, regional inequalities would also be prominent here. However, the effect of existing private institutions on educational services remains limited for the time being as pointed out by the UNDP (2006, p. 41):

> These foreign schools charge fees much higher than those in local schools, and are mainly attended by children of foreign expatriates and local rich people. They make no positive contribution to the access of education services to the poor; however, because of their limited numbers, negative impacts, for example, by draining skilled teachers from the domestic public and private sectors, are so far minimal.

The limited availability of skilled teachers suggests that their leaching into the private realm may become more intensive.

The situation in TVET is radically different as it is accorded less social prestige and is rightly or wrongly believed to offer lower returns to investment in education. Far less competitive and appealing, vocational and technical institutions attract students from poorer households. The quality of teachers and their level of training are particularly unsatisfactory. The main shortcoming is that this contingent of teachers is not stable and most of them have not been trained in terms of instructional skills (Dormeier-Freire and Vũ 2006, p. 33).[8] Monthly tuition fees are relatively low — from VND 20 thousand to VND 100 thousand. In contrast to higher education, a certain level of initial investment is necessary in some vocational channels (mainly for equipment). This suggests new investments in private vocational education may rapidly attract the most qualified teachers and wealthiest students and so undermine the public system. This is exacerbated by the low pay for public TVET teachers. This will also result in an increasing amount of pressure on the tuition fees system. Furthermore, TVET centres remain for the time being largely located in urban areas.

Usually, private actors are not involved in TVET except though charity and other forms of education stipends. In order to make it profitable, private investors may choose rather to locate their centres in provinces with stronger development potential and more fee-paying students. Current governmental and international projects try to promote a certain "decentralization" of TVET activities in remote areas, but again, the better-off and urban population will benefit first from the diversification of private education and training services provision.

It is difficult to analyse the impacts on non-degree vocational education provision, largely because this segment of the sector is so diverse. For skills provision, some non-public actors, or people-founded organizations, do provide short-term training to various sectors of the population, that is, in some provinces, such as Cần Thơ, community organizations provide skills programmes to migrants, generally with low levels of qualifications (typically sewing or hairdressing). This kind of skills development approach has been strongly associated with a social component that "resolves" unemployment without significant skills. Opening non-degree vocational education to private and non-public actors may stimulate the supply of informal education, but the impact will be limited if the current narrow social approach is maintained.

2. Quality and corruption

In education, quality can be understood and measured in many different ways. Quality in the education and training system is a cause for concern, particularly in light of Vietnam's accession to the WTO. As has been clearly highlighted by several authors, the quality of education and training varies greatly from one region to another, and depends on household ability to pay. As UNDP (2006, p. 39) reports "schools in more affluent areas have better quality facilities and learning materials than schools in remote and poor areas. As a result, the in-school performance and examinations required for entrance into higher levels of education constitute a relatively greater barrier for poor children".

Without adequate counter-measures, current trends premise the deepening of a two-tiered system with different layers of different levels of quality. The education and training system is already divided in different levels of quality where "mass education" cohabits with "quality education". As an example, today some classes in urban areas have twenty to twenty-five pupils; there are forty to forty-five in rural areas. Focused on the need to universalize access to education, the government has paid less attention to quality issues despite certain efforts in teacher training. There is an urgent need to launch curricular reform, establish a minimum level of quality, and re-establish educational values within the system.

Teachers are part of all three problems and their solution. They need to be further upgraded simultaneously with reform of the curriculum. A Teacher Training Upgrading and Strengthening Programme has been undertaken for more than ten years (since 1994), and Vietnamese teachers are relatively well trained compared with those in other countries at a similar socio-economical level of development. However, for teachers to adapt to the new context, more meaningful investments in teachers are required.

Finally, the role of the teachers must be re-evaluated not only in teaching, but also in ethical terms so that education again becomes an educational process rather than just another economic process.

There are, in addition, many quality issues related to certification and accreditation. For training programmes of less than one year, no certification of completion is delivered. A certain attention has to be paid to the certification and accreditation issue to avoid "diplomas mills", especially if the number of actors and programmes increases. Regulation and accreditation activities are essential governmental duties in a more open education and training system that is not just for higher education services, but also for the all the professional training programmes flourishing across the region.

Corruption and quality are intertwined. Corruption occurs in several educational practices. First, admission is one of the main objects of illicit transactions. The cost of admission to certain universities or institutions with a good reputation can be high. In this case, it affects higher education more than TVET, because higher education attracts the richest part of the population and has a higher social value. Another well known issue in academic corruption concerns diplomas. PhDs, Master's degrees, and certificates of all kinds can be bought. With the emergence of a new solvable demand, these activities have become more lucrative. In the higher education sector, 42 per cent of the students are young adults attending university courses during their employment. A university degree or diploma is considered a necessity to gain professional mobility and promotion opportunities, although the return on investment still seems low (except in the private sector). This new situation has of course contributed to propagating this kind of educational corruption.

In a situation where levels of corruption are high, the consequences of the WTO accession and its implications for educational services may create some further distortions and widen corrupt practices if no clear regulations are adopted.

3. Labour market.

One of the main aims of skills development is to equip individuals with skills to make them more "employable" or improve their access to labour markets. The labour-intensive industrialization mode still prevails in Vietnam and the labour market must absorb over one million new labour entrants per year. Several studies show that the labour market in Vietnam is segmented (ADB 2006, p. 1).

This means that workers with identical skills can receive not only different salaries, but also different non-wage benefits. The labour market is segmented across regions, and dependent on gender or formal-informal and rural-urban cleavages. Consequently, working conditions and occupational mobility may vary a lot from one individual to another, regardless of his educational attainment or skills level (ADB, 2006). In other words, there are different returns for individuals equipped with the same skills.

In the past, as some authors have pointed out, "labour segmentation worked for the mutual benefit of all market participants until the mid-1990s" (Henaff and Abrami 2004, p. 102). But the segmentation of the labour market can be seen in the long-term as a barrier to matching the skill level of workers with the needs of private enterprises. This segmentation is also jeopardizing the education and training responsiveness to market pressures at the moment, when demand for workers with a higher level of vocational proficiency seems to be emerging from the private sector and current economic reforms.

Further diversification of the skills development system is necessary. The WTO accession can have a positive effect in the adjustment of the skills development supply to market needs. But without transitional mechanism and "WTO-friendly" labour regulations, it can also increase the segmentation and discrepancies that are observable today.

CONCLUSION

Based on these elements, we can propose a series of hypotheses. First, some changes were already taking place in the education and training sector before Vietnam's WTO accession, especially with respect to liberalization and privatization. We would expect the accession to accelerate this existing trend. Second, and as underlined in the literature, the accession may concentrate the provision of education and training services in profitable urban areas, leaving rural and remote communities out. For the time being, the strongest demand for non-state education and training services is mainly located in urban areas. Alternatively, in some rural areas adjacent to urban areas or special industrial zones (such as Hưng Yên), local authorities are trying to cope with this situation by offering training programmes for farmers to equip them with the minimum skills required by the big factories located nearby. Third, we may expect the WTO accession to intensify competition for skilled and qualified workers; provinces may find it difficult to compete with "talented human resources" programmes (Dormeier-Freire, Henaff, and Martin 2004). In that context, besides the rural and urban cleavage, the disparities among regions and provinces may also deteriorate if competition appears to be the only driving mechanism.

In other words, disadvantaged social groups, which are already considered vulnerable (the poor, women, ethnic groups, migrants) in terms of access to education and training services, may see their situation exacerbating. The penetration of private actors and foreign actors, facilitated by the WTO accession, may create an unbalanced situation, and one classical argument would be the following (UNDP 2006, p. 30):

> [...] Internationally prominent educators continually caution prudence to developing countries in permitting the penetration of their education system to foreign private education service suppliers. They consider that these could undermine the public system by attracting the best teachers and lead to the creation of a two-tiered system, propagating elitist attitudes.

With no clear coping mechanisms, Vietnam is indeed vulnerable. The market opening may not threaten universal access to essential services, but it will likely worsen existing inequalities in the provision of education and training services. Income, which is already a social discriminant in terms of access, especially in higher education, will become a more important discriminant factor in various ways. The danger here is that fragmented education and training systems will emerge with different levels of quality for the different kinds of social groups. Other problems include the lack of scholarships and other education stipends for ethnic groups and other poor groups. It is unclear how the impact of the WTO accession will affect the frequency and magnitudes of corruption.

The accession of Vietnam to the WTO will have a set of contrasted effects on educational services. It is hoped that the increased diversification will match supply better with the demand for education and training and improve the skills development systems. The accession in itself is part of a larger process of socio-economic transformations that are already radically changing the educational and skills environment of the country. In that sense, the WTO impact will foster existing liberalization and privatization policies. Previous policies such as socialization have already triggered some profound changes in the provision of and access to certain skills, and the relationships between the different actors involved.

Some questions, however, do remain. The situation in terms of the inequalities of access to the educational system, will have to be analysed further. For the time being, private educational actors may have little effect in skills development, although in the near future, the situation may change. Furthermore, one of the layers of skills development, the TVET, suffers from traditional shortcomings. Only a dynamic strategy, and one that involves more than privatization, has to be promoted to make it clearly more attractive, especially at a time when IT enterprises, such Asus (a subcontractor for Hewlett Packard and Apple), have announced their intention to delocalize their manufacturing activities from China to Vietnam. The classical skills development approach, which is limited to a supply-driven technical and vocational education and training, has to be reformed. Pouring money into the disadvantaged skills development layers can only be effective within the framework of a clear strategy.

The question of balance between university graduates, technicians, and technical workers also has to be addressed in a country where the industrialization mode is labour-intensive and the majority of the population is still working in the agricultural sector. In that perspective, labour market segmentation, sometimes underestimated, could also expand with the new deregulations. As a matter of fact, it questions the link between the training provided, the labour market, and how employers view the skills provided by institutions. Here, as noted by Cheshier and Penrose (2007), business associations and private enterprises have to be able to voice their views.

In sum, in order to absorb the effects of WTO accession, the whole educational sector has to be strengthened to ensure a skills development system that matches the current socio-economic transformations. Clear policies, a transparent environment, an accreditation system, transitional regulations, and education and training stipends have to be adopted and/or adapted to limit the potential threats.

Notes

1. Such as the Prime Minister Nguyễn Tấn Dũng during his meeting with the Ministry of Labour representatives of the sixty-four provinces in May 2007.
2. It has to be mentioned that ongoing discussions also emphasize the links between basic education and skills development, notably on life skills and non-technical and vocational skills.
3. Article 35 of the 1992 Constitution states that education and training is the top national priority.
4. In fact, the first donors' meeting was held in Paris in 1993, just before the U.S. embargo was lifted.
5. For example, "Vietnam Vision till 2020", written by the Ministry of Science and Environment, or "Socioeconomic Development Strategy for the period 2001–2010" by the Ministry of Planning and Investment.
6. Prime Minister Nguyễn Tấn Dũng announced on 10 May 2007 that "the government of Vietnam will pour $1 billion into vocational training in an effort to improve workforce quality" (*Vietnam News Brief*, 14 May 2007).
7. Many articles or books have described the social inequalities in the education sector. Some are to be found in the bibliography of this article.
8. The "Top 200" report has some illustrations. One taken from a seafood company: "When workers come from the training centre they only have some general knowledge. Even the teacher lacks practical knowledge because the school lacks equipment. When they come to the company they cannot even tell the different types of shrimps." (UNDP 2007, p. 32)

References

Abrami, R. and N. Henaff. "The City and the Countryside: Economy, State and Socialist Legacies in the Vietnamese Labour Market". In *Reaching for the Dream, Challenges of Sustainable Development in Vietnam*, edited by E. Beresford, M. Tran Ngoc Angie. NIAS, Copenhagen, 2004.

Asian Development Bank. *Labour Segmentation and Poverty.* Briefing Note No. 12, 2006.

Centre for International Economics. *Vietnam Poverty Analysis.* AusAID, Canberra, 2002.

Chau Lam. *Vietnam Non-formal Education.* Education for all Monitoring Report 2008. Hanoi: UNESCO, 2007.

Cheshier, S. and J. Penrose. *Top 200, Industrial Strategies of Vietnam's Largest Firms.* UNDP Vietnam Policy Dialogue Paper, 2007.

Cheshier, S., J. Penrose and J. Pincus. *Flying Geese or Cooked Goose? Vietnam's Insertion into Regional and Global Trade Patterns.* Hanoi: UNDP, 2006.

Dormeier Freire, A., N. Henaff, and J-Y Martin. *Đổi mới et globalisation, vers un accroissement des inégalités en matière d'éducation?.* RUIG-Défi Social du Développement, <http://www.unige.ch/iued/new/recherche/ruig-dsd/re_pays.php>, Geneva, 2004.

Dormeier Freire, A. and Vũ Bích Thủy. "How Do National and International Actors Interact in Skills Development Strategies? The Analysis of Vietnam under Đổi Mới (1986–2004)", *Etudes Courtes* No. 9, IUED, Geneva, 2006.

―――. "Education and Training in Vietnam during Đổi Mới: between Successes and Uncertainties". Paper presented at the Geneva Graduate Institute of Development Studies (IUED) Conference "20 years of Doi Moi", Geneva, December 2006, 2007.

Duggan, S. "Educational Reforms in Vietnam: A Process of Change or Continuity?" Comparative Education 37, no. 2 (2001): 193–212.

General Statistics Office. *Vietnam Household Living Standard Survey.* Hanoi: Statistical Publishing House, 2002.

―――. *The 2006 Population Change, Labour Force and Family Planning Survey.* Hanoi: Statistical Publishing House, 2007.

GTZ (Deutsche Gesellschaft für Technische Zusammenarbeit). *Preventing Corruption in the Education System: A Practical Guide.* Eschborn: GTZ, 2004.

Henaff, N. and J-Y Martin (eds). *Observatoire de l'emploi et des ressources humaines au Vietnam.* Paris: IRD-Karthala, 2003.

Litchfield, L. and P. Justino. "Welfare in Vietnam during the 1990s, Poverty, Inequality and Poverty Dynamics". *Journal of the Asia Pacific Economy 9*, no. 2 (2004): 145–69.

London, J. "Rethinking Vietnam's Mass Education and Health Systems". In *Rethinking Vietnam*, edited by D. McCargo. London: Routledge, 2004.

Mekong Economics. "Vietnam Inequality Report 2005: Assessment and Policy Choices". Synthesis Paper of the "DFID Drivers of Inequality in Vietnam" Project, 2005.

Ministry of Education and Training. *Vietnamese Education Development Strategy to Year 2010*. Hanoi, 2000.

Nga Nguyệt Nguyễn. "Trends in the Education Sector from 1993–98". Hanoi: World Bank Policy Research Working Paper 2891, 2002.

Nguyễn, Lộc. "Vietnam's Education in the Transitional Period". Paper presented at the 28th Human Resources Development Working Group Meeting — APEC, Hồ Chí Minh City, 22–26 May, 2006.

Nguyễn Ngọc Thắng and Trương Quang. "International Briefing 18: Training and Development in Vietnam". In *International Journal of Training and Development 11*, no. 2 (2007): 139–49.

Oxfam. "Do as I Say, Not as I Do, The Unfair Terms for Vietnam's Entry to the WTO". Oxfam Briefing Paper 74, 2005.

Phạm Lan Hương and G. Fry. "Education and Economic, Political, and Social Change in Vietnam". In *Educational Research for Policy and Practice*, no. 3 (2004): 199–222.

Salomon, M., Vu Doan Kiet. "Doi Moi, Education and Identity Formation in Contemporary Vietnam". In *Compare: A Journal of Comparative Education 37*, no. 3 (2007): 345–63.

Saner, R. and S. Fasel. "Negotiating Trade in Educational Services within the WTO/GATS Context". Aussenwirtschaft, No. 59 (2003): pp. 275–308.

Trần Thăng Long, Nguyễn Thị Hương Giang. "Business Higher Education in Vietnam — Market Oriented Perspectives". Paper presented at the 2nd International Conference on Management Education for 21st Century, Hanoi, 2003.

UNDP (United Nations Development Programme). *Impacts of Basic Public Services Liberalization on the Poor and Marginalized People: The Case of Health, Education and Electricity in Vietnam*, Hanoi: UNDP, 2006.

Van Der Wende, M. "Globalisation and Access to Higher Education". In the *Journal of Studies in International Education 7*, no. 2 (2003): 193–206.

Varghese, N. "GATS and Higher Education: The Need for Regulatory Policies". Research Policies, IIEP. Paris: UNESCO, 2007.

Vietnam News Briefs. "Labour & Education, Vietnam Earmarks $1 bln for Vocational Training". Hanoi, 14 May 2007.

———. "Labour and Education Vietnam Needs $481 mln for Classroom Consolidation by 2010". Hanoi, 24 August, 2007.

Vu Quoc Ngu. "Social Disparities in Vietnam: The Case of Poverty Reduction and Educational Attainment". In *Social Inequality in Vietnam and the Challenges to Reform,* edited by P. Taylor. Singapore: Institute of Southeast Asian Studies, 2004.

World Bank. "Poverty, Vietnam Development Report 2004". Joint Donor Report to the Vietnam Consultative Group meeting, Hanoi, 2003.

————. *World Bank Development Indicators.* Washington: World Bank, 2007.

World Trade Organization. *Working Party on the Accession of Vietnam to the WTO.* Geneva: WTO, 2006.

INDEX

CPSIA information can be obtained at www.ICGtesting.com
Printed in the USA
LVOW071107221011

251526LV00001B/262/P